D1806903

V&R unipress

Susanne Reichl / Ute Smit (eds.)

#YouthMediaLife & Friends

Interdisciplinary research into young people's mediatised lifeworlds / Interdisziplinäre Forschung zu mediatisierten Lebenswelten Jugendlicher

With 37 figures

V&R unipress

Vienna University Press

MIX
Papier aus verantwor-
tungsvollen Quellen
FSC® C083411
www.fsc.org

Bibliographic information published by the Deutsche Nationalbibliothek
The Deutsche Nationalbibliothek lists this publication in the Deutsche Nationalbibliografie;
detailed bibliographic data are available online: https://dnb.de.

Publications of Vienna University Press
are published by V&R unipress.

© 2024 by Brill | V&R unipress, Robert-Bosch-Breite 10, 37079 Göttingen, Germany,
an imprint of the Brill-Group
(Koninklijke Brill NV, Leiden, The Netherlands; Brill USA Inc., Boston MA, USA; Brill Asia Pte Ltd,
Singapore; Brill Deutschland GmbH, Paderborn, Germany; Brill Österreich GmbH, Vienna, Austria)
Koninklijke Brill NV incorporates the imprints Brill, Brill Nijhoff, Brill Schöningh, Brill Fink,
Brill mentis, Brill Wageningen Academic, Vandenhoeck & Ruprecht, Böhlau and V&R unipress.
Unless otherwise stated, this publication is licensed under the Creative Commons License
Attribution-Non Commercial-No Derivatives 4.0 (see https://creativecommons.org/licenses/
by-nc-nd/4.0/) and can be accessed under DOI 10.14220/9783737016391. Any use in cases other
than those permitted by this license requires the prior written permission from the publisher.

Cover image: © Lisza-Sophie Neumeier
Printed and bound by CPI books GmbH, Birkstraße 10, 25917 Leck, Germany
Printed in the EU.

Vandenhoeck & Ruprecht Verlage | www.vandenhoeck-ruprecht-verlage.com

ISBN 978-3-8471-1639-4

Contents

Acknowledgements

A warm thank you to all our contributors: those who have participated in *#YouthMediaLife* activities locally and those who are based at other institutions and have contributed to our conference and this volume. We continue to learn so much from you and your fascinating research.

We would also like to express our sincere gratitude to the reviewers who provided valuable comments and constructive criticism on the contributions in our edited volume. Your feedback has helped to guarantee the high quality and interdisciplinarity of this publication.

To make interdisciplinary work possible at all, a great deal of communicative and administrative work is needed: thank you to our wonderful #YouthMediaLife team, Cornelia Schantl and Lisza-Sophie Neumeier, for having done an excellent job at keeping us going, and to the whole team of the *#YouthMediaLife21* conference. Lisza contributed crucially to this volume by taking over the correspondence, keeping an eye on the various versions of the contributions, devoting her finely honed editing skills to all the articles, and keeping the editors on track.

Dafna Lemish's pandemic insights on children and media research have been reprinted by kind permission of Taylor & Francis Ltd. We also wish to acknowledge the support we got from the publisher V&R unipress, in particular Mr. Oliver Kätsch, who answered all our email queries promptly and carefully.

Interdisciplinary work needs space, openness and trust. As colleagues from different disciplines, yet based at the same department, we have been given the space to work together in so many more ways than we used to beforehand. We'd like to thank each other for our productive and delightful collaboration.

Susanne Reichl & Ute Smit

Susanne Reichl / Ute Smit

Introduction

Choosing a title for an edited volume constitutes an act of identification: more than an indication of its content, a title ideally reflects some of the communicative intent behind its initiating project. Calling this volume *#YouthMediaLife & Friends*, we acknowledge both the shared event that it is based on – an academic conference – and the friendly spirit that has pervaded our scholarly community before and after the conference. With an academic event as its starting point, this book continues a long-standing tradition of how scholarly undertakings develop from presentations to book chapters, and how academics move between the roles of conference organisers and participants to editors and authors. The novelty aspect lies thus not in the overall procedure, but in other, arguably more relevant and exciting, aspects: the topic in focus, the constellation of contributors, and the nature of the conference and its academic exchange.

The conference, *#YouthMediaLife 2021*[1], took place at the end of March of that year and thus in the middle of a Covid-induced lockdown in Austria. As one of the first online conferences organised at our university, it required creativity and innovation on many fronts, such as appropriate technological solutions, online-friendly programme structuring including social events with a clearly Viennese cultural touch, and a large support team of fully committed IT and student helpers that made the three-day event a full success, allowing the almost 200 participants to give and listen to presentations, engage in academic discussion, enjoy the musical events, and extend their academic networks also beyond their own disciplines.[2]

A brief glance at this book's table of contents and list of contributors will confirm that this disciplinary breadth is also at the heart of the volume. Not only is it dedicated to a highly topical concern for 21st century societies, i.e. young

1 #YouthMediaLife. (2021). *International conference #YouthMediaLife2021.* #YouthMediaLife. https://youthmedialife2021.univie.ac.at/.
2 #YML21 Organising Committee. (2021, May 5). *#YML21 conference impressions.* #YouthMediaLife Blog. https://youthmedialife-blog.univie.ac.at/yml21-conference-impressions.

people's mediatised lifeworlds and their narrative constructions, it also displays an unusual mix of researchers, combining linguists, sociologists, anthropologists, psychologists and scholars in education, communication, literature and media studies. While some are located outside Austria, most contributors have been affiliated with our university. This is not accidental. It reflects that such an impressive range of disciplines does not happen ad hoc for a conference publication but is the result of years of intensive work and collaboration.

In our case, this has been made possible by an interdisciplinary research platform at the University of Vienna, bringing together more than 50 scholars strongly interested in "Mediatised Lifeworlds: Young People's Narrative Constructions, Connections and Appropriations". As indicated in this long title and captured more succinctly in the shorter name of *#YouthMediaLife*[3], the overall goal of this platform has been, since its inception in 2018, to investigate the role of stories and narratives in young people's everyday media practices. Particularly, we have been interested in the multimedial and multimodal universes and networks that young people participate in, in the ways they simultaneously construct and consume the narratives on offer, and in the complex processes that unfold as young people appropriate knowledge, skills and competences through their mediatised lifeworlds.

While this research interest spans a host of disciplines, integrating their approaches and insights, it also hinges on the central notions of narrative, media, youth, and lifeworld, whose joint operationalisation turned out to be the first task of the research platform. Put briefly, **narratives** are not only crucial for personal storytelling and being human, but they also form a culturally central communicative practice in times of media change. Just as the invention of writing revolutionised narratives in antiquity (Havelock, 1986), so have the recent technological advances profoundly impacted present-day mediated storytelling. One quite obvious aspect is that various modes, such as images or sound, complement the traditional verbal mode in constructing the respective narration. Linked to such new text-image constructions is a blurring of clear beginnings and endings in often co-narrated digital stories.

When turning to **media** and **mediatisation**, we take a contemporary theoretical perspective that does not consider media as a priori products that can be investigated in isolation from the social context they are part of. Rather, media are understood as part and parcel of people's social reality, of the social changes they find themselves in, and of their mutually positioning mediatisation practices (Hartmann, 2008; Hepp & Pfadenhauer, 2014). Our research focus is thus not on what media and their quantitative presence do to people, but on how

---

3 #YouthMediaLife. (n.d.) *Research platform mediatised lifeworlds.* #YouthMediaLife. https://youthmedialife.univie.ac.at/.

people act on and with media, for example when engaging in small storytelling in online communities (Bamberg & Georgakopoulou, 2008). Exemplifying people as 'produsers' (Bruns, 2006), such media practices stand for a change in modern media culture, questioning established role distinctions between user and producer, but also between professional and amateur media. Furthermore, such mediatised communication allows for a self-thematisation or mediated identity construction that, while important to all humans, is of particular relevance to young people in their endeavour to develop their selves and identities (Reichert, 2017).

Our focus on **youth**, however, is not primarily motivated by this age group's need for identity construction, neither by our professional preoccupation as educators. Rather, it recognises the pivotal role young people have as 'agents of change' (Großegger, 2017) for any large-scale societal development, with the digital mediatisation of the last decades being a prime example. Although generational labels by definition overgeneralise unduly, the often quoted collective of the 'digital natives' (Prensky, 2001) acknowledges the widely held perception that it was the millennials ("generation Y") and so-called generation Z, i. e. people born since the 1980s, who actually made the digital transformation mainstream (Aikat, 2020). Having little or no personal recollection of a time without social media, it is in particular generation Z for whom a distinction of 'old' vs 'new' media makes little sense and whose post-digital communicational practices merge the digital and analogue seamlessly. Rather than simply going for the latest tech device, post-digital choices are based on the practices that fulfil a user's needs most (Cramer, 2014). At the same time, this generation (or, indeed, any generation) is far from monolithic, but stands for highly diverse groups and individuals engaging in digital and mediatised practices in a multitude of ways.

To give centre stage to this diversity and complexity, the research platform has been operating with the concept of young people's **lifeworlds**. Originally introduced by early phenomenologists (Husserl, 1962; Schütz, 1974), the concept of 'Lebenswelt' has gained a central role in the German research and occupational field of social work. As recently argued by Björn Kraus (e. g. 2015), it aims to capture people's personal views of their everyday life, understanding such subjective constructions of realities as different from, but influenced by their objectifiable life conditions, such as material financial resources or immaterial social networks. When aiming to describe young people's *mediatised* lifeworlds, the main focus also lies on how they construct and perceive their practices, without neglecting the individual's life conditions, such as technological or societal access and support. Clearly, bringing together young people's mediatised lifeworlds and their narratives requires a more complex approach than a single discipline would allow.

This does not just concern research into young people's lifeworlds. It seems to us more generally that at this particular moment in time, the challenges for societies around the world demand more collaboration than ever. Rather than being an experimental academic playground, interdisciplinary work is essential if we want to address the multiple crises that our world seems beset by, and current research into those crises and ways of solving them is highly interdisciplinary (see, e.g., Teixeira de Melo, 2023, p. 80). Research into the consequences of the Covid pandemic, Anthropocene studies, mobility studies, environmental studies, migration studies, artificial intelligence, peace studies: these are just some examples that continue to demonstrate the power and the necessity of collaboration among the disciplines. And while "interdisciplinarity is no longer the new kid on the block" (Bijsterveld & Swinnen, 2023, p. 5)[4], it has not yet entered into standard practice and is not self-evident to many in the academic community.

Lau and Pasquini (2004, p. 49; 63) have referred to interdisciplinarity as "the floppy eared beastie," playing with the idea that individual projects grow into rather unruly (if endearing) amorphous objects unless contained by the constraints of the discipline, but also addressing a long history of attempts to define and redefine the concept itself. As they stress, a researcher's understanding of interdisciplinarity is strongly contingent upon their positionality, and it seems incumbent, then, to define our positionalities before we expound further on our understanding of interdisciplinarity.

Most contributions to debates on interdisciplinarity stress the importance of an institutional framework for this kind of work. In this respect we have been lucky: in the early years of the 21st century, the rectorate of the University of Vienna decided to harness the rich potential that the coexistence of 20 faculties and centres and more than 7500 researchers, engaged in 184 different study courses, promises. By financing research platforms as structural frameworks for interdisciplinary collaboration, they enabled a networking of the kind that allows researchers to go beyond their established disciplinary norms in order to ask less predictable questions than they are used to. Our research platform *#YouthMediaLife* was established in 2018 to investigate young people's media lifeworlds from a range of perspectives, bringing together experts from fields as diverse as computer science, cognitive psychology and German Studies. The structure of the research platform does not suggest one particular form of interdisciplinarity, nor did we try to impose an authoritative notion of what it should be. As Graff suggests (2015, p. 5), "[t]here is no single path to interdisciplinarity, no single model, no single standard for successful development."

---

4 See Graff (2015, p. 3), who points out a long history of interdisciplinary research, way before the late 20th century, for which it is often claimed.

To begin with, most members of our platform and contributors to this volume would see the nature of their work and their approach to research as already interdisciplinary. Many of the disciplines we are at home in, from cultural studies to teacher education, are based on a multitude of paradigms that escape rigid disciplinary delineation and classification. Obviously, whether you see yourself working in interdisciplinary research or not depends to a large extent on your own definition of your discipline.[5] Indeed, as Graff (2015, p. 5) argues in his book *Undisciplining Knowledge,* rather than being alternative to our modern understanding of academic disciplines, interdisciplinarity has always been part and parcel of them. Our own home disciplines, English literature and linguistics, have kept feeding into one another and been influenced by other fields of research, such as the cognitive sciences, psychology or the social sciences. Indeed, Ute Smit's main area of research, applied linguistics, combines discourse analysis with an interest in educational policies and institutions, and Susanne Reichl's focus on children's and young adult literature understands itself as a combination of literary and cultural studies with perspectives from psychology, education, and media studies. Understood by some as examples of "soft interdisciplinarity", these "interdisciplines" have always grown in the nurturing influence of interdisciplinary thought and interdisciplinary structures (see Graff, 2015, p. 6).

Apart from individual disciplines being interdisciplinary in themselves, the kind of interdisciplinarity that our research platform has practiced might best be characterized as what Theo van Leeuwen (2005, p. 6), referencing Novotny 1997, has called "a pluralist model": rather than establish a central discipline as the point of orientation, we share an interest in the same subject, but approach it from a range of diverse perspectives. No hierarchy exists among the various disciplines, and we each hope to contribute to the common aim: to find out more about young people's mediatised lifeworlds. While media studies or cultural studies might legitimately raise the claim to be the disciplines responsible for answering most questions in this respect, they will surely profit from the alternative or additional avenues that approaches such as developmental psychology, applied linguistics or cultural anthropology can provide. This reciprocal widening of horizons has entered into the conception of this volume, too: while the contributions are more or less bound to their disciplinary frames, we found it important to produce a volume that was comprehensible for non-specialist readers, too. In our review process, we made sure that each contribution was assessed both by a disciplinary expert and by a non-expert reader who specializes in another discipline. Non-expert reviewers were specifically advised to scruti-

---

5 See Lau and Pasquini (2004, p. 56–57), for an example of how geographers define themselves vis-à-vis their disciplines.

nize non-specialist accessibility and clarity of the writing, and the contributions have benefitted greatly from this particular focus.

This way of proceeding has become a practice in our communication across the disciplines in the research platform: rather than sticking to our own agendas, we have been forced out of our comfort zones and into the apparent wilderness of uncertain paradigms and unfamiliar standard procedures. We have been compelled to ask for clarification, to confront assumed truths, or to challenge seemingly evident statements, and often across the usually rather rigid levels of the academic hierarchy. Interdisciplinarity, as Bijsterveld and Swinnen (2023, p. 17) argue, requires "intellectual investment, interpersonal trust, and a sense of equality among the participants." As a number of academic voices have pointed out, the first step towards interdisciplinary work consists of putting a set of questions in the centre of interest, not a discipline and its methods (e. g. van Leeuwen, 2005, p. 8). These questions are based on individual researchers' academic curiosity, our main driving force, as well as on a generosity to engage in dialogue and put some effort into making our thoughts, sometimes encoded in disciplinary jargon, accessible to others.

In this volume, we did not set out to ask one overarching research question about young people's lifeworlds. Rather, we were relying on a diversity of questions, approaches, theories and answers that pay tribute to the diversity of the field of research. The contributions to this volume veer between inter- and multidisciplinarity, in a comfortable coexistence of two paradigms of collaboration: one in which we consciously cross boundaries to integrate two or more research traditions and questions, and one in which we read with interest and curiosity what our colleagues across the disciplinary boundaries have to say about questions that we, too, are interested in, and allow these ideas to merge. While some understandings of interdisciplinarity are strongly evaluative and distinguish between 'true' kinds (i. e., integrative models of interdisciplinarity) and 'merely additive' projects (see Teixeira de Melo, 2023, p. 81, for a summary of the debate), we are committed to both interdisciplinarity and multidisciplinarity, an integrative as well as an additive approach. We strongly believe that either has its value in contemporary enquiries into young people's media lifeworlds. Interdisciplinarity often feels to us as if we were "dabbling" in areas we know little about: Lau (in Lau & Pasquini, 2004, p. 52–3) writes of coming to geography from the perspective of literary studies and feeling like "a fraud" and an "impostor." Being firmly grounded in our disciplines helps us dare venture into interdisciplinary territory, just like we had to learn how to walk before we could run. Having the opportunity to ask questions at eye level, without having to fear professional face loss, has helped us take those steps into the unknown with a little more confidence.

Venturing out of our comfort zone, we are not just driven by a cold, distanced, academic curiosity. Our research platform can also be understood as an "affinity space" (Gee, 2004, p. 75–81), a term borrowed from the study of education and used to account for participatory cultures, such as fan communities: a space in which people come together to learn from one another because they have a common objective and a common interest, rather than any more essential qualities that bring them together. Appropriated for our research platform, our affinity space is not the consequence of academics working in a particular discipline, but a consequence of us being focused on and passionate about young people's media practices. As Gee (2004, p.77) stresses, these spaces can be nurturing if their affinity is to the cause and if the hierarchies are less important than the objective to share knowledge. The notion of affinity is particularly suitable for our context because we are hardly ever engaged in detached research questions. Rather, we often launch into hot debates about issues that matter to us, issues related to social change and social equality. Some of our contributions in this volume evidence the engagement with matters beyond the academy and point towards more humane ways of living with difference (see Hall, 1989, p. 10), a widening of democratic structures, and the dangers of totalitarian thought regimes, past and present. Many contributions aim at reading the ways in which young people interact with media critically, and actively fight against the simplifications and the cultural pessimism that has become a hallmark of journalistic discourses about young people's media use: neither a condemnation of a widespread dumbing down nor a celebration of utopian egalitarianism are likely to present themselves as solutions to the burning questions about democratic participation, sustainable ways of living, critical thinking, social cohesion and other questions of generations that feel left out and let down, and that have grown up in a post-digital age with seemingly endless opportunities of communication literally at their fingertips. The "transformative power" (Graff, 2015, p. 1) of interdisciplinary research is palpable in almost all the contributions gathered here.

As the result of a discussion and review process that involved interdisciplinary exchange, each contribution can be understood as influenced by engagement and dialogue across the disciplines. The research platform and its 2021 conference have acted as a contact zone under the umbrella of our joint interest in larger questions of young people's media practices. Various notions of interdisciplinarity coexist here: from vague, impressionistic inspiration by another discipline via the use of theoretical approaches and frameworks to the point in the review process at which the contributors were challenged to leave their home base in order to confront a criticism that came from outside their discipline. Because so many individual understandings exist of how disciplines might best be crossed at so many different stages of the academic communication process, we are not following a particular wording, definition or line of argumentation, instead offering this volume as a contribution to interdisciplinary research that hopefully encourages more collaborative work in young people's media life-worlds across the disciplines.

Reflecting the interdisciplinary nature of #YouthMediaLife, the 14 chapters of this volume highlight diverse practices and concerns of young people's media-tised lifeworlds, and do so from a range of disciplinary angles, following different methodological approaches. For purposes of orientation and clarity, the diverse material is divided into four sections (individual chapters are referred to by author surname/s):

The first section, **"Language and Community"**, concentrates on how media practices connect people and on how specific communities communicate. The types of community vary amongst the four chapters in this section: two are broader constellations of people, i. e. TikTok users (Jones) and students in Viennese upper secondary schools and a university (Ghamarian-Krenn & Schwarz), while the other two can be more narrowly demarcated by location and participation, as academics attending a particular academic conference (Neumeier) and students living in a specific student hall during a given time period (Bosso). A different grouping of the four chapters becomes evident as regards the age brackets in question: two are clearly focussed on young people (Ghamarian-Krenn & Schwarz; Bosso) while the other two (Jones, Neumeier) do not come with age restrictions, thus underlining that young people's lifeworlds are not always separable from those of other age groups. When turning to the media practices in focus, all four chapters topicalise the use and role of English, often as a lingua franca for communication amongst multilingual community members. While Ghamarian-Krenn & Schwarz pursue this interest in English from an informal language learning perspective, identifying the potential of media practices for the breadth and depth of English vocabulary knowledge for different student groups, the other three chapters investigate communicative and identity-construction practices, extending their analytical focus from a purely linguistic to a multi-modal one. Bosso analyses Facebook exchanges in a multicultural hybrid community and its shared communicative strategies. By combining multimodal content and sentiment analysis, Neumeier offers a genre analysis of conference tweets and their communicative functions. Jones, finally, zooms in on the lip-synching practices typically found on TikTok, and argues for their meaning potential as ranging from facilitating everyday racism to working against it in the form of linguistic activism.

The second section, **"Practices and Participation"**, investigates the role of young people's media practices in different kinds of participation. The age groups targeted in this section range from children for the first three chapters (Pirker & Mayrhofer; Dander; Boog-Kaminski, Loidl & Schäfer) to adolescents in the fourth (Jovicic). The practices in focus are diverse, as they combine using very specific mobile apps (Dander) versus digital media more generally (Jovicic), working with material and digital media in an educational project (Pirker & Mayrhofer) and collecting all kinds of real and virtual artefacts (Boog-Kaminski, Loidl & Schäfer). While all chapters offer interpretations of these practices for social participation, their respective framings differ. Dander and Boog-Kaminski, Loidl & Schäfer focus on children more generally, aiming to describe typical or expected practices and their possible implications when it comes to either so-called self-tracking apps (Dander) or collecting items as cultural practice more generally (Boog-Kaminski, Loidl & Schäfer). Pirker & Mayrhofer work with pupils in a lower secondary school, analysing their mainly visual practices for their educational relevance and acceptance within a religious instruction project which aims for critical personal evaluations of a biblical story. Jovicic, finally, zooms in on socio-economically marginalised adolescents in youth centres, evaluating their varied digital practices as indicative of fragmented biographies, marred by experiences of discrimination, poverty and limited career oppor-tunities, and thus reflecting a deeper conflict between succeeding in wider society versus participating in friendship and family groups. Overall, each framing allows for critical evaluations of young people's practices and their potential for social participation.

The third section, **"Perception and Emotion"**, contains three chapters that foreground the subjective construction of young people's respective lifeworlds through a combined focus on their perceptions and emotions. Zooming in on biographic objects, Sonnleitner argues for the mediating character such artefacts can acquire for individuals whose lived experience of language (Busch, 2017) comprises war-induced migration in childhood. With the focus on 'Mali', a social media series narrating events in a military mission in seemingly real time, Meister & Slunecko offer a multimedia, cross-platform dispositive analysis that identifies psychological framing and affect-inducing strategies employed in support of increased military recruitment. Investigating the meaning of emo-tions cross-nationally, Kawai & Ansorge identify different evaluations of black-and-white silhouette pictures between their large samples of Chinese and US Americans, while the younger participants show more similarity in their emo-tional reactions, arguably indicating a levelling effect of cross-nationally shared digital practices. Taken together, the three chapters differ noticeably between a selected few participants (Sonnleitner; Meister & Slunecko) vs. representative samples (Kawai & Ansorge), which is a clear indication of the respective qual-itative vs. quantitative methodological framing and also comes to the fore in the different treatment of 'perception' and 'emotion'. While the first two chapters conceptualize them as interrelated in what they aim to investigate, i.e. in-dividuals' emotionally infused perceptions of what happened in the past or might be relevant in the future, the third study investigates emotions as its object of enquiry and uses perception as a methodological take. Despite such discipline-related differences in conceptualisation, however, all three contributions identify people's perceptions and emotions as highly relevant levers for learning more about their subjective construction of their past, present or future lifeworlds.

The three chapters gathered in the fourth and final section, **"Crisis and Critique"**, are concerned with major socio-political crises and some of the impact they have had on young people: i.e. forced migration and online videos explaining refuge to children (Reschenhofer); National Socialism and children and young adult literature as propaganda (Blumesberger); and, finally, the recent pandemic and lessons learnt for how to research children's media practices (Lemish). Their respective units of research start from very focused and small, i.e. paratextual features of YouTube videos (Reschenhofer), widen to historical information on formal and informal distribution of children's literature (Blumesberger), and end up as broad as possible when offering general parameters for how to research children's mediated lifeworlds in the future (Lemish). All chapters offer in-depth critique of crisis-induced issues and provide suggestions for how to deal with the injustice in focus. On the practical side, for instance, Reschenhofer argues that thumbnails that are used to reference YouTube videos function as indicators of the intended audience; Blumesberger shows how historical accounts provide information on, for instance, circumventing censorship. Lemish, finally, identifies the pandemic-induced centrality of digital practices for all activities as a highly welcome experience for us researchers to investigate the *how* of children's mediatised practices across cultural and socio-economic contexts.

While these four sections offer a way to group the 14 chapters, it is certainly not the only one. We hope that the indications of internal differentiation included in the brief summaries above encourage readers to pick and choose the chapters of most relevance to their own interests. To help you along, please also turn to the chapter titles, provided in the table of contents, and their abstracts. Since these are bilingual, an explanation is needed: As indication of different academic traditions, authors were free to write their contributions in either German or English. To keep all chapters accessible also for non-German readers, we provide all abstracts in both languages. Additionally, the original titles were extended by adding translated versions, which also means that the first language of the title is the language the chapter is written in. We wish you happy browsing and reading as you join our *#YouthMediaLife & Friends* community!

References

Aikat, D. (2020). Millennials usher a post-digital era: Theorizing how generation Y engages with digital media. In J. Schulz et al. (Eds.), *Mediated millennials: Studies in media and communications* Vol. 19 (pp. 9–29). Emerald Publishing.

Bamberg, M., & A. Georgakopoulou (2008). Small stories as a new perspective in narrative and identity analysis. *Text & Talk, 28*(3), 377–396. https://doi.org/10.1515/TEXT.2008. 018.

Bijsterveld, K., & A. Swinnen (2023). Introduction. In K. Bijsterveld & A. Swinnen (Eds.), *Interdisciplinarity in the scholarly life cycle: Learning by example in humanities and social science research (*pp. 1–22). Palgrave Macmillan.

Bruns, A. (2006). Towards produsage: Futures for user-led content production. In F. Sudweeks, H. Hrachovec, & C. Ess (Eds.). *Proceedings: Cultural attitudes towards communication and technology* (pp. 275–284). Murdoch University, Perth.

Busch, B. (2017). Expanding the notion of the linguistic repertoire: On the concept of Spracherleben – the lived experience of language. *Applied Linguistics, 38*(3), 340–358. https://doi.org/10.1093/applin/amv030.

Cramer, F. (2014). What is 'post-digital'? *APRJA, 3*(1), 10–24.

Gee, J.P. (2004). *Situated language and learning: A critique of traditional schooling.* Routledge.

Graff, H. J. (2015). *Undisciplining knowledge: Interdisciplinarity in the twentieth century.* Johns Hopkins.

Großegger, B. (2017). Zwischen Freakout und Normcore: Jugend und Jugendkulturen in den späten 2010er Jahren. *Österreichisches Religionspädagogisches Forum, 25*(1), 7–16. doi:10.25364/10.25:2017.1.2.

Hall, S. (1989). *The Origins of Cultural Studies.* Transcript. Media Education Foundation.

Hartmann, M. (2008). Domestizierung 2.0: Grenzen und Chancen eines Medienaneignungskonzeptes. In C. Winter, A. Hepp, & F. Krotz (Eds.). *Theorien der Kommunikations- und Medienwissenschaft* (pp. 401–416). Springer VS.

Havelock, E. (1986). *The muse learns to write.* Yale University Press.

Hepp, A., & M. Pfadenhauer (2014). Mediatisierte Partizipation?: Kleine Formen der Beteiligung jenseits von Medienlogik. In F. Krotz, C. Despotovic, & M. Kruse (Eds.). *Die Mediatisierung sozialer Welten: Synergien empirischer Forschung* (pp. 235–262). Springer VS.

Husserl, E. (1962). *Die Krisis der europäischen Wissenschaften und die transzendentale Phänomenologie.* Hua IV.

Kraus, B. (2015). The life we live and the life we experience: Introducing the epistemological difference between "Lifeworld" (Lebenswelt) and "Life Conditions" (Lebenslage). *Social Work & Society, 13*(2), 1–9; https://d-nb.info/1080338144/34.

Lau, L., & M.W. Pasquini (2004). Meeting grounds: perceiving and defining interdisciplinarity across the arts, social sciences and sciences. *Interdisciplinary Science Reviews, 29*(1), 49–64. https://doi.org/10.1179/030801804225012437.

Prensky, M. (2001). Digital natives, digital immigrants Part 1. *On the Horizon, 9*(5), 1–6. https://doi.org/10.1108/10748120110424816.

Reichert, R. (2017). Defacement – Faciales Regime, "Selfies" und Gesichtsauflösung in Sozialen Medien. In M. Pfadenhauer & T. Grenz (Eds.). *De-Mediatisierung: Diskontinuitäten, Non-Linearitäten und Ambivalenzen im Mediatisierungsprozess* (pp. 113–126). Springer VS.

Schütz, A. (1974). *Der sinnhafte Aufbau der sozialen Welt: Eine Einleitung in die verstehende Soziologie.* Suhrkamp.

Teixeira de Melo, A. (2023). Toward a ("Dissolved") psychology of interdisciplinary and transdisciplinary relations: A complexity-informed proposal. *Review of General Psychology, 27*(1), 80–99. https://doi.org/10.1177/10892680221114860.

Van Leeuwen, T. (2005). Three models of interdisciplinarity. In P.A. Chilton & R. Wodak (Eds.). *A new agenda in (critical) discourse analysis: Theories, methodology and interdisciplinarity* (pp. 3–18). John Benjamins.

#YouthMediaLife. (2021). *International conference #YouthMediaLife2021.* #YouthMedia-Life. https://youthmedialife2021.univie.ac.at/.

#YML21 Organising Committee. (2021, May 5). *#YML21 conference impressions.* #Youth-MediaLife Blog. https://youthmedialife-blog.univie.ac.at/yml21-conference-impressions.

#YouthMediaLife. (n.d.) *Research platform mediatised lifeworlds.* #YouthMediaLife. https://youthmedialife.univie.ac.at/.

1. Language and community

Rodney H. Jones

Lip-synching and young people's everyday linguistic activism on TikTok

Abstract

Among the unique affordances of the video sharing app Tiktok is the ability it gives to users to *appropriate* the verbal performances of others and re-present them with their own bodies through practices of lip-synching. This often involves users appropriating the voices of people of races different from their own, which sometimes results in others critiquing the authenticity of their performances or criticizing them for 'cultural appropriation' or for perpetuating racial stereotypes. This chapter explores how young users of TikTok engage in voice appropriation and negotiate social norms surrounding it. It begins by describing how practices of lip- synching on TikTok raise broader issues around voice appropriation, racism, and the exploitation of people of colour who use the platform. It then discusses how concepts from sociolinguistics such as stylization, crossing, indexicality and (in)authenticity can help us to understand the ways lip-synching performances function in the linguistic marketplace of TikTok and the factors affecting people's negotiations of voice appropriation and authenticity. Finally, it demonstrates how the same technological affordances which facilitate practices of everyday racism (in the form of language mocking and cultural appropriation) also provide the tools for creators to 'call out' racist performances and engage in acts of 'everyday linguistic activism'.

Zu den einzigartigen Funktionen der Video-Sharing-App TikTok gehört die Möglichkeit, sich die verbalen Darbietungen anderer anzueignen und sie durch Lippensynchronisation mit dem eigenen Körper darzustellen. Dabei eigenen sich die Nutzer*innen häufig die Stimmen von Menschen anderer ethnischer Herkunft als ihre eigenen an, was manchmal dazu führt, dass andere die Authentizität ihrer Darbietungen kritisieren oder ihnen "kulturelle Aneignung" oder die Aufrechterhaltung rassistischer Stereotype vorwerfen. In diesem Kapitel wird untersucht, wie junge TikTok-Nutzer*innen mit Stimmaneignung umgehen und die damit verbundenen sozialen Normen aushandeln. Zunächst wird beschrieben, wie die Praktiken des Lippensynchronisierens auf TikTok umfassendere Fragen im Zusammenhang mit der Aneignung von Stimmen, Rassismus und der Ausbeutung von People of Color, die die Plattform nutzen, aufwerfen. Anschließend wird erörtert, wie Konzepte aus der Soziolinguistik wie Stilisierung, Crossing, Indexikalität und (Un-)Authentizität uns helfen können zu verstehen, wie Lippensynchronisationen auf dem sprachlichen Marktplatz von TikTok funktionieren und welche Faktoren sich auf die Aushandlung von Stimmaneignung und Authentizität auswirken. Schließlich wird aufgezeigt, wie dieselben technologischen Möglichkeiten, die rassistische Alltagspraktiken (in Form von Verhöhnung und kultureller Aneignung) ermöglichen, den Content Creators auch die Mittel an die Hand geben, rassistische Darbietungen anzusprechen und Handlungen des "alltäglichen sprachlichen Aktivismus" zu setzen.

In May of 2020, Australian singer Amy Shark was forced to apologize for posting a video on TikTok of her speaking in an Asian accent after her fans called out her "inappropriate" behavior. Shark's voice in the video, however, was not her own, but one of the many soundtracks available on TikTok for users to appropriate into their own performances. In other words, Shark was not "imitating" an Asian accent, but rather lip-synching someone else's imitation of one. In this case, the original offender was the part Mexican part Native-American comedian Anjelah Johnson, whose 2007 comedy routine featuring the persona of a Vietnamese nail salon worker had somehow, 13 years later, gone viral on TikTok.[1] Shark wasn't the only TikToker who lip-synched snippets from this routine. In fact, various versions of the snippet that Shark had appropriated had also been used by thousands of other creators of all different races.[2] But when Shark used the sound it became an opportunity for TikTokers (and Shark herself) to reflect on the "appropriateness" of this appropriation. In a tweet calling Shark out, African American comedian Nina Oyama reposted Shark's video with the message: "Don't forget to check on ur white friends in isolation to make sure they aren't doing stupid bullshit like this." In another tweet, she exhorted her followers: "Don't cancel amy shark (sic) just get her to delete it and maybe explain to her why it's bad" (Triscari, 2020). Notably, Oyama did not criticize Anjelah Johnson for her original performance.

Nothing in this example is particularly unusual in the world of TikTok. Every day, hundreds of thousands of creators appropriate the voices of other people into their videos, often lip-synching language varieties that are not their own from people who come from different racial or ethnic groups (or different regions or classes), and every day some of them get called out for appropriating voices that they do not have the "right" to use or lip-synching them in ways that might be construed as mocking, disrespectful, racist, or just "inappropriate". Sometimes, these acts of "calling out" themselves take on a viral quality, resulting in spirited debates about what kinds of voices different people should be allowed to use, as

---

1 See the original comedy routine at https://youtu.be/SsWrY77o77o.
2 See for example https://www.tiktok.com/music/nhạc-nền-Liz-Kim-Cương-700331502174054 2721 (Short URL: http://tinyurl.com/yckknzh7); https://www.tiktok.com/@aydinthedisneyne rd/video/6984852349856582917?is_copy_url=1&is_from_webapp=v1&q=do%20you%20like %20crystal%20gel&t=1658576371964 (Short URL: https://tinyurl.com/yupftkyb).

well as about broader issues about the meaning of "cultural appropriation" and what kinds of behaviors should be considered "racist".

In a way, this is what TikTok is all about. The main affordance of the app is the way it makes the soundtracks from everyone's videos available to other users, and the production and editing tools it provides that make lip-synching easy. This affordance, however, is also one of the reasons why TikTok has been implicated in the perpetuation of racist stereotypes, cultural appropriation and symbolic violence against women, people of color, and sexual minorities (Dersimonian, 2021; Guynn, 2022; Holt, 2019). As Parham (2020) puts it:

> Tiktok is built, by design, on appropriation—the original lip-syncing app required users to mime existing audio. TikTok hinges on how imaginatively users can build upon something that's already out there; it becomes all about the transformation. What sours this creative repackaging, mutates the joy into hatefulness, is when the content is estranged from its original context. The way someone or something can so quickly and easily be warped, diluted, recast as something other. The way one's culture can be stolen and made monstrous, made meaningless.

At the same time, TikTok's affordances for voice appropriation can also facilitate acts of "everyday activism" in which users engage in creative ways of "calling out" "inappropriate" appropriations and formulate other ways of appropriating the voices of others that are empowering, affirming, and challenge social and linguistic hierarchies (Alliare, 2022; Zwann, 2020). In this chapter, I will explore how a range of key concepts in sociolinguistics such as stylization, linguistic crossing, indexicality and authenticity, as well as more recent engagements with embodiment (Bucholtz & Hall, 2016) can help us to understand how young users of TikTok engage in voice appropriation and negotiate social norms surrounding it.

I will begin by introducing TikTok, with particular reference to the practices of lip-synching it facilitates and how these practices raise broader issues around voice appropriation, racism, and the exploitation of people of color who use the platform. Next, I will discuss how concepts from sociolinguistics such as stylization, crossing, indexicality and (in)authenticity can help us to understand the ways lip-synching performances function in the linguistic marketplace of TikTok and the factors affecting people's negotiations of voice appropriation and authenticity. Finally, I will discuss how the same technological affordances which facilitate practices of everyday racism (in the form of language mocking and cultural appropriation) also provide the tools for creators to "call out" racist performances and engage in acts of "everyday linguistic activism".

Voice appropriation on TikTok

TikTok is a short form video sharing platform owned by the Chinese company ByteDance. It was launched internationally in 2017, and a year later was merged with the app Musical.ly, a video platform that allowed users to create short lip-sync and comedy videos. At the time of writing, TikTok had over a billion active users outside of China, making it one of the most downloaded apps in the last decade. In 2021, visitors to the app's website exceeded visitors to Google (TikTok most popular website…, 2021), and in 2022 its engagement rate surpassed Facebook's, Twitter's and Instagram's (Cucu, 2022). The bulk of TikTok's users (approx. 60%) are young people between the ages of 16 and 24 (TikTok statistics, 2022), causing media commentators, marketers and academics alike to regard the platform as a "mirror of Generation Z" (Cervi, 2021, p. 198).

Videos on TikTok include a range of genres, including comedic videos (jokes, tricks), dance videos, documentary videos, explanatory videos (tutorials and lessons) and communal videos (challenges, memes, duets) (Schellewald, 2021). Among the most popular videos, however, are those in which creators use their bodies to perform other people's voices, including both the vocal tracks of popular songs, films and television programs, and vocal tracks from other TikTok creators' videos. Lip-synch videos can be considered a genre in themselves, but all of the other genres mentioned above also often incorporate lip-synching.

The key affordance of the app is the way that is allows users to appropriate and reuse sounds from one video to another, creating viral chains of appropriation and reappropriation of different people's voices. The interface includes a range of features that allow users to choose from a library of soundtracks (including both the soundtracks of other users' videos as well as commercial material such as popular songs and clips from movies and television shows), and to speed up or slow down the soundtrack or the video recording to better synchronize moves, gestures, and lip-movements to the sound. The viewing interface has icons for users to follow the creator of a video, to like the video, to comment on it, share it on other social media platforms, and to see other videos that have used this soundtrack and to reuse it in their own videos.

TikTok is often referred to as a social media platform, but in many ways, it doesn't conform to boyd and Ellison's (2007) famous definition of a social net-work site—it is not about creating a bounded network of friends. People are connected more by the voices and soundtracks that they reappropriate, the viral trends they participate in, and the "challenges" they take up. Thus, rather than durable networks of like-minded "friends", the kinds of "communities" facili-tated by TikTok are what Varis and Blommaert (2014) refer to as "light com-munities", loose, ephemeral groupings that gather briefly around particular discursive objects (memes, challenges, conspiracy theories). Zulli and Zulli

(2022) argue that voice appropriation is central to the way the platform encourages and shapes sociality by encouraging the imitation and replication of audio content through lip-synching. Creating content around a specific audio clip allows users to recognize and replicate their shared orientation towards a specific cultural product as well as their shared stances towards particular kinds of people or particular political or moral positions. Indeed, the use of certain soundtracks often comes to be associated with particular communities of users and functions as a way of promoting conviviality within those communities.

Because of the ludic, activity-based nature of the platform, Kurzrock (2019, p.1) imagines it as a "virtual playground" full of digital equipment and invented games that people can engage with together in various embodied ways. Indeed, a key aspect of users' ludic engagement with the platform is the way it allows them to "play" with their bodies, altering the way they look through the use of various filters and special effects, and altering the way they sound through the appropriation of other people's voices—an affordance I refer to here as *synthetic embodiment*. Synthetic embodiment is not just an affordance of TikTok, but a central affordance of digital media more generally—the ability they give people to fabricate new forms of embodiment by mixing and remixing different modes and materialities. Other examples include the avatars people inhabit in virtual worlds, digitally enhanced images created with apps like Snapchat and Instagram, and *Animoji* – animated emoji in which people merge their own voices and facial expressions with talking images of animals and other cartoon figures.

Synthetic embodiment is not just a matter of "play"; it also provides opportunities for users of digital media to "try on" different kinds of identities and experiment with different ways of being in the world. In an ethnography of urban skateboarders I conducted in the early 2000s (2011), for instance, I observed how skateboarders exploit the affordances of digital video to splice together footage of different tricks and moves and entrain them with the rhythm of their favorite music, in part, as a way of learning how to be skaters, and to, as I wrote (2011, p. 332) "imagine futures and contribute to their ongoing symbolic projects of self-formation." Gee (2003) has observed similar effects in his exploration of how players of video games make use of their avatars and in-game identities to experiment with different identities. The ability to "virtualize" and digitally "remix" the body/self can have profound psychological and social effects when it comes to things like learning, self-actualization, and community formation. But it can also have negative effects, leading to the exploitative commodification of certain kinds of bodies and selves, and the symbolic violence that comes from the perpetuation of caricatures and stereotypes (Lévy, 1998, see below).

The form of synthetic embodiment I'm most concerned with here is self-styling through the appropriation of another person's voice. This particular affordance, I argue, has profound implications for understanding issues of self and identity, as well as of commodification and symbolic violence. It presents opportunities for us to think about how *voices* speak to, from, and of embodied subjects, and their potential to create and disturb not just social identities but also relationships of power.

The ways TikTok allows for the separation (and reconfiguration) of voices and bodies is not entirely new. It can be located on a continuum of effects communication media more generally have had on the voice/body relationship over the past century. Bucholtz (2011) has noted how the development of communicative technologies such as the phonograph, the telephone and the sound film in the early 20th century produced dramatic shifts in language and subjectivity by facilitating the separation of voice from body. As soon as the voice and the body can be separated and reconfigured, she argues, questions immediately arise regarding what the "right voice" is for the "right body" based on prevailing language ideologies and social norms around things like gender, race and class. The ideologies of the voice dominant before the development of these technologies, Bucholtz (2011, p. 256) notes, "were rooted in essentialization and authentication, which comfortably imposed and reasserted hegemonic ideologies of social subjectivity." But, as a result of these new technologies, "voices have become … recontextualized through a process of linguistic re-embodiment, whereby [they] are detached from expectably raced, gendered, and classed bodies and jarringly reassigned to "inappropriate" bodies …"

These disruptions of expectations about what kind of voice can be legitimately paired with what kind of body have the potential to challenge dominant social orders, as has been the case with the lip-synching associated with drag performances, where the queering of the voice-body relationship is simultaneously playful and subversive. Butler (1999, p.175) has argued that what makes drag both alluring and revolutionary is the way it challenges the illusion of stable and objective gender identities, "play[ing] upon the distinction between the anatomy of the performer and the gender that is being performed."

But the effect of unsettling the voice-body relationship is, Bucholtz reminds us, not always an unsettling of hegemonic ideologies. Rather, sometimes the act of reassigning a voice to a body to which it does not belong can end up "re-inscribing" dominant ideologies, as with the blackface performances of minstrel shows, and with what Bucholtz and Lopez (2011) refer to as "blackvoice" sometimes used by white actors in Hollywood films. In fact, the appropriation of African American voices (mostly in the form of hip-hop soundtracks) by white TikTokers (and the stereotypical physical movements that accompany such performances, including mouthing the "n word") has been widely critiqued as a form of "digital blackface" (McLean, 2020; Parham, 2020). Like the animated GIFS featuring Black performers criticized by Kuo (2019, p. 182f.), the appropriation of Black voices allows non-Black creators to "puppeteer" and "playact" through Black identities which, as a result, take on the status of commodities.

It could be argued that synthetic embodiment of the kind exercised by creators on TikTok is by its very nature an exercise in caricature. It is not just that these "off the shelf" voices are inevitably paired with "off the shelf" bodily movements and gestures associated with certain stereotypical personae, but that the separation of voices and bodies seems to open up a space where caricature flourishes. In a study of the way people use Animoji, for instance, Herring and her colleagues (2020) found that speaking through Animoji filters seems to encourage playful verbal performances of stereotyped personae, with 85% of the Animoji clips in their corpus involving deviations from normal voice quality of the performer, and most of these including the stylization of ethnic and regional accents linked in sometimes racist ways to particular Animoji figures (e.g. a stereotyped Chinese accent being used with the panda animoji).

Whether a particular act of voice appropriation on TikTok is deemed "appropriate" or "inappropriate" (or somewhere in between), however, is not a matter of any universal norms of propriety. Rather, it is locally negotiated within and across particular communities and contingent on a range of factors including the social identity of the person doing the appropriating, the ways they position themselves in relation to the voice they have appropriated, and the way the voice and their particular appropriation of it are positioned vis-à-vis other performances using this voice, including both the original performance and the performance of other creators. Appropriating the soundtrack of a popular song, for instance, might also involve embodying the "style" of the artist, which, of course, when it comes to white creators embodying the styles of Black performers, is not unproblematic. At the same time, though, the voices and styles of celebrities also function as resources that young people use to claim a certain kind of cultural competence, displaying their ability to skilfully deploy, disassemble, and re-assemble various key cultural texts.

Another factor in judging the appropriateness of lip-synching performances involves the degree to which a snippet of sound has become what Abidin (2021) calls an "audio meme" and so come to be regarded as part of the vocal "commons" (Zwaan, 2020). In such cases, the "meaning" of a given act of appropriation comes less from its citation of a particular person or performance and more from its place in an ongoing stream of recontextualization. Assumptions creators make about the "common ownership" of cultural products, however, can also make them vulnerable to being "called out", as was the case when white TikTok celebrity Brittney Broski asserted in a video that many terms historically associated with African American Vernacular English (AAVE) had become part of the vocal "commons", which attracted fierce criticism, especially from Black creators (Mendez, 2020).[3]

Issues of voice appropriation become even more complicated when one takes into account the fact that, in the attention economy of TikTok, these snippets of other people's voices take on not just symbolic value, but also monetary value. While most of the work on the commodification of language has focused on the values assigned to particular codes or styles in various societies (e.g. Heller, 2010), when it comes to TikTok, it is people's *actual* voices and words that are turned into commodities, the value of which increases the more they are appropriated and circulated by other people. Creators on TikTok have a range of ways to profit from their activities, including being paid directly through TikTok's Creator Fund (for creators with more than 100,000 followers) and partnering with brands to promote their merchandise. All avenues to monetization on the platform, however, depend on creators' content "going viral", and either creating a sound that many other users want to appropriate or appropriating a popular sound from another creator in a particularly creative way that can increase the chances for a creator to attract views, likes and followers (Abidin, 2021). Further complicating these economies of attention are the economic interests of the platform itself and its desire to increase engagement by algorithmically seeding users' feeds with soundtracks that they are more likely to appropriate in the attempt to incubate new auditory memes.

The fame and economic rewards associated with viral soundtracks and dances, however, do not always flow to those who originally created them, laying bare another ideological dimension of voice appropriation that arises when cultural capital is distributed unequally among creators from different demographic backgrounds. Black creators and other creators of color, for example, regularly complain about white creators achieving fame by appropriating soundtracks or dances that originated in the Black community, the most publicized example being the "Renegade" dance which catapulted 15-year-old white creator Charli D'Amelio to fame and fortune while the actual creator of the dance, a 14-year-old Black girl named Jalaiah Harmon, received little attention. Such situations highlight the racial politics at play in the political economy of social media platforms and how the commodification of Black bodies and Black voices by privileged users helps to perpetuate racial inequality (Zwann, 2020).

---

3 In July of 2020, Broski posted a video defending her use of AAVE, saying: "The Nicki Minaj thing, "The big boobs? Chile, anyway," that's a meme, obviously. So when someone quoting that or when someone says "period," "sis," "snatch," all that, it's very much like internet culture. Like stan twitter. Stan culture has its own language."

Stylization, crossing and (in)authenticities

In many ways the practices of linguistic and embodied styling which creators engage in on TikTok make salient many of the points sociolinguists have been making about linguistic style over the past two decades, particularly its status as a form of *bricolage* in which people pick and choose from the communicative resources they have available to them and combine them in various ways to create or manage the identities they project to others (Eckert, 2008). Whenever people speak, they produce meaning not just based on what they say (semantic meaning), but also how they say it. The linguistic varieties, accents, and speech styles that they adopt are meaningful insofar as they point to or invoke particular kinds of identities or particular kinds of social situations. Sociolinguists call this kind of meaning "indexical meaning". When people, for example "talk posh", or "talk gangsta", they are invoking particular stereotypical personae, either aligning themselves to or distancing themselves from these personae.

In most cases, the speech styles that people adopt are associated with social identities that they can "legitimately" claim (that is, they "match" with their ethnicity, gender, class, and other features of their biographies). Sometimes, however, people adopt ways of speaking that are associated with people from different ethnicities, genders, classes, etc. Rampton (1995, p. 280) uses the term "crossing" to refer to instances when people adopt language or styles "not generally thought to belong to [them]." While such practices can often have clearly racist underpinnings, as in the case of white "Anglos" in America using "Mock-Spanish" for humorous effect (Hill, 2009), they can also, as Rampton (1995) shows in his detailed study of interactions among multi-ethnic teens in London, serve as a means by which young people negotiate ethnic difference and racial division in more positive ways. In the context of the multi-ethnic adolescent friendship groups Rampton studied, practices of crossing, he asserts, are not so much attempts to claim membership in an ethnic outgroup or mock or ridicule members of that outgroup, as they are attempts to develop allegiances with and claim membership in a multi-ethnic youth community. In this respect, practices of voice appropriation can function as a form of "everyday anti-racism" that challenges notions of "ethnic-absolutism" (2008, p. 4). At the same time, however, such practices can also raise questions about both authenticity and power within the wider context of societal race relations. In their studies of white teens in the U.S. who adopt features of African-American vernacular English, scholars such as Culter (1999) and Bucholtz (2011) point out that, while the aim of such practices is to index "authentic", "street-smart" identities, speakers often come off as "inauthentic" because the linguistic features they choose are usually based on broad stereotypes of African-American speech or "hip-hop style". At the same time, while adopting African-American English functions as a way for white teens to identify with stereotyped aspects of African-American masculinity, it also ends up reproducing "the "racialization" of African-American men as violent and dangerous, an image that legitimizes ferocious discrimination against this reference group" (Hill, 1999, p. 547). As Spitzmüller (2015) points out, all acts of stylization are essentially acts of "metapragmatic stancetaking" by which people do not just align themselves to or distance themselves from the kinds of people associated with the style they are imitating, but also by which they inevitably become agents in promoting or contesting particular ideologies of language, race, gender, etc.

While style in sociolinguistics has long been seen as a multimodal accomplishment, involving not just the voice, but also facial expressions, bodily movements, clothing and physical activities, most work on the stylization of others has focused primarily on the way people alter their voices to imitate the linguistic style of the outgroup. When creators choose "off the shelf" voices to lip-synch on TikTok, however, they are essentially outsourcing the linguistic labor of vocal stylization to the original speaker. The main locus of stylization is the body, with performers choosing facial expressions, gestures, dance movements, makeup, and items of clothing (as well as the electronic filters and adornments the app makes available) to go with the voice. Sometimes part of the performance involves mirroring, as closely as possible, the movements and facial expressions of the original performance, but at other times jarring dissonances are created between the style of the voice and the style of the bodily performance, generating "symbolically condensed dialogues" (Rampton, 199, p. 422) between the performing body and the voice that has been appropriated. But, as with drag, even when the performers' movements are closely entrained with the voice that they are lip-synching, there is always a disjuncture, a gap, a queering of the voice-body relationship which is at the heart of the practice. It is in this gap that issues of (in)authenticity and (in)appropriateness become salient.

Among the sociolinguists who have focused more on the embodied aspects of stylization are Goodwin and Alim (2010), who describe how a young white girl on a school playground makes use of embodied styling to mock a working-class African American girl. What is interesting is that the way she does this is not by "acting out" the voice she is imitating, but by combining the vocal performance associated with a wealthy white "Valley Girl" with gestures associated with working-class Black "Ghetto-Girls". To account for this, Goodwin and Alim introduce the term *transmodal stylization*, by which they mean more than just forms of multimodal, embodied styling, but modes of stancetaking that are enacted when different communicative modalities "simultaneously index multiple yet mutually elaborating culturally salient representations" (p. 179).

What Goodwin and Alim highlight with this concept is that sometimes stylization is not so much a matter of combining voices and bodies into "ideologically cohesive semiotic packages" but rather a matter of assembling resources in ways that "exploit semiotic dissonances between established meanings" (Bucholtz & Hall, 2016, p. 180). In fact, it might be argued that all stylization to some degree exploits dissonances, drawing attention to its own artifice. Coupland (2007, p.154), for instance, sees stylization as a matter of "strategic inauthenticity". What is different about the practices of styling made possible by TikTok is that the separation of the vocal and visual channels increases opportunities to exploit dissonances and to "play" with *inauthenticities*. And so, in the context of negotiating the appropriateness of various acts of appropriation, the real question is not whether or not a performance is "authentic" but rather what kinds of inauthenticities it gives rise to and what kinds of social meanings can arise in the gap between the voice and the body. Sometimes, of course, these inauthenticities produce symbolic violence in the form, for example, of mockery or the commodification of the other. But sometimes, inauthenticities can actually amplify affinities between different categories of people, challenge hegemonic orders of indexicality, and open up new possibilities for identity performance, empowerment and conviviality.

One example of this is famous Black TikToker ayaanahmed's rant about being accused of "catfishing" for wearing make-up[4] and the way it has been taken up by a whole range of different kinds of creators to celebrate their own makeup regimes, including many gay men who have used the soundtrack to claim affinity with ayaanahmed (as can be seen in white creator tylermilic_'s version where he uses ayaanahmed's voice in a campy performance of putting on his own make-up[5]). Each time a voice gets taken up by others, they recontextualize it, layering onto it their own storylines and embodied styles that do not entirely abandon the style of the original but build new indexicalities onto it.

More often than not, however, rather than producing straightforward affirmations or mockeries, the inauthenticities of voice appropriation in TikTok videos produce multiple and ambiguous meaning potentials (Hautea et al., 2021) in line with what Phillips and Milner (2017) see as the stance of ironic "ambivalence" that dominates much social media communication, especially among young people. A video of a young white girl playfully lip-synching the sexually explicit lyrics of a Black male hip-hop artist, for instance, can simultaneously communicate exploitive mockery, celebratory sexuality, and stinging gender critique.

---

4 https://www.tiktok.com/@ayaanahmed/video/6874648594381556994?is_copy_url=1&is_from
   _webapp=v1 (Short URL: https://tinyurl.com/39fzp7z2).
5 https://www.tiktok.com/@tylermilic_/video/6879881415723404546?is_copy_url=1&is_from_
   webapp=v1 (Short URL: https://tinyurl.com/4mns578v).

This semiotic ambivalence, of course, is, to some degree inherent in what Goffman (1974) refers to as "speak-fors" (instances when people perform the speech of others), chiefly because their communicative effects are not just a matter of producing connotative meanings, but of exploiting the indeterminacy of the communicative situation itself. Even in Rampton's (1995) study of crossing among multi-ethnic groups of adolescents, the "meaning" of a particular act of crossing can only be fully understood in terms of the specific social context in which it is used and the ways in which it has the potential to alter that context. Such observations, as Hill (1999, p. 543) argues, demonstrate the importance of attending to the ways social actors negotiate the linguistic boundaries of voice appropriation within "social and communicative space… where the grounds for inferences are shifting and fluid."

If the grounds upon which negotiations about linguistic crossing are built are shifting and fluid in physical contexts such as those studied by Rampton, they are even more unstable in the virtual world of TikTok where voices are shared and reshared at a lightning pace, generating ever new and changing trajectories of association and indexicality. A good example is the meme "Cash me ousside, how 'bout dah", which is the subject of Aslan and Vasquez's (2018) study of virality and metalinguistic commentary online. It started with the linguistic performance of a young white girl on the *Dr Phil* show who attempted to project a "tough", "streetwise" persona by appropriating features of AAVE. This performance later was turned into a stream of image-macro memes which mocked the performance, some explicitly riffing on its racialized nature, inciting a raft of metalinguistic commentary on the appropriateness of her appropriation. Later, however, when the soundtrack became an "audio meme" on TikTok, its grounding in its original context became increasingly tenuous. The sound clip ricocheted around the platform, ending up being used in contexts that seemed to have very little to do with the racialized performance of the original clip and the image-macro memes that it spawned, as for example, when cosplayers took to performing the soundtrack dressed as characters from Japanese anime[6,7]. In such cases it becomes difficult to trace neat lines of indexical relations and unravel how all the fields of connotation cohere. What seems more important than indexicality here is the iconicity[8] of these performances (Duemert, 2018), the way

---

6 https://www.tiktok.com/@cospeach/video/6702975122124311814?is_copy_url=1&is_from_we bapp=v1 (Short URL: https://tinyurl.com/c95cd89t) and https://www.tiktok.com/@cutie.cat.co splays/video/6691393179930856710?is_copy_url=1&is_from_webapp=v1 (Short URL: https:// tinyurl.com/2s38jye7).

7 https://www.tiktok.com/@cutie.cat.cosplays/video/6691393179930856710?is_copy_url=1&is_ from_webapp=v1 (Short URL: https://tinyurl.com/2s38jye7).

8 "Iconicity" has to do with the ways signs sometimes derive meaning based on their resemblance to what is being signified.

they create meaning through playing with (in)authenticities—creating varying degrees of resemblance and dissemblance to the original.

Part of the reason for this is that the main purpose of appropriating and circulating memes is often not so much to reproduce or critique the indexical meanings generated by previous iterations of the meme as it is to simply be part of the group of people circulating the meme. On TikTok, the main form that these playful practices of sharing take is "the challenge", in which users attempt to make their performances of viral soundtracks funnier and more "sharable" than others, which often ends up encouraging increasing dissonance between the voice being appropriated and the bodily performance associated with it.

These messy, entangled trajectories of indexicality, however, do not absolve users of accountability for the "appropriateness" of their performances. In fact, in some ways, lip-synching on TikTok actually ends up further problematizing acts of linguistic crossing by de-linking them from specific social interactions (and even specific bodies). Zwann (2020) argues that these decontextualized acts of voice appropriation often serve to expose the contradictions inherent in practices of crossing, making individuals *more* accountable for their appropriations and *more* vulnerable to being "called out" (see below). In this way, TikTok almost inevitably ensnares users into complex negotiations about appropriation and authenticity, privilege and power, and the validity of the various "micro hegemonies" (Blommaert & Varis, 2015) that govern the legitimacy of voice-body relationships on the platform.

TikTok and everyday linguistic activism

Just as the affordances for lip-synching create opportunities for cultural appropriation and everyday racism, they also create opportunities for young people to engage in everyday linguistic activism by exploiting the ambivalent voice-body relationships and the forms of "strategic inauthenticity" that the platform offers.

One way they do this is through making use of the various tools the platform provides for metapragmatic commentary. The "callout" is a specific kind of metapragmatic speech act in which a victim of "behind-the-back" talk or injustices is able to publicly accuse offenders and create an opportunity to respond to them (Goodwin, 1990). In some forms, like the Spoken Word performances Marquise Jones (2017) analyses, the callout is made particularly powerful through the ability it gives to the victim to characterize/caricature the offender through embodied performances of the offense. TikTok's affordances of allowing users to reproduce and rework the videos of others functions in a similar way, enabling perceived victims of inappropriate performances to *re-appropriate* those performances and recontextualize them in a dialogue in which the offenders become answerable for their behavior. They might, for example, use the "duet" function to create videos where they silently react in a split screen to the offender's performance[9], or they might comment upon it by inscribing written words, emojis, or filters on top of the offenders' video[10], or they might themselves produce caricatured performances of the offender's original caricature[11]. Sometimes callouts involve a combination of these techniques, as can be seen in rynstarr's performance of phrases white people have said to her (e.g. "Is that really your hair?", "Slaves were actually treated pretty well", "You're pretty, and I don't usually like Black girls") with a split screen next to her of white "frat boys" jive dancing, and the words: "Ranking these guys by the microaggressions they would have done to me in college" superimposed on top of the video.[12]

Another technique might be referred to as "re-meming", where creators take an existing trend and attempt to reframe it by layering a new trend on top of it. An example of this can be seen in the playful infiltration of the "Cash me ousside" meme by Japanese anime cosplayers (see above). A more serious example can be seen in the case of the soundtrack of Nicki Minaj's song Black Barbies[13], which became a popular feature in lip-synching performances of white creators. As a way of reclaiming this sound, Black performers took to appropriating it, with messages to other Black creators to do the same and text superimposed on their videos with questions like "Can an *actual* black woman get hype for using this sound?" Later supportive white creators started a new trend of appropriating the sound but *not* lip-synching to it, such as jennabeingdramatic, who superimposes the words "srry (sic) guys I can only sing what applies to me" over her video.[14]

The appropriation of other people's voices in ways that create dissonance does not always function to marginalize or belittle the original voice, but can sometimes be used as a way of creatively amplifying it. A good example of this can be

---

9 https://www.tiktok.com/@ambiezee/video/6805227482992610565?is_copy_url=1&is_from_ webapp=v1&q=racist%20lip-synching&t=1646845538962 (Short URL: https://tinyurl.com/ mr48d795).

10 https://www.tiktok.com/@sammy.idk0/video/7033963618236402946?is_copy_url=1&is_fro m_webapp=v1&q=racist%20lip-synching&t=1646845538962 (Short URL: https://tinyurl.co m/33e5byss).

11 https://www.tiktok.com/@ayaanahmed/video/6998966440434879749?is_copy_url=1&is_fro m_webapp=v1 (Short URL: https://tinyurl.com/mpnuexu2).

12 https://www.tiktok.com/@rynnstar/video/6926254857141767430?is_copy_url=1&is_from_w ebapp=v1 (Short URL: https://tinyurl.com/yckeyu7k).

13 The lyrics of the part of the song that was appropriated were: "I'm a fuckin' black barbie/ Pretty face, perfect body/ Pink seats in the 'Rari/ Always fuck him like I'm sorry…"

14 https://www.tiktok.com/@jennabeingdramatic/video/6975329023937252614?is_copy_url= 1&is_from_webapp=v1 (Short URL: https://www.tiktok.com/@jennabeingdramatic/video /6975329023937252614?is_copy_url=1&is_from_webapp=v1) see also https://www.tiktok.c om/@noelshaffer/video/6974887118556384518?is_copy_url=1&is_from_webapp=v1 (Short URL: https://tinyurl.com/58smhd69).

seen in the appropriation of the voice of US Congresswoman Alexandria Ocasio Cortez giving a speech in the House Chamber, in which she describes an encounter with a male colleague in which he called her "a fucking bitch", by teenage girls who lip-synched the video while putting on make-up[15]. Here what ends up being queered is not the voice, but rather the whole system of expectations that support not just misogynistic violence like that Representative Ocasio Cortez describes but also wider assumptions about femininity and authenticity. One of the creators who was part of this trend put it this way: "Unlike Instagram, which is very static—all you see is the end result, which can be judged as superficial, as women using make-up often are—TikTok shows the process and you can layer over context with these audios. It reveals how complicated and multifaceted we are, and that's really empowering."

Conclusion

In this chapter, I have suggested that online public spaces such as TikTok can provide an opportunity to witness the ways young people are grappling with questions about the rights and responsibilities that accompany different kinds of linguistic performances and are creatively exploiting the affordances of the platform to engage in everyday linguistic activism. As Zwann (2020, p. 11) notes, although lip-synching apps like TikTok "are filled to the brim with racial and gendered politics, complexities and challenges," they also have the potential to create a metapragmatic space where "new solutions, subversions and solidarities can arise."

In thinking about how normativities around appropriation and authenticity are worked out in digital media, Deumert (2018) argues, in the context of her analysis of linguistic creativity on digital platforms in South Africa, that semiotic negotiations of power and authenticity take place between the two poles of *mimesis* and *mimicry*. Mimesis is the affirmative creation of resemblances, the careful entrainment of voices with bodies, the fitting of the "right" voice with the "right" body. Mimicry is the transgressive creation of dissemblance, the entanglement of voices with bodies in which they don't belong, the dramatization of incoherencies. As Deumert sees them, these practices are not mutually exclusive, but overlap and interact, producing different forms of identity and non-identity between object and representation. More importantly, the indexicalities they produce are often not clear cut. Acts of mimesis can, in some contexts, be just as disruptive as acts of mimicry. Where the metapragmatic negotiation of the

---

15 https://www.tiktok.com/@lauriehernandez_/video/6882581814410480902?is_copy_url=1&is _from_webapp=v1 (Short URL: https://tinyurl.com/y32p6239).

boundaries of voice appropriation on platforms like TikTok take place is the gap between the two. It is in this gap, where the self is reimagined through the other, and the other is reimagined through the self, that young people are, sometimes earnestly, sometimes playfully, communally negotiating their situated understandings of what counts as "racist" and how to engage in "anti-racism".

References

Abidin, C. (2021). Mapping internet celebrity on TikTok: Exploring attention economies and visibility labour. *Cultural Science Journal, 12*(1), 77–103. https://doi.org/10.5334/c sci.140.

Agha, A. (2003). The social life of cultural value. *Language & Communication, 23*(3–4), 231–273. https://doi.org/10.1016/S0271-5309(03)00012-0.

Allaire, C. (2020, June 22). How TikTok went from dance videos to meaningful activism. *British Vogue*. https://www.vogue.co.uk/news/article/tiktok-activism-president-trump -rally.

Aslan, E., & Vásquez, C. (2018). 'Cash me ousside': A citizen sociolinguistic analysis of online metalinguistic commentary. *Journal of Sociolinguistics, 22*(4), 406–431. https:// doi.org/10.1111/josl.12303.

boyd, d.m. & Ellison, N. B. (2007). Social network sites: Definition, history, and scholarship. *Journal of Computer-Mediated Communication, 13*(1), 210–230. https://doi.org/10.111 1/j.1083-6101.2007.00393.x.

Blommaert, J. & Varis, P. (2013). Enough is enough: The heuristics of authenticity in superdiversity. In J. Duarte & I. Gogolin (Eds.), *Linguistic superdiversity in urban areas: research approaches* (pp. 143–160). Benjamins.

Bucholtz, M. 2011. *White kids language, race, and styles of youth identity*. Cambridge University Press.

Bucholtz, M. (2011). Race and the re-embodied voice in Hollywood film. *Language & Communication, 31*(3), 255–265. https://doi.org/10.1016/j.langcom.2011.02.004.

Bucholtz, M., & Hall, K. (2016). Embodied sociolinguistics. In N. Coupland (Ed.), *Sociolinguistics: Theoretical debates* (pp. 173–198). Cambridge University Press. https://doi.o rg/10.1017/CBO9781107449787.009.

Bucholtz, M., & Lopez, Q. (2011). Performing blackness, forming whiteness: Linguistic minstrelsy in Hollywood film. *Journal of Sociolinguistics, 15*(5), 680–706. https://doi.org /10.1111/j.1467-9841.2011.00513.x.

Butkowski, C. P., Dixon, T. L., Weeks, K. R., & Smith, M. A. (2020). Quantifying the feminine self(ie): Gender display and social media feedback in young women's Instagram selfies. *New Media & Society, 22*(5), 817–837. https://doi.org/10.1177/146144481 9871669.

Cervi, L. (2021). Tik Tok and generation Z. *Theatre, Dance and Performance Training, 12*(2) 198–204.

Coupland, N. (2007). *Style: Language Variation and Identity*. Cambridge University Press.

Cucu, E. (2022, February 24). 2022 Social media industry benchmarks. *Socialinsider.* https://www.socialinsider.io/blog/social-media-industry-benchmarks/.

Cutler, C. A. (1999). Yorkville Crossing: White teens, hip hop and African American English. *Journal of Sociolinguistics*, *3*(4), 428–442. https://doi.org/10.1111/1467-9481.00089.

Dersimonian, A. (2021, May 27). TikTok: A hotbed of cultural appropriation, and why it matters. *The American Genius.* https://theamericangenius.com/social-media/tiktok-hotbed-of-cultural-appropriation-why-it-matters/.

Deumert, A. (2018). Mimesis and mimicry in language – Creativity and aesthetics as the performance of (dis-)semblances1. *Language Sciences*, *65*, 9–17. https://doi.org/10.1016/j.langsci.2017.03.009.

Eberhardt, M., & Freeman, K. (2015). 'First things first, I'm the realest': Linguistic appropriation, white privilege, and the hip-hop persona of Iggy Azalea. *Journal of Sociolinguistics*, *19*(3), 303–327. https://doi.org/10.1111/josl.12128.

Eckert, P. (2008). Variation and the indexical field. *Journal of Sociolinguistics*, *12*(4), 453–476. https://doi.org/10.1111/j.1467-9841.2008.00374.x.

Eckert, P. (2019). The limits of meaning: Social indexicality, variation, and the cline of interiority. *Language.* https://doi.org/10.1353/LAN.2019.0072.

Gee, J. P. (2003). *What video games have to teach us about learning and literacy.* Palgrave-MacMillan.

Goffman, E. (1974) *Frame analysis.* Harper & Row.

Goodwin, M (1990). *He-said-she-said: Talk as social organization among Black children.* Indiana University Press.

Goodwin, M. H., & Alim, H. S. (2010). 'Whatever (neck roll, eye roll, teeth suck)': The situated coproduction of social categories and identities through stancetaking and transmodal stylization. *Journal of Linguistic Anthropology*, *20*(1), 179–194. https://doi.org/10.1111/j.1548-1395.2010.01056.x.

Guynn, J. (2022, August 24). It's not just Facebook and Twitter. TikTok is 'hatescape' for racism and white supremacy, study says *USA TODAY.* https://www.usatoday.com/story/tech/2021/08/24/tiktok-videos-hate-white-supremacy-racism-terrorism/8249286002/.

Hautea, S., Parks, P., Takahashi, B., & Zeng, J. (2021). Showing they care (or don't): Affective publics and ambivalent climate activism on TikTok. *Social Media + Society*, *7*(2), 20563051211012344. https://doi.org/10.1177/20563051211012344.

Herring, S. C., Dainas, A. R., Lopez Long, H., & Tang, Y. (2020). Animoji performances: 'Cuz I can be a sexy poop'. *Language@Internet*, *18*(1). https://www.languageatinternet.org/articles/2020/herring.

Hill, J. H. (1999). Styling locally, styling globally: What does it mean? *Journal of Sociolinguistics*, *3*(4), 542–556. https://doi.org/10.1111/1467-9481.00095.

Hill, J. H. (2009). *The everyday language of white racism.* John Wiley & Sons.

Heller, M. (2010). The commodification of language. *Annual Review of Anthropology*, *39*(1), 101–114. https://doi.org/10.1146/annurev.anthro.012809.104951.

Holt, B. (2019, November 1). Teens on TikTok have no clue they're perpetuating racist stereotypes. *Quartz.* https://qz.com/quartzy/1738478/how-teens-on-tiktok-are-perpetuating-racist-stereotypes/.

Jones, R.H. (2011b). C me sk8: Discourse, technology and 'bodies without organs'. In C. Thurlow & K. Mroczek (Eds.), *Digital discourse: Language in the new media* (pp. 321–339). Oxford University Press.

Kuo, R. (2019). Animating feminist anger: Economies of race and gender in reaction GIFs. In D. Ging & E. Siapera (Eds.), *Gender hate online: Understanding the new anti-feminism* (pp. 173–194). Palgrave Macmillan.

Kurzrock, E. (2022, February 23). Intensified play: Cinematic study of TikTok mobile app. *Medium.* https://ethankurzrock.medium.com/intensified-play-cinematic-study-of-tiktok-mobile-app-b8e848befaa8.

Kytölä, S., & Westinen, E. (2015). "I be da reel gansta"—A Finnish footballer's Twitter writing and metapragmatic evaluations of authenticity. *Discourse, Context & Media, 8,* 6–19.

Lorenz, T. (2020, February 13). The original Renegade. *The New York Times.* https://www.nytimes.com/2020/02/13/style/the-original-renegade.html.

Parham, J. (2020, August 4). TikTok and the evolution of digital blackface. *Wired.* https://www.wired.com/story/tiktok-evolution-digital-blackface/.

Phillips, W., & Milner, R. M. (2017). *The ambivalent internet: Mischief, oddity, and antagonism online.* Polity.

Marquis Jones, T. (2016). I'm callin you out!: Spoken Word as social (inter)action. *Texas Linguistics Forum 59,* 60–70.

Mendez, M. (2020, August 1). 'Kombucha Girl' slammed for saying AAVE is 'internet culture'. *The Daily Dot.* https://www.dailydot.com/irl/kombucha-girl-brittany-broski-aave/.

Newman, E. (2021, February 9). How make-up tutorials became Gen Z's favourite form of TikTok activism. *Dazed.* https://www.dazeddigital.com/head/article/51859/1/tiktok-makeup-tutorials-gen-z-activism-politics-aoc-blm-endsars.

Pew Research Center. (2019). Defining generations: Where Millennials end and Generation Z begins. *Pew* Research. https://www.pewresearch.org/fact-tank/2019/01/17/where-millennials-end-and-generation-z-begins/.

Rampton, B. (1995). *Crossing: Language and ethnicity among adolescents.* Addison Wesley Publishing Company.

Rampton, B. (1999). Styling the Other: Introduction. *Journal of Sociolinguistics, 3*(4), 421–427. https://doi.org/10.1111/1467-9481.00088.

Rampton, B. (2008). Everyday antiracism in ethnolinguistic crossing and stylisation. *Noves SL. Revista de Sociolingüística,* Winter, 1–6. http://www.gencat.cat/llengua/noves.

Schellewald, A. (2021). Communicative forms on TikTok: Perspectives from digital ethnography. *International Journal of Communication, 15,* 1437–1457.

Spitzmüller, J. (2015). Graphic variation and graphic ideologies: A metapragmatic approach. *Social Semiotics, 25*(2), 126–141. https://doi.org/10.1080/10350330.2015.1010323.

Triscari, C. (2020, May 4). Amy Shark apologises for 'inappropriate' TikTok video. *NME.* https://www.nme.com/en_au/news/music/amy-shark-apologises-for-inappropriate-tiktok-video-2658709.

TikTok most popular website of 2021. (2021, December 31). *BBC Newsround.* https://www.bbc.co.uk/newsround/59768051.

TikTok statistics—Everything you need to know. (2022, February 28).*Wallaroo Media.* https://wallaroomedia.com/blog/social-media/tiktok-statistics/.

Varis, P., & Blommaert, J. (2014). Conviviality and collectives on social media: Virality, memes, and new social structures. *Multilingual Margins: A Journal of Multilingualism from the Periphery*, 2(1), 31–44. https://doi.org/10.14426/mm.v2i1.55.

Zulli, D., & Zulli, D. J. (2022). Extending the Internet meme: Conceptualizing technological mimesis and imitation publics on the TikTok platform. *New Media & Society*, 24(8), 1872–1890. https://doi.org/10.1177/1461444820983603.

Zwann, J. (2020, June 15). Voices as commons: Secondary aurality, appropriation and the crowd. Retrieved 6 March 2022, from Academia website: https://www.academia.edu/49095843/Voices_as_Commons_Secondary_Aurality_Appropriation_and_the_Crowd.

Katharina Ghamarian-Krenn / Marlene Schwarz

Extramural engagement with English and vocabulary learning outcomes: A comparative account of research on Viennese teenagers and university students

Abstract

While vocabulary learning has long been considered as happening mostly in the classroom, recent research increasingly focuses on how extramural language contact is extending opportunities for lexical development and use beyond the walls of the classroom. This chapter presents a comparative analysis of two independent studies focusing on extramural English (EE) and its relation to vocabulary learning outcomes in Austria. The two studies target groups of learners differing in age and English proficiency and focus on two different types of vocabulary knowledge, namely knowledge of general and academic words. This allows for a fruitful comparison of compulsory English learning at secondary school and the self-chosen pursuit of English studies with an academic focus at the tertiary level. Using a self-developed EE questionnaire and receptive and productive vocabulary tests the two studies reveal several similarities: in both studies (1) engagement with EE is high despite the difference in age and educational contexts and (2) EE functions as a predictor variable for receptive but not for productive vocabulary knowledge.

Im Gegensatz zur häufigen Annahme, dass Fremdsprachenerwerb und Wortschatzerweiterung großteils im Klassenzimmer stattfinden, fokussiert die momentane Forschung zunehmend darauf wie außerschulischer Sprachkontakt mit Englisch (*Extramural English*) die Möglichkeiten der lexikalischen Verwendung und Entwicklung erweitert. Dieser Beitrag präsentiert eine vergleichende Analyse zweier eigenständiger Studien im Sekundar- und Tertiärbereich mit Fokus auf Extramural English (EE) und dessen Zusammenhang mit dem Vokabelerwerb im Kontext Österreichs. Dabei beleuchten die Studien nicht nur zwei verschiedene Alters- und Bildungsniveaus, sondern auch die Auswirkungen des außerschulischen Sprachkontaktes auf den generellen und akademischen Wortschatz. Die Ergebnisse beider Studien basieren auf selbstentwickelten EE-Fragebögen, sowie rezeptiven und produktiven Vokabeltestungen. Die vergleichende Analyse beider Studien zeigt, dass der außerschulische Kontakt hoch ist, unabhängig von Bildungskontext und Alter. Des Weiteren wurde Kontakt mit Extramural English von beiden Studien als Prädiktorvariable für rezeptives aber nicht für produktives Wortwissen identifiziert.

Keywords: *extramural English, informal vocabulary learning, receptive vocabulary knowledge, productive vocabulary knowledge*

1.   Introduction

Over the last two decades opportunities for engaging with foreign languages, and in particular English, have been growing enormously, leading to unprecedented possibilities for language development outside traditional school contexts (Nunan & Richards, 2015). This massive increase of English input is largely an unintended side effect of globalization, digitalization, and changing leisure activities. However, it is interesting because the amount of exposure in these informal environments far surpasses that of traditional classrooms and can lead to greatly improved language competence. Ten years ago, evidence for such informal language learning was largely anecdotal, but since then a newly emerging research field has begun to investigate extramural English (EE, Sundqvist, 2009) and informal second language learning (ISLL, Dressman & Sadler, 2020; Toffoli et al., in print). Such research aims to measure and understand the motivations, processes, and results of informal language learning and in a next step could lead to suggestions for adapting classroom teaching.

Greater vocabulary knowledge is one potential benefit of increased contact with extramural English and often the most tangible result of informal language learning for learners themselves (Kalaja et al., 2011, p. 52). As such, it has been the focus of much early research, but while some European countries already have established research traditions on informal (vocabulary) learning outside formal educational contexts, in particular the so-called subtitling countries[1] such as Belgium, Sweden and the Netherlands (e.g. Olsson & Sylvén, 2015; Peters, 2018; Peters et al., 2019; Puimège & Peters, 2019; Sundqvist, 2009; Verspoor et al., 2011), other countries, such as Austria, are still in their infancy regarding research on extramural practices.

This comparative analysis is based on two of the first studies aiming to relate vocabulary learning outcomes to engagement with EE in the Austrian context. Schwarz (2020) examined the general vocabulary size of 15- to 16-year-old students attending academic secondary schools in Vienna and Ghamarian-Krenn (2023) investigated knowledge of academic vocabulary knowledge among English major students at the University of Vienna. While the focus of the two studies is on different age groups and different areas of vocabulary development, they can be usefully compared with regard to EE practices in the context of Austria in the late 2010s and thus allow for interesting insights into a novel research environment.

---

1 Subtitling refers to the practice of broadcasting foreign-language TV programmes in the original version, which is often English, with subtitles in the respective country's language. Instead of subtitling other countries use dubbing or voice-over versions; for an overview see a study conducted for the European Commission (Media Consulting Group, 2009).

2.   Extramural English use and its relation to vocabulary learning

In the newly emerging research field, a wealth of different terms is currently used to describe informal out-of-school activities (Benson, 2011; Dressman & Sadler, 2020). In our studies we use the term *extramural English* (EE, Sundqvist, 2009; Sundqvist & Sylvén, 2016), which encompasses all forms of informal contact with English outside formal educational settings and incorporates both traditional and digital media. EE does not presuppose the presence of *learning*, it includes all informal activities in which learners *use* English. What is important though is that the language use is learner-driven rather than directed by teachers (Sundqvist & Sylvén, 2016, p. 6).[2] Hence, extramural activities typically are informal leisure activities, in which learners engage with English voluntarily during their spare time.

2.1.   Extramural activities at secondary and tertiary level

While engagement with EE has been researched across all educational levels beginning with children prior to formal education (e. g. Puimège & Peters, 2019) and pupils at primary level (e. g. Hannibal Jensen, 2017), young adults in secondary and tertiary education are the focus of the present studies. Taking a look at the types of extramural activities at secondary school level, listening to English music emerges either as the most practiced activity (e. g. Grau, 2009; Lai et al., 2015; Peters, 2018), or is among the most popular (e. g. Sundqvist, 2009; Sundqvist & Sylvén, 2014). Subsequently, consumption of video material, such as watching TV, films or video clips on various technical devices is ranked second in many studies (e. g. Grau, 2009; Lyrigkou, 2018; Peters, 2018). In comparison, the third place already displays more variation amongst studies. Nevertheless, many northern European studies report that playing computer games is the third most popular extramural activity (Peters, 2018; Sylvén & Sundqvist, 2012). In contrast, studies located in non-subtitling countries, such as Aniol (2011), Lyrigkou (2018) or Mirmán Flores and García Jiménez (2018), observe less prominent results regarding involvement in digital gaming.

Comparing these results to the findings at tertiary level reveals interesting similarities and differences. While listening to music (e. g. Kusyk, 2017; Liu, 2014; Orhon, 2018) and consumption of video material (e. g. Orhon, 2018; Trinder, 2015) remain immensely popular throughout the whole educational system,

---

2 It is also worth noting that while English is the most frequently used language for such informal activities, other languages could potentially also be used, as shown by the updated concept of *extramural L_n* (Sundqvist, 2019).

fewer studies have examined involvement in digital gaming at tertiary level, allowing for no valid comparisons across educational levels (e.g. Busby, 2021; Ferdous, 2013; Liu, 2014; Orhon, 2018). A noticeable difference is that participants involved in tertiary education display more interest in reading English texts, comprising books, novels, magazines, newspapers and academic texts (Hyland, 2004; Liu, 2014; Moncrief, 2011). Moreover, involvement in speaking activities ranging from face-to-face meetings to online video calls appears to be more varied at tertiary level. Prior educational levels appear to be characterized by reluctance regarding participation in speaking activities, but several studies at tertiary level report increased engagement in communicative English activities outside education (Lamb, 2002; Moncrief, 2011). Hence, some clear tendencies regarding EE engagement are visible across educational levels; however, such popularity rankings should be treated with caution, since extramural behaviour tends to be a highly individual phenomenon displaying large variation even within age groups (e.g. Lamb, 2004; Sylvén, 2006; Yi, 2005).

2.2.   Effects of EE on vocabulary knowledge

Concerning the relation between EE and vocabulary outcomes, studies on learners at secondary school from Sweden (Olsson & Sylvén, 2015; Sundqvist, 2009), Flanders (Peters, 2018; Peters et al., 2019), and the Netherlands (Verspoor et al., 2011) show that exposure to EE benefits vocabulary development. This finding is perhaps little surprising as these countries are known for their early exposure to English, particularly through subtitled English-language TV broadcasts. However, the evidence regarding effects of subtitled TV is inconclusive, with positive effects in some studies (Puimège & Peters, 2019) but not in others (Peters et al., 2019).

Investigating informal learning activities at university level, Li and Hafner (2022) find that exposure to EE has a significant positive effect on vocabulary knowledge. In addition, Lee (2019b) reports that, rather than the quantity of EE activities, it is their quality which is related to vocabulary knowledge. Furthermore, in a comparative study of learners at upper secondary school and university Peters (2018) showed that length of formal instruction is not as good a predictor of vocabulary size as exposure to EE, which is a highly interesting finding supported by previous studies (e.g. González-Fernández & Schmitt, 2015).

In more detail, all studies mentioned (Lee, 2019a; Li & Hafner, 2022; Peters, 2018; Peters et al., 2019; Sundqvist, 2009; Verspoor et al., 2011) report a significant relationship between EE and receptive vocabulary knowledge, which refers to word knowledge necessary for receptive language skills, such as reading or listening (Nation, 2013). This appears to hold true across educational levels. Conversely, productive word knowledge, intrinsic to speaking and writing a language, is much less well-researched and the existing results vary considerably. While Sundqvist (2009) and Olsson (2016) report a significant connection between EE exposure and productive vocabulary knowledge, Olsson and Sylvén (2015) and Lee (2019a) could detect no significant influence of the frequency of engagement with EE on vocabulary in text production or scores on productive vocabulary knowledge tests.

In addition to investigating the difference between receptive and productive word knowledge, studies comprise different types of vocabulary. For instance, some focus on general vocabulary, whereas others target specific vocabulary areas, such as knowledge of academic vocabulary, which is particularly frequent in academic genres (Nation, 2013).[3] Until recently, only few studies (Busby, 2021; Olsson & Sylvén, 2015; Sundqvist, 2009; Warnby, 2022) investigated the influence of EE exposure on academic vocabulary knowledge. In an early study, Sundqvist (2009, p. 151) noted that EE did not have the same impact on word knowledge across all frequency bands; in fact, EE seems to have less impact the more difficult and less frequent words are. This conclusion is supported by Busby's (2020) findings using the academic section of the Vocabulary Levels test: Her results show that EE involvement had no significant influence on form-meaning recognition knowledge of academic words in a multiple linear regression model. However, two other studies (Olsson & Sylvén, 2015; Warnby, 2022) contradict these findings by revealing significant links between EE activities and academic word knowledge. While Olsson and Sylvén (2015) relate a significant growth of academic vocabulary in written texts over time to EE engagement, Warnby (2021) found significant positive correlations between receptive academic form-meaning knowledge and seven EE activities, which overall explained 26% of the variance in the academic word knowledge score.

In sum, only few studies using diverse research instruments have been conducted so far, which highlights the fact that the studies presented in this chapter make two relevant contributions: They not only add a comparative perspective on two different age groups but additionally compare knowledge of different types of vocabulary.

---

3 Frequency, i.e. a given word's overall frequency in a language, is a pervasive factor in vocabulary research since it affects most or all aspects of lexical processing and acquisition (Schmitt, 2010, p. 13). Lexical items with a higher frequency are learned earlier and they are also processed and remembered better (Ellis, 2002; Schmitt, 2010). Commonly, vocabulary is thus sorted into so-called frequency bands, based on information drawn from large corpora, which contain thousands of texts from different genres and thus provide a good indication of overall frequency in a given language.

3.   Research questions

The aim of this analysis is to compare the findings of two original studies in-vestigating different groups of learners with regard to (1) the type and frequency of extramural engagement and (2) the effect of extramural activities on receptive and productive English vocabulary knowledge. Accordingly, the analysis focuses on the following research questions:

RQ 1: How does engagement with extramural English compare in two groups of Austrian learners of English differing in terms of age and proficiency level?

RQ 2: How do the two groups of learners compare in relation to the effect of engagement with extramural English on receptive and productive aspects of vo-cabulary knowledge?

4.   Introducing the methodology of the two studies

This comparative analysis of extramural activities and their relation to vocabu-lary outcomes is based on two independent studies concentrating on the same geographical setting. Both studies are situated in the Austrian capital Vienna: Schwarz (2020) collected data from tenth-grade students at seven academic secondary schools (AHS) in different districts, whereas Ghamarian-Krenn (2023) focuses on students at the Department of English and American Studies at the University of Vienna. The two participant groups thus differ markedly in relation to age (M_{sec}= 15.6; M_{uni}= 21.3) and English proficiency (B1-B2; B2-C1)[4], but also in relation to the goals of their English studies: While the teenage secondary school students have to study English as a compulsory subject that aims to develop their language competence in preparation for their A-level exams (*Matura*), the uni-versity students chose to specialize in English and concentrate on developing their academic English as a more specialized competence. This difference is reflected in the foci of the two studies: Schwarz (2020) tested secondary school students' overall vocabulary size, whereas Ghamarian-Krenn (2023) focused on knowledge of academic vocabulary. Nevertheless, both studies used the same measure of extramural contact in form of an in-depth questionnaire estimating participants' frequency of engagement with EE. After a short characterization of

---

4 These proficiency levels refer to the six-level scale (i. e. A1, A2, B1, B2, C1, C2) proposed in the
   Common European Framework of Reference for languages (Council of Europe, 2001). B1 and
   B2 indicate the two stages of independent user, whereas B2 and C1 refer to the transition stage
   from independent to proficient user.

the two samples, the research design, instruments, and data analysis techniques used in the two studies will be described and compared below.

4.1.   Participants

Both studies recruited their participants via educational institutions: in Schwarz (2020) complete English classes were invited to participate according to pre-set sampling criteria, and Ghamarian-Krenn (2023) invited all students in the year group to take part. Ultimately, participation was voluntary in both studies. Data collection was carried out by the researchers during class time at schools and at university.

Characteristic		Secondary school students (N = 189)		University students (N = 152)	
Gender	female	N = 109	58%	N = 117	77%
	male	N = 79	42%	N = 35	23%
Mean age	in years	M = 15.56 [15.46; 15.65]	SD = 0.68	M = 21.26 [20.67; 21.84]	SD = 3.66
Level of English	acc. to CEFR		B1-B2		B2-C1
Age of onset	in years	M = 7.81 [7.49; 8.12]	SD = 2.12	M = 7.43 [7.06; 7.81]	SD = 2.34
Length of English study	in years	M = 7.76 [7.45; 8.07]	SD = 2.16	M = 13.78 [13.07; 14.48]	SD = 4.37
Number of home languages	1	N = 84	45.16%	N = 1	0.7%
	2	N = 87	46.77%	N = 60	39.5%
	3	N = 11	5.91%	N = 54	35.5%
	4+	N = 4	2.15%	N = 37	24.3%

Table 1: Participant comparison of Schwarz (2020) & Ghamarian-Krenn (2023)

In Schwarz's (2020) study, the final quantitative sample included a total of 201 tenth-grade students from seven Viennese upper secondary schools. However, due to absences on the day of data collection for the questionnaire, only 189 participants can be used in most quantitative analyses, as can be seen in Table 1 above. In comparison, the study by Ghamarian-Krenn (2023) involves a total sample of 152 tertiary level students, divided into 117 female [77%] and 35 male [23%] students, which is an even larger gender imbalance than in Schwarz's (2021) study with 58% female and 42% male students. While these gender differences are in line with the proportions in the overall student populations, they can further be explained by the fact that at secondary school level, English is an obligatory school subject for all students, while at university students can choose if they want to pursue their English studies. Other visible differences are the level of language proficiency and the number of languages spoken. While Schwarz's (2021) secondary school participants have an estimated language proficiency of B1-B2, participants in Ghamarian-Krenn's (2023) study had to pass the university entrance exam and had a minimum English level of B2. Moreover, concurrent to the difference in age, Schwarz's (2021) secondary school participants spoke fewer languages than the tertiary-level students involved in Ghamarian-Krenn's (2023) study. While at secondary school level, 91.9% of the participants report speaking one to two home languages, the picture is becoming more complex at university with only 40.2% of the sample speaking one to two languages and 59.8% speaking three or more languages in their spare time.

4.2.   Research design

Schwarz (2020) was the first larger study to focus on extramural English practices among Austrian teenagers in academic upper secondary schools and as such it pursued three main aims: establishing an overview of contact with EE, exploring the relationship between EE and receptive and productive vocabulary size, and analysing learners' perspectives on EE and (vocabulary) learning. To achieve these aims, a cross-sectional study using a fully integrated mixed methods approach was conducted. The sequential QUAN-qual research design consisted of a larger quantitative strand followed by a more in-depth qualitative exploration to gain insights into learners' emic perspectives on EE and informal language learning. In the quantitative strand, which is the focus of this chapter, data were collected using a detailed questionnaire, an online language diary, and two vocabulary tests (see section 4.3).

Ghamarian-Krenn's (2023) study investigates the influence of EE involvement on the development of receptive and productive form-meaning knowledge of academic verbs, using purely quantitative methodology. Following a longitudinal research design, students filled in a detailed questionnaire on EE behaviour and then completed four vocabulary tests on different word knowledge aspects at three different points in time. While the longitudinal nature is intrinsic to the larger project, only the data of the first data collection involving EE engagement will be used for this contribution to make the two studies more comparable.

4.3.   Instruments

Schwarz (2020) developed a detailed questionnaire to gather information on participants' sociodemographic and linguistic background and to estimate frequency of engagement in different EE activities. The core part of the questionnaire is a comprehensive list of leisure activities, for which participants were asked to indicate how frequently they did these in English on a 5-point scale ranging from 'almost never' to 'almost every day'. All items were presented in German as the language of schooling to ensure that students understood them correctly. Ghamarian-Krenn (2023) adopted the same questionnaire with slight adaptations; for instance, the EE items in Schwarz (2020) also elicited how students engage in activities; for instance, whether they watch a film on TV, on DVD, or online. Since, however, her analysis showed that young adults in Austria all preferred similar modes of engagement, which are mostly internet-based, these distinctions were dropped by Ghamarian-Krenn (2023). Hence, for this comparative study slight adaptations, such as the derivation of summary variables, were necessary to support direct comparisons of the EE data from both age groups. The data on frequency of EE presented is based on a list of 38 EE activities used in both studies.

For Schwarz (2020), the practicalities of classroom-based research necessitated the selection of vocabulary measures that could quickly and easily be administered during lessons. Hence, *V_YesNo* (Meara, 2015), a checklist test containing pseudowords to discourage guessing and to correct for overestimation, was used to measure written receptive vocabulary size at the level of meaning recall. Students completed a pen-and-paper version of the test, which was then scored according to criteria set out by Meara and Miralpeix (2017). The test score provides an estimate of participants' receptive knowledge of the 10,000 most frequent words in English. In addition, *Lex30* (Meara & Fitzpatrick, 2000), an innovative measure using a word association task to elicit a sample of written words under time pressure, was used to test productive vocabulary size operationalized as recall of written word form. The sample of words elicited with the help of 30 cue words is scored in relation to word frequency; points are awarded for all response words not included in the 1,000 most frequent English words as knowledge of lower frequency words indicates greater productive vocabulary size. Similar to other indices of productive vocabulary knowledge based on free production (e.g., the Lexical Frequency Profile (Laufer & Nation, 1995) or computerized indices of lexical diversity (Jarvis, 2013), *Lex30* scores cannot be interpreted in terms of concrete size estimates, but can be used to rank participants in terms of vocabulary knowledge.

Focusing on receptive and productive form-meaning knowledge of academic verbs, Ghamarian-Krenn (2023) designed two tests to estimate participants' vocabulary knowledge. Both tests, the form-meaning recall [$\alpha = 0.89$] and the form-meaning recognition test [$\alpha = 0.90$], comprise 72 academic verbs from 10 frequency bands and display satisfactory measures regarding reliability, discrimination values and facility values, which additionally contributed to overall test validity (see α values above). Moreover, test validity was enhanced using a test evaluation questionnaire during the piloting phase in which the students were able to rate the test and note difficulties. Item formats in both vocabulary tests are based on the receptive and the productive versions of the Vocabulary Levels test (Laufer & Nation, 1999; Nation, 1990; Schmitt et al., 2001).

4.4. Data analysis

Statistical analyses were carried out using the software packages SPSS (IBM Corp. 2020, Version 27.0.), R (Version 3.5.1, R Development Core Team 2018) and RStudio (Version 1.2.1335, RStudio Team 2018). Since this comparative analysis is based on individual studies, some EE activities had to be re-categorized to obtain the same data structure (see section 4.3.) before descriptive analyses were carried out jointly. For tests of difference between independent sub-samples the non-parametric Wilcoxon rank-sum test, which is also known as and computationally equivalent to the Mann-Whitney U test, was used because the data often did not show a normal distribution. Pearson's r was used as effect size, as it is preferable to other options because of its simple interpretation (Field et al., 2012, p. 57f.). The interpretation of effect sizes follows the recommendations by Plonsky and Oswald (2014), which are based on a large meta-analysis of effects in quantitative L2 research. For the correlation coefficient r they suggest that .25 should be seen as small, .40 as medium, and .60 as large in terms of effect.

For the results on the relation between EE and vocabulary knowledge, we draw on the multiple regression analyses that were carried out for the individual studies. As a direct comparison of the findings is not possible due to the different foci and measures of vocabulary, a re-analysis was not necessary. For further details on data analysis in the individual studies, please see Schwarz (2020) and Ghamarian-Krenn (2023).

5. Findings and Discussion

In the following section both research questions will be addressed, starting with an analysis of EE engagement. Results will be presented successively for both studies and compared and contrasted in a second step.

5.1.   Research question 1: Extramural English activities

In response to research question 1, both studies show that the overall frequency of engagement with EE is high: In Schwarz (2020) 96.3% of secondary school students reported doing at least one EE activity (almost) every day and, with 97.4%, the figure for the university students in Ghamarian-Krenn (2023) is even higher.

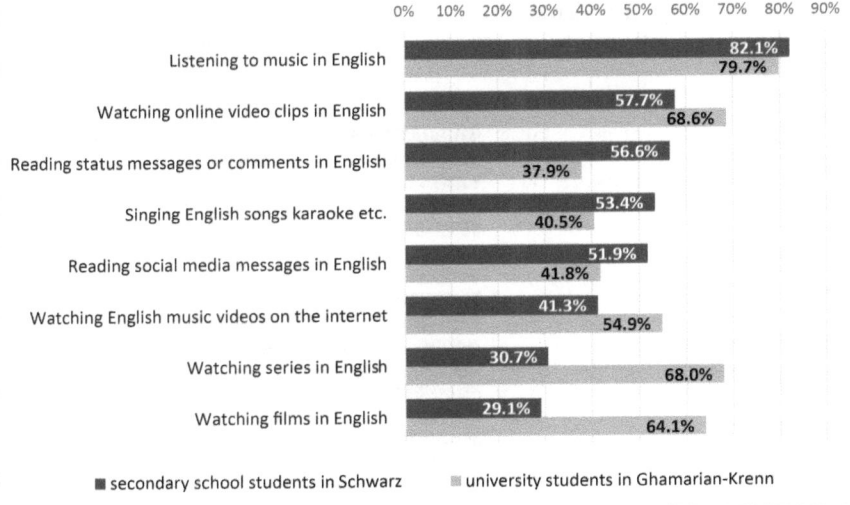

Figure 1: EE activities engaged in (almost) every day by more than 50 % in at least one of the two studies

Figure 1 displays the most popular EE activities, in which more than 50% of participants in at least one group engage on a daily basis. Results show that both groups have five "top activities" and that the two most common activities are listening to English-language music and watching online video clips in both cases. In addition, over 50% of the university students frequently watch films, series, and online videos, whereas teenage learners tend to read English on social media, both with regard to private messages and public posts, and sing (along to) music more often.

When also taking into account activities which are done at least a few times a week by over 50% in one of the groups (see Figure 2), the university students show greater diversity, with 18 common EE activities, than their younger counterparts with 10 activities. However, the types of activities largely overlap: both groups watch English-language films, series and video clips; engage with music; read on social media and use English in other online environments such as apps and search engines. In addition to these common activities across groups, university students read noticeably more in English than their younger counterparts in the form of books, print and/or online articles and informational texts. This might be explained by the increased independence of students at tertiary level, which requires participants to read more informational texts, such as manuals or recipes, and inform themselves about daily news in (online) resources available in English.

Furthermore, the tertiary students also report attending concerts, reading lyrics, and watching factually oriented TV programs such as documentaries or reports more frequently. They also use English productively to some extent in their leisure time when writing notes and thinking in English.

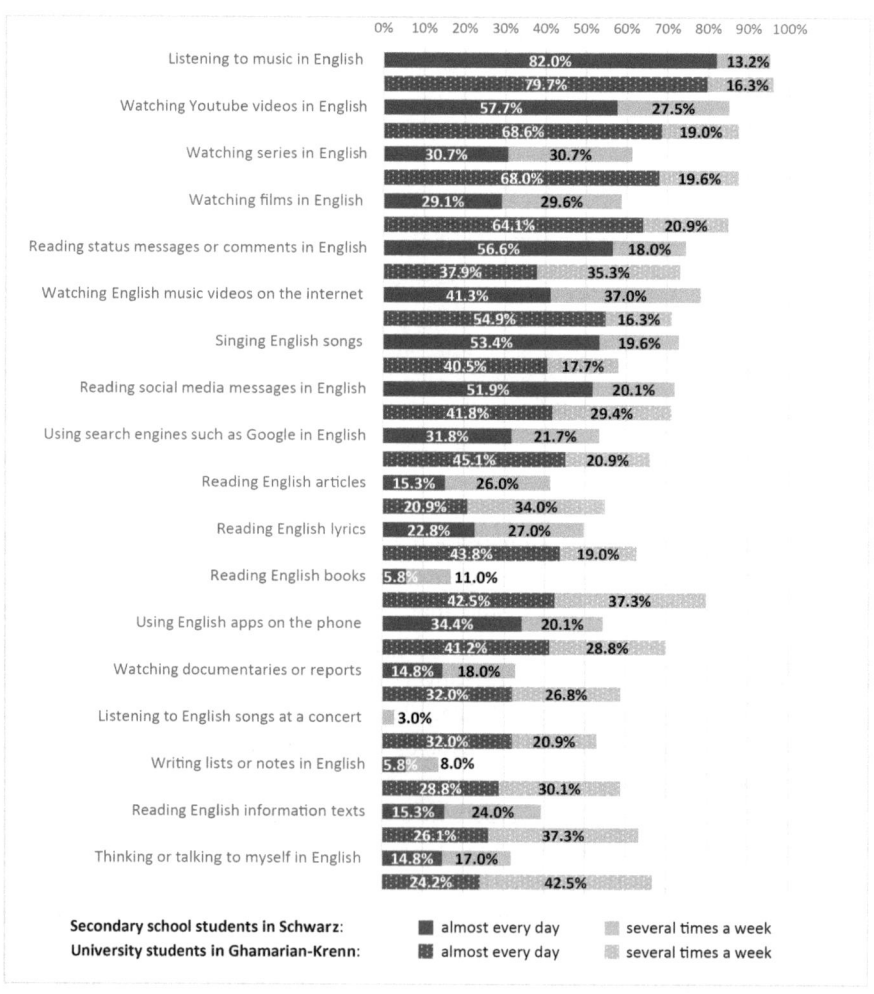

Figure 2: EE activities done at least a few times a week by over 50 % in at least one study

These results highlight that involvement in EE activities is high across educational levels. This finding corresponds to observations made by previous studies at secondary level, such as Olsson and Sylvén (2015) and Sylvén (2019), and sheds further light on university students' frequency of exposure to EE, a target population which has been rather neglected so far. Furthermore, the most popular EE activities are surprisingly similar across the two participant groups despite the difference in age, with the two top activities (i. e. music and video clips) showing near-complete overlap. Common EE activities in both groups thus typically (1) involve a screen, (2) take place in digital contexts, and (3) mostly involve listening/viewing or reading and thus primarily employ receptive language skills, particularly in the younger age group. Overall, these results are not surprising in that previous research has produced comparable findings both in Europe (e. g. Moncrief, 2011; Peters, 2018; Sundqvist, 2009) and further afield (e. g. Barbee, 2013; Lai et al., 2015; Orhon, 2018; see section 2). The fact that university students read more English than teenagers at secondary level is also supported by earlier studies (Ferdous, 2013; Hyland, 2004; Liu, 2014; Moncrief, 2011), but unlike these studies our analysis does not indicate that tertiary students engage in more extramural speaking activities; in fact, writing notes and thinking and/or talking to oneself were the only frequent activities involving a productive language skill.

The comparative analysis of the two participant groups further indicates that the students at tertiary level engage in more diverse activities. However, closer analysis reveals that in both age groups there is at least one individual who engages in all activities at least a few times a week. Hence, EE environments in both age groups generally seem to be characterized by a few widespread activities complemented by various individualized pursuits (Berns et al., 2007).

One activity that is conspicuous in its absence among the most frequent EE activities in our studies in comparison to previous research is gaming. While there are gamers in both studies with 31% of the university students and 28% of the adolescents enjoying single-player games and 23% in each group engaging in multiplayer games at least a few times a week, digital games are not a common point of contact with English in comparison to northern European studies (e. g. Peters, 2018; Sundqvist, 2009). Therefore, the results of these two studies are more in line with Aniol (2011), Lyrigkou (2018) and Mirmán Flores and García Jiménez (2018). Nonetheless, it is interesting to note that contrary to expectations and previous research (e. g. Peters, 2018), gaming is slightly more common among the university students than among the younger learners in this study, at least for single-player games (Greenberg et al., 2010; Sylvén & Sundqvist, 2012).

5.2.   Research question 2: The relation between Extramural English and vocabulary knowledge

This section first presents the two studies' findings on the effect of EE on general and academic vocabulary knowledge separately before drawing them together in an integrated comparison and discussion.

5.2.1. EE and vocabulary knowledge at secondary level

The tenth-grade students participating in Schwarz (2020) have an estimated mean receptive vocabulary size of approximately 4,800 lemmas[5] based on *V_YesNo* ($M = 4807.26$ [4590, 5053], $SD = 1498.8$). On average, they scored 38.23 points ([36.51, 39.92], SD = 11.41) on the productive vocabulary measure *Lex30*. While this score cannot be interpreted in absolute terms, it is comparable to previous studies on similar proficiency levels (e. g. Alejo González & Piquer Píriz, 2016; Walters, 2012).

The relationships between vocabulary size, EE and other potential influencing factors were first explored graphically and through bivariate analyses. Then two standard multiple regression models were computed for receptive and productive vocabulary size. Both models included the six predictor variables presented in Table 2 together with their operationalizations.

Predictor variable	Operationalization
Extramural English (EE)	Median score for frequency of engagement with extramural English activities
Length of English instruction	Years spent learning English
Socioeconomic status	Summary variable combining highest level of parental education and occupational prestige
Media access	Number of different media devices available at participants' homes
Gender	Gender (female/male)
Number of home languages	Number of languages spoken at home

Table 2: Predictor variables considered for multiple regression models in Schwarz (2020)

For receptive vocabulary size 117 complete cases were used to fit the multiple regression model. The percentage of missing values across the outcome variable and the six predictor variables varied between 0 and 25%; in total, 72 out of 189

---

5 A *lemma* is one way of counting lexical items. It includes the base word and its grammatical word forms within the same part of speech (i. e. those based on inflectional morphology). For instance, the lemma for the verb *develop* also includes the verb forms *develops, developed* and *developing,* but not the noun form *development.*

cases (38%) were incomplete.[6] Diagnostic plots and tests as well as model fit statistics for both regression analyses generally suggest that there are no concerns about unmet assumptions and influential data points. The regression model presented in Table 3 shows that receptive vocabulary size as measured by *V_YesNo* is predicted by EE and the number of years students spent learning English. The effects of the other predictors included in the model are not statistically significant. The standardized β coefficients indicate that frequency of engagement with EE explains slightly more variance in receptive vocabulary size than the number of years students spent learning English. The total R^2 value for the model was 21.3%, meaning that in combination the predictor variables explained 21% of the variance in *V_YesNo* scores.

	B	95% CI	*SE*	*p*	*β*
Constant	1864.41	[163.33, 3565.49]	858.36	.032*	
EE	461.81	[169.66, 753.96]	142.42	.002**	0.28
Length of English instruction	172.34	[54.17, 290.50]	59.63	.005**	0.25
SES	163.68	[-161.39, 488.74]	164.03	.321	0.11
Media access	116.53	[-40.98, 274.05]	79.48	.145	0.13
Gender (male)	165.68	[-338.83, 670.18]	254.57	.517	0.11
Number of home languages	-181.43	[614.64, 251.79]	218.60	.408	-0.08
N = 117, adjusted R^2 = .21					

Table 3: Coefficients of standard multiple regression model for V_YesNo scores

For productive vocabulary size a standard multiple regression model was built in parallel to the model for receptive vocabulary size. The percentage of missing values for *Lex30* across all seven variables ranged from 0 to 17%; in total 59 out of 189 cases (31%) were incomplete. The model for productive vocabulary size was thus fit on 130 complete cases and contains the same predictors as the model for receptive vocabulary size. A summary of the model is presented in Table 4: it only explains 8.5% of the variance in Lex30 scores and length of English instruction is the only significant predictor. Hence, frequency of engagement with EE does not emerge as a statistically significant predictor for productive vocabulary size.

---

6 Multiple imputation was considered as an option to deal with the issue of missing data, but since multiple imputation for multivariate models is a complex procedure which has a number of assumptions and should ideally include additional variables to predict missing data (Van Buuren, 2012), a decision to use listwise deletion and present a complete case analysis was finally reached.

	B	95% CI	SE	p	β
Constant	26.42	[13.85; 38.98]	6.34	<.001**	
EE	1.28	[-0.92; 3.48]	1.11	.251	0.10
Length of English instruction	1.23	[0.35; 2.11]	0.44	.006**	0.23
SES	2.03	[-0.37; 4.43]	1.21	.097	0.18
Media access	-0.14	[-1.34; 1.05]	0.60	.813	-0.02
Gender (male)	2.66	[-1.17; 6.59]	1.94	.172	0.23
Number of home languages	-0.05	[-3.06; 2.96]	1.52	.975	-0.00
N = 130, adjusted R^2 = .08					

Table 4: Coefficients of standard multiple regression model for Lex30 scores

The results on the relation between EE and vocabulary size among secondary school students thus suggest that EE affects receptive and productive vocabulary knowledge differently. While EE emerges as the strongest predictor of receptive vocabulary size among those considered in the multiple regression model, the outcomes for productive vocabulary size seem to suggest that it is not affected by engagement with EE. This outcome is not entirely surprising because the most common extramural activities mostly involve receptive language use, as shown in the previous section, and are therefore less likely to support the development of productive knowledge. However, it could also be the case that *Lex30* is not a sensitive enough measure to investigate this connection; clearly, further research is needed in this respect. Overall, Schwarz's (2020) findings indicate that the effect of EE on productive vocabulary is qualitatively different from and noticeably weaker than the effect on receptive vocabulary size.

5.2.2. EE and vocabulary knowledge at tertiary level

Out of Ghamarian-Krenn's (2023) 152 participants 51 participants had to be excluded due to missing values for one of the two examined variables, leaving a data set of 101 participants. As in Schwarz (2020), participants display a larger receptive vocabulary knowledge with a mean score of 59.63 points out of a maximum of 72 points. Hence, participants were able to answer 82.2% of the items on the form-meaning recognition test for academic words correctly. In comparison, students were only able to fill in 40.76 out of 72 items correctly in the form-meaning recall test testing productive knowledge, which amounts to 56.61%.

To analyse the relationship between EE activities and academic vocabulary knowledge a factor analysis was calculated, revealing that the items of the questionnaire can be grouped into the following categories:

	Sub-constructs	EXAMPLES
Extra-mural behavior	English music	I listen to English music; I sing English songs
	English video material	I watch films in English; I watch series in English
	English online	I use English apps on the phone; I use search engines, such as Google, in English
	English gaming	Playing computer games on the computer or gaming consoles; Playing games online with others
	Fiction reading	I read English books; I read English short stories
	Information-oriented reading	I read English articles; I read English information texts
	Communication-oriented reading	I read e-mails in English; I read social media messages in English
	Written communication	I write e-mails in English; I write social media messages in English
	Creative writing	I write English stories
	English speaking	I speak English in face-to-face interactions

Table 5: Subconstructs of Extramural behaviour

In a next step multiple linear regression models were used to examine the relationship between these categories of EE involvement and academic vocabulary knowledge. After the verification of all necessary preconditions[7], a multiple linear regression model investigating the influence of EE exposure on form-meaning recognition knowledge of academic verbs was calculated.

Considering the results of the multiple regression analysis depicted in Table 6, engagement with EE appears to significantly predict participants' knowledge of form-meaning recognition knowledge of academic verbs [$F(11, 89)= 1.96$, $p = 0.041$]. This indicates that EE involvement at the beginning of university studies appears to influence academic word knowledge. However, EE was only able to explain 9.6% of the total variance of the form-meaning recognition score, which implies that more factors appear to have an effect on form-meaning recognition knowledge at tertiary level.

Taking a closer look at the individual types of EE involvement, two categories stand out. While engagement in fiction reading appears to have a positive impact on academic verb development [$\beta = 0.281$, $t = 2.138$, $p = 0.035$], listening to music has a significant negative influence [$\beta = -0.362$, $t = -3.154$, $p = 0.002$]. All other EE variables can be considered as neutral, since they have no significant influence on academic form-meaning knowledge at this stage of tertiary education.

---

7 The necessary preconditions for model interpretation considered were suitable predictor variable to sample size ratio, multicollinearity and normality of residuals, amongst other measures. For more detail see Ghamarian-Krenn (2023).

	B	95% CI	SE	P	β
Constant	58.54	[53.543; 63.540]	2.52	0.000	
English music	-2.68	[-4.371; -0.992]	80.85	0.002**	-0.36
English video material	-1.59	[-3.278; 0.101]	0.85	0.065	-0.20
English online	0.07	[-1.530; 1.663]	0.80	0.934	0.01
English gaming	-0.25	[-1.747; 1.241]	0.75	0.737	-0.04
Communication-oriented reading	0.82	[-1.765; 3.404]	1.30	0.530	0.12
Information-oriented reading	-0.08	[-1.823; 1.657]	0.86	0.925	-0.01
Fiction reading	2.08	[0.146; 4.008]	0.97	0.035*	0.28
Written communication	-2.26	[-5.260; 0.734]	1.51	0.137	-0.30
Creative writing	1.20	[-0.461; 2.858]	0.84	0.155	0.18
English speaking	0.13	[-2.051; 2.312]	1.20	0.905	0.02
Number of daily activities	0.06	[-0.357; 0.482]	0.21	0.768	0.06
N= 101; adjusted R^2= 0.096					

Table 6: Coefficients of standard multiple regression model for form-meaning recognition score

Conversely to the relationship between EE and form-meaning recognition knowledge of academic verbs, EE appears to have no significant influence on form-meaning recall knowledge of the same words [$F(11, 89) = 0.79$, $p = 0.648$]. The linear multiple regression model summarized in Table 7 shows that the model could only predict 2.4% of the variation of the academic form-meaning recall scores. However, while no overall influence of EE can be detected, one category of extramural involvement, namely engagement in information-oriented reading, appears to be significantly linked to the vocabulary score. Interestingly, a negative effect of information-oriented reading on form-meaning recall knowledge of academic words can be detected [$β = -0.31$, $t = -2.498$, $p = 0.014$], meaning that students who are more involved in reading newspapers, magazines, instruction texts such as recipes or blogs and forum entries in English achieved a lower score on the form-meaning recall test of academic verbs.

	B	95% CI	SE	P	β
Constant	37,62	[30.842; 44.405]	3.41	0.000	
English music	-0.14	[-2.436; 2.149]	1.15	0.901	-0.02
English video material	0.40	[-1.893; 2.692]	1.15	0.730	0.04
English online	0.22	[-1.947; 2.386]	1.09	0.841	0.20
English gaming	-0.94	[-2.969; 1.085]	1.02	0.358	-0.11
Communication-oriented reading	1.33	[-2.181; 4.822]	1.77	0.454	0.15
Information-oriented reading	-2.97	[-5.327; -0.606]	1.19	0.014*	-0.31
Fiction reading	1.19	[-1.432; 3.808]	1.32	0.370	0.13

(Continued)

	B	**95% CI**	**SE**	**P**	**β**
Written communication	0.64	[-3.429; 4.703]	2.05	0.756	0.07
Creative writing	0.52	[-2.767; 1.737]	1.13	0.651	-0.06
English speaking	0.43	[-2.531; 3.389]	1.49	0.774	0.05
Number of daily activities	-0.22	[-0.792; 0.346]	0.29	0.439	-0.17
N= 101; adjusted R²=-0.024					

Table 7: Coefficients of standard multiple regression model for form-meaning recall score

5.2.3. Comparing EE and vocabulary knowledge at secondary and tertiary level

Similar to the parallels found regarding extramural activities of secondary and tertiary level students, many consistencies can be found regarding the impact of EE on vocabulary knowledge. Regardless of the vocabulary type researched, both studies reveal that involvement in EE activities significantly influences receptive vocabulary knowledge but appears to have no impact on productive vocabulary knowledge. This partially corresponds to previous findings regarding the influence of EE on vocabulary knowledge. While many EE studies (e.g. Busby, 2021; Ferdous, 2013; Lee, 2019a; Li & Hafner, 2022; Olsson, 2016; Peters, 2018; Peters et al., 2019; Sundqvist, 2009; Verspoor et al., 2011) provide support for a positive effect of EE on receptive vocabulary knowledge across educational levels, far fewer studies have investigated and found a significant connection to productive vocabulary knowledge (Lee, 2019a; Olsson, 2016; Sundqvist, 2009).

The lack of influence of EE on productive word knowledge detected in the two studies might be partially explained by the facts that receptive knowledge of new vocabulary is generally acquired before productive knowledge (Schmitt, 2010) and that participants in both studies mostly used their receptive language skills during EE activities, which might foster receptive but not productive knowledge of words. Indeed, similar to Webb (2005), Schwarz (2020) found an unexpected effect of so-called "niche activities" like programming, rapping, sports or creative writing, which are carried out by a small minority of participants but generally involve more productive language use than the most widespread EE activities. An analysis comparing the participants who engaged in such niche activities (*n* = 29) with the remainder of the group (*n* = 113) showed a significantly higher receptive vocabulary size, but no statistically significant effect on productive vocabulary size.

Similarly, Ghamarian-Krenn (2023) also found that a particular type of EE involvement, namely engagement in fiction reading, has a stronger positive effect on receptive academic vocabulary development than others. This result is supported by Busby (2021), who reports a similar significant positive influence of reading novels on general receptive vocabulary knowledge. However, while other studies, such as Busby (2021), Peters (2018) and Sundqvist (2009) additionally revealed positive effects of gaming, internet use and video consumption on general vocabulary knowledge, such correlations were not found in the present studies. The lack of a correlation with academic vocabulary knowledge in Ghamarian-Krenn might be explained by the fact that academic words are less salient in computer games and other informal EE activities, which therefore offer little opportunity for academic vocabulary growth. A case in point is the colloquial language of lyrics, which might explain that listening to English music even displays a negative effect on receptive academic word knowledge.

Overall, results revealed that extramural activities affect receptive and productive lexical knowledge differently, regardless of participant group and type of vocabulary researched: both studies found measurable and statistically significant effects of EE on receptive, but not on productive knowledge. However, it needs to be pointed out that this does not mean that no vocabulary knowledge at all is acquired. In fact, qualitative accounts of learners (Schwarz, 2020) indicate that some productive knowledge is acquired from incidental exposure, but it is likely that quantitative instruments are not sensitive enough to detect such effects.

6.   Conclusion

To summarize, the studies by Schwarz (2020) and Ghamarian-Krenn (2023) display several similarities regarding extramural engagement and the impact of EE on vocabulary knowledge across educational levels. Both studies have found consistently high engagement in EE activities, with tertiary students displaying a larger diversity of extramural habits. While both participant groups report high interest in listening to English-language music and consuming videos, students at tertiary level additionally show increased involvement in reading activities.

Concerning the influence of EE on general and academic vocabulary knowledge, both studies have found a significant impact on receptive word knowledge, while no influence on productive word knowledge could be detected, either for general or academic vocabulary. Whereas such a positive effect on receptive knowledge is well-established in previous research at both secondary and tertiary level (Lee, 2019a; Li & Hafner, 2022; Peters, 2018; Peters et al., 2019; Sundqvist, 2009; Verspoor et al., 2011), studies on productive knowledge are much scarcer and have produced mixed results (Lee, 2019a; Olsson & Sylvén, 2015; Sundqvist, 2009).

Nevertheless, it should be taken into account that both studies had a different research focus, using different vocabulary measures to investigate their research questions, i.e. two tests of general vocabulary knowledge, *V_YesNo* (Meara, 2015) and *Lex30* (Meara & Fitzpatrick, 2000), for Schwarz's secondary school students and self-designed form-meaning recall and form-meaning recognition tests of academic verbs for Ghamarian-Krenn's tertiary students. Moreover, while Schwarz's (2020) research can be described as cross-sectional, Ghamarian-Krenn's (2023) study is a longitudinal study, covering a time span of one year. To increase comparability between the different research designs only the first data collection point of her study was used, neglecting changes in results over time (for further information see Ghamarian-Krenn (2023)).

Overall, this comparative analysis of two independent studies contributes to the field by (1) providing first data on the Austrian context, (2) analysing EE practices in two groups differing in age and proficiency within this setting and (3) comparing the effects of extramural language learning and use on the two complementary areas of general and academic vocabulary knowledge. Further explorations of extramural practices in diverse populations are needed to create a more comprehensive picture (Sockett, 2014). Moreover, with regard to vocabulary and the differential effects on receptive and productive knowledge further research is clearly needed, too; ideally, in-depth analyses of students' actual behaviour, their strategies for dealing with unknown lexical items, and their vocabulary learning mechanisms in informal contexts should be conducted (Schmitt, 2019), for instance using observations or eye-tracking methods. However, considering that EE is an inherently private phenomenon, learners' own accounts might be more easily accessible in the near-future and can provide interesting insights into their EE worlds (Schwarz, forthcoming).

The fact that extramural activities are leisure activities which are firmly located in learners' private spheres also needs to be borne in mind when considering the implications of research on informal language learning. As mentioned in the beginning, the aim of such research ultimately is to make suggestions for the adaptation of classroom teaching to connect formal and informal learning environments. However, this next step needs to be taken with great care so as not to alienate learners, especially adolescents. EE is voluntary and non-instructed by nature (Sundqvist & Sylvén, 2016) and thus cannot and should not be "taught" at school or forcefully integrated into lessons. One first step for teachers could simply be to acknowledge the existence of extramural English and its beneficial effects on language development and to show a positive attitude towards this phenomenon by recognizing knowledge acquired outside school as relevant and valuable, giving learners' room to share experiences, or having an open ear for difficulties encountered outside class, if learners should want to share them.

7.   References

Alejo González, R., & Piquer Píriz, A. (2016). Measuring the productive vocabulary of secondary school CLIL students: Is Lex30 a valid test for low-level school learners? *VIAL (Vigo International Journal of Applied Linguistics)*, *31*, 31–53.

Anioł, M. (2011). New media and new literacies: Mapping extracurricular English language competences of Polish and Norwegian adolescents. In M. Kaczmarek (Ed.), *Health and well-being in adolescence: Part two. Media* (pp. 101–124). Bogucki Wydawnictwo Naukowe.

Barbee, M. (2013). Extracurricular L2 input in a Japanese EFL context: Exposure, attitudes, and motivation. *Second Language Studies*, *32*(1), 1–58.

Benson, P. (2011). Language learning and teaching beyond the classroom: An introduction to the field. In P. Benson & H. Reinders (Eds.), *Beyond the language classroom* (pp. 6–16). Palgrave Macmillan.

Berns, M., De Bot, K., & Hasebrink, U. (Eds.). (2007). *In the presence of English: Media and European youth*. Springer.

Busby, N. L. (2021). Words from where? *ITL – International Journal of Applied Linguistics*, *172*(1), 58–84. https://doi.org/10.1075/itl.19018.bus.

Council of Europe. (2001). *Common European Framework of Reference for languages: Learning, teaching, assessment*. http://www.coe.int/t/dg4/linguistic/Source/Framework _EN.pdf.

Dressman, M., & Sadler, R. (Eds.). (2020). *The handbook of informal language learning*. Wiley-Blackwell.

Ellis, N. C. (2002). Frequency effects in language processing: A review with implications for theories of implicit and explicit language acquisition. *Studies in Second Language Acquisition*, *24*, 143–188.

Ferdous, T. (2013). *Use of English beyond the classroom wall: A study of undergraduate students' out-of-class English learning activities* [PhD thesis]. BRAC University, Dhaka, Bangladesch.

Field, A., Miles, J., & Field, Z. (2012). *Discovering statistics using R*. SAGE.

Ghamarian-Krenn, Katharina. (2023). *Extramural English and academic verb knowledge: A longitudinal study of Viennese students majoring in English*. [PhD thesis]. University of Vienna.

González-Fernández, B., & Schmitt, N. (2015). How much collocation knowledge do L2 learners have? The effects of frequency and amount of exposure. *ITL – International Journal of Applied Linguistics*, *166*(1), 94–126. https://doi.org/10.1075/itl.166.1.03fer.

Grau, M. (2009). Worlds apart? English in German youth cultures and in educational settings. *World Englishes*, *28*(2), 160–174. https://doi.org/10.1111/j.1467-971X.2009.015 81.x.

Greenberg, B. S., Sherry, J., Lachlan, K., Lucas, K., & Holmstrom, A. (2010). Orientations to Video Games Among Gender and Age Groups. *Simulation & Gaming*, *41*(2), 238–259. https://doi.org/10.1177/1046878108319930.

Hannibal Jensen, S. (2017). Gaming as an English language learning resource among young children in Denmark. *CALICO Journal*, *34*(1), 1–19. https://doi.org/10.1558/cj.29519.

Hyland, F. (2004). Learning autonomously: Contextualising out-of-class English language learning. *Language Awareness, 13*(3), 180–202. https://doi.org/10.1080/0965841040866 7094.

Jarvis, S. (2013). Defining and measuring lexical diversity. In S. Jarvis & H. Daller (Eds.), *Vocabulary knowledge: Human ratings and automated measures* (pp. 13–43). John Benjamins.

Kalaja, P., Alanen, R., Palviainen, Å., & Dufva, H. (2011). From milk cartons to English roommates: Content and agency in L2 learning beyond the classroom. In P. Benson & H. Reinders (Eds.), *Beyond the language classroom* (pp. 47–58). Palgrave Macmillan.

Kusyk, M. (2017). The development of complexity, accuracy and fluency in L2 written production through informal participation in online activities. *CALICO Journal, 34*(1), 75–96. https://doi.org/10.1558/cj.29513.

Lai, C., Zhu, W., & Gong, G. (2015). Understanding the quality of out-of-class English learning. *TESOL Quarterly, 49*(2), 278–308. https://doi.org/10.1002/tesq.171.

Lamb, M. (2002). Explaining successful language learning in difficult circumstances. *Prospect, 17*(2), 35–52.

Lamb, M. (2004). 'it depends on the students themselves': Independent language learning at an Indonesian state school. *Language, Culture and Curriculum, 17*(3), 229–245.

Laufer, B., & Nation, I. (1995). Vocabulary size and use: Lexical richness in L2 written production. *Applied Linguistics, 16*(3), 307–322. https://doi.org/10.1093/applin/16.3.307.

Lee, J. S. (2019a). Informal digital learning of English and second language vocabulary outcomes: Can quantity conquer quality? *British Journal of Educational Technology, 50* (2), 767–778. https://doi.org/10.1111/bjet.12599.

Lee, J. S. (2019b). Quantity and diversity of informal digital learning of English. *Language Learning & Technology, 23*(1), 114–126.

Li, Y., & Hafner, C. A. (2022). Mobile-assisted vocabulary learning: Investigating receptive and productive vocabulary knowledge of Chinese EFL learners. *ReCALL, 34*(1), 66–80. https://doi.org/10.1017/S0958344021000161.

Liu, X. (2014). Students' perceptions of autonomous out-of-class learning through the use of computers. *English Language Teaching, 7*(4), 74–82. https://doi.org/10.5539/elt.v7n4p 74.

Lyrigkou, C. (2018). Not to be overlooked: Agency in informal language contact. *Innovation in Language Learning and Teaching, 16*(4), 1–16. https://doi.org/10.1080/17501229.20 18.1433182.

Meara, P. (2015). *V_YesNo: a Yes/No vocabulary test for English (v1.01)*. lognostics. http://www.lognostics.co.uk/tools/V_YesNo/V_YesNo.htm.

Meara, P., & Fitzpatrick, T. (2000). Lex30: An improved method of assessing productive vocabulary in an L2. *System, 28*(1), 19–30. https://doi.org/10.1016/S0346-251X(99)000 58-5.

Meara, P., & Miralpeix, I. (2017). *Tools for researching vocabulary*. Multilingual Matters.

Media Consulting Group. (2009). *Study on the use of subtitling: The potential of subtitling to encourage foreign language learning and improve the mastery of foreign languages*. https://publications.europa.eu/en/publication-detail/-/publication/e4d5cbf4-a839-4a8 a-81d0-7b19a22cc5ce/language-en.

Mirmán Flores, A., & García Jiménez, E. (2018). The influence of family environment on exposure to English among Spanish secondary school students. *Estudios Sobre Educación, 34*, 283–306. https://doi.org/10.15581/004.34.283-306.

Moncrief, R. (2011). Out-of-classroom language learning: A case study of students of advanced English language courses at Helsinki University Language Centre. In K. K. Pitkänen, J. Jokinen, S. Karjalainen, L. Karlsson, T. Lehtonen, M. Matilainen, C. Niedling, & R. Siddall (Eds.), *Language Center Publications 2. Out-of-classroom language learning* (pp. 107–118). University of Helsinki Language Centre.

Nation, I. (1990). *Teaching and learning vocabulary*. Heinle & Heinle.

Nation, I. (2013). *Learning vocabulary in another language* (2nd edition). Cambridge University Press.

Nunan, D., & Richards, J. C. (2015). Preface. In D. Nunan & J. C. Richards (Eds.), *Language learning beyond the classroom* (pp. xi–xvi). Routledge.

Olsson, E. (2016). *On the impact of extramural English and CLIL on productive vocabulary* [PhD thesis]. University of Gothenburg, Göteborg.

Olsson, E., & Sylvén, L. K. (2015). Extramural English and academic vocabulary: A longitudinal study of CLIL and non-CLIL students in Sweden. *Apples – Journal of Applied Language Studies, 9*(2), 77–103.

Orhon, Y. (2018). An investigation of out-of-class language activities of tertiary-level EFL learners. *Education Reform Journal, 3*(1), 1–14.

Peters, E. (2018). The effect of out-of-class exposure to English language media on learners' vocabulary knowledge. *ITL – International Journal of Applied Linguistics, 169*(1), 142–168. https://doi.org/10.1075/itl.00010.pet.

Peters, E., Noreillie, A.-S., Heylen, K., Bulté, B., & Desmet, P. (2019). The impact of instruction and out-of-school exposure to foreign language input on learners' vocabulary knowledge in two languages. *Language Learning, 69*(3), 747–782. https://doi.org/10.1111/lang.12351.

Plonsky, L., & Oswald, F. L. (2014). How big is "big"? Interpreting effect sizes in L2 research. *Language Learning, 64*(4), 878–912. https://doi.org/10.1111/lang.12079.

Puimège, E., & Peters, E. (2019). Learners' English vocabulary knowledge prior to formal instruction: The role of learner-related and word-related factors. *Language Learning, 69* (4), 943–977.

Schmitt, N. (2010). *Researching vocabulary: A vocabulary research manual*. Palgrave Macmillan.

Schmitt, N. (2019). Understanding vocabulary acquisition, instruction, and assessment: A research agenda. *Language Teaching, 52*(2), 261–274. https://doi.org/10.1017/S026144 4819000053.

Schmitt, N., Schmitt, D., & Clapham, C. (2001). Developing and exploring the behaviour of two new versions of the Vocabulary Levels Test. *Language Testing, 18*(1), 55–88.

Schwarz, M. (forthcoming). Learner perspectives on informal L2 vocabulary learning. In M. Kusyk, G. Sockett, & D. Toffoli (Eds.), *Language learning and leisure: Informal language learning in the digital age*. De Gruyter Mouton.

Schwarz, M. (2020). *Beyond the walls: A mixed methods study of teenagers' extramural English practices and their vocabulary knowledge* [PhD thesis]. University of Vienna, Vienna.

Sockett, G. (2014). *The online informal learning of English*. Palgrave Macmillan.

Sundqvist, P. (2009). *Extramural English matters: Out-of-school English and its impact on Swedish ninth graders' oral proficiency and vocabulary* [PhD thesis]. Karlstad University, Karlstad.

Sundqvist, P., & Sylvén, L. K. (2012). World of VocCraft: Computer games and Swedish learners' L2 English vocabulary. In H. Reinders (Ed.), *Digital games in language learning and teaching* (pp. 189–208). Palgrave Macmillan.

Sundqvist, P., & Sylvén, L. K. (2014). Language-related computer use: Focus on young L2 English learners in Sweden. *ReCALL, 26*(1), 3–20. https://doi.org/10.1017/S0958344013000232.

Sundqvist, P., & Sylvén, L. K. (2016). *Extramural English in teaching and learning: From theory to practice.* Palgrave Macmillan.

Sylvén, L. K. (2006). How is extramural exposure to English among Swedish school students used in the CLIL classroom? *Vienna English Working Papers (VIEWS), 15*(3), 47–53.

Sylvén, L. K. (2019). Extramural English. In L. K. Sylvén (Ed.), *Investigating language and content integrated learning insights from Swedish high schools* (pp. 152–167). Multilingual Matters.

Sylvén, L. K., & Sundqvist, P. (2012). Gaming as extramural English L2 learning and L2 proficiency among young learners. *ReCALL, 24*(3), 302–321. https://doi.org/10.1017/S095834401200016X.

Toffoli, D., Sockett, G., & Kusyk, M. (Eds.). (in print). *Language learning and leisure: Informal language learning in the digital age.* De Gruyter Mouton.

Trinder, R. (2015). *Online informal learning of English: How students use technology to supplement classes.* International Conference ICT for Language Learning (4th edn.). http://conference.pixel-online.net/ICT4LL/files/ict4ll/ed0008/FP/2161-ICL1391-FP-ICT4LL8.pdf.

Van Buuren, S. (2012). *Flexible imputation of missing data.* Chapman & Hall/CRC.

Verspoor, M. H., De Bot, K., & Van Rein, E. (2011). English as a foreign language: The role of out-of-school language input. In A. De Houwer & A. Wilton (Eds.), *English in Europe today: Sociocultural and educational perspectives* (pp. 147–166). John Benjamins.

Walters, J. (2012). Aspects of validity of a test of productive vocabulary: Lex30. *Language Assessment Quarterly, 9*(2), 172–185. https://doi.org/10.1080/15434303.2011.625579.

Warnby, M. (2022). Receptive academic vocabulary knowledge and extramural English involvement – is there a correlation? *ITL – International Journal of Applied Linguistics, 173*(1), 120–152. https://doi.org/10.1075/itl.21021.war.

Webb, S. (2005). Receptive and productive vocabulary learning: The effects of reading and writing on word knowledge. *Studies in Second Language Acquisition, 27*(1), 33–52. https://doi.org/10.1017/S0272263105050023.

Yi, Y. (2005). Asian adolescents' out-of-school encounters with English and Korean literacy. *Journal of Asian Pacific Communication, 15*(1), 57–77.

Lisza-Sophie Neumeier

Twitter for academic purposes: An analysis of scholarly communication through conference tweets

Abstract

Twitter has become a prominent social medium among academics of all disciplines.[1] In addition to postings about academic achievements, Twitter is frequently used at conferences to exchange knowledge or network within an academic community. Especially since, due to the Covid-19 pandemic, many conferences had to be moved to an online setting, social media functioned as an alternative channel for real-life conference communication. To investigate the use of Twitter in the context of conferences from an applied linguistic perspective, I have conducted a genre analysis with a data set consisting of all tweets posted shortly before, during and after a small social anthropology online conference. Multimodal content analysis and sentiment analysis were applied to the tweets to generate information about the communicative functions and the sentiments of conference tweets. The findings showed that scholars used Twitter for a range of different communicative functions, which were primarily assigned to organizational, self-promotional and networking-related aspects. Posting content-related tweets seemed to be a rather uncommon practice. Tweets related to networking and self-promotion were more likely to include multimodal content in the form of images. Furthermore, as expected, most tweets expressed a rather positive or positive sentiment. These results indicate that conference tweets form an important genre for academics and should be considered in EAP syllabi. Also, conference organizers should promote a conference hashtag if they wish to enable a digital backchannel.

Twitter hat sich unter Wissenschaftler*innen aller Fachrichtungen zu einem wichtigen sozialen Medium entwickelt. Vor allem auf Konferenzen wird Twitter genutzt, um Wissen auszutauschen oder sich innerhalb einer akademischen Gemeinschaft zu vernetzen. Insbesondere seitdem viele Konferenzen in ein Online-Setting verlegt wurden, fungieren soziale Medien als alternativer Kanal für die vor Ort stattfindende Konferenzkommunikation. Um die Nutzung von Konferenz-Twitter zu untersuchen, wurde in dieser Studie eine Genre-Analyse von Tweets, die kurz vor, während und nach einer kleinen sozialanthropologischen Online-Konferenz gepostet wurden, durchgeführt. Die Tweets wurden einer multimodalen Inhaltsanalyse und einer Sentimentanalyse unterzogen, um Infor-

---

1 Under the lead of Elon Musk, at the time of writing (August 2023), Twitter is undergoing a rebranding process, transitioning into 'X' (Conger, 2023). Since the current project used Twitter data from 2021, the platform will be referred to as 'Twitter' in the following.

mationen über die kommunikativen Funktionen und die Stimmungen der Konferenz-Tweets zu erhalten. Die Ergebnisse zeigten, dass Twitter für unterschiedliche kommunikative Funktionen genutzt wurde, die vor allem organisatorischen, selbstdarstellerischen und netzwerkbezogenen Aspekten zugeordnet werden konnten. Das Posten von inhaltsbezogenen Tweets schien eine eher unübliche Praxis zu sein. Tweets, die sich auf die Vernetzung und Selbstdarstellung bezogen, enthielten häufiger multimodale Inhalte in Form von Bildern. Außerdem drückten die meisten Tweets erwartungsgemäß eine eher positive oder positive Stimmung aus. Diese Ergebnisse deuten darauf hin, dass Konferenz-Tweets ein wichtiges Genre für Akademiker*innen darstellen und in EAP-Curricula aufgenommen werden sollten. Außerdem sollten Organisator*innen von Konferenzen einen Konferenz-Hashtag etablieren, wenn sie einen digitalen Rückkanal ermöglichen wollen.

1   Introduction

In March 2020, the Covid-19 pandemic unexpectedly changed life as most of us knew it: Most governments sent their countries into lockdown and in-person meetings of any kind were restricted to avoid the spread of the virus. Modern technology came into play at this point. Phone calls, video conferencing tools, and social media of all kinds constituted the only way to keep in touch with family and friends. However, not only private but also professional communication shifted to online settings. In the world of academia, remote work and distance learning were implemented. Academic conferences were canceled or postponed. However, after organizers had realized that the pandemic would persist, most conferences were moved into an online setting too. Here, Twitter, a social medium for microblogging, i.e., "[a] form of blogging that involves the development of short chunks of text" (Ince, 2019), played a leading role in academic exchange. Already before the pandemic, a whole body of literature on the multimodal genre of conference tweets showed that Twitter constitutes a crucial tool for scholarly communication at academic conferences (e.g., Mazarakis & Peters, 2015; Luzón & Albero-Posac, 2020). However, no study to this date that I am aware of has examined the use of Twitter at online conferences. Scholars researching English for Academic Purposes (EAP) have also stressed the need for research into digital academic literacies and multimodality in EAP contexts (Lillis & Tuck, 2016, p. 39; Paltridge & Starfield, 2016, p. 226). For this purpose, a data set of conference tweets posted at an online social anthropology conference called "ASA2021: Responsibility" (Association of Social Anthropologists) will be analyzed by means of a methodological design consisting of multimodal content analysis and sentiment analysis. In the present paper, firstly, the use of Twitter for academic purposes is described and relevant studies on conference Twitter use are reviewed. Secondly, the study design including the data set and twofold methodology is outlined. Thirdly, the results are presented and discussed. Lastly, limitations are revealed, and conclusions and implications are drawn.

2   Researching Twitter

2.1   Approaching conference tweets from an EAP perspective

The term "genre" refers to a range of concepts, which "discuss the ways in which texts and works of art are structured by their creators and received by readers and viewers" (Shaw, 2016, p. 243). "Genre" is typically associated with literature, music or film; however, for the purpose of the present paper, "genre" will be defined from an applied linguistic point of view as a "set of communicative purposes" which is context-specific to the respective needs of the communicative situation (Swales, 1990, p. 58). Additionally, examples of a specific genre tend to be similar with regard to their structure, register, style and intended readership (Swales, 1990, p.58). In the context of EAP, genre analyses are conducted to share knowledge about the production of academic genres with students, teachers, researchers, or even interested non-specialists (Shaw, 2016, p. 243). Typical EAP genres include abstracts, research articles, or MA theses. However, the analysis of genres is not limited to verbal features, but multimodal aspects can be considered as well. Examples of multimodal EAP genres are conference posters or dissertations including figures and diagrams. Furthermore, with the ever-increasing enhancement of the Web 2.0[2], digital genres also offer myriad possibilities for multimodal genre analysis (see Askehave & Nielsen, 2005), such as the analysis of websites or also more dynamic genres, such as social media postings in the academic context, which will be tackled in the present paper. More specifically, my aim is to analyze conference tweets to make their purpose more explicit.

In order to do so, it is crucial to first delineate the possibilities and limitations of conference tweets attributed to the microblogging platform's nature in the time period of question.[3] Concerning their length, tweets are limited to 280 characters. They are relatively free with regard to their structure due to the absence of a typical move structure or any other requirements that have to be met. However, adding (conference) hashtags or hashtags related to the topic of

---

2 The term "Web 2.0" describes nowadays' participatory nature of the websites compared to before the year 2000 ("Web 1.0"), when most web pages were rather static and did not involve interactive features (Butterfield et al., 2016).
3 However, it has to be borne in mind that this was the status quo in May 2022, when the data for this piece of research was collected. As Elon Musk took over the platform in October 2022, changes in its features, rules and regulations, but also the reputation of the platform have already happened and can be expected for the future (Hutchinson, 2022).

the tweet, in this case, academic Twitter (e. g., #PhDchat or #academicchatter) is common. So-called "mentions", i. e. tagging other people, such as other conference attendees, keynote speakers, presenters or organizers with their individual Twitter handles constitutes another conventional habit of conference Twitter users. In addition to these mentions and hashtags, emojis, GIFs, pictures, videos and links can be used as devices of stance and engagement (Luzón & Albero-Posac, 2020, p. 39). Anyone with a Twitter account can post about any conference if they are familiar with the conference's hashtag. Hence, posting is not reserved for conference organizers and attendees. In terms of accessibility of this text type, everyone with an internet connection can look up (conference) hashtags. Hence, a Twitter account is no prerequisite for reading (conference) tweets.

2.2   Twitter for academic purposes

Twitter plays a remarkable role in today's academic online communication. Already in an early international online survey conducted among 711 academics regarding their online social media use in connection to their work, 90% of the participants indicated the use of Twitter in their professional context (Lupton, 2014, p. 14). While other social media were not considered as useful for their academic work, 81% of the participants stated the usefulness of the microblogging platform Twitter for their profession, followed by academia.edu with disillusioning 23% (Lupton, 2014, p. 15). At academic conferences, Twitter is frequently used as a medium for digital "backchannel" microblogging as it enables real-time and non-verbal conversation, which does not interrupt the presenter (Ross et al., 2011, p. 215).

While defining the genre of conference tweets is challenging as they can take many different forms, they are characterized by the following key aspects: They are posted in the context of an academic conference. The tweeters are academics or university students. The topics of the tweets can, but do not have to include academic content (Weller et al., 2011, p. 3). Luzón and Albero-Posac (2020, p. 48) identify four different types of users of conference Twitter: organizers, attendees, non-attendees and publishing houses. Regarding the Twitter activity of these users, Reinhard et al. (2009, p. 167) defines three different stages at which conference tweets are posted: before, during, and after the conference. Before a conference, Twitter is usually used by organizers to maximize the feeling of anticipation for attendees by announcing conference events and reminding attendees to register. Attendees frequently use Twitter to exchange information about the trip and accommodations, in the case of on-site conferences. During a conference, organizers usually tweet to inform attendees about organizational aspects or changes in the schedule and to post pictures or links. The tweeting behavior of conference attendees varies with regard to their personal style and the academic conference community. Nevertheless, it usually includes the discussion of conference topics, sharing of photos and resources, networking among the attendees and self-promotion (Luzón & Albero-Posac, 2020, p. 38). After a conference, organizers commonly tweet to thank the attendees and to post statistics and reflections. Attendees sometimes also thank the organizers and share photos of the conference or links to their own blogs (Reinhard et al., 2009, p. 167).

2.3 Recent research on conference Twitter

As the current chapter presents a small-scale study on academic conference tweets, the following section will review research conducted on scholarly communication through tweets in the context of academic conferences of the past fifteen years. While all studies described below investigated the purposes of tweets, some of them also examined the users and sentiments of conference tweets (Ross et al., 2011; Parra et al., 2016). For all studies conducted with Twitter data posted before 2017, it is crucial to keep in mind that tweets were limited to 140 characters, which doubled to 280 characters in 2017 (Eberl, 2020, p. 131). This adjustment considerably modified the possibilities and, hence, the genre of conference tweets. This needs to be kept in mind when comparisons between data sets collected prior to 2017 and after 2017 are drawn.

One of the first studies on conference Twitter was conducted by Reinhardt et al. (2009), who used an online survey to inspect users and detect the purposes of tweeting at various conferences. They found that conference Twitter constituted an alternative option for communicating, discussing the conference topics and for exchanging and sharing resources (Reinhardt et al., 2009, p. 155). Nevertheless, a closer look reveals some limitations as the sample size was low with only 41 responses to the survey (Reinhardt et al., p. 149). Additionally, some of the works that are cited in the text are not mentioned in the list of references. Moreover, the academic discourse communities of the conferences of interest remain unspecified.

Luckily, the 2011 study by Ross et al., which investigated users, uses and affective factors of academic conference attendees, mentioned the conference discipline, i.e. digital humanities. This early piece of research on conference Twitter excels with its methodological novelty and diversity, including qualitative content analysis, a quantitative examination of user conversations, text analysis and a qualitative survey. Yet, the survey only got 11 responses, and the text analysis failed to yield fruitful results as, due to the length limitations of tweets, users invented abbreviations and jargon, which could not be identified with conventional tools for linguistic text analysis (Ross et al., 2011, p. 219). Therefore, the authors call for innovative methods to integrate linguistic text analysis in research on conference tweets, which will be operationalized with an innovative automated text mining method, more specifically sentiment analysis, in the present research project. Nevertheless, Ross et al.'s study (2011, p. 214) showed that "the digital backchannel constitutes a multidirectional complex space, in which users make notes, share resources and ask questions as well as establishing a clear online presence". The findings regarding the use of conference tweets are similar to most results obtained in that respect (e. g., Lee et al., 2017).

Also concerned with uses and users, Mazarakis and Peters (2015) investigated 1879 conference tweets of Science 2.0 conferences. The results of their tweet analysis were multifaceted. Concerning tweeting time, they found that most tweets were posted after lunch and coffee breaks, which implies that conference organizers could use these time slots for distributing important information. Furthermore, their findings showed that only a few users tweeted very frequently, while most users tweeted only occasionally (Mazarakis & Peters, 2015, p. 271). Their qualitative content analysis revealed that sharing conference content and resources was the purpose of over 80% of the conference tweets (Mazarakis & Peters, 2015, p. 269). Unfortunately, the methods used to find out about users and tweeting time remained opaque in their article.

A comprehensive piece of research, conducted by Parra et al. (2016), looked into purposes, sentiments, topical patterns and networks detected in conference tweets. They used tweets from 16 computer science conferences which took place over a span of five years. Their methods included network analysis, sentiment analysis and topic modeling (Parra et al., 2016, pp. 305 f.). Their analyses of the purposes of conference tweeting showed changing practices in Twitter use over time: In the 2009 conference contexts, Twitter was used for conversational purposes, i. e., replies and mentions, while in 2013, conference tweets evolved around informational aspects, i. e., retweets and tweeting URLs (Parra et al., 2016, p. 301). Concerning the sentiments, they found that conferences focusing on human-computer interaction exhibited emotions more consistently, and, in general, a higher number of positive sentiments compared to more analytical fields of research was detected (Parra et al., 2016, p. 311). While Parra et al. (2016) did not address the relationship between the purposes and sentiments of the conference tweets, my study aims to detect whether there is a tendency for certain communicative functions to express specific sentiments among the ASA2021 conference tweets.

Network analysis seems to be a rewarding method to detect the social network configuration structures of academic discourse communities. Like Parra et al. (2016), Lee et al. (2017, p. 767) also conducted a network analysis of three digital humanities conferences based on the Twitter feed of the conference hashtags.

Their secondary and tertiary focus constituted a content analysis of the uses of conference tweets as well as topic modeling (Lee et al., 2017, p. 773). Their results showed that the Twitter networks analyzed were closely-knit, but "led by a few individuals who were mostly at the cent[er] of the subgroups in the network" (Lee et al., 2017, p. 793). This is similar to Mazarakis and Peters' findings (2015, p. 271). As far as the uses of Twitter for the digital humanities conferences are concerned, they found similar results for all three conferences. For the 2016 conference, Lee et al. (2017, p. 790) categorized the tweets as follows: "topical discussions/conversations (29.3%), daily chatter (20.5%), jotting down notes/memos (18.3%), sharing photos/videos (15.5%), sharing resources (13.0%), and administrative/announcements (3.4%)".

The first study to analyze 280-character conference tweets was led by Luzón and Albero-Posac (2020). In the context of two applied linguistics conferences, they investigated the communicative functions and the use of semiotic resources to achieve these functions (Luzón & Albero-Posac 2020: 33). They used qualitative content analysis for the examination of the communicative functions and multimodal discourse analysis based on Bezemer and Kress (2008) for the in-depth investigation of semiotic resources which helped to realize the communicative functions (Luzón & Albero-Posac, 2020, p. 39). The first version of their code system was based on categories found by the research reviewed above (Ross et al., 2011; Mazarakis & Peters, 2015; Lee et al., 2017). By means of an inductive coding process of their Twitter data, they then created their final code system (see Table 1 for the categories). The results of their study show that the conference tweets were primarily posted for community building and networking, followed by engaging in informal intereraction and commentary as well as self-promotion (Luzón & Albero-Posac, 2020, p. 48). Also, Twitter features such as mentions, using hashtags, emojis, and retweets were used to achieve these communicative purposes. The study by Luzón and Albero-Posac (2020) is up to date, the first study to analyze tweets with 280 characters and it also considered multimodal aspects of the tweets. Additionally, the sample size of the data set (140 tweets) was similar to the number of tweets analyzed in the current project (118). Therefore, the code system by Luzón and Albero-Posac (2020) will be used for the analysis of the conference tweets in the present data set. Luzón and Albero-Posac (2020, p. 49) also call for more research on the communicative purposes of conference tweets in different disciplines, which is why a social anthropologist conference was chosen for the purpose of this paper.

Before turning to the study design of the present research project, I would sum up the most relevant findings of the reviewed studies as follows: Typical purposes of conference tweeting were "topical conversations", "jotting down notes", "sharing resources and photos/videos", "daily chatter" and "announcements" (e. g., Lee et al., 2017). Moreover, sentiments of conference tweets were primarily positive (e. g., Parra et al., 2016; Ross et al., 2011). Generally, most studies stressed the importance of the role of social media for scholarly networking (e. g., Lupton, 2014; Ross et al., 2011; Luzón & Albero-Posac, 2020). So far, to my knowledge, no studies have been conducted on Twitter use before, during and after academic conferences which were exclusively held online.

3   Methodology

Considering the above, my research project aims to shed light on the Twitter activity of an online conference of one specific academic discourse community by applying a novel research methodology to this text type, which will be described in detail below.

3.1   Research questions

My study intends to gain insights into the reasons for tweeting at conferences and whether the conference community tends to use emotional or rather neutral language for expressing themselves. Thereby, I also aim to be able to draw implications for digital academic practices of the 21st century.

Hence, the two research questions underlying this research project are as follows:

RQ I: What are the communicative functions of conference tweets posted before, during, and after a social anthropology online conference?

RQ II: Which sentiments do tweets posted in the context of a social anthropology online conference carry?

3.2   Data set

The data set consists of 118 multimodal initial Twitter postings tweets by 45 different users before, during and shortly after the social anthropologist conference ASA2021: Responsibility. The conference hosted by the *Association of Social Anthropologists* (ASA) was organized by the Department of Social Anthropology at the University of St. Andrews, Scotland, and held online from March 29 to April 2, 2021. Prominent topics for the conference contributions included extinction, health, disease, well-being, morality, and legality (Association of Social Anthropologists, 2021). This conference was chosen for the analysis as it was a small conference that took place in an online setting during a time of the pandemic when attending and organizing online conferences was new territory for most academic communities.

Twitter data was collected manually with the help of the conference's hashtag (#asaresponsibility). Concerning the choice of the timespan relevant to the analysis of the conference tweets, two prominent events marked the beginning and the end of the discourse on ASA2021: The first posting referring to the *Call for Papers* for the 2021 conference, i. e. 3 ½ months before the start of the event, constitutes the first tweet in the data set (@visualplague, 2020), whereas the last tweet (@CAP_Ltd, 2021) in the set announces the shipping of the conference prize draw and was posted a month after the end of the conference. All postings with the hashtag #asaresponsibility which were posted before the CfP referred to "ASA2020". Every tweet containing the hashtag #asaresponsibility that was posted between these two events was collected and subject to analysis. The tweets in the data set consist of a maximum of 280 characters each, some were posted in a thread, and many of them contain semiotic resources other than verbal text, such as pictures, emojis and hyperlinks. I am only interested in postings with the hashtag #asaresponsibility, rather than secondary postings (retweets, likes or comments). The methodology of the present article has a twofold nature and will be introduced below.

3.3   Multimodal content analysis (RQ I)

Qualitative content analysis helps to structure and identify patterns in large amounts of data (Grbich, 2007, p. 112). Hence, to detect the communicative functions of the conference tweets, a multimodal content analysis will be adopted and conducted with the help of MAXQDA 2022.[4] Communicative functions serve to classify "acts of communication or uses of a medium of communication" (Chandler & Munday, 2011). Therefore, for the purpose of this project, communicative functions are defined as multimodal acts of communication on Twitter. A tweet can contain one or more communicative functions. Figure 1 displays an example of a tweet used to announce their own talk, share conference pictures and announce conference events (see the hyperlink).

In the qualitative coding process according to Kuckartz (2018), all 118 tweets will be coded deductively based on the classification of communicative functions of conference tweets by Luzón and Albero-Posac (2020). It consists of four parent codes and 20 subcodes, as can be seen in Table 1.

---

4 To obtain the .mx22 file with the coded passages, please contact the author of this paper via email.

letha_laetitia
@letha_laetitia   ...

Me and @jshergonz are sharpening pencils and
thoughts for tonight's ASA Lab on drawing,
ethnography and responsible representation. Join us
at 8pm 📓 ✏️ See you there!
#Graphic_anthropology #ASAResponsibility
nomadit.co.uk/conference/asa...

1:18 PM · Mar 31, 2021

Figure 1: Example of coding Twitter data (@letha_laetitia, 2021)

Coding scheme Luzón and Albero-Posac (2020, p.38)

Organization	Announcing conference
	Calling for papers
	Announcing conference events
	Providing practical information
	Virtual chairing
Informal commentary and interaction	Commenting on others' presentations
	Engaging in discussion on others' presentations
	Evaluating conference and others' presentations
Community building	Announcing attendance
	Expressing regret (for non-attendance) or sadness for the end of the conference
	Keeping in touch after the conference
	Engaging in (disciplinary) humour
	Informing of social activities
	Sharing conference pictures
	Congratulating and thanking
	Sharing conference outputs and other useful resources
	Other
Self-promotion	Announcing one's own talk
	Sharing one's own outputs
	Advertising one's own publications

Table 1: Communicative functions of conference tweets (Luzón & Albero-Posac, 2020, p. 38)

As more than one code can be assigned to one meaningful passage, multiple coding is employed. For the iterative coding process, a codebook including a definition as well as an anchor example for each category was created (see Appendix). Nevertheless, as tweets do not only consist of verbal data but can also include other semiotic resources, the code system by Luzón and Albero-Posac (2020, p. 38) is not only applied to the text of the tweets: images, links and emojis are also considered in the analysis. Here, images play an essential role as they provide ample opportunities to add information to the text of a tweet, which is after all limited to 280 characters. Therefore, in the multimodal coding process, images are labeled as such and coded deductively. Ledin and Machin (2020, p. 10f.) list several ways of analyzing images within multimodal analysis, such as the examination of color in visual design, perspectives, angles, or representation of participants in a picture. Ledin and Machin (2020, p. 39f.) also introduce the concepts of denotation and connotation of an image, which goes back to Roland Barthes' levels of meaning. Just like words, images denote and connotate meaning:

> Denotation takes place on the primary level of signification and consists in what we think of as the literal, fixed, dictionary meaning of a word, ideally one that can be universally agreed upon. Connotation occurs on the secondary level of signification and consists of the changing associative meaning of a word. (Yan & Ming, 2015, p. 60)

Hence, while the rather neutral depiction of the content of an image refers to its denotation, the implicit communication of values, ideas and concepts through images relates to the connotation of a picture (Ledin & Machin, 2020, p. 39f.). For this chapter, only the first level of meaning, namely denotation, is taken into account.

3.4   Sentiment analysis (RQ II)

Although priority is given to the analysis of the communicative functions of conference tweets, sentiment analysis adds valuable insights into the affective world of the conference participants, organizers, non-attendees, or publishers. More specifically, sentiment analysis is a data mining technique and refers to the analysis of people's attitudes, emotions and sentiments towards entities captured in written text production (Liu, 2015, p. 1) to be subsequently used to support decision-making processes (Pozzi et al., 2017, p.1). This field of study can be located within the discipline of natural language processing, which is concerned with the development of computer applications with the goal of processing and analyzing a magnitude of naturally occurring language.

To understand how the Twitter users felt about the online conference that was chosen for this chapter, the verbal parts of the conference tweets are analyzed toward their sentiments (i.e., negative, slightly negative, neutral, slightly positive, positive or no sentiment at all). More specifically, a computer-automated corpus-based sentiment analysis is performed on the data set in MAXQDA 2022. The qualitative data analysis software accesses a lexical resource called Senti-WordNet 3.0 to determine the emotions expressed in the conference tweets. In SentiWordNet 3.0, which was created by Baccianella et al. (2010), numerical scores have been assigned to every synset, i.e., a set of synonyms. The values of these scores are positive for words with positive connotations, negative for words with negative connotations and approximating zero for neutral words (MAXQDA, 2022, p. 15). In the analysis, MAXQDA 2022 assesses the sentiment values of each word and calculates the mean values of the sentiment scores in each tweet to classify the tweet. Words without sentiment scores are categorized as "no sentiment" (MAXQDA, 2022, p. 15 f.). The software also allows classifying words to be ignored in the analysis. As this analysis aims to detect the sentiments towards entities concerning the conference and not the content of the conference itself, all presentation titles, hashtags and Twitter handles of accounts were excluded.

According to MAXQDA (2022, p. 16), the agreement between sentiment analysis controlled and carried out by humans compared to computer-automated sentiment analysis lies at only 60–70%. Nevertheless, manually assigning sentiment scores for each word in the tweets of the data set underlying this chapter would go beyond the scope and purpose of the project as the focus lies on the genre analysis of conference tweets. Therefore, MAXQDA 2022 will be used for the sentiment analysis.

4.   Results and discussion

4.1   Communicative functions of conference tweet

In the qualitative data analysis, a total of 267 verbal passages and images with communicative functions were detected in the data set. The distribution of communicative functions identified with regard to the parent categories is quite balanced with "organization" making up for 30% (80 instances), "self-promotion" accounting for 28.8% (77 instances), "community building" with 25.5% (68 instances) and, lastly, "informal commentary and interaction" with 15.7% (42 instances) (see Figure 2).

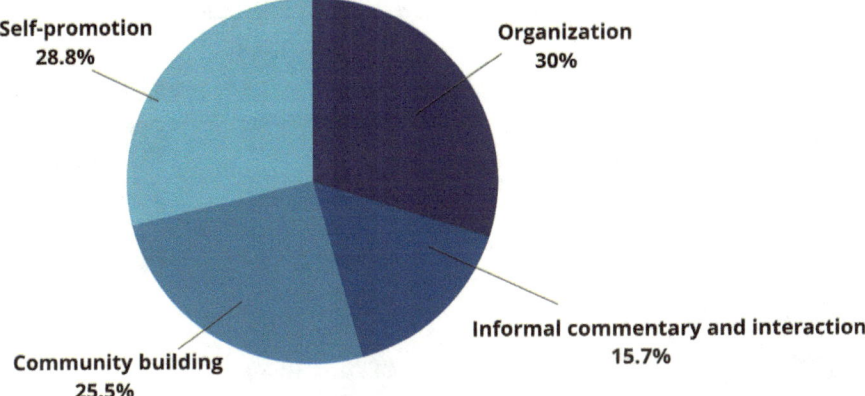

Figure 2: Distribution of communicative functions of conference tweets

Hence, the realms of organization, self-promotion, and community building are equally often addressed by Twitter users posting about ASA2021. Informal commentary and interaction, which occur less frequently, constitute an exception. Interestingly, this confirms the findings by Parra et al. (2016, p. 301), who discovered a shift from a focus on an informal use of conference Twitter to an increasingly informational use. A possible reason for this is that social media posting behavior changes over time as new features are introduced or as users move to different platforms. Hence, this finding could also be due to the fact that conversations about the presentations might have happened in a different environment: For on-site conferences, it is likely that they happened directly after the presentations. For the current online scenario, it has to be kept in mind that online conferences are held through conference platforms like Hopin, Moodle, or Discord, which include various alternatives for communication. Therefore, it is possible that a considerable amount of scholarly online communication took place in these more private conference settings. This explanation could also account for the large amounts of content-specific communication in conference tweets of the on-site conferences investigated by Reinhard et al. (2009, p. 155) and Mazarakis and Peters (2015, p. 269).

The overall distribution of the four parent codes is roughly in agreement with the results by Lee et al. (2017, p. 790). Yet, the number of tweets concerned with organizational matters is considerably higher in the present study. A reason for this could be that the organizers of the conference observed by Lee et al. (2017, p. 790) did not rely on Twitter as much as the organizers of ASA2021. This suggests that the distribution of communicative functions of conference tweets is case-specific. Concerning ASA2021, the following figure provides a detailed overview of the absolute frequencies detected for each communicative function (see Figure 3).

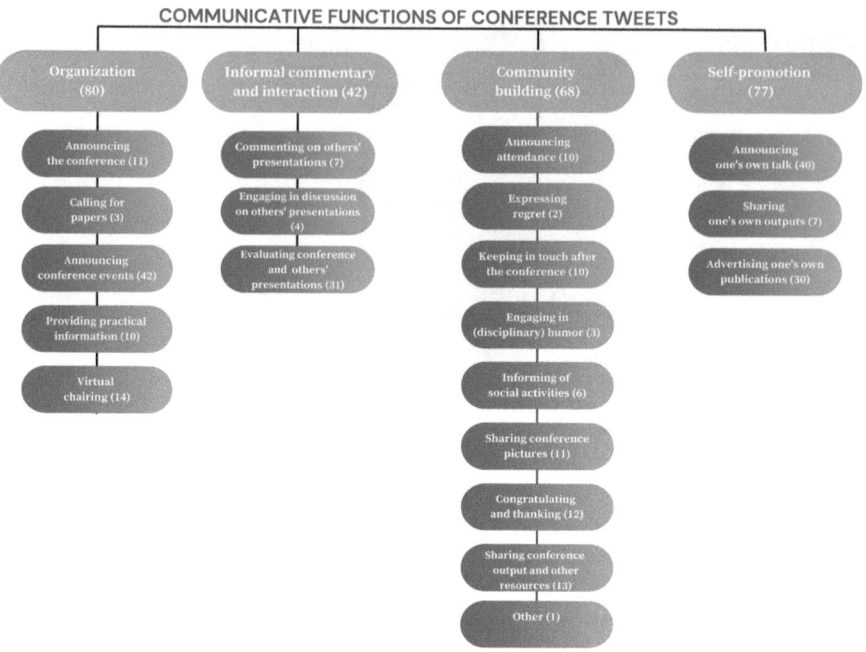

Figure 3: Total numbers of communicative functions of conference tweets

The subcodes "announcing conference events" (42 instances), "announcing one's own talk" (40 instances), "evaluating conference and others' presentations" (31 instances), and "advertising one's own publications" (30 instances) occur most frequently in the data set. By contrast, subcodes such as "calling for papers" (3 instances), "engaging in (disciplinary) humor" (3 instances), and "engaging in discussion on others' presentations" (4), were only identified a few times in the data set (see Figure 2). Again, a possible explanation for the low number of these communication functions might be that they were carried out in different online settings.

Discussing every subcategory in detail exceeds the limits of this paper. Therefore, in the following four subsections, examples of the two most prominent communicative functions for each parent category are provided.

Organization

When Twitter users post about organizational matters, "announcing conference events" is among the most frequent communicative functions of the data set (15.7%). The following example (see Figure 4) is paradigmatic for a conference tweet in which an inserted image takes over the function of adding verbal information. It illustrates that verbal and non-verbal features cannot always be clearly distinguished: While the limited space for text provides the reader with the date and general topic of the announced conference event, the inserted image, which mostly consists of text, offers additional information on the content of the talk, exceeding the usual tweet limit.

Visual Plague/ Global War Against the Rat 🐭
@visualplague

On March 29 #ASAResponsibility Aparecida Vilaça will be giving this year's Firth Lecture on Viruses, human-animal relations and response-ability in Indigenous Amazonia

Raymond Firth Memorial Lecture: *Viruses, human-animal relations and response-ability in Indigenous Amazonia*

Aparecida Vilaça (Museu Nacional - UFRJ)

Beginning with some recent reflections of Amazonian peoples concerning the animal origin of infection by Covid-19, I intend to discuss human-animal relations, which in this ethnographic region are based on a mythology that presupposes an indiscernibility between different types of beings. The sociocultural transformations arising from contact, especially Christianization, a theme central to Firth's work, will allow us to approach this topic from another angle, revealing some of the paths taken by the response-ability of these peoples to changes.

11:08 AM · Mar 22, 2021

Figure 4: Example of an announcement of conference events (@visualplague, 2021)

Another interesting communicative function constitutes "virtual chairing", accounting for 5.24% of all passages considered in the analysis. Virtual chairing includes the announcement of a conference event shortly before the event, as well as a preview of the content and the exact time of the event. The example in Figure 5 depicts a scenario where the Department of Social Anthropology, St. Andrews, announces the schedule for day three of the conference and the presidency of the memorial lecture. This is emphasized by the image posted with the tweet, which provides in-depth information on the content of the lecture.

However, this position is not only occupied by the conference organizers (@theasainfo, @StAndrewsAnthro), but also by the private accounts of conference organizers and other conference attendees (e. g., @visualplague), which is in line with the findings by Luzón and Albero-Posac (2020, p. 41), who also detected informative tweets about conference events and other organizational matters posted by non-organizers.

St Andrews Social Anthropology
@StAndrewsAnthro

Day 3 of #ASAResponsibility today! Panels start at
2.15pm, and then at 6.30pm we have the Ladislav
Holy Memorial Lecture: Peter Geschiere (Amsterdam)
will speak on 'Witchcraft' and the Accountability of
Conspiracy Thinking theasa.org/conferences/as...

Ladislav Holy memorial lecture:
Responsibility versus Responsibilization
Anthropologists, 'Witchcraft' and the
Accountability of Conspiracy Thinking

Peter Geschiere **(University of**
Amsterdam)

Chair: Roy Dilley (University of St Andrews)

What can anthropology contribute to analyzing
'responsibility'? Kinship - an anchor of our
discipline for Ladislav Holy and many others - suggests a focus on
taking responsibility. But 'witchcraft,' in many African settings seen
as the reverse of kinship, rather raises issues of responsibilization,
in the sense of tracing accountability. In her recent book
Mafiacraft, Deborah Puccio-Den signals that for both social
scientists and Sicilians such responsibilization became a major
challenge in order to grasp an unnamed form of agency that
insisted on hiding itself. Studying responsibility as
responsibilization might be relevant for present-day contexts,
marked all over the world by an avalanche of conspiracy theories
in which actors remain hidden, defying the border between
imaginary and real.

2:14 PM · Mar 31, 2021

Figure 5: Example of a virtual chairing situation (@StAndrewsAnthro, 2021)

Informal commentary and interaction

In the cases of rather informal communication among the scholars, "evaluating
conference and others' presentations" is the most prominent subcode, making
up 11.6% of all coded passages in the data set. Figure 6 displays a tweet in which
both the conference ("Great to be attending [...]") as well as a specific presentation are mentioned and assessed.

Not only evaluating the delivery but also commenting on the content of a
presentation is rare (2.62%). In the example shown in Figure 7, a conference
attendee wants to raise awareness of a pressing issue by referring to the shared
knowledge of the academic discourse community.

As also stated by Luzón and Albero-Posac (2020, p. 48), this example indicates
that informal commentary and interaction also contribute to the strengthening
of the conference community.

Sean Heath
@SeanmrHeath

Great to be attending the @theasainfo
#ASAResponsibility annual conference virtually.
Washing the dishes while watching "The limits of
collaboration" session this morning! Excited for the
week.

12:20 PM · Mar 29, 2021

Figure 6: Example of an evaluation of the conference and a presentation (@SeanmrHeath, 2021)

Nevertheless, as already mentioned above, the low number of occurrences of conference tweets within informal commentary and interaction could point to the outsourcing of conversation about the presentations to other platforms or also private messages through Twitter.

Sarah Schönbauer
@SarahSchonbauer

Great talk by @Bomm_L #ASAResponsibility about
how responsibility for plastics is shifted to the
younger generation. Something that should remind us
all on the climate change discourse. Younger
generations not yet in powerful positions being
responsible for collective futures...

12:39 PM · Apr 1, 2021

Figure 7: Example of a comment on a presentation (@SarahSchonbauer, 2021)

Community building

When it comes to networking, "sharing conference outputs and other useful resources" (4.87%) and "congratulating and thanking" (4.49%) occurs most often. Figure 8 shows a tweet with a link to the recording of the conference's memorial lecture.

Visual Plague/ Global War Against the Rat 🐀
@visualplague

The recording of the Ladislav Holy Memorial Lecture
delivered this year by Peter Geschiere at
#ASAResponsibility @theasainfo @StAndrewsAnthro
@univofstandrews is now available online

youtube.com
ASA2021: Ladislav Holy Memorial Lecture

6:00 PM · Apr 24, 2021

Figure 8: Example of making conference outputs available (@visualplague, 2021)

Figure 9 is a paradigmatic example of emphatically praising and thanking the contributors, organizers and administrators of the conference for their work.

Dr. Tridibesh Dey
@treeonplastics   ...

#ASAResponsibility was a carnival of fantastic
scholars and ideas. Really enjoyed it!

A big thanks to the local organising group
@StAndrewsAnthro, to @theasainfo and the
wonderful team of administrators, ever present, ever
helpful. Well done, folks.
Enjoy a well-deserved break!

5:27 PM · Apr 2, 2021

Figure 9: Example of thanking conference organizers and administrators (@treeonplastics, 2021)

Academic conferences provide ample opportunity for networking. However, if the conference happens online, the networking has to move into a digital space too. Therefore, tweets within these subcategories are crucial as these Twitter users identify themselves as part of an academic conference community. Conference tweets which aim to contribute to networking, hence, provide the opportunity to bridge the professional and the private identities of academics and build networks for professional, but also social and informal exchange, which is particularly essential for academics who are new in the field.

Self-promotion

"Announcing one's own talk" seems to be a common practice with 14.98% of all coded passages in the set. Figure 10 illustrates this category with an advertisement and a sneak peek of their conference presentation.

Another popular aim of conference tweets is "advertising one's own publications". Publications were promoted by authors and book publishers alike and this practice amounts to 11.24% of the coded passages.

Figure 11 displays a multimodal tweet including an emoji, i.e. the champagne bottle emoji to indicate celebration, and a visually-appealing flyer to support and emphasize the verbal part of the tweet, which announces a reception to celebrate the publishing house's new publications. Hence, posting conference tweets for the purpose of self-promotion is not only done by academics, but also by publishing houses (Luzón & Albero-Posac, 2020, p. 48).

letha_laetitia
@letha_laetitia   ···

Just want to say that @josesherwood_ & I will run
Lab01 at the next #ASAresponsibility [29March-1Apr
2021]. If you join us [online], we promise we'll make
you #draw your #ethnography!
#graphic_anthropology
#visual #methods

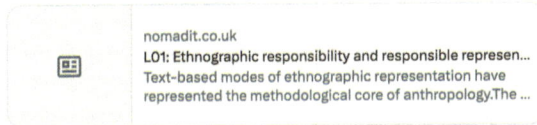

10:41 AM · Feb 3, 2021

Figure 10: Example of an announcement of someone's own talk [@letha_laetitia, 2021)

These results also corroborate the ideas of Ross et al. (2011, p. 214), who detected "establishing a clear online presence" as an important purpose of conference tweeting.

BerghahnAnthropology
@BerghahnAnthro   ···

🐦Calling all #ASAResponsibility participants: join us
for a "BYOB" reception tomorrow, 31 March at 15.45
to celebrate our new publications in
#SocialAnthropology! See more details about the
conference here: bit.ly/3czQ3FZ @theasainfo

2:24 PM · Mar 30, 2021

Figure 11: Example of an ad of publications (@BerghahnAnthro, 2021)

Images

Within the 118 conference tweets, a total of 56 images consisting of screenshots of video calls, conference abstracts, books, logos, and pictures were detected. These images were coded with the same code system as the verbal parts of the tweets.

Table 2 shows the occurrences of communicative functions identified in the images.

Code System	Visual
˅ 🔲 Communicative functions	
˅ 🔲 Organization	
🔲 Virtual chairing (14)	1
🔲 Providing practical information (10)	1
🔲 Announcing conference events (42)	11
🔲 Calling for papers (3)	
🔲 Announcing conference (11)	1
˅ 🔲 Informal commentary and interaction	
🔲 Evaluating conference and others' presentations (31)	
🔲 Engaging in discussion on others' presentations (4)	
🔲 Commenting on others' presentations (7)	
˅ 🔲 Community building	
🔲 Other (1)	
🔲 Sharing conference outputs and other useful resources (13)	2
🔲 Congratulating and thanking (12)	
🔲 Sharing conference pictures (11)	11
🔲 Informing of social actitvities (6)	
🔲 Engaging in (disciplinary) humor (3)	
🔲 Keeping in touch after the conference (10)	3
🔲 Expressing regret (2)	
🔲 Announcing attendance (10)	
˅ 🔲 Self-promotion	
🔲 Advertising one's own publications (30)	18
🔲 Sharing one's own outputs (7)	1
🔲 Announcing one's own talk (40)	16

Table 2: Relationship between images and communicative functions

Interestingly, the majority of the images (62.3%) express a communicative function related to self-promotion, whereas only 28.6% of the images are used for community building and 17.5% of the images help to convey organizational matters. Surprisingly, not a single image is used for informal commentary and interaction. Within the category "organization", the most frequent use of images is to announce conference events, making up for 26.2% of all instances in this subcategory. Concerning community building, it does not come as a surprise that 100% of the segments identified as the sharing of conference pictures was detected in the images. Taking a closer look at self-promotion, 60% of all cases of "advertising one's own publications" and 40% of the instances of "announcing one's own talk" were detected in the images. Hence, it can be inferred that visual content is primarily used for self-promotion. This suggests an inclination towards more information density and multimodal practices when it comes to self-promotion. It is likely that publishing houses use this practice to advertise their products on social media in order to make profit and that they probably also have paid staff for exactly this purpose. However, this finding could also imply that the scholar advertising their own work wants to leave a convincing impression and provide their fellow Twitter user with the whole picture by sharing more information and putting more effort into a posting. Considering this finding from an educational perspective, it suggests supporting the awareness-raising and fostering of the literacy of this online genre in the academic community, for example by means of teaching Twitter use for academic purposes in the context of advanced EAP courses.

4.2   Sentiments of conference tweets

In this section, first, the overall results of the sentiment analysis are reported and illustrated with examples. Second, the relations between sentiments and communicative functions are addressed.

Distribution of sentiments

The results of the sentiment analysis show that the majority of conference tweets (55.1%) have a rather positive sentiment and 16.1% have a positive sentiment. A neutral sentiment was detected in 24.6% of conference tweets and the rest is shared by rather negative sentiments (2.5%) and no sentiments (1.8%). Not a single tweet in the data set shows a purely negative sentiment. Figure 12 depicts the absolute frequencies of sentiments detected in the data set.

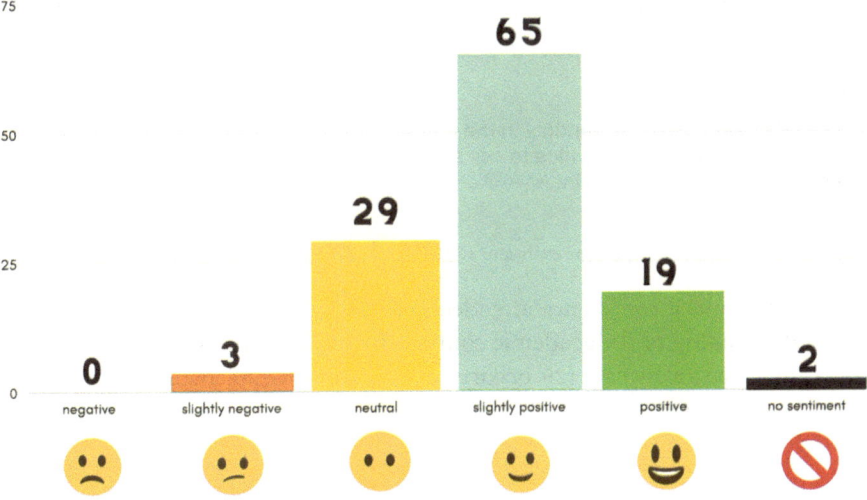

Figure 12: Absolute frequencies of sentiments in the data set

A prototypical example of a rather positive sentiment, which occurs 65 times, is illustrated in the following example:

Clare Chandler
@AnthroAMR   ...

Super to see #SocSciAMR research being presented at the Association of Social Anthropologists conference #ASAResponsibility with @cmyuill @dr_loreleijones. @JustinD_902 presents trajectories of global health architecture through rational drug use @FeverStudies 👏

👤 GlobalHealthDx and 5 others

1:08 PM · Mar 29, 2021

Figure 13: Tweet with a rather positive sentiment (@AnthroAMR, 2021)

Here, a conference attendee acknowledges the presentation of antimicrobial resistance in the context of the social anthropologist conference. An even more positive sentiment (19 cases) is depicted in the next tweet:

Dr Ben Hildred
@BHildred   ...

Aparecida Vilaça was outstanding in the Firth Memorial Lecture, and really nice to see some folks from @standrewsanthro again! #ASAResponsibility

6:47 PM · Mar 29, 2021

Figure 14: Tweet with a positive sentiment (@BHildred, 2021)

In this example, a conference attendee praises the keynote speaker and appreciates the reunion of the academic community of the University of St. Andrews. Regarding neutral tweets (29 occurrences), the following tweet shows an appropriate example.

CFP and call for labs is open for #ASAResponsibility until the end of the month @theasainfo

theasa.org
ASA2021: RESPONSIBILITY
Online, 29 March - 2 April 2021

10:32 PM · Dec 8, 2020

Figure 15: Tweet with a neutral sentiment (@visualplague, 2020)

This neutral post informs about the call for papers and labs with their dedicated deadline. Although rather negative sentiments only occur three times, the following exemplifies this category:

I am so missing in person conferences and all the fun!
@MScEnSoc @RohanJackson #ASAResponsibility

6:56 PM · Mar 29, 2021

Figure 16: Tweet with a rather negative sentiment (@NakaMookherjee, 2021)

In this case, a conference participant expresses regret about the online setting of the conference due to the circumstances of the Covid-19 pandemic at that time. We need to be aware that the rather negative tweet is not directed at the conference or its organizers, but rather expresses frustration with the situation caused by the pandemic.

Aligning with the prevalent positive sentiments found in the conference tweets studied by Parra et al. (2016) and Ross et al. (2011), the results of the present sentiment analysis confirm the predominant positivity of conference tweets.

Sentiments in relation to the communicative functions

Now that each sentiment has been illustrated with an example, the link between communicative functions and sentiments will be explored. Table 3 depicts each communicative function with its respective occurrences of positive, negative, neutral, rather negative, rather positive sentiment or no sentiment at all. For the interpretation of this table, it has to be borne in mind that each tweet was assigned one sentiment, while frequently more than one communicative function was detected within one tweet.

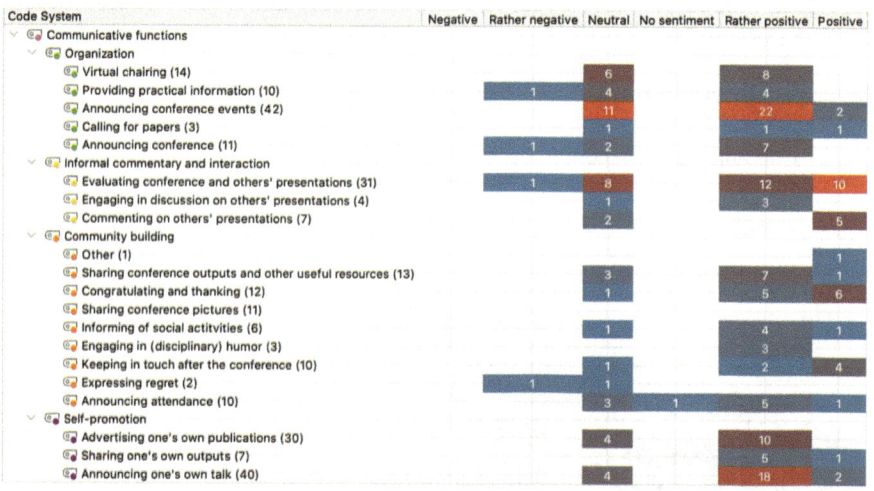

Code System	Negative	Rather negative	Neutral	No sentiment	Rather positive	Positive
Communicative functions						
Organization						
Virtual chairing (14)			6		8	
Providing practical information (10)		1	4		4	
Announcing conference events (42)			11		22	2
Calling for papers (3)			1		1	1
Announcing conference (11)		1	2		7	
Informal commentary and interaction						
Evaluating conference and others' presentations (31)		1	8		12	10
Engaging in discussion on others' presentations (4)			1		3	
Commenting on others' presentations (7)			2			5
Community building						
Other (1)						1
Sharing conference outputs and other useful resources (13)			3		7	1
Congratulating and thanking (12)			1		5	6
Sharing conference pictures (11)						
Informing of social activities (6)			1		4	1
Engaging in (disciplinary) humor (3)					3	
Keeping in touch after the conference (10)			1		2	4
Expressing regret (2)		1	1			
Announcing attendance (10)			3	1	5	1
Self-promotion						
Advertising one's own publications (30)			4		10	
Sharing one's own outputs (7)					5	1
Announcing one's own talk (40)			4		18	2

Table 3: Relations of communicative functions and sentiments

Regarding the absolute frequencies, it is evident that "announcing conference events" frequently co-occurs with rather positive (22 occurrences) and neutral (11 occurrences) sentiments. The evaluation of the conference or of conference events also shows rather positive (12 cases), positive (10 cases) and neutral sentiments (8 instances). Another salience can be identified in the rather positive sentiments detected in relation to "announcing one's own talk" (18 instances).

These findings confirm the implications drawn on the basis of the overall prevalence of positive conference tweets and the predominance of pictures within the category of self-promotion. Thus, the idea that conference tweets serve to position academics within an academic community by offering thorough and visually appealing multimodal information is further supported. Also, while non-academic Twitter is frequently used to rage about political decisions, for example, its use for academic purposes follows different goals: Here, Twitter is mostly used for promotional purposes, expressing membership and deepening conference and discourse community networks, which would explain the friendliness among the conference attendees.

5.   Conclusion and implications

This piece of research aimed to shed light on scholarly communication on Twitter before, during and after an academic conference held in an online setting. Based on a multimodal content analysis of conference tweets' communicative functions and a sentiment analysis, it can be concluded that in the context of academic online conferences, Twitter as a key microblogging medium for digital communication serves a variety of different communicative functions. The multimodal content analysis (RQ I) showed that for academics at all levels of hierarchy, conference tweets are an approachable genre offering many options for the integration of multimodality. Concerning the communicative functions, this study demonstrated that organizational, self-promotional and social aspects were almost equally important. Content-specific comments, however, were provided rarely, which might be a reflection of them happening outside of Twitter. The results of the multimodal content analysis also stressed the importance of networking and identified the diligence of conference Twitter users when it comes to self-promotion. Lastly, due to the nature of the communicative purposes of the conference tweets, the sentiment analysis (RQ II) confirmed that most tweets showed a positive or rather positive sentiment. Hence, as opposed to conventional EAP texts, which usually adopt a rather neutral to formal academic register, conference tweets exhibit a very emotional language use.

These findings raise intriguing implications for their application. In accordance with Lillis and Tuck (2016, p. 38) and Luzón and Albero-Posac (2020, p. 49), the results of this study emphasize the necessity of recognizing conference tweets as an EAP genre. Thus, as digital and multimodal literacies are increasingly important, the use of Twitter for academic purposes should be on the syllabus for advanced EAP courses. In this way, (junior) academics would be able to learn about the myriad possibilities of networking and positioning themselves in an academic discourse community. The findings also suggest that conference organizers should create Twitter hashtags for their conferences and advertise them during the conference in order to foster the digital backchannel, especially at conferences which take an online or hybrid form. These implications are arguably also applicable to comparable microblogging services that might replace Twitter in the future, such as LinkedIn.

Nevertheless, there are several limitations to the study at hand. Firstly, the generalizability of the results is limited due to the context-specificity of the conference community of ASA2021. Secondly, while computer-automated sentiment analysis is a useful text mining tool for large amounts of data, the classification of the tweets sometimes showed imprecisions in comparison to human intuition. Also, the lexicon SentiWordNet 3.0 was published in 2010, and, thus, cannot account for sentiments of newer concepts or words. Especially during the pandemic, new word creations have found their way into the dictionary and some words have received altered connotations (Grzega, 2021). Thirdly, another potential weakness is the realization of online conferences on conference platforms, creating space for outsourced and more private communication among scholars. This could account for the fact that Twitter users in the data set hardly discuss content-related aspects. Lastly, as only tweets with the hashtag #asaresponsibility were considered in the analysis, it is likely that some conference attendees, organizers, and publishers also tweeted about the conference without using the hashtag. These tweets remain unknown.

Therefore, future research on online conferences could also take communication through backchannels integrated into the conference platforms into consideration. Moreover, an in-depth multimodal analysis of how different semiotic resources are used to achieve communicative functions in online conference tweets could yield useful results. In addition, it has to be kept in mind that social media platforms are in constant change as they aim to cater to their users' needs, for example, by implementing new features. Due to Elon Musk's controversial acquisition of Twitter in October 2022, and the rebranding of Twitter into X in July 2023, this is a highly topical issue for the platform. Therefore, awareness of the variability of social media platforms should be raised among scholars conducting research on the use of as well as users of the platform.

References

@AnthroAMR. (2021, March 29). *Super to see #SocSciAMR research being presented at the Association of Social Anthropologists conference #ASAResponsibility with @cmyuill @dr_loreleijones. @JustinD_902 presents trajectories* [Tweet; image]. Twitter. https://twitter.com/AnthroAMR/status/1376491373097013249.

Askehave, I., & Ellerup Nielsen, A. (2005). Digital genres: A challenge to traditional genre theory. *Information Technology & People, 18*(2), 120–141. https://doi.org/10.1108/0959 3840510601504.

Association of Social Anthropologists. (2022, March 14). *ASA2021: Responsibility*. The ASA. https://theasa.org/conferences/asa2021/.

Baccianella, S., Esuli, A., & Sebastiani, F. (2010). Sentiwordnet 3.0: An enhanced lexical resource for sentiment analysis and opinion mining. In N. Calzolari, K. Choukri, B. Maegaard, & J. Mariani (Eds.), *Proceedings of the international conference on language resources and evaluation, LREC 2010, 17–23 May 2010, Valletta, Malta* (pp. 2200–2204). European Language Resources Association. http://nmis.isti.cnr.it/sebastiani/Publicati ons/LREC10.pdf.

@BerghahnAnthro. (2021, March 30). *Calling all #ASAResponsibility participants: join us for a "BYOB" reception tomorrow, 31 March at 15.45 to celebrate our new publications* [Tweet; image]. Twitter. https://twitter.com/BerghahnAnthro/status/137687308196530 9959.

@BHildred. (2021, March 29). *Aparecida Vilaça was outstanding in the Firth Memorial Lecture, and really nice to see some folks from @standrewsanthro again! #ASAResponsibility* [Tweet]. Twitter. https://twitter.com/BHildred/status/1376576714248163331.

Butterfield, A., Ekembe Ngondi, G., & Kerr, A. (2016). *A Dictionary of computer science* (7th ed.). Oxford University Press. https://doi.org/10.1093/acref/9780199688975.001.0001.

@CAP_Ltd. (2021, May 19). *Getting ready to send our lucky conference prize draw winners their new books. We have more conference prize draws in* [Tweet; image]. Twitter. https://twitter.com/CAP_Ltd/status/1394952234958524416.

Chandler, D., & Munday, R. (2011). *A dictionary of media and communication*. Oxford University Press. https://doi.org/10.1093/acref/9780199688975.001.0001.

Conger, K. (2023, August 3). *So what do we call Twitter now anyway?* The New York Times. https://www.nytimes.com/2023/08/03/technology/twitter-x-tweets-elon-musk.html.

Eberl, M. (2020). Double trouble: Are 280-character tweets comparable to 140-character tweets? In S. Rüdiger & D. Dayter (Eds.), *Studies in corpus linguistics* (Vol. 98, pp. 131–146). John Benjamins Publishing Company. https://doi.org/10.1075/scl.98.06ebe.

Grbich, C. (2007). *Qualitative data analysis: An introduction*. SAGE.

Grzega, J. (2021). From Corona party to coronapaniek: Cross-linguistic critique of COVID-related contributions to Wiktionary. *Langauge@Internet, 19*, 1.

Hutchinson, A. (2022, December 19). *A look at all the changes implemented by Elon Musk at Twitter in his time as chief twit*. Social Media Today. https://www.socialmediatoday.com /news/How-Twitter-Has-Changed-Under-Elon-Musk/639041/#:~:text=Elon%20Musk %20has%2C%20however%2C%20announced,live%20location%20will%20be%20suspe nded.%E2%80%9D.

Ince, D. (2019). Microblogging. In *A dictionary of the internet* (4th ed.). Oxford University Press.

Kuckartz, U. (2018). *Qualitative Inhaltsanalyse. Methoden, Praxis, Computerunterstützung* (4th ed.). Beltz Juventa.

Ledin, P., & Machin, D. 2020. *Introduction to multimodal analysis* (2nd ed.). Bloomsbury.

Lee, M. K., Yoon, H. Y., Smith, M., Park, H. J., & Park, H. W. (2017). Mapping a Twitter scholarly communication network: A case of the association of internet researchers' conference. *Scientometrics, 112*(2), 767–797. https://doi.org/10.1007/s11192-017-2413-z.

@letha_laetitia. (2021, February 3). *Just want to say that @josesherwood_ & I will run Lab01 at the next #ASAresponsibility [29March–1Apr 2021]. If you join us [Tweet; link].* Twitter. https://mobile.twitter.com/letha_laetitia/status/1356900527200681984.

@letha_laetitia. (2021, March 31). *Me and @jshergonz are sharpening pencils and thoughts for tonight's ASA Lab on drawing, ethnography and responsible representation. Join us* [Tweet; image]. Twitter. https://twitter.com/letha_laetitia/status/1377218714353987586.

Lillis, T., & Tuck, J. (2016). Academic literacies: A critical lens on writing and reading in the academy. In K. Hyland & P. Shaw (Eds.), *The Routledge handbook of English for academic purposes* (pp. 30–43). Routledge.

Liu, B. (2015). *Sentiment analysis: Mining opinions, sentiments, and emotions.* Cambridge University Press. https://doi.org/10.1017/CBO9781139084789.

Lupton, D. (2014). *'Feeling better connected': Academics' use of social media.* News & Media Research Center, University of Canberra. https://semanticscholar.org/paper/%E2%80%98Feeling-better-connected%E2%80%99%3A-academics%E2%80%99-use-of-media-Lupton/cc4f9d7c07e30fadd4b559882a66e83cccc4468b.

Luzón, M. J., & Albero-Posac, S. (2020). 'Had a lovely week at #conference2018': An analysis of interaction through conference tweets. *RELC Journal, 51*(1), 33–51. https://doi.org/10.1177/0033688219896862.

Mazarakis, A., & Peters, I. (2015). Science 2.0 and conference tweets: What? Where? Why? When? *The Electronic Journal of Knowledge Management, 13*(4), 269–282.

@NakaMookherjee. (2021, March 29). *I am so missing in person conferences and all the fun! @MScEnSoc @RohanJackson #ASAResponsibility* [Tweet; link]. Twitter. https://twitter.com/NakaMookherjee/status/1376578925858537473.

Paltridge, B., & Starfield, S. (2016). Ethnographic perspectives on English for academic purposes research. In K. Hyland & P. Shaw. (Eds.), *The Routledge handbook of English for academic purposes* (pp. 218–229). Routledge.

Parra, D., Trattner, C., Gómez, D., Hurtado, M., Wen, X., & Lin, Y.-R. (2016). Twitter in academic events: A study of temporal usage, communication, sentimental and topical patterns in 16 computer science conferences. *Computer Communications, 73*, 301–314. https://doi.org/10.1016/j.comcom.2015.07.001.

Pozzi, F. A., Fersini, E., Messina, E., & Liu, B. (Eds.). (2017). *Sentiment analysis in social networks.* Morgan Kaufman.

Reinhardt, W., Ebner, M., Beham, G., & Costa, C. (2009). How People are using Twitter during Conferences. In V. Hornung-Prähauser & M. Luckmann (Eds.), *Creativity and innovation competencies on the web: Proceedings of the 5th EduMedia conference, Austria, 4–5 May 2009* (pp. 145–156). EduMedia.

Ross, C., Terras, M., Warwick, C., & Welsh, A. (2011). Enabled backchannel: Conference Twitter use by digital humanists. *Journal of Documentation, 67*(2), 214–237. https://doi.org/10.1108/00220411111109449.

@SarahSchonbauer. (2021, April 1). *Great talk by @Bomm_L #ASAResponsibility about how responsibility for plastics is shifted to the younger generation. Something that should remind* [Tweet]. Twitter. https://twitter.com/SarahSchonbauer/status/1377571223228592130.

@SeanmrHeath. (2021, March 29). *Great to be attending the @theasainfo #ASAResponsibility annual conference virtually. Washing the dishes while watching "The limits of collaboration" session* [Tweet]. Twitter. https://twitter.com/SeanmrHeath/status/1376 479465010823171.

Shaw, P. (2016). Genre analysis. In K. Hyland & P. Shaw. (Eds.), *The Routledge handbook of English for academic purposes* (pp. 243–255). Routledge.

@StAndrewsAnthro. (2021, March 31). *Day 3 of #ASAResponsibility today! Panels start at 2.15pm, and then at 6.30pm we have the Ladislav Holy Memorial Lecture* [Tweet; link and image]. Twitter. https://twitter.com/StAndrewsAnthro/status/1377232951856013317.

Swales, J. (1990). *Genre analysis: English in academic and research settings* (1st ed.). Cambridge University Press.

@treeonplastics. (2021, April 2). *#ASAResponsibility was a carnival of fantastic scholars and ideas. Really enjoyed it! A big thanks to the local organising group* [Tweet]. Twitter. https://twitter.com/treeonplastics/status/1378006254933663744.

VERBI Software. (2022, June 21). *22 – Analyzing tweets.* MAXQDA. https://www.maxqd a.com/help-mx20/analyze-tweets-surveys/analyze-sentiments-of-tweets.

@visualplage. (2020, December 8). *CFP and call for labs is open for #ASAResponsibility until the end of the month @theasainfo.* [Twitter; link]. Twitter. https://twitter.com/visualpl ague/status/1336423463020613632.

@visualplague. (2021, April 24). *The recording of the Ladislav Holy Memorial Lecture delivered this year by Peter Geschiere at #ASAResponsibility @theasainfo @StAnd-rewsAnthro @univofstandrews is* [Tweet; link]. Twitter. https://twitter.com/visualplague /status/1385987132305649666.

Weller, K., Dröge, E., & Puschmann, C. (2011). Citation analysis in Twitter: Approaches for defining and measuring information flows within tweets during scientific conferences. In M. Rowe, M. Stankovic, A.-S. Dadzie, & M. Hardey. (Eds.), *Proceedings of the ESWC2011 Workshop on 'Making Sense of Microposts': Big things come in small packages* (pp. 1–12). CEUR-WS.

Yan, S., & Ming, F. (2015). Reinterpreting some key concepts in Barthes' theory. *Journal of Media and Communication Studies, 7*(3), 59–66. https://doi.org/10.5897/JMCS2014.0412.

Appendix

Parent code	Sub code	Definition	Anchor example
Organiza-tion			
	Virtual chair-ing	organizers (or under special circumstances also attendees) an-nounce talks, panels or keynote speeches by providing in-formation on the topic and the pre-senter immediately before the event	"Day 3 of #ASAResponsibility today! Panel starts at 2.15pm, and then at 6.30pm we have the La-dislav Holy Memorial Lecture: Peter Geschiere (Amsterdam) will speak on 'Witchcraft' and the Accountability of Conspiracy Thinking theasa.org/conferences/as..." (@StAndrewsAnthro, 2021)

(Continued)

Parent code	Sub code	Definition	Anchor example
	Providing practical information	information concerning the conference is announced, e. g. registration or changes in the schedule	"#ASAResponsibility conference early bird registration is now open. All welcome https://theasa.org/conferences/asa2021/registration" (@theasainfo, 2021)
	Announcing conference events	conference events are mentioned, announced, organized by attendees, but not by the presenters themselves (not immediately before the event)	"Besides great panels, the annual @theasainfo conference #ASAResponsibility held online @StAndrewsAnthro later this month also features two amazing plenaries. The first being on extinction with @liana_chua @Gsodikoff & @DaceDzenovska as speakers https://theasa.org/conferences/asa2021/" (@visualplague, 2021)
	Calling for papers	CfP is distributed	"CFP and call for labs is open for #ASAResponsibility until the end of the month @theasainfo https://www.theasa.org/conferences/asa2021/" (@visualplague, 2020)
	Announcing conference	conference is mentioned, announced, advertised	"[…] #ASA2021 is going to be a fantastic virtual conference!! " (@ElenaKotsira, 2020)
Informal commentary and interaction			
	Evaluating conference and others' presentations	a value judgement about the conference or talks, keynote speeches, panels by others is made	"Plenaries @theasainfo #ASAResponsibility @StAndrewsAnthro @univofstandrews reflect major challenges of our times: Extinction & Epidemics, with stellar speakers: @liana_chua, […]" (@visualplague, 2021)
	Engaging in discussions on others' presentations	content-related topics are discussed with presenters	"Responsibility. How do we speak of it? Is it a scream, an act against the law, a silent attempt to do something within our own comfort zone? Is it exposure, to what extent? If we talk, who shall we address for responsibility to be found!? #ASAResponsibility #ODID #OpenArms" (@Alessan15234107 31.03.2021)

(Continued)

Parent code	Sub code	Definition	Anchor example
	Commenting on others' presentations	A statement about a talk, speech or presentation by others is posted	"Great talk by @Bomm_L #ASAResponsibility about how responsibility for plastics is shifted to the younger generation. Something that should remind us all on the climate change discourse. Younger generations not yet in powerful positions being responsible for collective futures…" (@SarahSchonbauer, 2021)
Community building			
	Sharing conference outputs and other useful resources	results, links and further information related to the conference are distributed	"[…] -if you were in the audience (or missed out) and want to read more, see our @jennifer_cree se 31.03.2021 full @HDRM_Project paper on COVID and doctor wellbeing: https://mdpi.com/1660–4601/18/4/2051" (@jennifer_creese, 2021)
	Congratulating and thanking	organizers, presenters, attendees, etc. are thanked and/or praised	"A big thank-you to @StAndrewsAnthro , @theasainfo and @NomadITnews for putting together such a wonderful programme at #ASAResponsibility in these difficult times and running it so amazingly well. Hope you are enjoying a well deserved spring break! @RohanJackson @ComradeMets" (@egorovavayi, 2021)
	Sharing conference pictures	photos taken before, during or after the conference are posted	 (@AnthroAMR, 2021)
	Informing on social activities	social activities are mentioned or advertised	"[…] Join us for the closing party (DJ included) at 18:30 https://theasa.org/conferences/asa2021/panels#timetable" (@visualplague, 2021)

(Continued)

Parent code	Sub code	Definition	Anchor example
	Engaging in (disciplinary) humour	jokes are made	"Me and @jshergonz are sharpening pencils and thoughts for tonight's ASA Lab on drawing, ethnography and responsible representation. […]" (@letha_l-aetitia, 2021)
	Keeping in touch after the conference	content-related or non-content-related discussions continue until after the conferences	"#ASAResponsibility was a carnival of fantastic scholars and ideas. Really enjoyed it! A big thanks to the local organized group @StAndrewsAnthro, to @theasainfo and the wonderful team of administrators, ever present, ever helpful. Well done, folks. Enjoy a well-deserved break!" (@treesonplastics, 2021)
	Expressing regret	non-attendees of the conference or of specific talks, panels, etc. express their dissatisfaction with not having been able to attend a certain event/the conference or expression of regret due to other circumstances (eg. online setting)	"I am so missing in person conferences and all the fun! @MScEnSoc @RohanJackson #ASAResponsibility" (@Naka-Mookherjee, 2021)
	Announcing attendance	attendees mention that they will be/are attending the conference	"Great to be attending the @theasainfo #ASAResponsibility annual conference virtually. Washing the dishes while watching "The limits of collaboration" session this morning! Excited for the week." (@SeanmrHeath, 2021)
Self-promotion			
	Advertising one's own publications	Presenters and publishing houses announce and advertise their written works	"[…] Conference discounts on many exciting books, including mine: https://combinedacademic.co.uk/social-anthropology-2021/…" (@visualplague, 2021)

(Continued)

Parent code	Sub code	Definition	Anchor example
	Sharing one's own outputs	presenters distribute their results	"A great turnout this morning at the fascinating panel organised by Daniel Knight, Martin Demant Frederiksen and Fran Markowitz on time as vertiginous, featuring an excellent paper by our very own @AnthDurham 1 30.03.2021 Elena Miltiadis. @PhantElena @StAndrewsAnthro #ASAResponsibility" (@AnthDurham1, 2021)
	Announcing one's own talk	presenters announce and advertise their own talk, panel or speech	"Our Lab "Ethnographic responsibility and responsible representation: Drawing as an alternative mode of representation and knowledge production" will happen on Wednesday 31 March, 8–9.30pm. See you there! #ASAresponsibility https://nomadit.co.uk/conference/asa2021/p/10106" (@letha_laetitia, 2021)

References

@Alessan15234107. (2021, March 31). *Responsibility*. How do we speak of it? Is it a scream, an act against the law, a silent attempt to [Tweet]. Twitter. https://twitter.com/Alessan15234107/status/1377233786656669698.

@AnthroAMR. (2021, March 29). *Super to see #SocSciAMR research being presented at the Association of Social Anthropologists conference #ASAResponsibility with @cmyuill @dr_loreleijones. @JustinD_902 presents* [Tweet; image]. Twitter. https://twitter.com/AnthroAMR/status/1376491373097013249.

@AnthDurham1. (2021, March 30). *A great turnout this morning at the fascinating panel organised by Daniel Knight, Martin Demant Frederiksen and Fran Markowitz on time* [Tweet]. Twitter. https://twitter.com/AnthDurham1/status/1376832944388591618.

@egorovayi. (2021, April 5). *A big thank-you to @StAndrewsAnthro , @theasainfo and @NomadITnews for putting together such a wonderful programme at #ASAResponsibility in these difficult times* [Tweet; image]. Twitter. https://twitter.com/egorovayi/status/1379094245844389893.

@ElenaKotsira. (2020, December 29). *WOW! I woke up to a load of such exciting paper submission for our #ASAResponsibility panel Heal02 that I almost* [Tweet]. Twitter. https://twitter.com/ElenaKotsira/status/1343894621995347971.

@jennifer_creese. (2021, March 31). Thanks to #ASAresponsibility for the opportunity to talk about Irish doctors' family caregiving dilemmas in #covid19 – if you were in [Tweet]. Twitter. https://twitter.com/jennifer_creese/status/1377302891787120644.

@letha_laetitia. (2021, March 10). *Our Lab "Ethnographic responsibility and responsible representation: Drawing as an alternative mode of representation and knowledge production" will happen on* [Tweet; link]. Twitter. https://twitter.com/AnthDurham1/status/1376832944388591618.

@letha_laetitia. (2021, March 31). *Me and @jshergonz are sharpening pencils and thoughts for tonight's ASA Lab on drawing, ethnography and responsible representation. Join us* [Tweet; link; image]. Twitter. https://twitter.com/letha_laetitia/status/1377218714353987586.

@NakaMookherjee. (2021, March 29). *I am so missing in person conferences and all the fun! @MScEnSoc @RohanJackson #ASAResponsibility* [Tweet; link]. Twitter. https://twitter.com/NakaMookherjee/status/1376578925858537473.

@SarahSchonbauer. (2021, April 1). *Great talk by @Bomm_L #ASAResponsibility about how responsibility for plastics is shifted to the younger generation. Something that should remind us.* [Tweet]. Twitter. https://twitter.com/SarahSchonbauer/status/1377571223228592130.

@SeanmrHeath. (2021, March 29). *Great to be attending the @theasainfo #ASAResponsibility annual conference virtually. Washing the dishes while watching "The limits of collaboration" session* [Tweet]. Twitter. https://twitter.com/SeanmrHeath/status/1376479465010823171.

@StAndrewsAnthro. (2021, March 31). *Day 3 of #ASAResponsibility today! Panel starts at 2.15pm, and then at 6.30pm we have the Ladislav Holy Memorial Lecture* [Tweet]. Twitter. https://twitter.com/StAndrewsAnthro/status/1377232951856013317.

@theasainfo. (2021, February 19). *#ASAResponsibility conference early bird registration is now open. All welcome* https://theasa.org/conferences/asa2021/registration [Tweet; link]. Twitter. https://twitter.com/theasainfo/status/1362809153115275266.

@treesonplastic. (2021, April 2). *#ASAResponsibility was a carnival of fantastic scholars and ideas. Really enjoyed it! A big thanks to the local organized group @StAndrewsAnthro* [Tweet]. Twitter. https://twitter.com/treesonplastics/status/1378006254933663744.

@visualplague. (2020, December 8). *CFP and call for labs is open for #ASAResponsibility until the end of the month @theasainfo* https://www.theasa.org/conferences/asa2021/ [Tweet; link]. Twitter. https://twitter.com/visualplague/status/1336423463020613632.

@visualplague. (2021, February 18). *Plenaries @theasainfo #ASAResponsibility @StAndrewsAnthro @univofstandrews reflect major challenges of our times: Extinction & Epidemics, with stellar speakers: @liana_chua, Janet Cox* [Tweet]. Twitter. https://twitter.com/visualplague/status/1362435612645679107.

@visualplague. (2021, March 7). *Besides great panels, the annual @theasainfo conference #ASAResponsibility held online @StAndrewsAnthro later this month also features two amazing plenaries. The* [Tweet; link]. Twitter. https://twitter.com/visualplague/status/1368592331843178499.

@visualplague. (2021, March 31). *Conference discounts on many exciting books, including mine:* https://combinedacademic.co.uk/social-anthropology-2021/... [Tweet; link]. Twitter. https://twitter.com/DaceDzenovska/status/1377263415845126144.

@visualplague. (2021, April 2). *A big thanks to everyone who participated in #ASAResponsibility @theasainfo @StAndrewsAntrho @univofstandrews & to NomadIT @ACE_UniStA & student volunteers for* [Tweet; link]. Twitter. https://twitter.com/visualplague/status/1378032843436273668.

Rino Bosso

Developing intercultural communication strategies through Facebook: A longitudinal investigation of VELF exchanges

Abstract

On the basis of a two-year longitudinal investigation, this study explores how the *habitat factor* (Pölzl & Seidlhofer, 2006) comes into play in Facebook exchanges among international students who happen to live at the same student dormitory in Vienna. The 94 study participants are members of what can be understood as a *multicultural hybrid community*, for they "overcome both physical and linguistic barriers to communication by exploiting the affordances of virtual environments" (Bosso, 2021, p. 17). The physical barriers which lead to the use of a Facebook group are the walls that surround them, for they all live in studio flats for single occupancy, whereas the linguistic barriers are due to the lack of a shared native language and are overcome through the use of Virtual English as a Lingua Franca (VELF) as their "communicative medium of choice" (Seidlhofer, 2011, p. 7). As the analysis of naturally-occurring VELF interactions shows, the *habitat factor* becomes manifest in the code-mixing strategies of *insertion, compounding,* and *congruent lexicalisation* (Muysken, 2000) leading to hybrid word-formation between English, used as the base language, and German, the inserted language which is dominant in the Austrian habitat. Despite their different linguacultural backgrounds, over time these international students develop shared communication strategies for enhancing mutual understanding via "the flexible adaptation of English, and of other linguistic and non-verbal resources, to [their own] online communicative needs" (Bosso, 2020, p. 291).

Auf Basis einer zweijährigen longitudinalen Untersuchung, erforscht diese Studie wie der *Habitat Factor* (Pölzl & Seidlhofer, 2006) zu den Facebook-Interaktionen zwischen internationalen Student*innen, die zufällig im selben Studentenwohnheim in Wien leben, beiträgt. Die 94 Studienteilnehmer*innen sind Mitglieder einer multikulturellen hybriden Gemeinschaft, da sie "sowohl physische als auch sprachliche Kommunikationsbarrieren überwinden, indem sie die Möglichkeiten virtueller Umgebungen nutzen" (Bosso, 2021, S. 17). Die physischen Barrieren, die zur Nutzung einer Facebook-Gruppe führen, sind die Wände, von denen die Student*innen umgebenden sind, denn sie leben alle in Einzimmerwohnungen zur Alleinbenutzung. Aufgrund des Fehlens einer gemeinsamen Erstsprache werden die sprachlichen Barrieren durch die Nutzung von Virtual English as a Lingua Franca (VELF) überwunden, welches als "kommunikatives Medium der Wahl" (Seidlhofer, 2011, S. 7) gilt.

Wie die Analyse natürlich vorkommender VELF-Interaktionen zeigt, manifestiert sich der *Habitat Factor* in den Code-Mixing-Strategien der *Einfügung, Zusammensetzung* und *kongruenten Lexikalisierung* (Muysken, 2000), was zu einer hybriden Wortbildung führt, und zwar zwischen Englisch, welche als Basissprache dient, und Deutsch, die hinzugefügte Sprache, welche im österreichischen Habitat vorherrscht. Trotz ihrer unterschiedlichen sprachkulturellen Hintergründe entwickeln diese internationalen Student*innen im Laufe der Zeit gemeinsame Kommunikationsstrategien zur Verbesserung des gegenseitigen Verständnisses durch "die flexible Anpassung des Englischen und anderer sprachlicher und nonverbaler Ressourcen an [ihre eigene] Online-Kommunikationsbedürfnisse" (Bosso, 2020, S. 291).

Introduction

Over the last couple of decades, the Internet has allowed billions of people around the world to get and keep in touch with each other, thereby augmenting the possibilities for both synchronous and asynchronous intercultural contact despite spatial and temporal divides between interactants. Furthermore, internet-based platforms and applications can also enhance intercultural contact at the local level by complementing face-to-face exchanges between members of local communities, thus becoming part of their daily communicative routines. In the latter scenario, communication can be hybrid on two counts. Firstly, interactions may oscillate between physical places and virtual spaces, whereby offline and online meaning-making processes often become intertwined. For instance, as discussed in this chapter, a Facebook group can be used by international students who live at the same student dormitory in Vienna to ask for information about the student dormitory or the city of Vienna, in order to better understand the physical context they all share. Secondly, in multicultural social formations, meaning-making processes can be linguistically hybrid: while English as a Lingua Franca (ELF) is often used "among speakers of different first languages for whom English is the communicative medium of choice" (Seidlhofer, 2011, p. 7), linguistic material from other languages can also be drawn upon, especially from those languages that are predominantly used in the physical place. As pointed out by Pölzl and Seidlhofer (2006), a habitat factor is often at play in ELF exchanges, which makes them "'locally colored' and variable according to local context" (Pölzl & Seidlhofer, 2006, p. 154).

In their online meaning-making processes on Facebook, the international students who participated in the present study often enrich their utterances in English with individual lexical items or whole phrases in German, which is the dominant language in the Viennese habitat. To borrow some terminology put forward by Muysken (2000), it is as if these students used English as "the base or matrix language" (Muysken, 2000, p. 155), whereby "the base language tends to be the community language of the migrant group, the inserted language the dominant national language" (Muysken, 2000, p. 156). These considerations seem to be confirmed by observing all of the Facebook discussion threads analysed in the present chapter: The matrix language is always English (the community language), and the inserted language is always German (the dominant national language in Austria). Furthermore, cases of code-mixing are also apparent, which corroborates Seidlhofer's view that ELF communication can be conceived of as "a hybrid, a composite kind of English, [whereby] elements of the other language(s) are adjusted to suit the virtual encoding rules of English" (Seidlhofer, 2011, p. 112).

The present paper explores how semiotic hybridity can be strategically exploited in naturally occurring Virtual English as a Lingua Franca (VELF) exchanges on Facebook, and how it develops over time into a salient feature of intercultural communication strategies. As will be shown in the following sections, VELF appears "to be characterized by the flexible adaptation of English, and of other linguistic and non-verbal resources, to the online communicative needs of multicultural social formations" (Bosso, 2020, p. 291). Therefore, while building on the existing ELF literature, this VELF study pays particular attention to how members of a specific multicultural community learn with and from each other how to employ hybrid semiotic resources effectively in order to achieve mutual understanding in their particular context of utterance production.

1   VELF: Sketching the scene

ELF research has become a vibrant field of enquiry into creative uses of English worldwide, especially among non-native speakers. Despite the extensive number of valuable studies carried out, some aspects of ELF communication are still underrepresented in the literature. In particular, previous research has sidelined the investigation of speech acts, the contribution of multimodality to meaning-making processes, the analysis of written exchanges (especially in online settings), as well as the investigation of informal learning processes within long-lasting multicultural social formations. All of these will be addressed in turn.

Most ELF studies to date (e.g. Jenkins, 2000; Seidlhofer, 2011; Mauranen, 2012) have centered around the analysis of face-to-face, spoken interactions, which have often been transcribed and collected in corpora of naturally occurring interactions. The annotation schemes employed in the tagging of ELF corpora seem to have focused predominantly on lexicogrammar and phonology, thereby sustaining analyses aimed at revealing creative patterns of language use in terms of forms and sounds. Examples thereof include the ELFA (2008), the VOICE (2013), and the ACE (2019) corpora. However, one crucial aspect of meaning-making processes, namely the expression of illocutionary forces to achieve particular perlocutionary effects, seems to be underrepresented in the ELF literature. To date, there is no open access corpus of spoken ELF communication that has been pragmatically annotated in terms of speech acts, nor by considering aspects of spoken communication, such as suprasegmentals, that can add layers of pragmatic meaning to the mere sequence of words used in utterances.

Besides pragmatics, what also seems to be underrepresented in the ELF literature is an investigation of the written modality of communication, especially in virtual settings. Exceptions include the studies carried out by Grazzi (2013) and Vettorel (2014). While the former did not carry out any linguistic analysis and focused instead on the advantages for students of using online platforms for developing writing skills, the latter investigated the lexicogrammar of ELF use in blogs. Once again, the focus lies on formal rather than on functional aspects of language use, and the number of studies addressing ELF communication in online settings is minimal. However, given the pervasiveness of online communication in both the private and the professional lives of a vast share of the world's population, the Internet arguably represents a virtual space with great potential for allowing intercultural contact generally and primarily via VELF.

Another aspect of ELF communication which has not received enough attention in the literature is multimodality. The very label English as a Lingua Franca suggests that the focus of analysis is on the use of verbal signs, i. e. on the *Lingua*. Consequently, multimodal aspects of face-to-face communication, such as facial expressions, gestures, gaze, or body postures, have only been addressed in a few research projects – consider, for instance, Konakahara (2016) and the ViMELF corpus (2018). But while it may be reasonable for ELF studies focusing on phonology or lexicogrammar to only analyze the verbal signs in utterances, in studying the pragmatics of VELF communication, one cannot simply ignore the elephant in the room, for semiotic hybridity is particularly prominent on social media platforms, such as Facebook. Herring (2019) conceives of these as *Interactive Multimodal Platforms*, "on which two or more semiotic modes – typically, text plus audio, video, and/or graphics – are available to support interactive human-to-human communication" (Herring, 2019, p. 42). Recent research on online communication has revealed, for instance, that nonverbal signs, such as emoticons, can be used as paralinguistic devices and function as intensifiers, thus complementing and enhancing the meaning expressed verbally (e. g. Derks et al., 2008). Other studies have reported on the use of emoticons as structural markers, thus replacing punctuation marks, such as periods and exclamation marks, but never a question mark (e. g. Amaghlobeli, 2012). Dresner and Herring (2010), instead, pointed to the fact that emoticons can influence the illocutionary force of an utterance: For example, the sequence of verbal signs that seem to express a complaint can be downgraded to a mere assertion by using a winking face at the end of the utterance (Dresner & Herring, 2010, p. 257). Non-verbal signs in online communication can therefore be used as aids to structure texts and, crucially, to manage rapport with interactants. In fact, those emojis, pictures and videos that are so often used in online communication add layers of pragmatic meaning to the written utterances, just as suprasegmentals do in the case of spoken ones. That is, they have pragmatic meaning.

In order to understand the pragmatics of VELF, though, it is not only essential to consider both verbal and non-verbal features in online utterances, for it is also crucial to explore the contextual circumstances in which the online utterances are embedded, understanding how a multicultural community comes into being in the first place. Hence, the need "to proceed by way of clearly situated qualitative studies with a strong ethnographic element" (Seidlhofer et al., 2006, p. 21). Therefore, an understanding of meaning-making processes in ELF exchanges, whether these occur face-to-face or in virtual spaces, cannot solely be derived from activities such as corpus compilation and analysis, but it must also be informed by ethnographic work.

Of course, ethnographic work needs time, and so does learning. A longitudinal perspective, therefore, seems to be the best suited to explore learning processes within a given social formation. It represents the best way to understand the dynamics leading to the use, uptake and re-use of innovative form-function relationships over time within specific communities. Importantly, this approach can be applied both to formal educational settings as well as to informal ones. As to the former, a longitudinal approach to ELF data collection and analysis was pioneered by Smit (2010). Over a period of three years, she investigated class-room discourse via ELF in a hotel management programme in Austria, thereby focusing on the "dynamic developments taking place socioculturally and inter-actionally [for] such developmental processes can hardly be captured cross-sectionally, [and] require the chronologically wider, diachronic perspective of-fered in longitudinal studies" (Smit, 2010, p. 86).

Inspired by the longitudinal approach put forward by Smit (2010), the present study represents an attempt to link the dots between the underrepresented ELF research areas described above. It does so by exploring the informal learning processes of use, uptake, and re-use of innovative form-function relationships, of *ad hoc* online communication strategies that, over time, sediment into a shared repertoire. By focusing on the online, informal exchanges between study participants on Facebook, which are realized outside of formal educational settings, this paper seeks to explore how linguistic resources are drawn upon and put to use to make meaning, and what patterns seem to emerge over time.

As mentioned in the introduction, the case study described in the following sections is that of a community of international students who have lived at the same student dormitory in Vienna for extended periods of time. Additionally, they have a Facebook group they regularly use in order to accomplish a wide range of communicative acts, but especially those of information seeking and giving. This community seems to display some of the traits of a Community of Practice (CoP) that were put forward by Lave and Wenger (1991), and further elaborated by Wenger (1998). These traits include having a "joint enterprise" that is carried out via "mutual engagement" and by employing a "shared repertoire" (Wenger, 1998, p. 73). In the case of the international student community mentioned above, the joint enterprise consists in making sense of a new physical reality, the Viennese habitat most of them are unfamiliar with when they arrive at the dormitory. Since most of them only speak very little German, they use English as their primary communicative resource for helping each other and sharing information. In this respect, it is also a joint enterprise for members of this specific social formation, as is the case with ELF communities more generally, to negotiate among themselves effective ways of communicating (see also House, 2003; Smit, 2010). In the community under observation in this study, the use of the meaning-making potential of the main communicative resource English appears to be increasingly enriched over time with lexical elements in German. Furthermore, multimodal aspects of online communication are also used to realize pragmatic meaning. By using these hybrid ways of communicating, community members develop their own endonormative conventions. This is, therefore, a particular kind of a CoP, namely a Multicultural Hybrid Community (MHC), which can be understood as "*a relatively long-lasting multicultural social formation, whose members overcome both physical and linguistic barriers to communication by exploiting the affordances of virtual environments*" (Bosso, 2021, p. 17).

2   Study design: Methodology for data collection and analysis

Exploring meaning-making processes requires an understanding of the situational context in which these are activated. Even if a researcher might be particularly interested in the investigation of disembodied, online communication, as is the case with VELF exchanges, it is vital to adopt hybrid ethnography for data collection, in order to "explore how people design, encounter, and use the Internet in their physical, real world lives" (Jordan, 2009, p. 185). This approach of "[c]onducting research in a manner that accounts for the hybrid field responds to the contemporary reality in which fully online and fully offline methodologies offer useful – but not sufficient – tools" (Przybylski, 2021, p. 5).

The MHC members who participated in this study are international, tertiary-level students who share the same physical place over extended periods of time.

Most of them live in studio flats for single occupancy and are therefore separated by physical barriers. On the one hand, the walls that surround them protect their private sphere but, on the other, they isolate them from the other inhabitants of the dormitory. The very structure of the physical setting limits their possibilities of interacting face-to-face. However, one of them, Samuel[1], created a private Facebook group "to get to know the people [he lives] with [...] to have a platform to communicate, to share events, to talk about problems, [...for] a Facebook group gives you the possibility to reach a wide audience with really little effort" (from an interview with Samuel).

The private Facebook group of the student dormitory was regularly used by MHC members during the data collection phase of this longitudinal study, from October 2014 to September 2016. In this period, the 94 MHC members who agreed to participate in this study were involved in 789 VELF exchanges of varying lenghts, accounting for over 56,000 words, and hundreds of non-verbal signs, such as pictures, emojis, and Facebook likes. The VELF exchanges were collected after having received informed consent from the 94 study participants by copying the VELF exchanges on Facebook into Word files. These have then been manually annotated with the multimodal annotation tool MAXQDA which, from the 2020 release onwards, offers the opportunity to annotate both images and texts within the same document. The kind of annotation performed is pragmatic and focuses on communicative acts, that is to say, on the illocutionary forces associated with both the verbal and non-verbal elements of utterances. In addition to this, instances of creative word formations have also been annotated, whether resulting from the exploitation of English morphological resources alone or from the combination of morphological material in English and other languages (usually German).

It might be important to mention that I did not participate in the VELF exchanges in the virtual field setting (the Facebook group) despite my presence in the actual physical setting. My decision to be only an observer of the VELF exchanges between MHC members was motivated by the need to avoid any interference in the development of the ethnographic object: naturally occurring, non-elicited VELF exchanges. The preservation of the ethnographic object is of the utmost importance in an applied linguistic qualitative research project, for "qualitative research takes place in the *natural setting*, without any attempts to manipulate the situation under study" (Dörnyei, 2007, p. 38, emphasis in original). Therefore, even if, on the one hand, I got to know my informants relatively well in the physical setting, on the other hand, I also needed to step back from the

---

1 This and other study participants' names used in the present chapter as well as in previous publications are pseudonyms that are used in place of real names to protect the privacy of participants in this study.

virtual setting in order to "achieve an acceptable degree of 'objectivity'" (Duranti, 1997, p. 85).

A longitudinal observation of VELF exchanges within Facebook groups of this kind can be beneficial to an understanding of how informal learning occurs when ELF users accommodate to each other's communicative behavior over extended periods of time. These informal learning processes may become manifest, for instance, when there is a gradual uptake and re-use of lexical items in the habitat language which are embedded in the matrix language English. As pointed out by Smit (2010) in the report on her longitudinal study of ELF communication in higher education, among students "[t]here was the strongly held belief that community members developed linguistically towards each other", resulting in the integration of some expressions of the habitat language in the student group's shared repertoire in the course of their studies (Smit, 2010, p. 408).

Like any other instance of communication, effective ELF communication is also bound to using linguistic forms that suitably convey the intended pragmatic meaning in relation to a specific context of use. Consequently, learning how to realize ELF discourse effectively is a context-specific process that unfolds over time in the natural habitat shared by interactants.

The habitat-triggered code-mixing practices between English and German observed in the present study arguably sustain the realization of indexical reference to the physical place MHC members share. As the analysis of VELF exchanges carried out in the following sections will show, MHC members expediently combine both English and German linguistic resources for achieving their specific, local communicative goals, but they do not merely do this by inserting lexical items in German into the English matrix. Code-mixing processes between the lingua franca and the habitat language may also lead to hybrid word-formation patterns. The underlying processes and pragmatic functions of such code-mixing practices will be investigated in the following sections.

3 Exploiting the habitat factor: insertion, compounding and congruent lexicalization

The online use of words as they naturally occur in the habitat may function for MHC members as pre-constructed phrases, as if they were idiomatic expressions, whose re-use "makes both production and processing of text easier" (Seidlhofer & Widdowson, 2009, p. 27). According to Schaller-Schwaner's observations (2015), ELF users come to share a "common background knowledge [...which] provides shared schemata and terminology for comprehension beyond intelligibility as a property of the code" (Schaller-Schwaner, 2015, p. 345). This terminology for comprehension is at times drawn upon from the local physical habitat in which the interactions are embedded, and it can take different forms, as well as serve different functions, as explained below.

3.1   Using hybrid word-formation to build a shared repertoire

Several lexical items in German become over time active elements in the linguistic repertoire of MHC members and can be combined with English linguistic resources via *compounding*, or *congruent lexicalization* (Muysken, 2000).

An example of this process, which leads to hybrid word-formation, can be appreciated in the VELF exchange initiated by Alicia on the 3rd of October 2014:

Alicia: is there bier in the automats?
Samuel: Nope... (Because you would have to proof your age...)

The hybrid post produced by Alicia is emblematic of different code-mixing practices. In the creative information-seeking act she produces, Alicia merges English and German resources. English is used as the matrix language, and only function words are drawn from this code: "*is there* bier *in the* automats?". These words in English provide the co-text in which the German content words are inserted and linked to each other. Instead of translating these into English as "beer" and "vending machines", Alicia tries to reflect the linguistic reality that both she and her fellow student dormitory residents experience in the physical environment they share, thereby realizing indexical reference to the physical place more readily than it would be the case with translation.

However, *insertion* is not the only code-mixing type employed here. In fact, the two content words in German undergo some form of adaptation to the conventions of English spelling and morphology when inserted into the utterance above. In the first place, both words are common nouns, and in written German, unlike written English, these should always be capitalized. Furthermore, the second content word, "automats", is pluralized. However, the bound morpheme used to make the plural is not the -en morpheme that would typically be used in German, but the -s morpheme which is used to create regular plurals in English. This is, therefore, an instance of *congruent lexicalization*, whereby Alicia merges heterogeneous linguistic resources into "a shared grammatical structure" (Muysken, 2000, p. 3). Creative word-formation processes of this kind often occur in ELF interactions. As Seidlhofer (2011) explains, "an infinite number of words can be coined that are morphologically "possible" but not attested in ENL, including words which have been drawn from other languages and have become Englishized so to speak by adaptation" (p. 116).

Besides formal considerations concerning the exploitation of the habitat factor, and whether it comes into play in instances of insertion or congruent lexicalization, what is even more interesting to derive from the longitudinal observation of VELF interactions is how some habitat-related terms become part of the MHC members' linguistic repertoire and are consistently repeated in similar contexts of utterance production.

A few weeks later, on the 16th of October, Ilona also asks for information concerning the vending machines at the student dormitory:

> Ilona: Anybody knows why snack automat doesn't work? [1]
> Samuel: Because it breaks down every couple of weeks... ☺ [1]
> Ilona: That's sad ☹

Here Ilona creates the hybrid compound noun "snack automat", which consists of one noun in English and one in German. The need for this compound noun is context-dependent: at the student dormitory, there are three vending machines, one for cold drinks, one for coffee, and one for snacks. With her creative compound, Ilona realizes indexical reference to one specific object in the physical place.

The use of the lexical item "automat" occurs in other Facebook posts, too. In the next one, produced on the 26th of October, one of the residents also posts a request for information. It is a Sunday, and tobacconists are closed in Vienna, so they would like to know where it would be possible to buy a packet of cigarettes. Berta is willing to help:

> Berta: You can buy it from the "automat" in TheMall[2]

Unlike the previous examples, Berta flags the German term "automat" visually by means of double quotes. These are perhaps meant to signal that a corresponding lexical item in English does not come to mind in that very moment, and this seems to be what is inferred by Samuel, who contributes to the discussion as follows:

> Samuel: jup, there is a vendig machine in TheMall, but you need a bank card to prove your age.

In the utterance above, Samuel provides a translation for the lexical item "automat", namely "vendi[n]g machine". In this exchange, translation results from a joint enterprise, whereby one user signals a foreign term with typographic means, such as quotes, and another provides a corresponding translation during the same interaction. However, it is interesting to note that while in the whole VELF corpus there are six occurrences of the term "automat", the sole instance of the

---

2 "TheMall" is used in this text in place of another lexical item in order to conceal the exact location of the student dormitory where study participants live.

use of its English equivalent "vending machine" occurs in the exchange above. Except for the example above, MHC members do not seem to need to translate the term "automat" into English, as if it had become part of their shared repertoire and background knowledge.

Linguistic hybridity appears to be widely accepted within the MHC under observation and not to give rise to any misunderstandings. On the contrary, the exploitation of the habitat factor may arguably function as a clarity enhancement strategy in Facebook discussion threads that focus on exchanging information about the physical place. This also seems to be the case with the following interaction between Enrico and Sierra on the 3rd of December 2014:

> Enrico: Hi folks…. please, does anybody know anything about parking next to the house? I know that there are some time periods to be paid for but where can be bought the parking ticket?? Thanks in advance!!!!

Here Enrico is looking for information on where to purchase the parking tickets for the car parking lots next to the student dorm, and Sierra replies as follows:

> Sierra: yep at ubahn station…in the same automat where you buy Fahrkarte!

Sierra creates a hybrid post in which the habitat factor is particularly prominent: Only function words are in English, whereas all content words, namely those that carry the most communicative value, are in German: "ubahn station" (underground station), "automat" (ticket machine), and "Fahrkarte" (transport ticket). This seems to be in line with Muysken's observation that there tends to be an asymmetry in code-mixing when it comes to the use of grammar and lexical categories. Function words "tend to come from the base or matrix language" (Muysken, 2000, p. 155), whereby "the base language tends to be the community language of the migrant group, the inserted language the dominant national language" (Muysken, 2000, p. 156). These considerations seem to be confirmed by observing all of the Facebook discussion threads in the present subsection: The matrix language is always English (the community language), and the inserted language is always German (the dominant national language in Austria).

Interestingly, it also seems to be the case that once interlocutors read a linguistically hybrid message, they tend to mirror this linguistic behavior and reply with hybrid messages themselves. In fact, while in his first post Enrico did not include any non-English words, in thanking Sierra he suddenly accommodates a "Danke" in his own reply:

> Enrico: OK, coool! Danke! ☺

Importantly, however, Enrico's use of a word in German, "Danke", does not serve the purpose of realizing indexical reference, of engaging relevant aspects of the physical context, so to say. It seems to be motivated by the need to manage rapport with Sierra because, by thanking her in German, Enrico is accommodating Sierra's hybrid communication style into his own reply.

A couple of months later, on the 13th of February 2015, Sally produces her own instance of hybrid word-formation via compounding:

> Sally: Hey people ☺ I bought 2 bottles of sparkling water (Vöslauer mild) by mistake. I actually don't drink water with gas. So I left the bottles by the coffee automat on the table. Feel free to take them ☺

Sally informs the whole MHC that she is willing to give away two bottles of sparkling water. In so doing, she specifies the brand and type "(Vöslauer mild)" and glosses the term in English "water with gas". She then provides clear indications of where she left the bottles, namely "by the coffee automat". In line with the terminological choices made by her fellow student dormitory residents in previous posts, she does not translate the term "automat" into English. The term has become part of her linguistic repertoire and can be used for some creative word-formation processes. In this case, in inserting a lexical item in German into her VELF utterance, Sally does not use the German "Kaffeeautomat" but realizes a compound noun whereby meaning is compositional: The first lexical item in English "coffee" specifies what kind of "automat" she is referring to. This is the same kind of creative, hybrid compounding strategy employed by Ilona on the 16th of October with her "snack automat".

The analysis of the examples in the present subsection has shown how MHC members seem to align on exploiting the habitat factor in their VELF exchanges with specific reference to the term "automat". Study participants did not merely insert this term into their VELF utterances for, in their code-mixing practices, they also created hybrid coinages via compounding (i.e. "snack automat" and "coffee automat") and hybrid plural forms (i.e. "automats") leading to congruent lexicalization.

But while it might be interesting in itself to consider how specific terms borrowed from the physical habitat become part of the linguistic repertoire that MHC members can draw upon, it is even more interesting to observe that study participants seem to derive from these *ad hoc* realizations some strategies for creative word-formation, which they re-apply in subsequent Facebook posts. However, as discussed in the next subsection, there are further pragmatic functions that are realized by study participants when exploiting the habitat factor.

3.2   Filling lexical gaps with the habitat language

While members of the MHC under observation in this study are capable communicators in English, there might occasionally be cases in which a target lexical item in English is unknown to the utterer or does not come to mind. This is, of course, a major communicative problem, for the intended meaning cannot be expressed. Therefore, some MHC members use the habitat language as a resource for filling a lexical gap in their VELF utterances. This is to say that code-switching to a language other than English can be motivated by the need to fill a lexical gap within the part of the VELF utterance expressed in English. This represents a strategy for eliciting an equivalent term in English from the audience, which the utterer does not know, or cannot recall. Similar strategies have been described in the ELF literature on spoken communication. Klimpfiger, for instance, calls this strategy "appealing for assistance" (Klimpfinger, 2007, p. 38).

On the 10th of December 2014 Sally, a native speaker of Russian, Samuel, a native speaker of German, and Ilona, a native speaker of Kazakh, have the following VELF exchange:

> Sally: Hey guys! Does anyone have this thing to measure human's height, the volume of waist, etc. ? I forgot the word. "Meter" auf Deutsch oder. .? ☹
>
> Samuel: maßband in german - or measure tape in english ☺
>
> Sally: Thank you Samuel ☺ so does anyone have measure tape/maßband ? ☺
>
> Ilona: Sally yes we have 000[3]

Sally initiates the discussion above because she intends to express the illocutionary force of request for an object. However, she is confronted with a communication problem: she cannot remember how to say *tape measure* in English and, therefore, adopts two strategies within the same utterance. Firstly, she glosses the term in English: "Does anyone have this thing to measure human's height, the volume of waist, etc. ?", therefore providing some cues as to what the desired object might be used for. Secondly, she admits that she cannot recall the corresponding term in English and so tries to provide some additional cues by switching to German: "'Meter' auf Deutsch oder. .? ☺" ["Meter" in German, right?], whereby the use of the inverted quotes to mark the term "Meter" and that of the confused face emoji she places at the end of the utterance suggest that she is not sure of the term she puts forward.

Samuel provides the following information: "maßband in german - or measure tape in english ☺". Therefore, he corrects the German term used by Sally and suggests its translation into English, thereby proposing, however, the coinage

---

3 Whenever occurring in the data, the number of the apartment in which study participants live has been substituted with the dummy number '000'.

"measure tape" (instead of *tape measure* or *measuring tape*). "Measure tape" seems to be a word-by-word translation of the compound noun "maßband" and hence, a case of covert translation. It is this non-conformist form which is picked up by Sally and re-used in her next utterance, who is grateful for she can now name the object she needs to utter her communicative act of request, both in English and in German: "Thank you Samuel ☺ so does anyone have measure tape/maßband ? ☺". What we see here is, therefore, an instance of active co-construction of meaning (Mauranen, 2006), whereby interactants negotiate meanings and then agree on a term to be used for expressing these.

Ilona has the requested object and is willing to lend it to Sally: "Sally yes we have 000", whereby 000 stands for Ilona's apartment number and functions here as a directive: "come pick it up at my place". Sally presses the Like button next to Ilona's post, thereby also uttering a communicative act in its own right: "on my way", "be right there".

In the VELF exchange examined above, Sally has identified her own communicative problem, namely, a lexical gap in her utterance that would prevent her from asking for an object she needs. In order to solve this problem, she has first glossed the term and has also suggested a candidate term in German. Therefore, she has employed two strategies to ensure the achievement of her goal, and these proved successful, for Sally's message was understood by other MHC members, and she was offered a "measure tape" by Ilona.

The analysis of habitat-enhanced code-mixing practices illustrated in the present subsection has exemplified one additional pragmatic function, namely that of solving potential communicative problems arising from lexical gaps in an English utterance by means of the mere insertion of German lexical items into the English matrix. However, at times hybridity in VELF utterances is not only linguistic, but more generally semiotic. There may be instances of rather complex VELF posts in which meaning-making is realized through the use of different languages and also different semiotic modes, as described below (for more examples see Bosso 2020).

3.3   Exploiting multimodality for meaning-making

On the 19th of July 2016 and, therefore, towards the end of the second year of data collection, Beatrice, a native speaker of Cantonese Chinese and of Hong Kong English, Emily, a native speaker of British English, and Madison, whose native language is Serbian, engage in the following VELF exchange. Beatrice's pretext for writing is that she is seeking information on how to find the pick-up station, which is mentioned in a notice of attempted delivery she finds in her mailbox:

Beatrice: Does anyone know where is this abholstation? Or where is the church…?

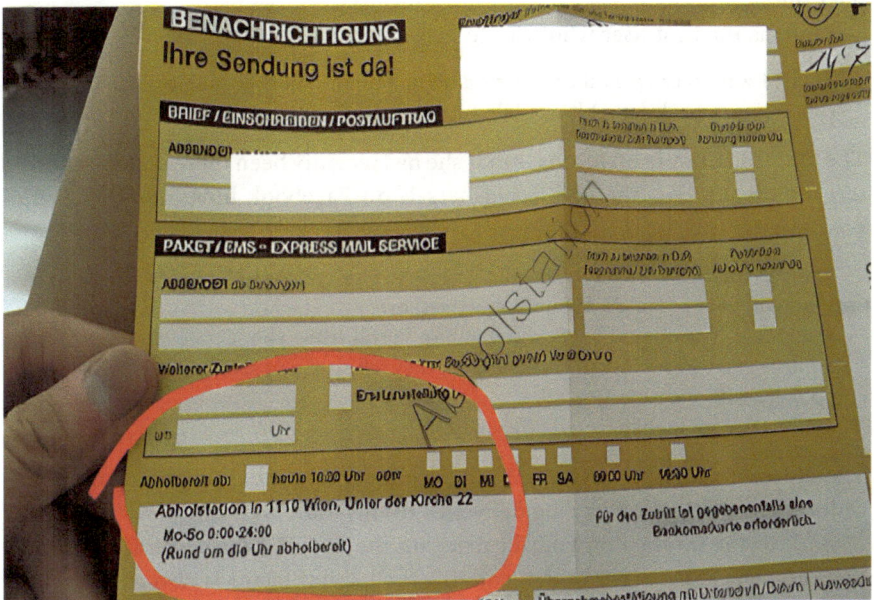

When addressing her audience, Beatrice seems to rely on an assumed shared experience with notices of attempted delivery in German. Assuming this shared experience among Facebook group members seems reasonable, for they all live in the same student dormitory in Vienna. Furthermore, Beatrice tries to help her audience to recall such an experience by creating a multimodal text consisting of verbal signs in English and German, and a picture of a notice of attempted delivery. As we can see from the picture, Beatrice has circled in red one specific part of it, thus drawing the audience's attention to the most salient information they require to help her. This information is also repeated in her questions, for Beatrice asks her peers whether they know where to find two named entities: an "abholstation" (pick-up station) and a "church". The first named entity appears in her text in German, as shown in the notice. Using this lexical item as it naturally occurs in the German-speaking habitat Beatrice and her audience share allows for the effective realization of indexical reference. However, her use of the second named entity in English, namely "church", seems to result from a misunderstanding. "Church" is the direct translation from German into English of the lexical item "Kirche". The co-text in which "Kirche" appears in the notice, however, is "Unter der Kirche", which is the proper name of a rather long street in Vienna, and does not offer any specific indications as to where the "abholstation"

is to be found in relation to a specific church: The pick-up station is not "Under the Church".

Emily is the first user who tries to help Beatrice:

> Emily: I went there the other day it's a bit of a nightmare, but yeah u go all the way to simmering + go down a bit of a hill, turn left at some point and its next to billa

The first thing Emily mentions is that she has recently been there. Furthermore, a few months earlier, she had asked herself on Facebook how the collection of packages sent to the student dormitory works:

> Emily: is it possible to get packages delivered to StudentDorm? how…? do you just have to stay in your room all day until it arrives, or?
> Samantha: if it doesn't fit in the mailbox they'll leave you a note with the package number and where you can get it.. usually they take it to a post office and you can pick it up there with the note ☺
> Emily: Ok cool thanks ☺

Therefore, through a previous VELF exchange, Emily has acquired some procedural knowledge concerning deliveries to the student dormitory.

Back to the interaction with Beatrice on the 19th of July, while at first Emily does not repeat the term "abholstation", the habitat factor is also at play in her post, in which the toponym "simmering" (one of Vienna's districts) and the proper name "billa" (an Austrian supermarket chain) are mentioned in her indications. However, Emily's indications are somewhat vague (e. g. "turn left at some point"). It is perhaps because of these vague indications that Beatrice writes a second post:

> Beatrice: Lol thanks… I wonder when did the postman came…. cuz i was always in my room at the daytime but i never heard he knocked my door ☺

Beatrice does not seem to be entirely convinced by Emily's reply. While she thanks her interlocutor, her thanking is preceded by "Lol" (i.e. "lots of laughs"), whereby laughter might be triggered by nonunderstanding (see also Matsumoto, 2018). The suspension marks following the word "thanks" might also be suggestive of nonunderstanding. The combination of this abbreviation with suspension marks may represent Beatrice's strategy for managing rapport with an interlocutor who has tried to help but has not met her expectations. Beatrice does not seem to want to signal nonunderstanding explicitly, but she tries to keep the interaction going: She, therefore, goes on with the rhetorical question "I wonder when did the postman came"[4], provides some additional information, and

---

4 According to the Electronic World Atlas of Varieties of English (available at https://ewave-atlas.org/valuesets/59738) double marking of past tense is a level B feature of Hong Kong English, which is neither pervasive nor extremely rare.

concludes her utterance with the emoji grinning face with sweat 😅, which can be taken to convey the idea of "tension or embarrassment" (Emojiall, Emoji Dictionary, 2019: s.v. *grinning face with sweat*)

Emily replies as follows:

> Emily: i know! the postmen are so annoying they often don't even try knocking - also i wanna know why they have started putting the packages at such far away abholstations

In her reply, Emily seems to focus on rapport management by showing a supportive attitude ("i know! the postmen are so annoying they often don't even try knocking"). She also asks a rhetorical question ("i wanna know why they have started putting the packages at such far away abholstations"), thus complaining about the fact that "abholstations" are far from the student dormitory. Emily, therefore, aligns with Beatrice's attitude towards the circumstances, and her style. She mirrors Beatrice's linguistic choices, for she employs the same named entity "abholstation". However, Emily does not solely repeat this lexical item, for she also modifies it. In particular, she pluralizes it, but instead of using the morphological rules of German to this end and adding the -en suffix for regular plurals, she uses the -s suffix for regular plurals in English, just like Alicia did on the 3rd of October 2014 in her utterance "is there bier in the automats?". The hybrid form "abholstations" produced by Emily, therefore, results from the exploitation of the *virtual language* (Widdowson, 2003), whereby a German noun in its base form is pluralized by adding a derivational suffix in English.

While Emily shows empathy for, and alignment with, Beatrice, both in terms of tone of the message and linguistic choices, she does not seem to suspect that Beatrice might not have entirely understood her indications. In fact, Emily does not provide any further explanations as to how to reach the pick-up station. This is perhaps why Madison joins the interaction to provide further indications:

> Madison: U3 then bus 69A from Simmering to Unter der Kirche if you don't feel like walking. Also, bus 72A to Bleriotgasse is a direct line (it stops in front of TheMall but it doesn't go that often so the first option is usually better).

Madison's post appears to be more focused on knowledge transfer rather than on rapport management. He provides detailed information about what means of transportation can be used to reach the pick-up station and where to get off. The best option he suggests would be to take the "U3 then bus 69A from Simmering to Unter der Kirche": he thereby hints at the fact that "Kirche" is not to be considered in isolation (i. e. Beatrice should not look for a "church") but as part of the German compound noun "Unter der Kirche", which is the proper name of the bus stop Beatrice needs to get off at.

In the VELF exchange discussed in this subsection, a picture of a notice of attempted delivery was combined with verbal signs in order to utter a communicative act of request for information. Furthermore, emojis and suspension marks were used to manage rapport while signalling non-understanding. These multimodal strategies supported an effective negotiation of meaning among the interactants, which points our attention to the fact that non-verbal elements at times play a crucial role in the realization of pragmatic meaning in VELF exchanges.

4   Conclusions

As the analysis of the VELF exchanges carried out in this chapter has shown, MHC members seem to overcome the limitations to communication imposed by the student dormitory's physical structure by resorting to a Facebook group, thereby developing effective online communication strategies. Despite their different linguacultural backgrounds, study participants increasingly accommodate to each other in their VELF exchanges. They develop shared communication patterns that sustain mutual understanding; they build rapport and a sense of community online and thence offline. In short, MHC members initiate the socialization process online, and through their VELF exchanges, they regulate their shared life in the physical place. Of course, it would not have been possible to make these observations if a longitudinal approach to data collection had not been employed, for manifestations of learning processes leading to the development of a shared repertoire and community building can arguably only be witnessed through an extended observation of chronological developments. Furthermore, this study has benefited from an interdisciplinary approach consisting of hybrid ethnographic methods for data collection and corpus linguistics for data analysis. It is thanks to the direct observation of both the virtual and the physical field settings inhabited by study participants and to the enlightening interviews carried out with some of them that an understanding of meaning-making processes in the hybrid habitat described above was possible.

In this chapter, the analysis of multilingual phenomena in VELF exchanges has focused on code-switching practices whereby, in the same utterance, an alternation between English and another language is present. As the exchanges between MHC members analyzed here have exemplified, English appears to be their "communicative medium of choice" (Seidlhofer, 2011, p. 7), and hence the primary resource they employ for meaning-making. However, this is often complemented by using German, which is the dominant language in the physical environment inhabited by the MHC members. Code-mixing practices have been explored in relation to the habitat factor (Pölzl & Seidlhofer, 2006), whereby a habitat-related term in a language other than English is inserted into the matrix language, the latter being English. While VELF exchanges are instances of disembodied interactions, they are nevertheless strongly related to the study participants' physical context, and VELF communication among MHC members has also been shown to be as "'locally colored' and variable according to local context" (Pölzl & Seidlhofer, 2006, p. 154) as spoken ELF communication is.

As was observed during the analysis of VELF discourse, habitat-enhanced code-mixing practices are not only manifest in instances of insertion of a lexical item in German into the English matrix. More creative instances of language use can be witnessed when hybrid word-formation takes place via compounding (e.g. "snack automat"; "coffee automat") or congruent lexicalization (e.g. "automats"; "abholstations"), through the exploitation of the virtual language (Widdowson, 2003).

But besides considerations as to the forms that habitat-enhanced code-mixing practices might take, it is crucial to understand how these are functionally motivated. By exploiting the habitat factor, MHC members manage to realize indexical reference to the physical place they share more readily: They reduce cognitive load by simplifying both active production and receptive processing. Furthermore, using the dominant language in the physical habitat can help them solve some communicative problems in their VELF utterances. In fact, when a target lexical item in English is unknown or cannot be recalled, the insertion of a lexical item or phrase in German serves to fill a lexical gap in the VELF utterance. In short, the exploitation of the habitat factor seems to develop over time into a set of shared strategies among MHC members, which supports mutual understanding and helps them overcome communicative problems. Multimodality further supports meaning-making processes and sustains rapport management.

These findings remind us of what might seem obvious, namely that learning processes related to communication strategies are by no means confined to formal classroom settings. This contribution will hopefully inspire the interest of other researchers and prompt them to replicate the methodology described above to find out more about informal learning processes and VELF use among members of other multicultural hybrid communities across the globe. Apart from providing more insights into this highly relevant form of communication, such studies might also allow for research turning to the interface of informal and formal English language education and in what ways the latter could take on board the varied colors of English in the globalized world and in the virtual spaces out there.

References

Amaghlobeli, N. (2012). Linguistic features of typographic emoticons in SMS discourse. *Theory and Practice in Language Studies, 2*(2), 348–354. https://doi.org/10.4304/tpls.2.2.348-354.

Bosso, R. (2020). Exploring the pragmatics of computer-mediated English as a lingua franca communication: Multimodal and multilingual practices. In A. Mauranen & S. Vetchinnikova (Eds.), *Language change: The impact of English as a lingua franca* (pp. 291–310). Cambridge University Press.

Bosso, R. (2021). "Seriously?! Do we really have such pigs here?!": Exploring complaints in virtual English as a lingua franca exchanges. In A. Rosca & A. Sevilla-Pavón (Eds.), *Building up telecollaborative networks for intercultural learning in the digital age* (pp. 13–26). Comares.

Derks, D., Bos, A., & von Grumbkow, J. (2008). Emoticons and online message interpretation. *Social Science Computer Review, 26*(3), 379–388. https://doi.org/10.1177/0894439307311611.

Dresner, E., & Herring, S. (2010). Functions of the nonverbal in CMC: Emoticons and illocutionary force. *Communication Theory, 20*, 249–268. https://doi.org/10.1111/j.1468-2885.2010.01362.x.

Education University of Hong Kong. (2021, August 22). *ACE – Asian Corpus of English.* https://corpus.eduhk.hk/ace/index.html.

Emojiall. (n.d.). Grinning face with sweat emoji. In Emoji Dictionary. Retrieved March 8, 2021, from https://www.emojiall.com/en/emoji/%f0%9f%98%85.

Grazzi, E. (2013). *The sociocultural dimension of ELF in the English classroom.* Anicia.

Herring, S. (2019). The coevolution of computer-mediated communication and computer-mediated discourse analysis. In P. Bou-Franch & P. Garcés-Conejos Blitvich (Eds.), *Analyzing digital discourse: New insights and future directions* (pp. 25–67). Palgrave Macmillan.

House, J. (2003). English as a lingua franca: A threat to multilingualism? *Journal of Sociolinguistics, 7*(4), 556–578. https://doi.org/10.1111/j.1467-9841.2003.00242.x.

Jenkins, J. (2000). *The phonology of English as an international language: New models, new norms, new goals.* Oxford University Press.

Jordan, B. (2009). Blurring boundaries: The "real" and the "virtual" in hybrid spaces. *Human Organization: Summer 2009, 68*(2), 181–193. https://doi.org/10.17730/humo.68.2.7x4406g270801284.

Klimpfinger, T. (2007). "Mind you, sometimes you have to mix": The role of code-switching in English as a lingua franca. *Vienna English Working Papers, 16*(2), 36–61.

Konakahara, M. (2016). The use of unmitigated disagreement in ELF casual conversation: Ensuring mutual understanding by providing correct information. In K. Murata (Ed.), *Exploring ELF in Japanese academic and business contexts: Conceptualization, research and pedagogic implications* (pp. 70–89). Routledge.

Lave, J., & Wenger, E. (1991). *Situated learning: Legitimate peripheral participation.* Cambridge University Press.

Matsumoto, Y. (2018). Functions of laughter in English-as-a-lingua-franca classroom interactions: A multimodal ensemble of verbal and nonverbal interactional resources at miscommunication moments. *Journal of English as a Lingua Franca, 7*(2), 229–260. https://doi.org/10.1515/jelf-2018-0013.

Mauranen, A. (2006). Signaling and preventing misunderstanding in English as lingua franca communication. *International Journal of the Sociology of Language, 177*, 123–150. https://doi.org/10.1515/IJSL.2006.008.

Mauranen, A. (2012). *Exploring ELF: Academic English shaped by non-native speakers.* Cambridge University Press.

Max Planck Institute for Evolutionary Anthropology. (2021, September 22). *eWAVE-The electronic world atlas of varieties of English.* https://ewave-atlas.org/.

Muysken, P. (2000). *Bilingual speech: A typology of code-mixing.* Cambridge University Press.

National Research Council of the National Academies. (2011). *Assessing 21st century skills: Summary of a workshop.* National Academic Press.

Pölzl, U., & Seidlhofer, B. (2006). In and on their own terms: The "habitat factor" in English as a lingua franca interactions. *International Journal of the Sociology of Language, 177*, 151–176. https://doi.org/10.1515/IJSL.2006.009.

Przybylski, L. (2021). *Hybrid ethnography: Online, offline, and in between.* Sage.

Schaller-Schwaner, I. (2015). The habitat factor in ELF(A) – English as a lingua franca (in academic settings) – and English for plurilingual academic purposes. *Language Learning in Higher Education, 5*(2), 329–351. https://doi.org/10.1515/cercles-2015-0016.

Seidlhofer, B. (2011). *Understanding English as a lingua franca.* Oxford University Press.

Seidlhofer, B., & Widdowson, H. (2009). Accommodation and the idiom principle in English as a lingua franca. In K. Murata & J. Jenkins (Eds.). *Global Englishes in Asian contexts: Current and future debates* (pp. 26–39). Palgrave Macmillan.

Seidlhofer, B., Breiteneder, A., & Pitzl, M.-L. (2006). English as a lingua franca in Europe: Challenges for applied linguistics. *Annual Review of Applied Linguistics, 26*, 3–34. https://doi.org/10.1017/S026719050600002X.

Smit, U. (2010). *English as a lingua franca in higher education: A longitudinal study of classroom discourse.* De Gruyter.

Trier University of Applied Sciences. (2021, July 11). *ViMELF-Corpus of Video-Mediated English as a Lingua Franca Conversations.* https://www.umwelt-campus.de/en/camp us/organisation/fachbereichuwur/sprache-kommunikation/indi/en/applied-research/ case-project.

University of Helsinki. (2021, September 22). *ELFA – The Corpus of English as a Lingua Franca in Academic Settings.* https://www.helsinki.fi/en/researchgroups/english-as-a-l ingua-franca-in-academic-settings.

University of Vienna. (2020, September 10). *VOICE-The Vienna-Oxford International Corpus of English.* http://voice.univie.ac.at.

VERBI Software. (2020). MAXQDA. (Version Analytics Pro 2020 Student) [Computer software]. https://www.maxqda.com/de/neu-in-maxqda-2020.

Vettorel, P. (2014). *English as a lingua franca in wider networking: Blogging practices.* De Gruyter Mouton.

Wenger, E. (1998). *Communities of practice: Learning, meaning, and identity.* Cambridge University Press.

Widdowson, H. (2003). *Defining issues in English language teaching.* Oxford University Press.

2. Practices and participation

Viera Pirker / Florian Mayrhofer

Bild als Kritik: Image-Kommunikation in einem Unterrichtsprojekt

Abstract

Die Bedeutung visueller Kommunikation hat sich in der Kultur der Digitalität umfassend erweitert. Für die Interrelation von Bild und Kommunikationsform(en) steht paradigmatisch der Bildtypus Selfie. Dieser Beitrag unternimmt eine Tiefenschau in ein Unterrichtsprojekt, in dem Schüler*innen medienproduktiv handeln. Angesiedelt im Religionsunterricht, zielt das Projekt mit der Methode der interaktionalen Bibeldidaktik auf ein besseres Verstehen der Umgangsweisen von Schüler*innen mit einem biblischen Text. Mit Selfies erzählen die Schüler*innen eine biblische Geschichte in Bildern nach. Die hier vorgelegte Analyse stellt die Nutzung von Bildern als implizite Form subversiver Positionierung im diskursiven Kontext der Disziplinarmacht Unterricht zur Diskussion. Spezifisch für den empirischen Forschungsansatz ist die Analyse von visuellen Erzeugnissen mit der Dokumentarischen Methode und die anschließende Triangulation mit den Selbstdeutungen der Schüler*innen in der unterrichtlichen Präsentation. So werden sowohl Bildpraktiken als auch kommunikative Strukturen rekonstruiert.

Die kleinschrittige, retardierende Analyse der Produkte und der Gesprächsprozesse macht auf verschiedenen Ebenen fragile Momente der Kritik sichtbar: Der Unterricht gibt starke Orientierungsschemata vor, die den Zugang der Schüler*innen zum Gegenstand prägen. Diese handeln rollenkonform, nutzen aber kreativ die mediale Umsetzung in Bildern, um ihre Agency zum Ausdruck zu bringen. Sie kritisieren damit subversiv die ihnen gestellte theologische „Story". Die Dechiffrierung der verschiedenen Ebenen zeigt die Tiefenstrukturen eines komplexen, sozialräumlich interaktiven Gefüges.

The significance of visual communication has expanded comprehensively in the culture of digitality. The image type selfie is paradigmatic for the interrelation of image and form(s) of communication. This article takes an in-depth look at a teaching project in which pupils act in a media-productive way. Set in religious education classes, the project aims at a better understanding of pupils' ways of dealing with a biblical text using the method of interactional Bible didactics. The pupils use selfies to retell a biblical story in pictures. The analysis presented here discusses the use of images as an implicit form of subversive positioning in the discursive context of the disciplinary power of teaching. Specific to the empirical research approach is the analysis of visual products with the documentary method and the subsequent triangulation with the students' self-interpretations in the classroom presentation. In this way, both visual practices and communicative structures are reconstructed.

The small-scale analysis of the products and the discussion makes fragile moments of critique visible on various levels: The lessons provide strong orientation schemes that shape the students' access to the subject matter. They act in conformity with their roles, but creatively use the media implementation in images to express their agency. In doing so, they subversively criticise the theological „story" set before them. Deciphering the different levels reveals the deep structures of a complex, socio-spatially interactive structure.

0.   Einleitung

Konsequenzen des Medienwandels für Bildung und Persönlichkeitsentwicklung von Heranwachsenden lassen sich in vielfältiger Weise in Bildungszusammenhängen und im schulischen Unterricht wahrnehmen. Gerade die Veränderungen im Rahmen von sich ausweitenden Bildpraktiken, die sich mit den modernen Medien und dem Durchbruch der digitalen und mobil vernetzten Smartphone-Fotografie spätestens seit den 2010er Jahren beobachten lassen, haben großen Einfluss darauf, wie sich Schüler*innen heute sehen, und zeigen, wie sie lernen und reflektieren. Sie kulminieren exemplarisch in der Bildpraktik des „Selfies". Davon wird auch der Religionsunterricht, der in vielen deutschsprachigen Ländern als reguläres Schulfach im Fächerkanon verortet ist, beeinflusst. Religionspädagog*innen widmen sich vermehrt der sich wandelnden Lebenswelt Jugendlicher und untersuchen Auswirkungen der digitalen Transformation in verschiedenen Facetten (z. B. Gojny et al., 2016; Nord & Zipernovszky, 2017). In diesem Beitrag wird eine Tiefenschau in ein Unterrichtsprojekt im Rahmen des römisch-katholischen Religionsunterrichts unternommen, in dem Schüler*innen einer siebten Schulstufe der Allgemeinbildenden Höheren Schulstufe (AHS) in Österreich medienproduktiv tätig wurden und mit der Bildpraktik Selfie sich selbst ins Bild setzen sollten. Gefragt wurde danach, ob sich Jugendliche in einem unterrichtlichen Zusammenhang auf visuelle Prozesse der Selbsteinschreibung einlassen, ob sie Abgrenzungen, Weiterentwicklungen und Kritik in Bild und Wort formulieren oder welche semantische, aber auch analytisch-reflexive Kompetenz Schüler*innen in Bezug auf zeichenhafte Kommunikation zu einem religiösen Thema mitbringen und anwenden. Im Verlauf des Forschungsprozesses wurde zunehmend erkennbar, dass die Schüler*innen Bilder als Kritik einsetzten und auf diese Weise eine eigenständige Image-Kommunikation in das Unterrichtsprojekt einbezogen haben. Diese Erkenntnis stellt den Fokus dieses Beitrags dar.

1.   Medienwandel? Rolle der Bildlichkeit in Digitalisierungsprozessen

Dass Digitalisierung und Prozesse des Medienwandels weit mehr sind als die bloße Ergänzung unseres Alltags um neue elektronische Hilfsmittel, wie Computer oder Smartphone (Rettberg, 2019, S. 435), haben in den vergangenen Jahren unterschiedliche (soziologische) Autoren betont (u. a. Castells, 1996; Reckwitz, 2017; Nassehi, 2019). Prägnant auf den Punkt gebracht hat dies Felix Stalder, wenn er von einer „Kultur der Digitalität" (2016) spricht und beschreibt, dass mit dem Medienwandel auch ein Wandel von *Praktiken* und somit einer gesamten *Kultur* einhergeht. Diese veränderte Kultur hat dann auch Einfluss darauf, wie wir miteinander kommunizieren. Schon seit längerem ist von einem „image turn" (Fellmann, 1991), einem „pictorial turn" (Mitchell, 1992) oder einem „iconic turn" (Boehm, 1994) die Rede, welcher unsere Kommunikation immer stärker durchzieht und bei dem Christa Maar und Hubert Burda (2004) sogar von einer „neue[n] Macht der Bilder" sprechen. Das Bild ist also aus der menschlichen Kommunikation heute nicht mehr wegzudenken. Gerade die Verbreitung von Smartphones ermöglichte eine ubiquitäre und cumquitäre Bildproduktion und führte zu einer regelrechten Explosion öffentlich zugänglicher Bilder.[1] So wurden allein bis Mitte 2015 täglich 350 Millionen Bilder auf der Plattform Facebook geteilt. Ulla Autenrieth (2014a) untersuchte die Verwendung von Bildern in Social-Media-Netzwerken und konnte darin fünf zentrale Funktionen von Bildern entdecken. Diese benennt sie einerseits als Identitäts-, Beziehungs-, Informations- und Content-Management sowie andererseits als Entertainment (S. 160 f.). Bilder mutierten also durch den digitalen Wandel von reinen Erinnerungsobjekten zu einem veritablen Kommunikationsmedium. Sie visualisieren die Kommunikation des Alltags (S. 14) und haben wesentliche „kommunikative […] Funktionen für die Identitäts- und Beziehungsaushandlungen jugendlicher Userinnen und User" (S. 16). Bilder repräsentieren dabei den*die Profilinhaber*in innerhalb des kommunikativen Zusammenhangs und werden so auch zu einem „Werkzeug der Identitätsarbeit" (S. 16). Diese Funktionen überschneiden sich in vielerlei Hinsicht mit den von Christina Schachtner (2018) beschriebenen vier Praktiken der Subjektivierung im Kontext einer digitalen Welt, insbesondere mit der Suche nach Rollen bzw. neuen Rollen („Verwandeln") wie auch mit der Praktik des „Vernetzens", d. i. vernetzte Kommunikation, die vor allem auf Anerkennung abzielt (S. 171).

---

1 So zeigen die neuen Daten des Jugend-Internet-Monitors 2022 für Österreich, dass bild- bzw. videobasierte Plattformen wie Youtube (95 %, +2 % im Vergleich zu 2021), Instagram (81 %, -3 %), Snapchat (70 %, -5 %) oder TikTok (70 %, +13 %) weit verbreitet sind und ihre Verwendung großteils immer noch am Wachsen ist (Saferinternet.at, 2022).

1.1   Selfie – Ein Beispiel für digitale Praktik

Für die Interrelation von Bild und veränderter Kommunikationsform(en) steht paradigmatisch der Bildtypus Selfie (Ullrich, 2019), dem sich auch in jüngster Zeit religionspädagogische Forschungen widmeten (u. a. Gojny et al., 2016). Interesse in religionspädagogischer Hinsicht weckten hier vor allem anthropologische wie ethische Implikationen und Herausforderungen, die sich aus dem digitalen Wandel für religiöse Bildungsprozesse ergeben. Obwohl Selfies nicht der am meisten geteilte Bildtypus sind, ist dieser kennzeichnend für den Wandel hin zu einer auch durch Selbstinszenierung geprägten Medienwelt bei Kindern und Jugendlichen. Hierbei ist bezeichnend, dass sich Bildproduzent*innen in einem Selfie bildlich festhalten und dadurch im Bild Subjekt, Objekt und Rezipient*in des Bildes in eins fallen (Ullrich, 2016, S. 2). Jerry Saltz (2014) betonte besonders deren „instant", also unmittelbar bildkommunikativen, Charakter und Wolfgang Ullrich (2019) spricht bei Selfies gar von einer „mündlichen Sprechkultur" (S. 54), in der das Bild intuitiv konzipiert wird und als solches vor allem als „Statusmitteilung" (S. 8) fungiert, um so mit anderen eine Verbindung herstellen zu können sowie Reaktionen bei anderen hervorzurufen (S. 35). Dazu werden Selfies in der Regel über Soziale Medien wie Instagram oder Snapchat geteilt und so in einen spezifischen kommunikativen Kontext eingebettet, der mit Textunterschriften und Captions/Hashtags nach eigenen linguistischen Gesetzmäßigkeiten unterlegt ist (Glanz, 2018; Gojny & Kürzinger, 2020). Nach Felix Stalder (2016) stehen Selfies für ein „Verfahren des Sich-Einschreibens in die Welt" (S. 122), welches sich durch Momente der Auswahl (Lenkung von Aufmerksamkeit), der Verlinkung (Erstellung neuer Zusammenhänge) und der Veränderung (Weg-, Hinzunahme) auszeichnet und so stark durch Referentialität als eine der drei zentralen Formen einer Kultur der Digitalität charakterisiert ist. Dies schafft zum einen stets neue Bedeutungen, zum anderen konstituiert sich durch diese Praktiken auch das Subjekt selbst in der Welt (S. 96–128). Auch lassen sich in Selfies Logiken der Vermarktung im Alltäglichen entdecken, die zum Ziel haben, das Gegenüber visuell zu beeinflussen und zu überzeugen (Holiday et al., 2016; Autenrieth, 2019, S. 261). Sie sind strukturiert durch Praktiken einer „Visual Rhetoric" (Holiday et al., 2016, S. 177) und des „Visual Storytelling[s]" (Bozdag & Kannengießer, 2019, S. 361). Dies hat zur Folge, dass sich Praktiken und soziale Beziehungen des Alltags vielfach eine Konstruktionslogik von Theatralisierung einfügen (Autenrieth, 2019, S. 261). Bei der Erforschung von Selfies werden bisher unterschiedliche Schwerpunkte gesetzt: Zum einen ist eine zentrale Frage jene nach Selbst(re)präsentation. Jill Walker Rettberg (2019) konnte hierbei zeigen, dass keine klare Trennung zwischen Selbstpräsentation und Selbstrepräsentation sinnvoll scheint:

The short answer is that they can be seen as either because the two terms provide two different ways of looking at this phenomenon. A representation is an object, a sign that is seen as constructed in some way, [...]. A presentation is an act, [...] the way that the person acts to present themselves. (S. 430)

Beide Formen kommen in Forschungsarbeiten zum Tragen. Neben Selbst(re)präsentation wird zugleich nach Identität und Sozialität gefragt (Diefenbach & Christoforakos, 2017; Thumim, 2017). Dies geschieht durchaus kritisch (Senft & Baym, 2015; Autenrieth, 2014b, S. 53f.): So ist im medialen Diskurs (z. B. ARTE, 2017), aber auch in empirischen Untersuchungen häufig von einer Korrelation mit einer narzisstischen Störung die Rede (Fox & Rooney, 2014). Anders interpretiert dies Ulla Autenrieth (2019, S. 259) im Rückgriff auf Roberts et al. (2010), indem sie die verstärkte Beschäftigung der Jugendlichen mit ihrer Außenwirkung vielmehr mit der Entwicklungsaufgabe in Beziehung setzt, die an die Jugendlichen selbst herangetragen wird. Diese bestünde in der Herausbildung der eigenen Identität in der Pubertät. Deswegen handle es sich auch nicht so sehr um eine „generation me", sondern um ein „developmental me", wie Roberts et al. (2010) dies benennen. Auch Wolfgang Ullrich (2019) greift den vielfach an Selfies herangetragenen Vorwurf des Narzissmus auf und entlarvt ihn mit einem Hinweis auf den Soziologen Richard Sennett (1986): Selfie-Kritiker*innen seien in der „Logik der Moderne gefangen, der zufolge das Private und Innere das Eigentliche ist, das Äußere und Öffentliche hingegen einen sekundären, immer auch defizitären Status hat. Dabei gehört es zu den Pointen von Sennetts Theorie, gerade den Öffentlichkeitsskeptikern, die die Bildung des Selbst als wichtigste und damit zugleich intimste Angelegenheit deklarieren, Narzissmus zu unterstellen" (S. 31).

1.2   Zum Phänomen der Kritik

Als weiterer theoretischer Hintergrund dieses Projekts gilt es, das Verständnis von Bildern als Medium subversiver Positionierung zu ergründen. Diese Praktik ist unter anderem in Social Media aus Memes oder aus dem Phänomen des Protests durch Bilder (Schankweiler, 2019) bekannt. „Das Bildermachen und das Teilen von Bildern beeinflusst immer stärker, wie vor allem eine jüngere Generation soziales Leben überhaupt denkt" (S. 11). Jugendliche haben vielfältige Erfahrungen mit kritischen und Kritik übenden Bildzeugnissen, also mit Praktiken der Zeugenschaft, die durch die Kamera erfolgen, beispielsweise in Revolutionen und Unterdrückungssystemen, die durch bildpolitische Praktiken in Social Media codiert und ausgeübt werden, häufig in vorläufiger Ästhetik, sei es in Selfies, in Memes und rekreierenden Inszenierungen (S. 49–52).

Kritik, im alltäglichen Wortsinn als „Prüfen", „Zweifeln" oder auch „als nicht
normfreie ‚Beurteilungskunst'" (Niesyto, 2010, S. 61) verstanden, beinhaltet in
Beziehung auf den Umgang mit Medien einerseits die Kritik der Mediennutzung,
der Mediensozialisation und der Medien in der Theorie und als Phänomene,
wobei die klassische Medienkritik einer „Denkweise [entspringt], die eigenständige Handlungsmöglichkeiten der Subjekte unterschätzt [...]" (Niesyto,
2010, S. 61). Mediensozialisation vollzieht sich zunehmend als Selbstsozialisation
auf selbstgewählten Plattformen und in hoch diversen Medienzugängen. Zudem
ist die Bedeutung der eigenständig kreativen Gestaltung von Medien für Jugendliche gewachsen. Die Dynamik der Mediensozialisation steht mit schulischen Bildungsprozessen in Wechselbeziehungen. Gerade in der kreativen Gestaltung agieren Schüler*innen als kritische Subjekte, indem sie Machtsysteme
und Vorgaben stützen, erfüllen oder auch hinterfragen. Diese Deutung, dieses
Verständnis von Kritik schließt an die Theorie der Machtverhältnisse und der
Konstellation von Macht und Wissen nach Michel Foucault (1992) an. Ihm zufolge wird Macht nicht besessen, sondern bezeichnet die Beziehung zwischen
Menschen als Individuen und Gruppen, die einander mit ausgefeilten Diszipli-
nierungstechniken und -praktiken begegnen. Auch wenn Foucault keine eigene
pädagogische Theorie entwickelt hat, sind insbesondere seine an räumlicher
Kontrolle orientierten Ansätze, aber auch die Gestaltung der Beziehungen, der
Zeit und der Leistung im pädagogischen Diskurs auf große Resonanz gestoßen
(Kupfer, 2011; Rottlaender, 2018; Grabau & Rieger-Ladich, 2014, S. 63). Foucault
(1992, S. 11) selbst sieht die pädagogische Kunst in ihrem eigenen Anteil an der
Regierungskunst. Menschen stehen gerade im Bereich der schulischen Erziehung
unter intensiver Beobachtung, in deren Ausprägungen sich Disziplinarmacht
vollzieht. Damit sie ausgeübt werden kann, ist ein Diskurs im Sinne einer Anhäufung von Wissen vorgeordnet, aus dem heraus festgelegt, festgestellt und
begründet werden kann, was der Norm und der an ihr ausgerichteten Diszipli-
nierung entspricht. Je mehr Wissen Einzelne oder Gruppen besitzen, desto mehr
Teilhabe am System der Beherrschung ist ihnen möglich. Die Erziehungssysteme
nehmen unmittelbar teil an der Macht durch ihren gesellschaftsstrukturierenden
Auftrag der Segregation und Allokation, ebenso, wie sich eine individualisie-
rende Didaktik und die Dynamik der Leistungsbeurteilung und -bewertung als
eine Ausübung der Disziplinarmacht vollzieht. Die Dynamik der Kritik, die
Foucault als kulturelles Erzeugnis in Form von „kleinen polemisch-professio-
nellen Aktivitäten" beschreibt, analysiert er in dem 1978 gehaltenen Vortrag
„Was ist Kritik", indem er sie an die Dynamik der Aufklärung bei Immanuel Kant
annähert. Beide, Kritik und Aufklärung, führt er auf die Gemeinsamkeit zurück,
nämlich „eine bestimmte Art zu denken, zu sagen, zu handeln auch, ein bestimmtes Verhältnis zu dem, was existiert, zu dem, was man weiß, zu dem, was
man macht, ein Verhältnis zur Gesellschaft, zur Kultur, ein Verhältnis zu den

anderen auch – etwas, was man die Haltung der Kritik nennen könnte" (Foucault, 1992, S. 8).

Kritik charakterisiert und definiert Foucault als „die Kunst, nicht dermaßen regiert zu werden" (1992, S. 12). Er erkennt darin ein Sich-ins-distanzierende-Verhältnis-Setzen zur Umgebung, die ein Subjekt „nicht auf diese Weise und um diesen Preis" (Foucault, 1992, S. 12) annehmen will. In der Kritik werden die Grenzen der Wahrheit, des Rechts, der Autorität durch deren jeweilige Befragung ausgelotet und aufgezeigt, ohne notwendig bereits über eine Alternative zu verfügen. Auf diese Weise entsteht Kritik in den „Beziehungen zwischen der Macht, der Wahrheit und dem Subjekt" (Foucault, 1992, S. 15) und kann als Distanzierung von einem Zustand der Unmündigkeit gelesen werden. In den Worten Foucaults:

> Wenn es sich bei der Regierungsintensivierung darum handelt, in einer sozialen Praxis die Individuen zu unterwerfen – und zwar durch Machtmechanismen, die sich auf Wahrheit berufen, dann würde ich sagen, ist die Kritik die Bewegung, in welcher sich das Subjekt das Recht herausnimmt, die Wahrheit auf ihre Machteffekte hin zu befragen und die Macht auf ihre Wahrheitsdiskurse hin. Dann ist die Kritik die Kunst der freiwilligen Unknechtschaft, der reflektierten Unfügsamkeit. In dem Spiel, das man die Politik der Wahrheit nennen könnte, hätte die Kritik die Funktion der Entunterwerfung. (Foucault, 1992, S. 15)

Dem „Wissen" (als akzeptabel geltende Erkenntnisverfahren und -wirkungen) und der Macht („viele einzelne, definierbar und definierte Mechanismen [...], die in der Lage scheinen, Verhalten oder Diskurse zu induzieren", Foucault, 1992, S. 32) ist eine methodologische Funktion zu eigen: „[M]it ihnen sollen nicht allgemeine Wirklichkeitsprinzipien ausfindig gemacht werden, es soll gewissermaßen die Analysefront, es soll der relevante Elementtyp fixiert werden" (Foucault, 1992, S. 32). Kritik hat in diesem Verständnis Anteil an der Befragung, Hinterfragung, auch Entlarvung von Wissen und von Macht. In ihrer Form ist sie offen, auch „fragil und unbeständig" (Foucault, 1992, S. 40): In einem kommentierenden Wort, Glosse und Geste, bildlich gesprochen aber auch in der Karikatur, dem Selfie oder einem Meme, setzt sich ein Subjekt gegen die bestehenden Dispositive ab, ent-unterwirft sich.

Im vorliegenden Zusammenhang wird die Anregung von Grabau und Rieger-Ladich aufgenommen, „den Blick für widerständige Praktiken zu öffnen, die sich dem Kontrollprinzip nicht fügen" (2014, S. 73 f.), wobei dieser Blick in der interaktionalen und materialen Dimension des Unterrichtsprojekts eingesetzt wird. Die Kritik, die in die mediengebundenen Elaborate und Praktiken der Schüler*innen eingeschrieben ist, wird im vorliegenden Zusammenhang nicht als juveniler Übermut abgetan, sondern als Ausdruck des Sich-ins-Verhältnis-Setzen zum Dispositiv der unterrichtlichen Macht wahrgenommen. Im Hintergrund steht ein Verständnis von religiöser Bildung, wie es Andrea Lehner-Hartmann (2014) in Anschluss an Helmut Peukert charakterisiert. Dem folgend geht es in religiöser Bildung darum, „sich ein Bewusstsein und darin auch ein Verhältnis zu anderen Personen, Dingen und sich selbst zu schaffen und im Horizont von Geschichte und des Lebens mit anderen handlungsfähig zu werden" (Lehner-Hartmann, 2014, S. 34), worin ein zentrales Ziel religiösen Lernens liegt, nämlich die „Ausbildung religiöser Urteilskraft" (Lehner-Hartmann, 2014, S. 34). Dies umfasst die Fähigkeit, sich selbständig ein Urteil darüber zu bilden, „ob religiöse Traditionen und Praktiken dem Menschsein mit seinen Grenzerfahrungen und Ambivalenzen gerecht werden, die menschliche Realität nicht ernstnehmen und ideologisch oder illusionär verschleiern oder gar zur psychischen Aufrüstung missbraucht werden, um Menschen für andere Zwecke gefügig zu machen [...]" (Lehner-Hartmann, 2014, S. 34).

2.   Religions- und mediendidaktische Einbettung

Auch im religionspädagogischen Diskurs nehmen Untersuchungen mit Bezug auf Mediatisierung, Digitalität und Social Media zu (Nord & Zipernovsky, 2017; Pirker, 2019a; Pirker, 2019b; Gojny & Kürzinger, 2020). Gerade diese Ausgangslage zeugt von der Wichtigkeit der Auseinandersetzung mit dem Medienwandel im Kontext von (religiösen) Bildungsprozessen, dem sich das hier vorgestellte Projekt widmet. So sollen nach dieser theoretischen Verortung nun der Kontext des Forschungsprojektes sowie die fachdidaktische Einbettung vorgestellt werden.

Religiöses Lernen vollzieht sich nicht ausschließlich rezeptiv, sondern die involvierten Subjekte verwenden immer auch Medien, um entweder ihre Religiosität oder religiöse Haltung und Positionierung zum Ausdruck zu bringen – in Texten, Symbolen, Riten u.v.a. Daher „zählt zu den zentralen religionspädagogischen Herausforderungen, Heranwachsende zur religiösen Selbstexpression und zur Partizipation an religiösen Vollzügen zu befähigen. (Religiöse) Medien diesbezüglich aktiv verwenden und gestalten zu können, ist eine religiöse Schlüsselkompetenz" (Gärtner, 2015). Dieses Anliegen wurde für das hiesige Forschungsprojekt aufgegriffen, didaktisch geplant und forscherisch begleitet.

Es geschieht ganz im Sinne des *DigComp 2.2: Digital Competence Framework for Citizens* der EU-Kommission (European Commission, 2022), welches im Kompetenzbereich „3. Digital Content Creation" die Kompetenz „3.1 Developing Digital Content: To create and edit digital content in different formats, to express oneself through digital means" (S. 27) vorsieht. Der didaktische Entwurf lässt sich dem Leistungslevel 2 zuordnen, das folgende Kompetenzen formuliert: „At basic level and with autonomy and appropriate guidance where needed, I can *identify* ways to create and edit simple content in simple formats" und „*choose how I express myself through the creation of simple digital means*" (European Commission, 2022, S. 27). Ebenso lässt sich ein Bezug zur Kompetenz „3.2 Integration and re-elaborating digital content: To modify, refine and integrate new information and content into an existing body of knowledge and resources to create new, original and relevant content and knowledge" (European Commission, 2022, S. 29) herstellen. Diese Dimension formuliert auf Leistungslevel 2 „[a]t basic level and with autonomy and appropriate guidance where needed, I can: select ways to modify, refine, improve and integrate simple items of new content and information to create new and original ones" (European Commission, 2022, S. 29). Religiöse Bildung, wie sie im Projekt formuliert wurde, leistet daher auch einen wesentlichen Beitrag zu digitaler Bildung von Schüler*innen.

Im Hintergrund der didaktischen Planung stand eine partizipative Mediendidaktik, die sich selbst in der kritischen Erziehungswissenschaft und näherhin auch in der konstruktivistischen Didaktik und Mediendidaktik verortet sieht. Diese wird als Querschnittsaufgabe verschiedener Fachdidaktiken (Mayrberger, 2019, S. 183 f.) – so auch der Religionsdidaktik – gesehen und bietet dadurch vielerlei Anknüpfungspunkte. Grundlegend zeichnet sich eine partizipative Mediendidaktik dadurch aus, dass sie verschiedene Bedingungsebenen (Gesellschaft, Bildungskontext, Akteur*innen, Beziehung untereinander) daraufhin untersucht, in welchem Zusammenhang sie mit Medien als prägendem Kontext stehen und wie sie an unterschiedlichen Punkten allen im Lehr-/Lernprozess involvierten Akteur*innen die Möglichkeit bietet, sich einzubringen (Mayrberger, 2019, S. 189–196). Der Lehr-/Lernprozess kennzeichnet sich durch fünf Phasen (Analyse der Gestaltung, Planung, Durchführung, Prüfung und Planungsanpassung), die jedoch iterativ zu denken sind, und ermöglicht das Konzept nach den unterschiedlichen Bedürfnissen zu aktualisieren und anzupassen (Mayrberger, 2019, S. 197 f.). Diese grundlegenden Überlegungen aufgreifend wurde die Projektidee didaktisch entwickelt, die ein religionsunterrichtliches Thema (Passion Jesu; Schuld) mit einem mediendidaktischen Thema (Selfies; Selbstdarstellung) verbindet. Es greift Medien als prägenden Kontext auf. In Bezug auf Mayrbergers Verlaufsmodell (2019, S. 200) ist das didaktische Konzept einerseits durch den vorgegebenen Projektauftrag zu Beginn eher fremdbestimmt, im Laufe des Arbeitsprozesses (v. a. in den Phasen des eigenständigen Arbeitens der Schüler*innen) ermöglichte es aber ein großes Maß an Selbstbestimmung. Von der Planung her war es durch die institutionellen Vorgaben schulischen Unterrichts stark präsentisch geplant. Virtuell wurde es dort, wo Schüler*innen konkrete Werkzeuge wie das Smartphone oder Bearbeitungssoftware zum Einsatz brachten. Dies lag jedoch im Ermessen der Schüler*innen. Im Verlauf der Erstellung der Endprodukte gab es immer wieder kurze Phasen der Anpassung (z. B. ob noch Zeit, Material etc. benötigt wurde; wie die Bilder gestaltet werden dürfen etc.). Die didaktische Planung lässt sich folgendermaßen schematisch kurz zusammenfassen:

	Thema der Einheit	Didaktische Zielsetzung	Kompetenzen
1+2	Was meint „Schuld" und „Versöhnung"?	Begriffe und Bilder zum Thema „Schuld" werden gesammelt und gemeinsam geordnet, um einen ersten Zugang und Überblick zum Thema zu erhalten.	Ich kann erklären, was mit „Schuld" alles gemeint sein kann und wie wir Menschen damit umgehen. Ich kann beschreiben, wo in unserem Leben „Schuld und Versöhnung" eine Rolle spielen.
3+4	Wer macht sich wie schuldig beim Kreuzweg Jesu?	Die Passionserzählung nach Markus wird anhand eines Puppentheaters in Stationen nachgespielt, um einen inhaltlichen Zugang zu erhalten. Der Projektauftrag für die nächsten Stunden wird besprochen.	Ich kann „Schuld-Erfahrungen" beim Kreuzweg Jesu erkennen und beschreiben.
5+6	Arbeitsphase in Kleingruppen	In Kleingruppen werden Selfies und Plakate erstellt.	Ich kann von „Schuld-Erfahrungen" beim Kreuzweg Jesu in Selfies erzählen. Ich kann selbständig und wo nötig unter Anleitung Wege zur kreativen Gestaltung und Bearbeitung einfacher Inhalte in einfachen Formaten identifizieren und auswählen. Ich kann selbständig und wo nötig unter Anleitung Wege der Modifikation, Verfeinerung, Verbesserung und Integration einfacher Elemente neuer Inhalte und Informationen auswählen, um neue Inhalte zu produzieren.
7+8	Präsentation und Reflexion der Ergebnisse I	Im Plenum werden die Elaborate präsentiert und von den Schüler*innen kommentiert sowie gemeinsam anhand von Impulsfragen sowohl religionsdidaktisch wie mediendidaktisch reflektiert.	Ich kann reflektieren, ob der Arbeitsauftrag erfüllt wurde. Ich kann Verbesserungsvorschläge für zukünftige ähnliche Arbeitsprozesse erstellen.

Tabelle 1: Didaktische Verlaufsplanung

Die im Forschungsprojekt analysierten Projektarbeiten wurden entlang der oben beschriebenen Planung – jedoch aufgrund äußerer Faktoren in leicht veränderter Form – im Rahmen des römisch-katholischen Religionsunterrichts in einer 7. Schulstufe an einer Wiener AHS im Zeitraum Mai bis Juni 2019 sowohl im Unterricht selbst als auch in der Freizeit außerhalb der zur Verfügung gestellten Unterrichtsstunden erstellt. Dies wird als Bereitschaft zur intensiveren Auseinandersetzung und als Motivation für den Arbeitsprozess interpretiert. Im Vorfeld fanden in den Einheiten 1–3 eine Auseinandersetzung mit dem Begriff „Schuld", wie er für die 7. Schulstufe im Lehrplan vorgesehen ist, und eine ausführliche, multiperspektivische Erarbeitung[2] der Passionserzählung nach Markus statt. Fokussiert wurde auf die Endgestalt des Textes mit seiner erzählten Welt bzw. dem erzählten Inhalt und nicht historisch-kritischen Fragen. Insofern fiel die theoretisch-methodische Entscheidung auf ein literarisch-interpretatives Verfahren (Klumbies, 2018, S. 183 f.).

Die nachfolgende Aufgabe bestand darin, die Passionserzählung in Kleingruppen durch Selfies nachzuerzählen und sich selbst in die Geschichte einzuschreiben, unter der Perspektive der individuellen Schuldgeschichten in dieser Erzählung. Durch das Aufgreifen schuldhafter Momente in der Erzählung sollte den Schüler*innen ein reflexiver Schutzraum geboten werden, um ein solches im pädagogischen Kontext nicht einfach zu behandelndes Thema zur Sprache zu bringen. Diesen Schutzraum eröffnet die Passionserzählung selbst, indem der biblische Text als Bühne fungiert, auf der die Thematik von Schuld als existenzielle menschliche Grunderfahrung wahrgenommen und reflektiert werden kann (Grümme, 2012, S. 355). Dies schien gerade deswegen notwendig, da häufig schnell „auf die angebliche Schlechtigkeit und Bosheit der Kinder und Jugendlichen" (S. 352) bzw. des Menschen allgemein Bezug genommen wird. Auch wird Schuld vorschnell in „naturalisierenden Schuldzuschreibungen" (S. 355) als notwendiges Existenzial charakterisiert, ohne das befreiende Existenzial einer – christlich gesprochen – göttlichen Liebe ins Spiel zu bringen. Aus religionspädagogischer Sicht ist das Thema Schuld nur im Zusammenhang mit dem befreienden Existential verantwortungsvoll im Religionsunterricht einzuspielen (S. 355). Der genaue Projektauftrag lautete daher: „Erzählt in 3 Kleingruppen eine kurze Episode zum Thema *Schuldig-Werden* im Kreuzweg mit einer Selfie-Story (3–5 Selfies) nach."[3]

Darüber hinaus stellen die in der Passionserzählung vorherrschenden Momente der Schwachheit und Gebrochenheit menschlicher Existenz einen Ge-

---

2 Anhand einer gekürzten Fassung wurde mit selbstgebastelten Figuren in zehn Stationen die Passionserzählung nach Markus nacherzählt und die Schüler*innen dazu aufgefordert, bei jeder ‚Station' ein Schaubild mit den Figuren zu stellen. Die Methode folgt Hecht (2018).
3 Nähere Ausführungen zur didaktischen Einbettung finden sich bei Pirker und Mayrhofer (2020, S. 103 f.).

gensatz zu dem in Social-Media-Kontexten häufig konstruierten „Happy Life"
(Gojny, 2016, S. 33) dar. Dadurch besteht die Möglichkeit, der Gebrochenheit des
Lebens, abseits der Ausklammerung in Social Media, Raum zu geben und sie zu
thematisieren. Durch ihre besondere Raumsemantik und das Spiel der Licht-
verhältnisse zwischen Hell und Dunkel (Klumbies, 2018, S. 188) bietet sich die
Version des Evangelisten Markus für bildhafte Darstellungen an und wurde aus
diesem Grund als Textgrundlage gewählt.

Mit den Selfies sollten die Schüler*innen in weiterer Folge eine Selfie-Story auf
einem Plakat mit Überschrift, Hashtags und Bildunterschriften gestalten, wie
dies den Schüler*innen aus Social-Media-Plattformen bereits bekannt war. Die
jeweiligen Gruppenarbeiten wurden anschließend im Unterricht vorgestellt.
Sowohl die Endprodukte der Gruppenarbeiten als auch die unterrichtliche Präsentation waren Gegenstand der Untersuchung des Forschungsprojektes.

3.   Forschungskontext, methodischer Zugang und Reflexion

Der Feldzugang nimmt Anleihen aus der Aktionsforschung (Altrichter et al.,
2018), die eine systematische Reflexion des eigenen Unterrichts durch eine
Lehrkraft impliziert. Das Forschungsinteresse, die Konzeption des Projekts und
die Auswertung wurden im Team vorbereitet. Florian Mayrhofer setzte als Lehrer
der Lerngruppe das didaktische Projekt im Unterricht um. Die Aufbereitung und
Analyse der Daten fand in notwendiger Distanz zur eigenen Praxis im Team und
verschiedenen Resonanzgruppen statt.

Gegenstand der Analyse waren nur die Werkstücke der Gruppenarbeit und
deren Präsentation im Unterricht. Diese Unterrichtsgespräche wurden zunächst
nach dem TiQ-Regulatorium (Talk in Qualitative Social Research) transkribiert.[4]
Die unterschiedlichen Gattungen (Bild und Unterrichtsgespräch) können durch
die Anwendung der Dokumentarischen Methode in eine gemeinsame Analyse
integriert werden. Für die Sprach- und Bildanalyse folgten wir der Theorie Ralf
Bohnsacks (2011) und Aglaja Przyborskis (2004; 2018), erweitert um die vertie-
fenden Bild-Instrumentarien von Bohnsack et al. (2015).

Die drei in Schüler*innengruppen entstandenen Produkte wurden einzeln als
Bilder, die reflektierte Relationen von Bild und Text beinhalten, analysiert. Eine
Triangulation erfolgte durch die Analyse der Gruppenpräsentationen im Kontext
des Unterrichtsgesprächs. Anschließend wurden die drei Projektergebnisse in

---

4 Die Audioaufzeichnung der Präsentationen wurde für eine weitere Auswertung mit dem
Transkriptionssystem „TiQ" aufbereitet, das für die Dokumentarische Methode vielfach zur
Anwendung kommt (Przyborski & Wohlrab-Sahr, 2014, S. 167 f.).

einer komparativen Analyse auf ihre kommunikativen Strukturen hin untersucht.

Die theoretische und fachdidaktische Verortung konkretisierte die Forschungsfrage: *Wie vollziehen Schüler*innen visuelle Prozesse der Selbsteinschreibung in Selfies?* Die Projekte haben im Forschungsprozess auf unterschiedlichen Ebenen neue Einsichten generiert. Zum einen für die Religionspädagogik: Wie verstehen Schüler*innen eine biblische Geschichte? Welche Bildwelten und Lebenswelten kommen wortwörtlich *ins Bild*? Zum anderen für das classroom management, insbesondere durch eine entstehende Gruppendynamik: Wie setzen sie einen Unterrichtsauftrag um? Wie funktioniert eine Kleingruppe und prägt den gesamten Prozess sowie das System der Klasse? Während die Selfie-Thematik im Forschungsprojekt angezielt wurde, ist die Dimension der Kritik erst in der Analyse der Schüler*innen-Elaborate zum Vorschein gekommen. Im vorliegenden Rahmen fokussiert die Analyse auf eine zentrale Erkenntnis des Projekts: die visuelle Formulierung von Kritik in den Bildpraktiken der Schüler*innen.

4. Kritik in den Bildpraktiken von Schüler*innen

Nach diesen theoretischen Ausführungen werden drei ausgewählte Bilder aus den Gruppenelaboraten in verdichteter Form in Bezug auf den Aspekt der Kritik in den Bildpraktiken dargestellt. Die oben beschriebenen Schritte der Analyse werden hier auf die Fragestellung dieses Beitrags fokussiert und gebündelt. Eine detaillierte Analyse der gesamten Gruppenelaborate findet sich bereits an anderer Stelle und soll hier nicht wiedergegeben werden (Pirker & Mayrhofer, 2020; Mayrhofer, 2021).

4.1   Gruppe #snitch – Judas-Selfie

Das zur Analyse ausgewählte Bild ist dem Plakat der Gruppe #snitch entnommen. Die Gruppe besteht aus fünf Schülerinnen, die sich dadurch auszeichnen, dass sie einen selbstverständlichen Umgang mit Selfie-Praktiken pflegen und klar Hashtags als Bildinterpretamente einsetzen. In der Umsetzung greifen die Schülerinnen die Themen der Unterrichtsreihe auf (Passion und Schuld) und erzählen diese auch nahe am biblischen Text. Sie verlegen das Geschehen jedoch in ihren eigenen Alltag. Fokussiert wird die Story der Bildfolge auf die beiden Figuren des Judas und Jesus, die zugleich ein oppositionelles Paar bilden. Andere Elemente der Passion werden weggelassen (z. B. Petrus, der von einer anderen Gruppe ins Zentrum gerückt wird). Die Umsetzung der Bildpraktiken zeigt sich besonders im dritten der sechs Bilder, das die Gefangennahme Jesu als Thema hat (siehe Abb. 1).

Im Vordergrund ist die Figur des Judas zu sehen, die zugleich die Bildproduzentin des Selfies ist. Perspektivisch leitet das Selfie den Blick in den Hintergrund, wo die Szene der Gefangennahme durch drei andere Schülerinnen dargestellt wird. In Bezug auf die Bildpraxis Selfie (Ullrich, 2019) wird diese von den Schülerinnen zur Gänze adaptiert und umgesetzt. Zum einen findet eine klare Kommunikation mit den Betrachter*innen des Bildes statt. Die Judasfigur blickt aus dem Bild heraus direkt die Betrachter*innen an, lächelt und setzt die in Social-Media-Kontexten häufig gebräuchliche „Daumen-hoch-Geste" ein. Diese Geste stellt eine zweifache Verbindung dar: Einerseits erzeugt sie eine Verbindung zu den Betrachter*innen des Bildes, andererseits lenkt der gebogene Daumen den Blick zurück auf die Gefangenenszene, welche durch die Figur des Judas als positiv bewertet wird (auch durch die zufrieden lächelnde Mimik). Zugleich ist das Bild durch einen sehr spontanen Charakter gekennzeichnet. Dies fand auch Bestätigung durch die Schülerinnen selbst in ihrer unterrichtlichen Präsentation:

S1w: Hier, das ist der (.) Judas, der (2) ⌐ Lm: wieder, mhm ⌐ verraten hat, deswegen lächelt er auch, weil er einen guten Job gemacht hat. (ZZ. 169–172)

Abbildung 1: Judas-Selfie, Gruppe #snitch (anonymisiert durch VP & FM)

Worin liegt hier jedoch das kritische Potenzial der Schülerinnen? Die geübte Kritik der Schülerinnen im Bild wird durch ein komplexes Gefüge der verschiedenen Ebenen von Story, Selfie und Captions deutlich: Das Bild wird zunächst mit zwei Captions versehen: „#geschnappt" und „#snitch". Der erste Hashtag stellt die Verbindung zum Geschehen in Bild 1 her und umschreibt das Geschehen im Bildhintergrund, die Gefangennahme. Interessant ist jedoch die zweite Caption. Im Hashtag #snitch wird Kritik am Geschehen geübt: Snitch bedeutet Verräter und wird aus der Alltagswelt der Schülerinnen importiert. Das Bild erfährt dadurch eine (Be-)Wertung durch die Schülerinnen, die zwar auf der einen Seite die traditionell überlieferte Rolle des Judas als einem Verräter par excellence übernimmt, doch in einem gewissen Spannungsfeld zur Selbstdarstellung der Judasfigur im Selfie steht. Wie bereits erläutert, kommentiert „Judas" das Geschehen als positiv durch die Daumen-hoch-Geste. Es entsteht ein Gegensatz zwischen positiver und negativer Bewertung. Die Schülerinnen greifen den bekannten Topos des Verrats auf, wenden diesen durch einen Begriff aus ihrer Alltagswelt ins Jetzt und üben dadurch Kritik am Verrat. Die Schülerinnen framen das Geschehen als ungerecht und die Judasfigur im Bild als Verräter.

Kritik wird jedoch auch an der Logik der Erzählung und insbesondere an der Figur des Jesus geübt: Die Schülerinnen folgen einem Orientierungsmuster, gemäß dem sich jede Story durch eine sinnvolle Logik auszeichnet. Dies wird zunächst an der Szene im Garten Getsemani erkennbar, wo sie bewusst die Figur des Judas bei den schlafenden Jüngern positionieren:

> S3w: Und hier schläft Judas mit, weil er, (.) die dürfen halt nicht erfahren, dass er einen Plan ausheckt. (ZZ. 187 f)

Die Orientierung an einer sinnvollen Logik wird allerdings auch in einer tieferliegenden Schicht erkennbar. Die Figur des Jesus, wie sie sich in der neutestamentlichen Vorlage findet, ergibt für die Schülerinnen keinen Sinn. Eine Messiasfigur, die sich einem göttlichen Plan und dem Leiden ohne Widerstand hingibt[5], folgt nicht der Logik der Schülerinnen, weshalb sie diese umkehren und in eine kraftvoll protestierende Figur verwandeln. Die Jesus-Figur zeichnet sich – auch in den anderen Bildern des Plakats – durch ihre besondere Stärke und kraftvolle Gesten aus. Sie protestiert und wehrt sich gegen das Geschehen. Das findet Bestätigung in der verbal stockend vorgebrachten Präsentation der Schülerinnen:

> S1w: [...] die da, die, man sieht da, dass jemand hier, wenn man ganz genau hinschaut, sieht man da, dass je-, sieht man da, dass jemand gequält wird ⌞Lm: Ok (.)⌝ und das ist Jesus, der sich versucht zu wehren. (ZZ. 172–175)

In der Bildkomposition folgt die Darstellung im Hintergrund auch jener, wie sie aus Fotografien des Civil Rights Movements in den USA der 1960er bekannt ist, in der sich schwarze US-Bürger*innen der Festnahme durch weiße Polizisten widersetzen (Berger, 2011, S. 117).[6] Genau dieses Orientierungsschema findet

---

5 Bspw. zeichnet Burkett (2002, S. 155–173) die narratologische Struktur vom geheimen, leidenden und kommenden Messias nach.

6 Die Gruppenarbeiten fanden noch vor Beginn der enormen Ausweitung des Bewusstseins für die #BlackLivesMatter-Bewegung in Europa nach der Ermordung von George Floyd statt, weswegen dieser Vergleichshorizont noch nicht in die Analyse einbezogen werden kann.

sich so in der gewaltvollen Szene im Bildhintergrund, die von der Judasfigur festgehalten wird, und bildet somit eine Kritik am biblischen Original.

4.2   Gruppe Emoji – Kreuzigung

Abbildung 2: Kreuzigung, Gruppe Emoji (anonymisiert durch VP & FM)

Das Bild der zweiten Gruppe, die aus zwei Jungen und zwei Mädchen bestand, zeigt das letzte der vier Bilder des Plakats, die Kreuzigungsszene (Abb. 2). Sowohl in der Gestaltung als auch der linearen, klaren und sachlichen Strukturierung unterscheidet sich dieses Gruppenelaborat von den anderen. Das Layout aller Bilder ahmt eindeutig die aus Social-Media-Plattformen geläufigen Designs von Polaroid-Bildern nach. Diese wurden feinsäuberlich per Hand von den Schüler*innen zugeschnitten und in einem imaginären Raster angeordnet. Die Orientierung drückt sich nicht nur im Layout des Plakats aus, sondern auch in der Konzentration auf wesentliche Merkmale der jeweiligen Szene in den Bildern. Das hier analysierte Bild zeigt im Bildvordergrund die Bildproduzentin, die, wie auch zwei andere Schüler*innen, durch Überlagerung mit einem Emoji[7] anonymisiert dargestellt ist. Die klare, reduzierte Optik ist auch im vierten Bild

---

7 Emojis sind aus Emoticons weiterentwickelte Piktogramme. Ihre ursprüngliche Funktion bestand hauptsächlich darin, Gefühle auszudrücken (Siever, 2019). Je nach kulturellem Kontext können sie ganze Begriffe ersetzen. Beißwenger und Pappert (2019) stellten fest, dass ihre Verwendung in Whatsapp-Texten vor allem der Lesbarmachung des Textes und der Sichtbarmachung von Beziehung gilt.

vorherrschend. Im rechten unteren Bildviertel wird der Gekreuzigte dargestellt. Die linke Bildhälfte ist von drei Figuren zu zwei Dritteln ausgefüllt. Die einzige nicht anonymisierte Figur zeigt mit dem Finger auf den gekreuzigten Jesus und erinnert in der Bildsprache an Matthias Grünewalds berühmte Kreuzigungsszene des Isenheimer Altars (1512–1516) mit Johannes dem Täufer, der mit einem überdimensionierten Finger auf das Kreuz verweist. Im hiesigen Kontext stellt dies jedoch einen spottenden Soldaten dar. Die Anonymisierung zeigt zum einen ein Vertrautsein mit digitalen Bildpraktiken, zum anderen eine Orientierung, die an anderer Stelle als „Selbstkontrolle" ausgewiesen wurde (Mayrhofer, 2021, S. 262). Darin spiegelt sich ein erstes Moment der Kritik. Drei der vier Schüler*innen zeigen ihr Gesicht nicht. Die Emojis fungieren damit als Strategie der Anonymisierung und nicht als Ausdruck der Emotionalität.[8] Kritik erfährt daher die Bildpraktik Selfie mit ihrem Orientierungsschema der Selbstdarstellung. Die Schüler*innen in den Bildern positionieren sich gemäß dem Arbeitsauftrag zwar in den Bildern, aber eine Selbstabbildung im vollen Wortsinn wird durch die Anonymisierung unterlaufen. Gerade die Auswahl der Emojis erzeugt zusätzlich eine Opposition zwischen dem grausamen gezeigten Inhalt und der fröhlichen Emotion der Emojis, die nicht zueinander passen. Theoretisch hätten auch andere, situationsadäquatere Emojis zur Verfügung gestanden. Es wurden jedoch gerade fröhliche Emojis eingesetzt.

Dies unterstreicht die Abgrenzung vom Arbeitsauftrag, die auch in der Art und Weise, wie die Schüler*innen das Bild in Szene setzen, deutlich zu Tage tritt. Die Szene wird nämlich durch die gewählte Perspektive geschickt theatralisiert und in eine Kulissenbühnen-Optik (Kotte, 2013, S. 258–262) mit mehreren Ebenen verwandelt. Diese Optik leitet die Betrachter*innen über jeweils drei Ebenen, dargestellt durch die Figuren im linken Bildrand, zur Figur im rechten unteren Bildrand, den gekreuzigten Jesus, und zieht den Blick der Betrachter*innen regelrecht in das Bild hinein. Damit umgehen die Schüler*innen die Selbst-Positionierung im Bild des Arbeitsauftrags, wie sie die Bildpraxis Selfie fordert. Zugleich zeugt dies von einer Distanz zwischen gezeigtem Inhalt und den Schüler*innen selbst. Ähnlich einem Geschehen auf einer Leinwand wird das Geschehen abgebildet, allerdings ohne sich dabei selbst zu positionieren oder involvieren lassen zu müssen. Dies wird besonders in der Zusammenschau mit der oberen Bildreihe des Plakats (Bild 1 und 2) erkennbar, in welcher das Geschehen im Vordergrund und nicht primär im Mittel- und Hintergrund zu finden ist. Es entsteht dort durch die Anordnung der Figuren vielmehr ein szenischer Raum, in dem die einzelnen Figuren miteinander kommunizieren. Schreiben sich die Schüler*innen zudem durch eine leichte, legere Körperhaltung, eine im

---

8 Eine weitere Orientierung ist hier auch die Kategorie Geschlecht, da geschlechterstereotype Emojis für jeweils Burschen und Mädchen ausgewählt werden.

Ärmel versteckte Hand oder der Hand in der Jackentasche in eine typische
Haltung des schulischen Pausengesprächs ein, stechen in den beiden Bildern der
unteren Bildreihe die petrifizierten Posen[9] hervor (kleine, symbolische Handlungen, die den Inhalt kompakt zusammenfassen, wie dies die Geste des Hin-
hörens beim Hahnenschrei darstellt). Einschreibung in das Geschehen findet
daher nur dort statt, wo die Schüler*innen eine ihnen bekannte Situation vor-
finden – wie dies z. B. bei einem Gespräch in lockerer Runde der Fall ist.

4.3   Gruppe Helden aus Jerusalem

Abbildung 3: #jesusislit, Gruppe Helden (anonymisiert durch VP & FM)

Die Geschichte „Helden aus Jerusalem" haben vier Schüler entwickelt. Um sie zu
inszenieren, haben sie eine Computerspiel-Optik gewählt, in der sie sich selbst als
Avatare hineingeschnitten haben (Abb. 3). Am vorderen Bildrand erscheint ein
„Talking Head", der Erzähler dieser völlig neuen Geschichte. Wir haben das
vierte Bild von sechs ausgewählt, die Schüler haben dieses mit dem Hashtag
„#jesusislit" versehen.

Zunächst erfolgt eine kurze Bildbeschreibung, um die Dynamik des Bildes
leichter zu dechiffrieren. Die Bildmitte nimmt eine hoch aufgerichtete Figur in
Oranten-Haltung ein. Die durch einen Schüler verkörperte Figur erscheint auch
auf anderen Bildern, doch nur hier leuchten ihr Gesicht, Haare und Sonnenbrille
weiß. Im hinteren Mittelgrund fliegt links oben ein anderer Schüler mit Bart und
Hörnern, der sogenannte „Ziegenmann", von einem Schwert durchbohrt, durch
das Bild. Auf der anderen, rechten Seite, nahe bei „Jesus", ist ein dritter Schüler in
mehrere Einzelteile zerteilt. Rechts davon am Bildrand befindet sich der vierte
Schüler in Sprunghaltung, beide Beine weit gespreizt und angewinkelt, die Arme
nach oben gestreckt und die Hände zum Victory-Zeichen erhoben. „lit" bedeutet

---

9 Zur näheren Bestimmung und Charakterisierung von *Habitus*, *Pose* und *Petrifikation* siehe
   Bohnsack & Przyborski (2015).

als jugendsprachlicher Slangbegriff „cool" oder „toll", assoziiert aber auch Jesus als Empfänger eines Lichts: „Jesus ist erleuchtet."

In der Präsentation erzählen die Schüler gemeinsam, was in diesem Bild passiert.

S7 m: Ähm Jesus ruft in den Him- Himmel hinauf und macht ein Ritual ⌐ S3w: F=fett ⌐ , de-, das (.) den Tempel dazu bringt (.) zu erleuchten. Der Ge- Gehilfe besiegt auch die Wächter, (.) durch Frustration begeht der Ziegenmann @Selbstmord@ ⌐ Lm: ok ⌐ (2) ähm (.) mit seiner Machete.? (3) (ZZ. 597–601)

Die Gruppe hat während der intensiven Erarbeitung des Projekts ihre Ergebnisse weitgehend geheim gehalten und keine Rücksprache mit dem Lehrer gesucht, sondern auf einen Überraschungseffekt gesetzt. Aufgefordert, als erste zu präsentieren, hat die Gruppe selbstbewusst darauf bestanden, als letzte an die Reihe zu kommen. Sie beginnen die Präsentation mit einer Einleitung, mit der sie sich auf grundsätzlicher Ebene von der im Religionsunterricht präsentierten „Story" der Passion absetzen:

S9 m: Ahm ⌐ Lm: Ja. ⌐ das ist die Geschichte der Kreuzigung von Jesus. ⌐ Lm: mhm ⌐ Wir haben sie so abgeändert, wie sie sich wirklich zugetragen hat. (ZZ. 566–571)

Die Schüler zeigen in ihrem Elaborat, dass sie über weitreichende Bildkompetenz, referentielle Praktiken und technische Raffinesse verfügen. Die Bildkompetenz ist eher als „intuitiv" zu charakterisieren: Die Äußerungen in der Präsentation lassen auch bei Rückfragen keinen tiefergehenden Reflexionsgrad erkennen. Indem sie auf die Optik und Logik von Videospielen zurückgreifen, erzählen sie jedoch eine Bildgeschichte, die den Rahmen des Arbeitsauftrags in jeder Hinsicht sprengt. Sie transformieren die Passionserzählung zu einer Heldengeschichte mit Elementen der Befreiung und Rettung, die mit Überraschung, Magie und Macht operiert. Motive der Passionserzählung lassen sich nur ansatzweise identifizieren und werden von den Schülern kaum in Wort oder Bild gebracht.

Die Schüler üben in dieser Arbeit Kritik, indem sie sich entschieden haben, das kreative Projekt zu einer Grenzverschiebung zu nutzen. Sie haben ihr rollenförmiges Verhalten verlassen und das religionsunterrichtliche Orientierungsschema zugunsten ihres eigenen Orientierungsrahmens hin verschoben. Sie öffnen mit ihren Bildern, mit ihrer Story ein Portal in eine andere Welt, mit selbstgesetzten Regeln. Sie verfehlen das Thema nicht versehentlich, sondern verweigern die biblische Erzählung. Auf formaler Ebene haben sie dies hervorragend, technisch aufwändig und kreativ umgesetzt. Auf inhaltlicher Ebene hingegen haben sie sich dem Arbeitsauftrag aktiv entzogen und die Erzählung grundständig transformiert, ja sogar invertiert, wie es im Bild selbst zu sehen ist.

Mit ihrer „Story" überschreiten sie provokativ eine unterrichtliche Grenze, sie machen Jesus zu einem „Helden" im herkömmlichen Sinn.

Für die Schüler stehen biblische Welt und Medienwelt nebeneinander, die mit dem Selfie-Projekt intendierte perspektivische Einschreibung in die biblische Erzählung wird verweigert. Sie trennen mit den einmontierten Selfies des „Erzählers" (vorne links) vielmehr klar zwischen einer erzählenden und einer erzählten Ebene, sie erzeugen einen fiktionalen Bühnenraum, der sie nicht existenziell angeht – die „Story" wird theatralisiert. Die Macht der digitalen Bilder (Pirker, 2021) und der damit verbundenen Narrationen wird in ihrem Projekt besonders deutlich: Die klare Orientierung an visuellen und narrativen Vorgaben des Gamedesigns verdrängt die eigentlich zu erzählende Geschichte in die Bedeutungslosigkeit.

Die Schüler ermöglichen in dieser Projektarbeit einen tiefen Einblick in ihren eigenen Orientierungsrahmen, der von gegenwärtigen medialen Eindrücken, sozialen und erzählerischen Praktiken sowie damit einhergehenden spezifischen Fiktionalitätskonzeptionen geprägt ist. Darin wirkt diese Schülerarbeit zutiefst authentisch sowie paradigmatisch.

5.   Fazit

In diesem Projekt wurde das komplexe sozialräumlich interaktive Gefüge eines Unterrichtsprojekts retardiert betrachtet, insbesondere im Blick auf kreative Elaborate der Schüler*innen, die diese im Rahmen des Religionsunterrichts erstellt und abschließend in der Lerngruppe präsentiert haben. In der Analyse der Produkte und der Gesprächsprozesse kommen auf verschiedenen Ebenen fragile Momente der Kritik zum Vorschein. Abschließend seien drei Erkenntnisse formuliert:

(1) Der Unterricht gibt starke Orientierungsschemata vor, die den Zugang der Schüler*innen zu einem Thema fundamental prägen. Hier zu nennen ist vor allem das Orientierungsschema der Machtverhältnisse im schulischen Kontext, das sich vor allem durch den Arbeitsauftrag und die verschiedenen Rollen im Unterrichtsgeschehen (Lehrperson, Schüler*innen) zeigt. Diese Erkenntnis ist zwar nicht neu, tritt aber in der Analyse verhältnismäßig deutlich hervor und lässt – im Sinne der Dokumentarischen Methode – darauf schließen, dass dieses Schema für die Schüler*innen im Arbeitsprozess eine leitende Funktion eingenommen hat. Dies ist insofern erstaunlich, als die Unterrichtsform einer Gruppenarbeit intendiert, das sonst im schulischen Alltag herrschende Orientierungsschema von Macht und Kontrolle wenn schon nicht außen vor zu lassen, doch zumindest abzuschwächen.

(2) Die Schüler*innen handeln rollenkonform, doch sie nutzen die kreative Bildarbeit als Gelegenheit, den gesetzten Rahmen zu durchbrechen. Mit den Mitteln ihrer Prozessgestaltung wie mit Mitteln des kreativen Ausdrucks üben sie Kritik an gegebenen und nicht ausgesprochenen Regeln, an didaktischen Machtverhältnissen und an unterrichtlichen Zuschreibungen. Sie hinterfragen Wissen, indem sie neues Wissen kreieren, und sie loten darin auch die Spannung zwischen dem Medium „Selfie" und den erforderlichen Inhalten der Inszenierung aus. Angesichts dessen stellt sich berechtigterweise die Frage, inwiefern die Bildkritik nicht schon immer Teil jeglicher kreativen Aufgabenstellungen im Unterricht gewesen ist und sich die Bildpraxis „Selfie" von anderen digitalen Bildpraktiken und anderen Erarbeitungen durch Schüler*innen in konventionelleren Aufgabenstellungen unterscheidet. Positiv hervorzuheben ist, dass die hier gewählte Bildpraxis des Selfies den Schüler*innen einen relativ weiten Aktionsraum der eigenen Positionierung ermöglicht, beginnend bei völliger Identifikation mit biblischen Figuren bis hin zu einer möglichst großen Distanzierung, indem z. B. die biblische Szene tatsächlich *als* ein Theaterstück im Hintergrund wie auf einer Bühne inszeniert wird. Die Schüler*innen gewinnen Handlungsspielräume und bewahren sich ihre Agency in der konkreten medialen Umsetzung. So entscheiden sie sehr genau, was und wie sie sich auf den Bildern des Projekts zeigen. Das genuine Potential der Selfies sehen wir gerade darin begründet, dass diese Bildpraxis die Positionierung der*des Bildproduzent*in zum Geschehen ausdrücklich herausfordert. Kann dies bereits als Ausbildung religiöser Urteilskraft gewertet werden? Eine Antwort darauf scheint schwierig zu sein. Doch lässt sich in den unterschiedlichen kritischen Anfragen an den Wahrheitsgehalt biblischer Erzählungen eine Exaktheit der Positionierung erkennen, die eine umfangreiche Basis für eine weitere Aufarbeitung und Vertiefung im Verlauf des Unterrichtsprozesses anbietet.

(3) In einer formalen Erfüllung des äußeren Auftrags setzen die Gruppen sich in ein abgrenzendes Verhältnis zu der Story, die ihnen religionsunterrichtlich nahegebracht wird. Über weite Strecken haben sie die Kompetenzen und Ziele im Blick, wobei die Gruppe „Helden aus Jerusalem" einen anderen Weg wählt. Erkennen, Beschreiben und Erzählen von Schuld-Erfahrungen in der Passion kommen nur auf Rückfrage durch die Lehrperson bei der Präsentation zur Sprache. Dafür haben die Schüler dieser Gruppe die digitalen Kompetenzziele in den Vordergrund gestellt. So interpretieren die Schüler*innen die ihnen gestellte Geschichte frei um, sie spielen mit ihren Bildern, mit Körpern, mit Avataren, mit ihrem „image". Sie nutzen selbstverständlich die von den Spiel-Narrationen inspirierte Bandbreite kreativer digitaler Bildkulturen. Für Lehrpersonen eröffnet das einen Einblick in die religiöse Gedankenwelt der Schüler*innen, erfordert jedoch zugleich eine enorme Dechiffrierungskompetenz mit Blick auf mediale Praktiken und theologische Muster.

Literaturverzeichnis

Altrichter, H., Posch, P., & Spann, H. (2018). *Lehrerinnen und Lehrer erforschen ihren Unterricht: Unterrichtsentwicklung und Unterrichtsevaluation durch Aktionsforschung*. Klinkhardt.

ARTE [Documentaries and Philosophy] (2017, March 7). *Philosophie – Me, my selfie and I* [Video]. YouTube. https://www.youtube.com/watch?v=y8JXqNQ27Mo.

Autenrieth, U. (2014a). *Die Bilderwelten der Social Network Sites: Bildzentrierte Darstellungsstrategien, Freundschaftskommunikation und Handlungsorientierungen von Jugendlichen auf Facebook und Co*. Nomos.

Autenrieth, U. (2014b). Das Phänomen ‚Selfie': Handlungsorientierungen und Herausforderungen der fotografischen Selbstinszenierung von Jugendlichen im Social Web. In J. Lauffer & R. Röllecke (Hrsg.), *Lieben, Liken, Spielen: Digitale Kommunikation und Selbstdarstellung Jugendlicher heute; medienpädagogische Konzepte und Perspektiven; Beiträge aus Forschung und Praxis; prämierte Medienprojekte* (S. 53–59). kopaed.

Autenrieth, U. (2019). Bilder in medial vermittelter Alltagskommunikation. In K. Lobinger (Hrsg.), *Handbuch visuelle Kommunikationsforschung* (S. 249–268). Springer VS. https://doi.org/10.007/978-3-658-06508-9.

Beißwenger, M., & Pappert, S. (2019). *Handeln mit Emojis: Grundriss einer Linguistik kleiner Bildzeichen in der WhatsApp-Kommunikation*. Universitätsverlag Rhein-Ruhr.

Berger, M. A. (2011). *Seeing through race: A reinterpretation of civil rights photography*. University of California Press.

Boehm, G. (1994). Die Wiederkehr der Bilder. In G. Boehm (Hrsg.), *Was ist ein Bild?* (S. 11–38). W. Fink.

Bohnsack, R. (2011). *Qualitative Bild- und Videointerpretation: Die dokumentarische Methode* (2., durchgesehene und aktualisierte Auflage). Verlag Barbara Budrich.

Bohnsack, R., Michel, B., & Przyborski, A. (Hrsg.). (2015). *Dokumentarische Bildinterpretation: Methodologie und Forschungspraxis*. Verlag Barbara Budrich.

Bohnsack, R., & Przyborski, A. (2015). Pose, Lifestyle und Habitus in der Ikonik. In R. Bohnsack, B. Michel, & A. Przyborski (Hrsg.), *Dokumentarische Bildinterpretation. Methodologie und Forschungspraxis* (S. 343–363). Verlag Barbara Budrich.

Bozdag, C., & Kannengießer, S. (2019). Visual Storytelling in der Kommunikationsforschung. In K. Lobinger (Hrsg.), *Handbuch Visuelle Kommunikationsforschung* (S. 361–376). Springer Fachmedien Wiesbaden. https://doi.org/10.1007/978-3-658-06508-9_20.

Burkett, D. R. (2002). *An introduction to the New Testament and the origins of Christianity*. Cambridge University Press.

Castells, M. (1996). *The rise of the network society* (Bd. 1). Blackwell Publishers.

Diefenbach, S., & Christoforakos, L. (2017). The Selfie Paradox: Nobody Seems to Like Them Yet Everyone Has Reasons to Take Them. An Exploration of Psychological Functions of Selfies in Self-Presentation. *Frontiers in Psychology, 8*(7). https://doi.org/10.3389/fpsyg.2017.00007.

European Commission. Joint Research Centre. (2022). *DigComp 2.2: The digital competence framework for citizens. With new examples of knowledge, skills and attitudes*. Publications Office. https://data.europa.eu/doi/10.2760/490274.

Fellmann, F. (1991). *Symbolischer Pragmatismus: Hermeneutik nach Dilthey*. Rowohlt Taschenbuch Verlag.

Fox, J., & Rooney, M. C. (2015). The Dark Triad and trait self-objectification as predictors of men's use and self-presentation behaviors on social networking sites. *Personality and Individual Differences, 76*, 161–165. https://doi.org/10.1016/j.paid.2014.12.017.

Foucault, M. (1992). *Was ist Kritik?* (W. Seitter, Übers.). Merve Verlag (Original publiziert 1978).

Gärtner, C. (2015). Medien. *WiReLex – Das Wissenschaftlich-Religionspädagogische Lexikon im Internet*. https://doi.org/10.23768/wirelex.Medien.100024.

Glanz, B. (2018, September 18). Rhetorik des Hashtags. *Pop-Zeitschrift*. Entnommen am 25. Juli 2022, von https://pop-zeitschrift.de/2018/09/18/social-media-september-von-be rit-glanz/.

Gojny, T., & Kürzinger, K. S. (2020). Selfies. *WiReLex – Das Wissenschaftlich-Religionspädagogische Lexikon im Internet*. https://doi.org/10.23768/wirelex.Selfies.200806.

Gojny, T., Kürzinger, K. S., & Schwarz, S. (Hrsg.). (2016). *Selfie – I like it. Anthropologische und ethische Implikationen digitaler Selbstinszenierung*. Kohlhammer.

Grabau, C., & Rieger-Ladich, M. (2014). Schule als Disziplinierungs- und Machtraum. Eine Foucault-Lektüre. In J. Hagedorn (Hrsg.), *Jugend, Schule und Identität* (S. 63–79). Springer Fachmedien. https://doi.org/10.1007/978-3-658-03670-6_4.

Grümme, B. (2012). *Menschen bilden? Eine religionspädagogische Anthropologie*. Herder.

Hecht, A. (2018). Biblische Figuren stellen. In M. Zimmermann & R. Zimmermann (Hrsg.), *Handbuch Bibeldidaktik* (2., revidierte und erweiterte Auflage, S. 583–588). Mohr Siebeck.

Holiday, S., Lewis, M. J., Nielsen, R., Anderson, H. D., & Elinzano, M. (2016). The selfie study: Archetypes and motivations in modern self-photography. *Visual Communication Quarterly, 23*(3), 175–187. https://doi.org/10.1080/15551393.2016.1223548.

Klumbies, P.-G. (2018). Das Markusevangelium. In M. Zimmermann & R. Zimmermann (Hrsg.), *Handbuch Bibeldidaktik* (2., revidierte und erweiterte Auflage, S. 183–191). Mohr Siebeck.

Kotte, A. (2013). *Theatergeschichte: Eine Einführung*. Böhlau.

Kupfer, A. (2011). Michel Foucault: Schule als Disziplinaranstalt. In A. Kupfer (Hrsg.), *Bildungssoziologie. Theorien – Institutionen – Debatten* (S. 67–78). VS – Springer Fachmedien. https://doi.org/10.1007/978-3-531-93263-7_7.

Lehner-Hartmann, A. (2014). *Religiöses Lernen: Subjektive Theorien von ReligionslehrerInnen*. Kohlhammer.

Maar, C., & Burda, H. (Hrsg.). (2004). *Iconic Turn: Die neue Macht der Bilder*. DuMont Literatur und Kunst Verlag.

Mayrberger, K. (2019). *Partizipative Mediendidaktik: Gestaltung der (Hochschul-)Bildung unter den Bedingungen der Digitalisierung*. https://content-select.com/de/portal/media /view/5df0cbfa-0f08-484b-a559-3116b0dd2d03.

Mayrhofer, F. (2021). Visuelles Storytelling mit Selfies als digitale Bildpraktik im Religionsunterricht. In A.-H. Massud & C. Hild (Hrsg.), *Religiöse Bildung bis 2030: Hürden und Chancen* (Bd. 1, S. 251–271). Empirische Pädagogik.

Mitchell, W. J. T. (1992). The Pictoral Turn. *Artforum, 30*, 89–94.

Nassehi, A. (2019). *Muster: Theorie der digitalen Gesellschaft*. C.H. Beck.

Niesyto, H. (2010). Kritische Anmerkungen zu Theorien der Mediennutzung und -sozialisation. In D. Hoffmann & L. Mikos (Hrsg.), *Mediensozialisationstheorien. Modelle und Ansätze in der Diskussion* (2., überarbeitete und erweiterte Auflage, S. 47–66). Verlag für Sozialwissenschaften.

Nord, I., & Zipernovszky, H. (Hrsg.). (2017). *Religionspädagogik in einer mediatisierten Welt.* Kohlhammer.

Pirker, V. (2019a). Bilder als Bedeutungsträger. Konstruktion und Darstellung von Identität und Authentizität in Social Media. *euangel. magazin für missionarische pastoral, 3.* Entnommen am 25. Juli 2022, von https://www.euangel.de/ausgabe-3-2019/aesthetik/bilder-als-bedeutungstraeger/.

Pirker, V. (2019b). Das Geheimnis im Digitalen. Anthropologie und Ekklesiologie im Zeitalter von Big Data und Künstlicher Intelligenz. *Stimmen der Zeit, 144*(2), 133–141.

Pirker, V. (2021). Zur Macht der Bilder. Theologische Anthropologie im Kontext digitaler Bildkulturen. In W. Beck, I. Nord, & J. Valentin (Hrsg.), *Theologie und Digitalität. Ein Kompendium* (S. 155–179). Herder.

Pirker, V., & Mayrhofer, F. (2020). „Das Evangelium nach Mika": Visuell-interaktionale Bibeldidaktik zur Passionserzählung. *Österreichisches Religionspädagogisches Forum, 28*(1), 99–123. https://doi.org/10.25364/10.28:2020.1.6.

Przyborski, A. (2004). *Gesprächsanalyse und dokumentarische Methode: Qualitative Auswertung von Gesprächen, Gruppendiskussionen und anderen Diskursen.* Springer Fachmedien Wiesbaden GmbH.

Przyborski A. (2018). *Bildkommunikation. Qualitative Bild- und Medienforschung.* De Gruyter.

Przyborski, A., & Wohlrab-Sahr, M. (2014). *Qualitative Sozialforschung: Ein Arbeitsbuch* (4., erweiterte Auflage). Oldenbourg Verlag.

Reckwitz, A. (2017). *Die Gesellschaft der Singularitäten: Zum Strukturwandel der Moderne.* Suhrkamp.

Rettberg, J. W. (2019). Self-Representation in Social Media. In J. Burgess, A. Marwick, & T. Poell (Hrsg.), *The SAGE Handbook of Social Media* (S. 429–443). SAGE Publications Ltd.

Roberts, B. W., Edmonds, G., & Grijalva, E. (2010). It is developmental me, not generation me: Developmental changes are more important than generational changes in narcissism – Commentary on Trzesniewski & Donnellan (2010). *Perspectives on Psychological Science, 5*(1), 97–102. https://doi.org/10.1177/1745691609357019.

Rottlaender, E. (2018). *Überwachen und Strafen im deutschen Schulsystem.* Universitäts- und Stadtbibliothek Köln.

Saferinternet.at. (2022). Jugend-Internet-Monitor. https://www.saferinternet.at/services/jugend-internet-monitor/.

Saltz, J. (2014). Art at arm's length: A History of the selfie. *Vulture.* https://www.vulture.com/2014/01/history-of-the-selfie.html.

Schachtner, C. (2018). Subjekt werden in einer digitalisierten Welt. *Katechetische Blätter, 143*(3), 169–174.

Schankweiler, K. (2019). *Bildproteste: Widerstand im Netz.* Wagenbach.

Senft, T., & Baym, N. (2015). What does the selfie say? Investigating a global phenomenon. Introduction for the selfie special issue. *International Journal of Communication, 9,* 1588–1606.

Sennett, R. (1986). *Verfall und Ende des öffentlichen Lebens. Die Tyrannei der Intimität* (R. Kaiser, Übers.). Fischer (Original publiziert 1974).

Siever, C. M. (2019). ‚Iconographetic communication' in digital media emoji in WhatsApp, Twitter, Instagram, Facebook – From a linguistic perspective. In E. Giannoulis & L. R. A. Wilde (Hrsg.), *Emoticons, kaomoji, and emoji: The transformation of communication in the digital age.* Routledge.

Stalder, F. (2016). *Kultur der Digitalität.* Suhrkamp.

Thumim, N. (2017). Self-(re)presentation now. *Popular Communication, 15*(2), 55–61. https://doi.org/10.1080/15405702.2017.1307020.

Ullrich, W. (2019). *Selfies: Die Rückkehr des öffentlichen Lebens.* Wagenbach.

Valentin Dander

Self-Tracking von Kindern und Jugendlichen als distribuierte Praxis

Abstract

Dieser Beitrag führt zunächst allgemein in das Thema Self-Tracking ein und referiert einen aktuellen Forschungsstand zu Self-Tracking, insbesondere von Jugendlichen. Zum Self-Tracking durch Kinder liegen keine empirischen Studien vor, obwohl es seit einigen Jahren Produkte auf dem Markt gibt, die sich explizit an Kinder ab sechs Jahren richten. Der empirische Teil des Texts berichtet von der subjektivierungs- und diskurstheoretischen Untersuchung eines Werbeclips für den Activity Tracker für Kinder, *Fit Bit Ace 2*. Theorie und empirischer Teil stützen wechselseitig die Feststellung, dass der Ausdruck „Self-Tracking" allgemein und mehr noch mit Blick auf kindliche Nutzungsszenarien zu kurz greift. Diese Folgerung stützt sich darauf, dass zum einen gängige Nutzungsweisen Akteur*innen weit über die unmittelbar anwendende Person involvieren und dass zum anderen das Tracking nur einen unter vielen Teilaspekten darstellt. Stattdessen wird das Geschehen des Self-Trackings demnach als eine distribuierte sozio-technische Praktik beschrieben. Die Analyse des Werbeclips destillierte neoliberale Subjektivierungsangebote heraus. Demnach operieren die Subjektivierungsangebote vielfältig: Kinder werden als Kinder *und* als kleine Erwachsene adressiert; sie sollen spielerisch *und* ernst, Teamplayer*innen *und* Gegenspieler*innen zugleich sein. Ihre Leistung *und* ihre Erholung sollen optimiert werden. Ergänzend zu dieser eher eindimensionalen Betrachtungsweise der Subjektivierungsangebote spürt das Fazit möglichen Ambivalenzen und emanzipatorischen Potenzialen von Praktiken des Self-Trackings nach.

This paper first introduces the topic of self-tracking in general and maps a current state of research on self-tracking, especially on self-tracking by adolescents. There are no studies on self-tracking by children, although there have been products for several years that are explicitly aimed at children from the age of six. The empirical part of the paper reports on the analysis of an advertising spot for an activity tracker for children (*Fit Bit Ace 2*), based on theories of subjection and discourse. The theoretical and empirical parts support the conclusion that the term „self-tracking" falls short in general and even more so with regard to children's usage. This conclusion is based on the fact that, first, modes of use involve actors far beyond the immediate user and that, second, tracking is only one among many operations, entangled with self-tracking. Instead, the phenomenon of self-tracking is described as a distributed socio-technical practice. The analysis distilled neoliberal offers of subjection. According to this, the offers of subjection operate ambiguously: children are addressed as children *and* as small adults; they are supposed to be playful *and* serious, team players *and* antagonists at the same time. In addition to this rather one-dimensional view of the subjecting addressings, while neglecting responses by users, the final section traces possible ambivalences and emancipatory potentials of self-tracking practices along with existing, mostly qualitative studies on the subject matter.

1.   Einleitung

Die Sensorisierung und Vernetzung von Menschen und „Dingen" bringt eine umfangreiche Verdatung des Alltagslebens mit sich. Dieses Sammeln von Daten entspricht meist einem Fremdtracking. Zeitgleich und in Teilen damit verwoben, werden digitale Praktiken des Self-Trackings, des Sammelns und Auswertens von Daten über sich selbst etabliert – auch zunehmend von Heranwachsenden (Brüggen & Schober, 2020; Dander, 2017). Über Wearables und/oder entsprechende Smartphone-Apps werden etwa Bewegung, Ernährung, psychische oder emotionale Zustände über verschiedene Parameter gemessen, analysiert und an die Nutzer*innen rückgemeldet. Auf diese Weise sollen diese Aspekte des eigenen Lebens wahrnehmbar, veränderbar, vergleichbar und zur Selbsterkenntnis und Selbstoptimierung eingesetzt werden (Damberger & Iske, 2017).

Inzwischen geraten auch Kinder und Familienkonstellationen in den Fokus kommerzieller Hersteller von Fitness-Anwendungen (meist Hardware/Software-Assemblagen). Auf diese Weise wird über Sorgeberechtigte eine weitere Ebene der Kontrolle eingezogen und entsprechend in Werbebotschaften vermittelt. Als Nutzer*innen der Daten können sowohl die Nutzer*innen der Geräte selbst als auch Unternehmen, Werbekund*innen und Sorgeberechtigte aufgefasst werden. So vollzieht sich das Daten-Sammeln und -Auswerten externalisiert und verteilt: Geräte und Programme tracken und übersetzen die gesammelten Daten in Visualisierungen. Hieran wird deutlich, inwieweit Self-Tracking in seinen Funktionalitäten und Nutzungsweisen über ein reines Sammeln von Daten hinausreicht. Weder kann wörtlich lediglich von einem *Self*-Tracking im Sinne von „ausgehend von der primärnutzenden Person selbst" ausgegangen werden, noch enden diese Praktiken beim Self-*Tracking*, insofern ein reines Tracking das Verarbeiten und Auswerten von Daten nicht notwendig impliziert. Diese argumentative Bewegung, welche darauf zielt, die griffige Wendung Self-Tracking anhand der Empirie zu verkomplizieren, wird im folgenden Textverlauf unterfüttert.

Der Beitrag nimmt seinen Ausgang in grundlegenden definitorischen Bestimmungen von Self-Tracking und führt kontextualisierend in damit verbundene soziotechnische Konstellationen ein (Abschnitt 2). Darauf folgen aktuelle Forschungsbefunde zur Nutzung von Self-Tracking-Anwendungen durch Jugendliche und Kinder im Kontrast zu jener Erwachsener mit einem Fokus auf die Bundesrepublik Deutschland (Abschnitt 3). Abschnitt 4 führt beispielhaft in einer kursorischen Analyse des Werbematerials zur *Fitbit Ace*-Produktserie in die Adressierung von Kindern ab sechs Jahren ein. Hierbei werden die Subjektivierungsangebote expliziert, mit welchen Self-Tracking-Nutzende allgemein und Kinder wie Sorgeberechtigte im Besonderen konfrontiert werden. Der abschließende, fünfte Abschnitt skizziert demgegenüber, ergänzend zum Fazit, emanzipatorische Potenziale, die im Kontext von Bildung oder Aktivismus mit Praktiken des Self-Trackings einhergehen können.

2. Was ist Self-Tracking?[1]

Zeitdiagnostische Analysen und Problematisierungen einer Kultur der datenbasierten Automatisierung, Vermessung und Überwachung werden in den letzten Jahren unter Schlagworten wie Big Data (Reichert, 2014; Sander, 2020), Surveillance Capitalism (Zuboff, 2019), Algorithmisierung oder Algorithmuskulturen (Seyfert & Roberge, 2017), Datenkolonialismus (Couldry & Mejias, 2019), Metriken (Mau, 2018), Scoring (Gapski & Packard, 2021), Social Sorting und Profiling (Lyon, 2014) uvm. vorgetragen und entlang verschiedener Schwerpunktsetzungen konkretisiert. All diese Beschreibungsformen setzen in je verschiedener Weise auf Infrastrukturen und Materialitäten, Diskurse und verschiedene Rationalitäten, Praktiken, Institutionalisierungen und De/Regulierungen, und Technologien im engeren wie im weiteren Sinne auf. Die Stoßrichtungen der Problematisierungen oder Kritiken richten sich beispielsweise auf inhärente Verwertungslogiken personenbezogener Daten (Dander, 2020; Sarikakis, 2012; Share Lab et al., 2016), disziplinierende und normalisierende Subjektivierungsweisen (Mämecke, 2021; Schöttler, 2016), Diskriminierungsformen (Allert, 2020; Eubanks, 2017; Noble, 2018) und sozial-ökologische Konsequenzen von komplexen Softwareanwendungen (Crawford, 2021).

Ermöglicht werden die beschriebenen und problematisierten Prozesse durch eine im globalen Norden annähernd flächendeckende Marktsättigung in Bezug auf mobile internetfähige Endgeräte (Smartphones), die sich durch stetig steigende Prozessorleistungen und Speichermedien (oder Zugang zu Cloud-basierten Ressourcen) auszeichnen. Ebenso ansteigend sind die Übertragungsraten in der Internetanbindung, wie auch die Vernetzbarkeit verschiedener Geräte und Gegenstände über Schnittstellen wie NFC, Bluetooth, etc. Harald Gapski (2015, S. 64) benennt im Kontext von Big Data mit *Vernetzung, Sensorisierung, Data-*

---

1 Die Ausführungen in Abschnitt 2 wurden in leicht veränderter Form von Dander (2023) übernommen.

fizierung, Algorithmisierung und *Monetarisierung* fünf maßgebliche „Treiber bzw. ermöglichende Faktoren" für eine signifikante gesellschaftliche Entwicklung.

Self-Tracking nimmt im bislang beschriebenen Kontext eine spezifische Position ein, insofern sich das Tracking, also das Daten-Sammeln, üblicherweise intentional und bewusst auf sich selbst richtet. Der Soziologe Stefan Selke beschreibt Self-Tracking als einen Typus von Gesundheitsmonitoring, welches neben *Human Tracking, Human Digital Memory* und *Sousveillance* i. S. v. *Gegen-Überwachung* wiederum einen von vier Grundtypen von „Lifelogging" darstelle. Self-Tracking als Praxis, um „in Echtzeit biometrische Daten des eigenen Körpers zu vermessen und damit eine präventive Lebensführung zu ermöglichen" (Selke, 2016, S. 6), zielt hierbei auf (zunächst physische) Gesundheit und Körperfunktionen, jedoch zunehmend auch auf Emotionen, Stimmungen und Verhaltenstracking oder -steuerung (etwa von Suchtverhalten o. ä.) (Selke, 2016, S. 6).

Insbesondere die Momente der Sensorisierung und der Vernetzung verschiedener Geräte und Nutzer*innen können als spezifische Bedingungen für die Ermöglichung einer breitenwirksamen Nutzung von Self-Tracking-Anwendungen genannt werden: *Wearables* wie *Fitness-Tracker* oder *Smartwatches*, aber auch Smartphones, sind mit einer Vielzahl von Sensoren ausgestattet, die es erlauben, verschiedene Körperfunktionen zu tracken. Zur Standardausstattung von Fitness-Trackern gehören etwa ein Beschleunigungssensor (*Accelerometer*), ein Luftdruckmesser (*Barometer*), ein Lagesensor (*Gyroskop*), ein Pulsmesser sowie ein Kompass.[2] Die meisten dieser Sensoren sind auch in Smartphones integriert, sodass diese selbst als Self-Tracking-Device genutzt werden können. In Kombination mit Fitness-Trackern werden sie oft zu verlinkten Geräte-Hubs (engl. *hub* kann z. B. mit Drehscheibe übersetzt werden), auf welchen die Daten gesammelt, analysiert, prozessiert und geteilt werden können. Vielfach wird der Begriff ‚Wearables' für am Körper tragbare elektronische Geräte verwendet. Allerdings bezieht etwa Statista in diese Kategorie auch smarte Kopfhörer mit ein, was in Bezug auf Self-Tracking-Praktiken und -Technologien nach einer Präzisierung als „wristworn wearables" verlangt (Statista, 2022).[3]

Self-Tracking-Praktiken wurden insbesondere am Beispiel der *Quantified Self-*Bewegung (QS) untersucht, deren Gründer und Mitglieder seit knapp 15 Jahren unter dem Motto „Self knowledge through numbers" („Selbsterkenntnis durch Zahlen") auf die emphatische Quantifizierung des eigenen Körpers und Verhaltens zielt (Damberger & Iske, 2017; Mämecke, 2021; Meißner, 2016; Schöttler,

---

2 So z. B. die Angaben des Herstellers *Fitbit* für seine eigenen Geräte auf der zugehörigen Website (Fitbit LLC, 2022).
3 Smarte Kopfhörer machen global betrachtet sogar den größten Anteil von Wearables aus (IDC Corporate, 2022).

2016, S. 202). In diesem Kontext kommen mitunter sehr individuelle technische Lösungen zum Einsatz, um die je eigenen Ziele am besten erreichen zu können. Diese reichen mitunter über konkrete körper- oder gesundheitsbezogene Ziele hinaus und beziehen stärker erkenntnis- oder normalisierungskritische Aspekte in die Selbstexpertisierung mit ein (Heyen, 2020). Aus der Innenperspektive werden die eigenen Praktiken als ermächtigend wahrgenommen. Die Außenperspektive der medialen Berichterstattung ergibt eher ein dystopisches Bild, wie eine diachrone Diskursanalyse nachzeichnet (Hepp et al., 2021). Diese rückt Aspekte wie neoliberale Selbstoptimierung, übersteigerte Selbstkontrolle oder mit Blick auf Krankenversicherungssysteme auch die Erosion gesellschaftlicher Solidarität in den Vordergrund. Auf diese Weise folgt die Berichterstattung tendenziell einer technodeterministischen Interpretation (Hepp et al., 2021, S. 48f.).

Allerdings kann nur ein kleiner Teil der Self-Tracking-Aktivitäten der *Quantified Self*-Bewegung zugerechnet werden (Schöttler, 2016, S. 202). Der größere Anteil der Nutzer*innen verlässt sich im Unterschied zu QS beim Self-Tracking auf vorgefertigte Angebote der kommerziellen Anbieter in diesem Sektor. Der Markt für körper- und gesundheitsbezogene Wearables wächst stark, wie Marktdaten des Branchenverbands *gfu Consumer & Home Electronics GmbH* (Gesellschaft zur Förderung der Unterhaltungselektronik) nahelegen – so seien sowohl der Stück-Absatz als auch der Umsatz von 2020 auf 2021 in Deutschland um etwa 20 % angewachsen (Drechsler, 2022). Weltweit decken fünf Firmen fast drei Viertel des Marktes ab, so werden Xiaomi, Apple, Huawei, Fitbit und Samsung als erfolgreichste Hersteller von *Wristworn Wearables* genannt.[4] Vielfältiger ist der Markt für Self-Tracking-*Apps*. Alleine *Google Play* weist Anfang 2022 unter der Suchanfrage „Self Tracking Apps" 250 Applikationen mit sehr verschiedenen Schwerpunktsetzungen aus, die jedoch alle diesem Segment zugeordnet werden (Google Play, 2022). Die im Folgenden angeführten Aspekte beziehen sich nicht nur, aber überwiegend auf diese kommerziellen Angebote.

3. Wer praktiziert Self-Tracking wie?

Self-Tracking im oben genannten Sinne wird bereits seit einigen Jahren angewandt. Allerdings ließen sich im Vorfeld eines 2017 erschienenen Artikels kaum Hinweise dafür finden, dass es sich bei Self-Tracking zum damaligen Zeitpunkt um ein für Jugendliche relevantes gesellschaftliches Feld handelte (Dander, 2017). Zum einen lag das daran, dass keine aussagekräftigen Studien vorlagen. Zum anderen wiesen Marktlage und Mediennutzungsstudien zu Jugendlichen keine nennenswerten Zahlen auf: So kam die Verbraucherzentrale NRW (Marktwäch-

---

4 Siehe auch hierzu die Marktanalyse von IDC von Ende 2022 (IDC Corporate, 2022).

ter, Verbraucherzentrale NRW e.V., 2017) in einer repräsentativen Erhebung zum Ergebnis, dass lediglich 3 % der 14–18-jährigen Internetnutzenden in Deutschland Wearables anwendeten (kabellose Kopfhörer dürften damals noch nicht damit gemeint worden sein).

Diese Situation hat sich mittlerweile deutlich gewandelt. Für 2021 verzeichnet die jährlich durchgeführte, für Deutschland repräsentative JIM-Studie des Medienpädagogischen Forschungsverbundes Südwest in 44 % der Haushalte mit Jugendlichen im Alter von 12 bis 19 Jahren eine Ausstattung mit Wearables (Feierabend et al., 2021a, S. 5).[5] 25 % der befragten Jugendlichen geben an, selbst ein solches Gerät zu besitzen. Der Anstieg im Vergleich zum Vorjahr (2021 zu 2020) wird allerdings nur mit einem Prozentpunkt ausgewiesen. 2019 waren es hingegen nur 13 % (Feierabend et al., 2020). Der Abschnitt zur Medienbeschäftigung (Feierabend et al., 2020, S. 13–15) weist Wearables nicht aus, während sportliche Aktivitäten allgemein unter den Freizeitaktivitäten zu den wichtigsten zählen (Feierabend et al., 2020, S. 11). Wie diese Leerstelle zu erklären ist, bleibt eine offene Frage: Nehmen die Jugendlichen Wearables nicht als Medien wahr? Nutzen sie sie schlichtweg nicht?[6] Wurden sie nicht abgefragt und daher nicht genannt? Oder wurden sie erfragt, aber es gab keine Positivantworten?[7]

Zum Vergleich mit der Gesamtbevölkerung in Deutschland ab 16 Jahren: 35 % gaben in einer ebenfalls repräsentativen Umfrage von Bitkom Research (Klöß, 2021, S. 13) im Mai 2021 an, das Zählen von Schritten und Stufen durch Fitness- und Gesundheitsanwendungen zu nutzen. 16 % nutzen Sport-Apps („mit denen man Ergebnisse mit anderen teilen kann") oder messen ihre Herzfrequenz, 8 % messen ihre Schlafqualität oder ihr Stresslevel. Die Ambivalenz der Fitness- und Gesundheitsanwendungen zeigt sich in der Zustimmung zu den beiden Aussagen „Die Hinweise setzen mich manchmal unter Druck" und „Die Hinweise motivieren mich, aktiv zu werden" – beiden Aussagen stimmt etwa die Hälfte der Befragten Nutzer*innen zu (Klöß, 2021, S. 18).

Während inzwischen zahlreiche qualitative Studien zu Self-Tracking-Praktiken Erwachsener durchgeführt wurden, ist das Feld mit Blick auf jugendliche oder

---

5 Auch hier werden als Beispiele für Wearables durchwegs lediglich Smartwatches genannt. Es ist also anzunehmen, dass kabellose Kopfhörer in der Studie ebenfalls nicht unter Wearables subsumiert werden.

6 Mit Blick auf US-Jugendliche und gesundheitsbezogene Smartphone-Apps gibt es Hinweise darauf, dass ein Download nur selten zu einer konkreten Nutzung führt (Wartella et al., 2016, S. 16f.).

7 In der KIM-Studie zu 2020, die alle zwei Jahre die Mediennutzung von Kindern (6–13 Jahre) in Deutschland ausweist, finden sich keine Hinweise auf Wearables, Self-Tracking, digitale Fitnessgeräte oder einschlägige Smartphone-Nutzung wie etwa das Zählen von Schritten etc. (Feierabend et al., 2021b). Gleiches gilt für die miniKIM-Studie für Kinder im Alter von zwei bis fünf Jahren (Kieninger et al., 2021).

kindliche Nutzungsweisen sehr überschaubar. 2020 publizierte das JFF in München Ergebnisse einer explorativen Studie zu „Self-Tracking im Freizeitsport" bei Kindern und Jugendlichen von 12 bis 18 Jahren (Brüggen & Schober, 2020). In Forschungswerkstätten (12–13 J.) und Interviews (15–18 J.; nur aktive Self-Tracking-Nutzer*innen) wurden Fragen zu faktischen und möglichen Nutzungsweisen von Self-Tracking beforscht. Für die älteren interviewten Jugendlichen zeigten sich u. a. folgende Nutzungsformen und Sinngebungen: Sie wollten ihre sportliche Leistung verbessern, betteten das Self-Tracking teilweise in karriere- und ausbildungsbezogene Projekte ein, wiesen ein unterschiedlich detailliertes Wissen über Tracking durch Unternehmen auf und nahmen dieses weitestgehend in Kauf. Allerdings zeigten sie sich teils zurückhaltend, was das Teilen von eigenen Daten über Social Media oder das Vergleichen von Ergebnissen mit anderen über Social Media betrifft (Brüggen & Schober, 2020, S. 16–18). Die Multifunktionalität und Medienkonvergenz des Smartphones wurde von einem Jugendlichen explizit problematisiert. Einerseits sollte es das Training unterstützen und würde dabei also benötigt, andererseits sorgten andere Smartphone-Anwendungen und -Funktionen aber für störende Ablenkung (Brüggen & Schober, 2020, S. 21).

In den konkreten Praktiken schienen zudem subversive Spuren auf, wenn die Jugendlichen Self-Tracker*innen sich gegen vorgesehene Nutzungsweisen sperrten oder Verschiebungen vornahmen. Neben der Konfiguration der in den Apps angebotenen Datenschutzeinstellungen oder der bewussten Nicht-Nutzung von technischen Funktionen des Daten-Teilens wurde etwa mit verfälschten Dateneingaben gearbeitet oder reflexiv mit Parametern in den Apps verfahren, die als unzutreffend eingeschätzt wurden (Brüggen & Schober, 2020, S. 16–18).

Empirisch wird künftig zu beforschen sein, inwieweit die vorliegenden, reichhaltigen Erkenntnisse über erwachsene Self-Tracker*innen auch auf jene im Kinder- und Jugendalter anteilig zutreffen. So ist etwa von einer Selbstexpertisierung und Selbstverwissenschaftlichung die Rede (Houben & Prietl, 2018; Zillien & Fröhlich, 2018). Self-Tracking-Apps können auch für eine erinnernde Identitätsarbeit genutzt werden, wie eine Fallanalyse einer Studentin ergab (Dehmel & Burgfeld-Meise, 2020, S. 46). Gewisse Konstellationen können Kontrollsysteme angezeigt erscheinen lassen, wenn etwa Angehörige mit einer Alzheimer- oder Demenzerkrankung getrackt werden können (Hagendorff & Hagendorff, 2019). Als ambivalent erscheint das möglicherweise distanziertere Verhältnis zum eigenen Körper, welches teils im Sinne eines Verlustes, teils als Erkenntnis- und Reflexivitätsgewinn aufgefasst wird.

Aus Mangel an vorliegenden Erkenntnissen über konkrete Self-Tracking-Praktiken von Kindern nehmen wir an dieser Stelle einen Perspektivwechsel von den Praktiken zum Produkt vor: Im nächsten Kapitel wird am Beispiel von *Fitbit Ace* nachvollzogen und analysiert, wie die Produktserie eines Fitness-Trackers für Kinder gestaltet und beworben wird, um Kinder und ihre Eltern als Kund*innen zu gewinnen.[8]

4.   Ambivalente Subjektivierungsangebote in Werbespots für *Fit Bit Ace*

4.1   Theorie und Verfahren: subjektivierungstheoretische Diskursforschung

Die analytische Auseinandersetzung mit dem Material, einem Werbespot, bedient sich subjektivierungs- und diskurstheoretischer Grundlagen. Subjektivierung wird als ein andauernder Prozess des Subjekt-Werdens aufgefasst, die keineswegs strukturdeterministisch zu verstehen, sondern mit Foucault und Butler stets in enger Verschränkung von Unterwerfung und Ermöglichung zu denken ist (Rose, 2019, S. 68f.). Entsprechend wird das Subjekt nicht als autonom, sondern als fundamental verstrickt in Machtrelationen aufgefasst (Jäger, 2010). Zumindest der Auseinandersetzung mit diesen Relationen kann es sich nicht entziehen, wobei an verschiedenen Stellen darauf hingewiesen wurde, dass programmatische Diskurse des Herrschens sich keinesfalls unidirektional in Subjekte einschreiben, wie Gouvernementalitätsanalysen mitunter nahelegten (Alkemeyer & Villa, 2010). Dies gilt für Programme als *Vorschriften* genauso wenig wie für Programme als *Software* oder *Hardware*, also für Mediendispositive. Ähnlich wie in der Adressierungsanalyse, etwa bei Rose (2019; Reh & Ricken, 2012), werden im Folgenden die subjektformierenden Ansprachen untersucht und im vorliegenden Artikel als „Subjektivierungsangebote" bezeichnet. Im Material liegt jedoch lediglich die Anrede vor; die für ein „rekursives soziales Geschehen" so bedeutsame Ebene der „Antworten [...] auf Re-Adressierungen" (Rose, 2019, S. 74) wie auch die praktische Auseinandersetzung mit Subjektivierungsangeboten fehlt, genauso wie die diskursiven Praktiken im Anschluss an die Subjektivierungsangebote.

Die Analyse folgt ausgewählten Leitfragen: Welche Subjektpositionen werden wie aufgerufen? In welcher Relation stehen sie zueinander? In welche Normhorizonte werden sie eingebettet? Welche Differenzierungen nehmen in der Konstruktion von Identität/Differenz, von positiv/negativ etc. eine wichtige Rolle ein? Welche Diskurskontexte werden implizit und explizit einbezogen?

---

8 Im Folgenden werden nicht in jedem Fall anderweitig Sorgeberechtigte explizit genannt. „Eltern" wird jedoch als weite und nicht notwendigerweise biologische Kategorie aufgefasst, bezieht sich also auf alle Personen, die in einem juristischen oder eltern-ähnlichen Sorgeverhältnis zu Kindern stehen. Gleiches bezieht sich auf „Familie" im Sinne aller familienähnlichen Konstellationen, auch jenseits heterosexueller Kleinfamilienmodelle.

Ein Werbespot ist per se auf die Veränderung von Wirklichkeit in der Zukunft ausgerichtet. Er soll eine neue Normalität erzeugen, die zugleich etwas Besonderes darstellt. Auf diese Weise bringen die Subjektivierungsangebote in Summe einen Teil dessen hervor, was als „sociotechnical imaginary" bezeichnet werden könnte, als stabilisierte (oder noch zu stabilisierende) kollektive Vorstellungen von erstrebenswerten Zukünften (Williamson, 2017, S. 16f).

Da das Material der vorliegenden Analyse ein audiovisueller Werbespot ist, dessen visuelle Anteile für die leitende Forschungsfrage nach den Subjektvierungsangeboten im Werbespot durchaus relevant sind, reicht ein ausschließlicher Blick auf Sprache in der Analyse nicht aus. Gleichwohl war eine umfassende, multimodale Sequenzanalyse nicht leistbar. Der Einbezug visueller Anteile beschränkt sich demnach eher auf die Oberfläche der Darstellung und auf Repräsentationslogiken (von Menschen und Gegenständen). Gleiches gilt für die Tonspur.

4.2 Material: ein Werbespot für den Activity Tracker für Kinder Fit Bit Ace 2

Das Modell *Ace* des Activity Tracker-Herstellers *Fit Bit* ist ein wasserabweisendes „Armband für Kinder", das mit einem Werbespot vom April 2018 für Kinder ab 8 Jahren beworben wurde (Fitbit Europe, 2018). 2019 wurde *Fitbit Ace 2*, 2021 *Ace 3* veröffentlicht. Beide nennen 6+ Jahre als angestrebtes Alterssegment (Fitbit, 2022; Wikipedia, 2022).[9] Die Unterschiede zwischen den Modellen beziehen sich überwiegend auf geringfügige Design-Entscheidungen wie Größe, Farben, Armbandlänge oder auf technische Leistungsfähigkeit wie Wasserresistenz, Stärke des Bluetooth-Senders, Akkulaufzeit etc. Die eingeblendete Textspur im 69 Sekunden langen Werbespot zu *Fitbit Ace 2* auf YouTube, welcher den Hauptgegenstand der Analyse bildet, liest sich wie folgt (Hervorhebungen im Original):

> „Früh übt sich
> wer große **Ziele** erreichen will
> Bewegungs-**Erinnerungen**
> Tracking deiner Schritte & aktiven Minuten
> Von **Erholung**
> Schlaf Tracking
> bis Aufstehen und **Alles-Geben**
> Verstellbare Armbänder passen sich den Kids an
> und überall
> und **dazwischen** überall
> **Wasserabweisend** bis zu 50 m Tiefe

---

9 Details zu *Fitbit Ace 3* waren zum Zeitpunkt des Schreibens an diesem Beitrag noch kaum aufzufinden, daher bezieht sich der Großteil des Abschnitts auf *Fitbit Ace 2*.

Denn **große** Ziele
verlangen **große** Schritte
Robust und für jeden Spaß zu haben
Frische Farben, Prints & Ziffernblätter
weil klein ganz **groß** sein kann
Bis zu 5 Tage Akkulaufzeit
Und wenn wir alle **zusammen** loslegen
Familienkonto – Elternansicht & Kinderansicht
erreichen wir alles
Wettkämpfe, Benachrichtigungen & Motivation
Ziele feiern
fitbit ace 2 – Aktivitäts-Tracker für Kinder ab 6" (Fitbit, 2019)[10]

Im Hintergrund des Werbespots läuft ein zügiger, aktivierender und positiv gestimmter Pop-Song mit Textzeilen wie: „You can be big, you can be anything; just follow your heart, reach up for the stars" und „Dreamin' what you wanna dream, cause what you're after, you'll find on the inside".[11] Die Bilder zeigen verschiedene Konstellationen in, der Anmutung nach, heterosexuellen und harmonischen Familiensettings, teilweise auch Kinder unter sich. Außer beim Schlafen im eigenen Bett sind die Kinder nicht alleine zu sehen, sondern sind gemeinsam beim Spiel aktiv und weisen freudige Gesichtsausdrücke auf. Zu sehen ist dabei fast durchgängig das Fitness-Armband. Die Farbschemata (Geräte, Inserts und Zuordnung der Nutzer*innen) folgen nur in Teilen stereotypen Geschlechterkodes (blau/rosa). Es sind überwiegend weiße Personen zu sehen, unter den Kindern ist eine *Person of Color*.

4.3   Analyse: Subjektivierungsangebote

Sprachlich werden in den Einblendungen auf einer ersten, technischen Ebene die zentralen technischen Spezifika der Fitness-Tracker angeführt (Bewegungs-Erinnerungen, Schritt-Tracking, Wasserresistenz, Akkulaufzeit, Konto-Einstellungen und Wettkampf-Modi). Auf einer direkten Anspracheebene werden wechselnd Kinder und Eltern adressiert. Diese zweite, narrative Ebene wird teils in erster Person Plural präsentiert („wenn wir alle zusammen loslegen", „erreichen wir alles"), die sowohl Familienkonstellationen als auch die Gesamtcommunity der Nutzer*innen meinen kann. Die Kinder sind hierbei im „wir" mitgedacht. Die Formulierung der Funktionen folgt zumindest einmal einer persönlichen Direktansprache der Kinder in der Einzahl („Tracking deiner

---

10 Anfang Januar 2023 ist das Video auf „privat" gestellt, also nicht öffentlich zugänglich.
11 Interpret*in und Titel des Tracks konnten anhand einer kursorischen Recherche nicht ausfindig gemacht werden.

Schritte"). Die Anpassungsfähigkeit der Geräte legt auf einer inhaltlichen Ebene nahe, dass die Kinder als Nutzer*innen im Mittelpunkt stehen. Zugleich sind die Eltern Adressat*innen, insofern die Kinder auch in dritter Person aufscheinen („Verstellbare Armbänder passen sich den Kids an").

Die Größe wird mehrfach angesprochen – in Bezug auf „große Ziele", die gleich zweifach genannt werden, aber auch: „große Schritte" und ganz allgemein („weil klein ganz groß sein kann") sowie im Liedtext („you can be big, you can be anything"). Damit ist auf der narrativen Ebene die Hauptachse markiert, die alle Aspekte organisiert: Größe habe nichts mit dem Alter zu tun, sondern kann durch Übung erreicht werden. Durch die Nutzung des Trackers werden die Kinder als kleine Erwachsenen-Subjekte adressiert. Das Gerät besitzen und nutzen zu dürfen, erhält gleichsam Initiationscharakter. Zugleich wird ihnen in Aussicht gestellt, durch die Nutzung (weiter) wachsen zu können. Ziel und Mittel zugleich ist Aktivität: alle zusammen, alles geben, alles erreichen.

Die Ambivalenz von Aktivität und Erholung ist im Text abgebildet. Allerdings wird selbst die Erholung in Form der Schlafqualität getrackt und kann optimiert werden. „Alles-Geben", Zielstrebigkeit und „Spaß" gehen Hand in Hand, wobei die wettbewerbs- und gamification-förmigen Spielmechaniken unterstützen sollen. Somit werden *spielerische* und *ernsthaft-effiziente Subjektivitäten* evoziert und nahegelegt, die sich saumlos miteinander verbinden lassen. Auch die Ambivalenz von Kooperation (zusammen alles erreichen) und Konkurrenz („Wettkämpfe") erzeugt eine gewisse Spannung: als Teamplayer*innen-Subjekte können die Kinder zielbezogen kooperieren (und feiern), allerdings benötigen sie für ihre Zielsetzungen Gegenspieler*innen. Insgesamt werden in den Spots (definier- und messbare) Ziele betont, wobei ebenso eindeutige Spielregeln befolgt werden sollen. Auf diese Weise kann die eigene Aktivität – wie Schritte oder Schlaf – optimiert und können erreichte Ziele gefeiert werden. So wird schließlich ein *achtsames Subjekt* aufgerufen, das nachhaltig mit sich selbst wirtschaftet und – mit Hilfe des Geräts – um sein Bedürfnis nach Ruhe weiß, damit es am nächsten Tag erneut Höchstleistungen erbringen kann.

Die Begleitsoftware eröffnet verschiedene Perspektiven für Eltern und Kinder, wie ebenfalls deutlich gemacht wird. In den etwas kürzeren, ansonsten aber inhaltlich sehr ähnlich gelagerten Werbespots für *Fitbit Ace 3* finden sich an der entsprechenden Stelle geringfügige Abweichungen zwischen der englisch- und der deutschsprachigen Version: „schützt die Privatsphäre – Einstellungen durch Eltern" bzw. „choose what kids see – parental controls" (Fitbit Europe, 2021; Fitbit MEA, 2021). Darin könnte eine Reaktion auf die in deutschsprachigen Ländern zu erwartende höhere Sensibilität für Datenschutzfragen zum Ausdruck kommen. Während im deutschsprachigen Text die Kontrolle der Kinder durch ihre Eltern als Argument für besseren Schutz der Privatsphäre angeführt wird, geht dabei die kindliche (oder auch jugendliche) Perspektive verloren, die potenziell auch gegenüber Eltern ihre Privatsphäre behaupten möchte (Wagner et al., 2010, S. 21 f). Im englischsprachigen Text steht der Kontakt der Kinder mit unliebsamen Inhalten oder Personen im Vordergrund.

5.   Self-Tracking als distribuierte Praxis um kindliche Selbste

Die Nutzer*innen der späteren *Fitbit Ace*-Modelle sind zwar in erster Instanz Kinder ab sechs Jahren. Ihre Steuer- und Kontrollmöglichkeiten sind aber gegenüber ihren Eltern deutlich eingeschränkt. Sofern sie keine eigenen Smartphones oder vergleichbare Geräte zur Verfügung haben, fungieren Geräte der Eltern als Instanzen des Daten-Sammelns, der Auswertung und auch der Präsentation für die Nutzenden. Darüber hinaus werden soziale Nutzungsformen nahegelegt, die verschiedene Geräte und ihre Nutzer*innen in ein gamifiziertes Verhältnis zueinander setzen können – auch jenseits von Familienkonstellationen. So wird in der Detailbeschreibung von Fitbit Ace 2 unter „Witzige Motivation & Anreize" genannt, dass Abzeichen Kinder u. a. motivieren sollen „ihre Freunde zu übertreffen". Anfang 2023 steht hier stattdessen „sich mit ihren Freunden zu messen" (Fitbit, 2022). Schließlich werden diese Datensammel-Praktiken von jenen der Unternehmen und potenziell von weiteren datennutzenden Firmen oder anderen überlagert. Es ist demnach – noch weniger als bei erwachsenen Self-Tracker*innen – keineswegs ausreichend festzustellen, dass „eine Person sich selbst trackt".

Die Funktions- und Anwendungsweisen, die hier nahegelegt werden, reichen weit über das reine Tracken hinaus: Das „Tracken", also das Aufzeichnen von Spuren, das Daten-Sammeln, nimmt im Spektrum der Funktionstypen von Self-Tracking-Geräten nur einen kleinen Teil ein (Reifegerste & Karnowski, 2020, S. 108). Als ebenso wichtig können Praktiken wie das Einordnen von Daten (etwa anhand von Referenzdatensätzen), das Rückmelden im positiven wie im negativen Sinne (Bewegungserinnerungen oder Meldungen erreichter Ziele), das Auswerten der Daten mit Blick auf Trainingspläne und -verläufe sowie schließlich die spielerische, motivierende, vergleichende oder rein kommunikative Funktion im Zusammenspiel mit anderen Nutzer*innen angesehen werden. Während verschiedene Instanzen am Sammeln der Daten beteiligt sind, verlagert sich die bewusste Sammelpraxis der beteiligten Kinder auf das Sammeln von Punkten in gamifizierten Nutzungssettings (Mosca, 2012; Schollas, 2014). Inwieweit auf diese Weise das zu erlangende Wissen über den eigenen Körper auf eine nur sehr vermittelte Ebene von Spielregeln, Abzeichen usw. verschoben wird, bleibt eine offene Frage.

In Summe wird anhand des Materials und seines Kontexts deutlich, dass die Relationen der beteiligten Instanzen deutlich über das hinausreichen, was ein simples Verständnis von Self-Tracking im Wortsinn impliziert. Self-Tracking lässt sich demnach allgemein, aber noch deutlicher angesichts der skizzierten kindlichen Nutzer*innen, als eine komplexe sozio-technische Praktik in distribuierten Konstellationen mit zahlreichen faktisch oder potenziell beteiligten menschlichen wie nicht-menschlichen Akteuren kennzeichnen.[12] Hierfür bieten weder das „Self" noch das „Tracking" eine hinreichend angemessene Beschreibungsweise.

Als interessant erweist sich jenseits dieses begrifflichen Aspekts, dass sämtliche kreativen Anteile der Gerätenutzung, wie etwa subversive Gebrauchsweisen im Sinne eines Cultural Hacking (Missomelius, 2018) in den Werbespots völlig ausgeblendet werden (z. B. Wechsel der Nutzenden, Fitbit dem Hund anlegen, Deaktivieren etc.). Allerdings greift Fitbit in der Werbestrategie an einer Stelle selbst auf künstlerisch-ästhetische Übersetzungsprozesse zurück, um neue Perspektiven auf Stress und Fitness zu eröffnen: In der „Fitbit Stress Symphony", die seit Dezember 2020 auf YouTube online steht, werden laut Textbox u. a. anonymisierte Fitbit Daten in eine mehr als 3-minütige, visualisierte orchestrale Chronik zum Jahr 2020 übertragen.[13]

6. Fazit und Ausblick

Dieser Beitrag lieferte zunächst allgemeine Einordnungen von Self-Tracking-Praktiken Erwachsener und Jugendlicher anhand der bestehenden Forschungslage. Darüber hinaus gab er Einblicke in Subjektivierungsangebote in einem Werbespot für *Fitbit Ace 2*, einen Activity-Tracker für Kinder. In der Analyse wurde skizziert, inwiefern die Nutzer*innen – Kinder wie Eltern – mit verschiedenen Subjektivierungsangeboten konfrontiert werden, die Nähen zu neoliberalen Subjektivitäten aufweisen: spielerische und leistungsfähige Subjekte, sich verausgabende und selbst-achtsame Subjekte, kooperative und kompetitive Subjekte. Einerseits fügt sich die „Self"-Wendung nahtlos in die genannten gouvernementalen Subjektkonzeptionen (Selbstverantwortung, Selbstdisziplin, Selbstkontrolle etc.) (Fach, 2004). Komprimiert formulieren Houben und Prietl unter Verweis auf Foucault:

---

12 In einer ethnografischen, praxistheoretisch angelegten Studie arbeitet Wiedemann heraus, auf welche Weise sich in Self-Tracking-Praktiken Geräte, Zahlen, Grafiken, Sinnlichkeit des Körpers usw. miteinander verweben (Wiedemann, 2019).

13 Kernthemen des Unternehmens – Gesundheit, Fitness, Stress und Resilienz – werden hierbei mit markanten, auch politischen Stationen aus dem ersten Pandemiejahr verbunden, wie etwa mit Bildern von Demonstrationen im Kontext der Black Lives Matter Bewegung (Fitbit Europe, 2020).

„Als datengetriebene Technologien des Selbst [...] können Selbstvermessungspraktiken also sowohl Visualisierungs- und Objektivierungsvorhaben, Kontroll-, Normalisierungs und Optimierungsprojekten, als auch Singularisierungsanforderungen dienen." (Houben & Prietl, 2018, S. 363)

Andererseits wird im Werbespot gerade das *Selbst*-bezügliche fraglich; wenn nämlich in diesem Beitrag ein Verständnis von Self-Tracking als Praktik „sich selbst trackender Selbste" durch eine Deutung als komplexe sozio-technische Praktik in distribuierten Konstellationen abgelöst wurde. Galt diese Feststellung bereits für bisherige Self-Tracking-Praktiken, so muss sie angesichts der komplexeren Nutzungsarrangements in familialen Konstellationen umso nachdrücklicher formuliert werden. Adressiert werden im Werbespot Eltern und Kinder jeweils in sich, aber auch zusammen als elterliches, kindliches oder familiales Kollektivsubjekt. Die Hardware, der Activity Tracker, ist omnipräsent und so anpassungsfähig, dass er in allen Alltagssituationen und möglichst ohne Pause (Wasserfestigkeit und Akkulaufzeit) am Leib getragen werden kann und wie eins mit den kindlichen Körpern wird.

Schließlich bleibt erneut zu betonen, dass konkrete Nutzungspraxen, soweit es der Forschungsstand zum Gegenstand einzuschätzen erlaubt, den „socio-technical imaginaries" (Williamson, 2017) in Form der herausgearbeiteten Subjektivierungsangeboten im Werbespot nicht umfänglich entsprechen. Bis hierher klingt das Analyseergebnis so dystopisch und einseitig, wie es Hepp et al. (2021) dem Mediendiskurs zu Self-Tracking attestieren. Um dem gegenzusteuern, sollen abschließend bildungsbezogene und gesellschaftspolitische Fluchtlinien skizziert werden, die in Auseinandersetzung mit der bestehenden Literatur die Ambivalenzen und emanzipatorischen Potenziale von Self-Tracking in den Blick nehmen.

Insbesondere mit Blick auf Optimierungskritiken kritisiert etwa Mämecke (2021, S. 137–139) eine dort vielfach verkürzte Perspektivierung des Gegenstands. Spezifische Praktiken des Self-Trackings können seines Erachtens in Form einer „[p]rogressiven Selbstverdatung" (Mämecke, 2021, S. 235–237) emanzipatorische politische Handlungsoptionen eröffnen. Bildungstheoretisch lassen sich Self-Tracking-Praktiken interpretieren, insofern sie ambivalente Transformationen der Selbst- und Weltverhältnisse anregen können. Idealiter wird Self-Tracking zum Reflexionsanlass über die viel kritisierten Problematisierungsebenen Optimierung, Objektivierung, Normalisierung etc. Zugleich wird eine Selbstthematisierung ermöglicht (Dehmel & Burgfeld-Meise, 2020), die jene Anteile miteinschließt, die nicht von der technischen Apparatur abhängig sind, sondern auch unabhängig davon einer Befragung unterzogen werden können.

Ein Umgang mit Self-Tracking-Anwendungen und -Geräten, der die vorgegebenen Spielregeln auszudehnen, subvertieren und umzudeuten weiß, könnte in dieser Hinsicht einen brauchbaren Startpunkt markieren (Richter & Allert, 2017, S. 249f; Rode, 2018) – auch für pädagogische Einsatzszenarien. Wie funktionieren Gerät und Software? Wie kann gegen die Regeln gespielt, wie können diese ausgehebelt werden? Im Kunstprojekt *Unfit Bits* werden Activity Tracker unter dem Motto „Free your fitness data from yourself" bspw. auf Metronome geschnallt (Brain & Mattu, 2015). Auf eine solche Weise lassen sich Überwachungsdispositive unterlaufen, Optimierungsanforderungen vergessen und Rationalisierungsbemühungen ästhetisieren.

„Selbstbestimmung heißt im Zusammenhang mit Self-Tracking immer auch Selbstproblematisierung und Befreiung meint immer auch die Befreiung von zweifelhaften Wünschen und Gewohnheiten" (Mämecke, 2021, S. 239). Wie Mämecke darlegt, ist ein solcher Prozess der Emanzipation weniger als ein einsamer, individualisierter zu denken, sondern vielmehr als kollektive Arbeit in und an einem „quantifizierten Wir" (Mämecke, 2021, S. 247) – und ist auf diese Weise an einem Kreuzungspunkt von Politischem und Pädagogischem anzusiedeln.[14] Und vielleicht steckt, sehr großzügig gelesen, selbst im „Wir" im Werbespot für *Fit Bit Ace 2* ein utopischer Schimmer, der das Gemeinsame vor das *Selbst*-bezogene „Ich" stellt.

Literatur

Ajana, B. (2018). Communal self-tracking: Data philantropy, solidarity and privacy. In B. Ajana (Eds.), *Self-tracking. Empirical and philosophical investigations* (pp. 125–141). Palgrave Macmillan.

Alkemeyer, T., & Villa, P.-I. (2010). Somatischer Eigensinn? Kritische Anmerkungen zu Diskurs- und Gouvernementalitätsforschung aus subjektivationstheoretischer und praxeologischer Perspektive. In J. Angermüller & S. van Dyk (Hrsg.), *Diskursanalyse meets Gouvernementalitätsforschung: Perspektiven auf das Verhältnis von Subjekt, Sprache, Macht und Wissen* (S. 315–335). Campus. http://deposit.d-nb.de/cgi-bin/dokse rv?id=3487812&prov=M&dok_var=1&dok_ext=htm.

Allert, H. (2020). Algorithmen und Ungleichheit. *merz – medien+erziehung, 03*, 26–32.

Brain, T., & Mattu, S. (2015). *Unfit Bits*. Unfit Bits. http://www.unfitbits.com/.

Brüggen, N., & Schober, M. (2020). *Erfahrungen von Kindern und Jugendlichen mit Self-Tracking im Freizeitsport. Explorative Studie im Rahmen des Projekts „Self-Tracking im Freizeitsport"*. Bayerisches Staatsministerium für Umwelt und Verbraucherschutz.

---

14 Auch die Debatten um den Einsatz der Corona Warn App in Deutschland und ähnlicher Contact-Tracing-Apps zur Pandemie-Eindämmung in anderen Ländern verweist auf den gemeinwohlorientierten Community-Aspekt, der in Forschung zu Self-Tracking meist weniger im Vordergrund steht. Für eine weitere Ausnahme siehe den Beitrag zu „Communal Self-Tracking" von Btihaj Ajana (2018).

Couldry, N., & Mejias, U. A. (2019). *The costs of connection: How data is colonizing human life and appropriating it for capitalism.* Stanford University Press.

Crawford, K. (2021). *Atlas of AI: Power, politics, and the planetary costs of artificial intelligence.* Yale University Press.

Damberger, T., & Iske, S. (2017). Quantified Self aus bildungstheoretischer Perspektive. In R. Biermann & D. Verständig (Hrsg.), *Das umkämpfte Netz. Medienbildung und Gesellschaft* (S. 17–36). Springer VS. https://doi.org/10.1007/978-3-658-15011-2_2.

Dander, V. (2017). Self-Tracking als Gegenstand medienpädagogischer Jugendarbeit? *merz – medien+erziehung – zeitschrift für medienpädagogik, 05,* 39–47.

Dander, V. (2020). Grundzüge einer Kritischen Politischen Ökonomie von Big Data Analytics – und ihre bildungstheoretischen Implikationen. In S. Iske, J. Fromme, D. Verständig, & K. Wilde (Hrsg.), *Big Data, Datafizierung und digitale Artefakte* (S. 75–95). Springer Fachmedien. https://doi.org/10.1007/978-3-658-28398-8_5.

Dander, V. (2023). Self-Tracking Mal Anders: Bildungspotenziale der SeLeMA-App. In A. Tsirikiotis, J. Schmidt, & V. Ketter (Hrsg.), *Digitale Hochschulbildung? Bildungsprozesse Studierender und Lehrender im Zeitalter der Digitalisierung* (Bd. 3) (S. 169–190). transcript. https://doi.org/10.1515/9783839448038-008.

Dehmel, L., & Burgfeld-Meise, B. (2020). Vergissmeinnicht! Self-Tracking-Apps auf dem Smartphone als Erinnerungsräume junger Erwachsener. *merz – medien+erziehung, 06,* 38–47.

Drechsler, J. (2022, März 16). Wearables weiterhin mit starken Zuwächsen. *gfu. Consumer & Home Electronics.* https://gfu.de/wearables-weiterhin-mit-starken-zuwaechsen/.

Eubanks, V. (2017). *Automating inequality: How high-tech tools profile, police, and punish the poor.* St. Martin's Press.

Fach, W. (2004). Selbstverantwortung. In U. Bröckling, S. Krasmann, & T. Lemke (Hrsg.), *Glossar der Gegenwart* (1. Aufl.). S. 228–235). Suhrkamp.

Feierabend, S., Rathgeb, T., Kheredmand, H., & Glöckler, S. (2020). *JIM-Studie 2020. Jugend, Information, Medien. Basisuntersuchung zum Medienumgang 12- bis 19-Jähriger.* Medienpädagogischer Forschungsverbund Südwest (mpfs). https://www.mpfs.de/fileadmin/files/Studien/JIM/2020/JIM-Studie-2020_Web_final.pdf.

Feierabend, S., Rathgeb, T., Kheredmand, H., & Glöckler, S. (2021a). *JIM-Studie 2021. Jugend, Information, Medien. Basisuntersuchung zum Medienumgang 12- bis 19-Jähriger.* Medienpädagogischer Forschungsverbund Südwest (mpfs). https://www.mpfs.de/fileadmin/files/Studien/JIM/2021/JIM-Studie_2021_barrierefrei.pdf.

Feierabend, S., Rathgeb, T., Kheredmand, H., & Glöckler, S. (2021b). *KIM-Studie 2020. Kindheit, Internet, Medien. Basisuntersuchung zum Medienumgang 6- bis 13-Jähriger.* Medienpädagogischer Forschungsverbund Südwest (mpfs). https://www.mpfs.de/studien/kim-studie/2020/

Fitbit. (2019, März 6). *Introducing Fitbit Ace 2.* https://www.youtube.com/watch?v=7iVrKHKsAGw.

Fitbit. (2022). *Aktivitäts-Tracker Fitbit Ace 2.* Fitbit. https://www.fitbit.com/global/de/products/trackers/ace2.

Fitbit Europe. (2020, Dezember 7). *Introducing the Fitbit Stress Symphony.* https://www.youtube.com/watch?v=o1k5umcNPEI.

Fitbit Europe. (2021, Februar 10). *Fitbit Ace 3: Tracker für Kids ab 6.* https://www.youtube.com/watch?v=RtW-3e1vV8s.

Fitbit Europe. (2018, April 3). *Wir präsentieren: Fitbit Ace—YouTube.* YouTube – Kanalinfo. https://www.youtube.com/watch?v=-VkdmMqRpRo&list=PLkPhw7XICKpblEw x8lF3CL5Qe_XecrBZY&index=46.

Fitbit LLC. (2022). *Fitbit Development: Sensor Guides.* Fitbit Developer. https://dev.fitbi t.com/build/guides/sensors/.

Fitbit MEA. (2021, März 9). *Introducing Fitbit Ace 3.* https://www.youtube.com/watch? v=rtnV4kzcZ5E.

Gapski, H. (2015). Medienbildung in der Medienkatastrophe – Big Data als Herausforderung. In H. Gapski (Hrsg.), *Big Data und Medienbildung* (S. 63–79). http://www.pedoc s.de/volltexte/2016/11634/pdf/Gapski_2015_Big_Data_und_Medienbildung.pdf.

Gapski, H., & Packard, S. (Hrsg.). (2021). *Super-Scoring? Datengetriebene Sozialtechnologien als neue Bildungsherausforderung.* kopaed.

Google Play. (Jan. 2022). Suchergebnisse für „self tracking apps". https://play.google.com /store/search?q=self+tracking+apps&c=apps&hl=en_US&gl=US&pli=1.

Hagendorff, T., & Hagendorff, J. (2019). Zum Verhältnis von Überwachung und Fürsorge aus medienethischer Perspektive. In I. Stapf, M. Prinzing, & N. Köberer (Hrsg.), *Aufwachsen mit Medien. Zur Ethik mediatisierter Kindheit und Jugend* (S. 183–198). Nomos. https://doi.org/10.5771/9783845293844-183.

Hepp, A., Alpen, S., & Simon, P. (2021). Beyond empowerment, experimentation and reasoning: The public discourse around the quantified self movement. *Communications, 46*(1), 27–51. https://doi.org/10.1515/commun-2019-0189.

Heyen, N. B. (2020). From self-tracking to self-expertise: The production of self-related knowledge by doing personal science. *Public Understanding of Science, 29*(2), 124–138. https://doi.org/10.1177/0963662519888757.

Houben, D., & Prietl, B. (2018). Strukturdynamiken, Reproduktionsmechanismen und Subjektformen der Datengesellschaft. In D. Houben & B. Prietl (Hrsg.), *Datengesellschaft: Einsichten in die Datafizierung des Sozialen* (S. 323–382). Transcript.

IDC Corporate. (2022, Dezember 21). *IDC Tracker Expects Wearables Growth to Stall as Macroeconomic Pressures Continue.* IDC: The premier global market intelligence company. https://www.idc.com/getdoc.jsp?containerId=prUS49980022.

Jäger, S. (2010). Subjekt und Subjektivierung. In S. Jäger & J. Zimmermann (Hrsg.), *Lexikon Kritische Diskursanalyse: Eine Werkzeugkiste.* Unrast.

Kieninger, J., Feierabend, S., Rathgeb, T., Kheredmand, H., & Glöckler, S. (2021). *MiniKIM 2020. Kleinkinder und Medien: Basisuntersuchung zum Medienumgang 2- bis 5-Jähriger in Deutschland.* Medienpädagogischer Forschungsverbund Südwest. https://www.mpf s.de/fileadmin/files/Studien/miniKIM/2020/lfk_miniKIM_2020_211020_WEB_barrier efrei.pdf.

Klöß, S. (2021). *Die Zukunft der Consumer Technology 2021. Marktentwicklung & Mediennutzung, Trends & Technologien.* Bitkom e.V. https://www.bitkom.org/sites/defaul t/files/2021-09/210817_ct_studie_2021.pdf.

Lyon, D. (2014). Surveillance, Snowden, and big data: Capacities, consequences, critique. *Big Data & Society, 1*(2), 1–13. https://doi.org/10.1177/2053951714541861.

Mämecke, T. (2021). *Das quantifizierte Selbst: Zur Genealogie des Self-Trackings.* transcript. https://elibrary.utb.de/doi/book/10.5555/9783839456033.

Marktwächter, Verbraucherzentrale NRW e.V. (2017). *Wearables, Fitness-Apps und der Datenschutz: Alles unter Kontrolle? Eine Untersuchung der Verbraucherzentralen.* Verbraucherzentrale NRW e.V. https://ssl.marktwaechter.de/sites/default/files/download s/mw-untersuchung_wearables_0.pdf.

Mau, S. (2018). *Das metrische Wir. Über die Quantifizierung des Sozialen* (Sonderausgabe für die Bundeszentrale für politische Bildung). Suhrkamp.

Schöttler, C. (2016). Self-Tracking zwischen Emanzipation und digitaler Überwachung. Die Rolle Big Datas für ein autonomes Verhalten. *Communicatio Socialis, 49*(2), 201–210. https://doi.org/10.5771/0010-3497-2016-2-201.

Selke, S. (2016). Einleitung. Lifelogging zwischen disruptiver Technologie und kulturellem Wandel. In S. Selke (Hrsg.), *Lifelogging: Digitale Selbstvermessung und Lebensprotokollierung zwischen disruptiver Technologie und kulturellem Wandel* (S. 1–21). Springer VS.

Seyfert, R., & Roberge, J. (Hrsg.). (2017). *Algorithmuskulturen, Über die rechnerische Konstruktion der Wirklichkeit.* transcript. https://doi.org/10.14361/9783839438008.

Share Lab, Joler, V., & Petrovski, A. (2016). Immaterial labour and data harvesting. *Share Lab.* https://labs.rs/en/facebook-algorithmic-factory-immaterial-labour-and-data-har vesting/.

Statista. (2022). *Marktanteile der Hersteller am Absatz von Wearables weltweit im 1. Quartal der Jahre 2021 und 2022.* Statista. https://de.statista.com/statistik/daten/studie/432983 /umfrage/marktanteile-der-hersteller-am-absatz-von-wearables-weltweit-nach-quartal/.

Wagner, U., Brüggen, N., & Gebel, C. (2010). *Persönliche Informationen in aller Öffentlichkeit? Jugendliche und ihre Perspektive auf Datenschutz und Persönlichkeitsrechte in Sozialen Netzwerkdiensten. Teilstudie im Rahmen der Untersuchung „Das Internet als Rezeptions-und Präsentationsplattform für Jugendliche "im Auftrag der Bayerischen Landeszentrale für neue Medien (BLM).* JFF – Institut für Medienpädagogik in Forschung und Praxis. https://www.jff.de/fileadmin/user_upload/jff/projekte/konvergenz studien/JFF-Bericht_Datenschutz_Persoenlichkeitsrechte.pdf.

Wartella, E., Rideout, V., Montague, H., Beaudoin-Ryan, L., & Lauricella, A. (2016). Teens, health and technology: A national survey. *Media and Communication, 4*(3), 13–23. https://doi.org/10.17645/mac.v4i3.515.

Wiedemann, L. (2019). *Self-Tracking. Vermessungspraktiken im Kontext von Quantified Self und Diabetes.* Springer VS.

Wikipedia. (2022). List of Fitbit products. In *Wikipedia.* https://en.wikipedia.org/w/inde x.php?title=List_of_Fitbit_products&oldid=1130627050#Trackers.

Williamson, B. (2017). *Big data in education. The digital future of learning, policy and practice.* SAGE Publications.

Zillien, N., & Fröhlich, G. (2018). Reflexive Selbstverwissenschaftlichung. Eine empirische Analyse der digitalen Selbstvermessung. In T. Mämecke, J.-H. Passoth, & J. Wehner (Hrsg.), *Bedeutende Daten: Modelle, Verfahren und Praxis der Vermessung und Verdatung im Netz* (S. 233–249). Springer Fachmedien. https://doi.org/10.1007/978-3-658-11781-8_11.

Zuboff, S. (2019). *The age of surveillance capitalism: The fight for a human future at the new frontier of power.* PublicAffairs.

Julia Boog-Kaminski / Sonja Loidl / Iris Schäfer

Analoge und abstrakte Wunderkammern: Zur Praxis des Sammelns in der Kinder- und Jugendmedienkultur

Abstract

Kinder sammeln alles: Spielzeug, Steine, Schneckenhäuser, Bücher, Briefmarken, tote Tiere[1] und heutzutage vermehrt: Bubbles, Points und Likes. Der Sprung von der Sammlung realer hin zu virtuellen Dingen ist jedoch keineswegs so groß, wie vermutet werden könnte, dienen doch beide Tätigkeiten der Akkumulation, Differenzierung und Strukturierung der Welt. Sie fördern die Auseinandersetzung mit der unmittelbaren Umgebung sowie mit dem Selbst des Kindes, das Präferenzen und Strategien entwickeln muss, um der begehrten Objekte habhaft zu werden. Dennoch lässt sich in dem Wechsel von der analogen hin zur abstrakten bzw. digitalen „Wunderkammer" eine Akzentverschiebung ausmachen, der wir im vorliegenden Beitrag nachgehen wollen. Nachdem aus (Medien-)pädagogischer und psychoanalytischer Perspektive Schlaglichter auf die historischen und kulturellen Eigenheiten des Sammelns geworfen werden, wird am Beispiel von ausgewählten Medienanalysen die doppelte Natur dieser Aktivität herausgestellt. Unabhängig davon, ob es sich um reale oder fiktive Sammlungsgegenstände handelt, changiert die kulturelle Praxis des Sammelns zwischen Zielgerichtetheit und Arbitrarität, Regression und Transformation und kann damit den medialen (Identitäts-) Bildungsmöglichkeiten im Kinder- und Jugendalter einen weiteren Aspekt hinzufügen.

Children collect everything: toys, stones, snail shells, books, stamps, dead animals and nowadays increasingly: bubbles, points and likes. However, the leap from collecting real things to collecting virtual things is by no means as great as might be assumed. Both activities serve to accumulate, differentiate and structure the world. They promote the engagement with the immediate environment as well as with the child's self, which must develop preferences and strategies in order to get hold of the desired objects. Nevertheless, in the shift from the analogue to the abstract or digital cabinet of curiosities, a shift in emphasis can be discerned: After highlighting the historical and cultural characteristics of collecting from a (media-)pedagogical and psychoanalytical perspective, the double nature of this activity will be focused on using selected media analyses as examples. Regardless of whether the objects collected are real or fictitious, the cultural practice of collecting os-

---

1 Siehe dazu die umfassende empirische Studie von Ludwig Duncker, Katharina Hahn und Corinna Heyd, die 2014 leitfadengestützte Interviews mit 30 Kindern über ihre privaten Sammlungen führten (Duncker et al., 2014).

cillates between purposefulness and arbitrariness, regression and transformation. Thus, it can add another aspect to the possibilities of media (identity) education in childhood and adolescence.

1.   Kurze Geschichte des Sammelns

In der Forschung wird Sammeln als anthropologische Konstante gewertet, die im Neolithikum beginnt und bis in die Gegenwart reicht (Wilde, 2015, S. 40–57). In allen Epochen der Menschheitsgeschichte wird es als ökonomische wie ästhetische Praxis eingesetzt, die Ordnungs-, Tausch- und Wissenszwecken dient. Neben fassbaren Gütern speichern bereits die sesshaft gewordenen Steinzeitmenschen Geschichten und Erfahrungen zu den Objekten. So wird der reine Nutzwert um einen „symbolischen Wert" erhöht. Harald Tesan (2011) spricht vom Sammeln daher als Kulturtechnik, „das heißt, es ist eine sowohl kulturell vermittelte als auch Kultur vermittelnde Handlungsweise" (S. 11).

Dies ist besonders mit der Entwicklung des Buchdrucks im Mittelalter nachvollziehbar. Hier entstehen nach den neolithischen und antiken Sammlungen von Realia höchst abstrakte Informations- und Erinnerungsspeicher in Form von Lexika und Bibliotheken (Wilde, 2015, S. 44). Doch erst mit der Renaissance und vor allem der Frühen Neuzeit wird das Sammeln als kulturelle Praxis zu einer grundlegend epistemologischen Angelegenheit. Nun werden, neben *Naturalia, Artificialia* und *Scientifica* der näheren Umgebung, auch Kuriositäten aus fernen Ländern in den Haushalten zusammengetragen und mit ihnen das Wissen über diese Dinge (Wilde, 2015, S. 45f.). Den entscheidenden Anstoß dafür geben die Entdeckungsreisen vom 15. bis zum 17. Jahrhundert, insbesondere die Eroberung Amerikas. Mit den fremden Fundstücken professionalisieren sich Sammler- und Tauschbörsen, die neben den materiellen Waren vor allem mit ihren immateriellen Kenntnissen handeln. Eine immer größere Anzahl an Raritätenkabinetten und sogenannten „Wunderkammern" entsteht, die ihren Wert aus der Seltenheit und Schwierigkeit der Beschaffung ihrer Objekte generieren. Dabei darf natürlich nicht vergessen werden, dass gerade diese Sammelpraxis koloniale Ansprüche und Machtverhältnisse widerspiegelt. Die Gegenstände wurden oft gewaltsam erobert und reproduzieren rassistische Weltbilder, die später auch in die Museen gelangten (Hoins & Mallinckrodt, 2015, S. 10–13).

Ob kunstvolle Schmiedearbeiten, Elfenbeinschnitzereien, Tierpräparate, Spielautomaten, Astrolabien oder Miniaturkunstdrechseleien; ob seltene Muscheln und Korallen, riesige Straußeneier und Zähne von Tieren, ob Literatur, physikalische oder chirurgische Instrumente und optische Spiegel – sie alle finden in diesen Kammern ihren Platz (Beßler, 2012, S. 14–19). Es sind *Kuriosia*, die schon dem lateinischen Wortstamm *cura* nach auf eine verstärkte Fürsorge und Aufmerksamkeit ihrer Sammler verweisen und die Sammlungen immer mehr eines reellen Nutzens entheben (Wilde, 2015, S. 46). Selbst Gebrauchsobjekte werden in diesem Zusammenhang zu Kunstwerken: die Vorform des Museums ist geschaffen. In ihnen wird versucht „den Makrokosmos in den Mikrokosmos [...] [zu] projizieren" (Pomian, 1994, S. 113) und die Welt damit be*greif*bar zu machen.

Die Wunderkammern tragen folglich zu einem ganz entscheidenden Aspekt des Sammelns bei: der Bildung. Sie dienen, neben der Konservierung und Speicherung, genuin der Wissenserzeugung sowie Wissensvermittlung. In ihrem Zentrum steht das Staunen und die Neugierde (*curiositas*), die ebenfalls als stärkste Antriebsmotive für das kindliche Sammeln herausgehoben werden: „die Sammelfaszination [hat] etwas zu tun [...] mit einem ursprünglichen Staunen über die Vielfalt und Erscheinungsfülle der Welt" (Duncker et al., 1999, S. 63). Eben dies motiviert offenbar auch die Menschen der Spätrenaissance mittels der Wunderkammern sowohl in ein „kontemplatives Versinken" über die Geheimnisse der Welt einzutreten als auch diese zu entschlüsseln: „Die Sehlust und das Unterhaltungsbedürfnis des Auges verbinden sich mit dem Wunsch nach Denken und beginnender Aufklärung" (Duncker, 2018, S. 66f.).

Mit dieser Frühphase der Museen sowie ihrer tatsächlichen Etablierung im 19. Jahrhundert verschiebt sich der Wert von Sammlungen noch stärker in Richtung eines Erkennen- und Wissenkönnens. Neben den Privathaushalten als Orte individueller, informeller Bildung werden nun institutionelle Orte geschaffen, die eine weitaus gezieltere „Sammelpolitik" betreiben (Duncker, 2018, S. 50). Eigenschaften wie Sachlichkeit, Anschaulichkeit und Verantwortung sowie das sinnvolle Auswählen aus einer Masse an Gegenständen rücken in den Fokus. Sie werden auch von den Schulen als Kriterien für ihre Realien-Sammlungen übernommen, mit denen den Schüler*innen u. a. Tiere und Pflanzen, aber auch Kunstwerke nähergebracht werden sollen.

1.2 Kindliches Sammeln: Zwischen Pädagogik und Pathologie

Die Hauptfunktion des Museums und der Schule wird als sinnvolle Selektion der angehäuften Materialien und des mit ihnen verbundenen Wissens verstanden (Wilde, 2015, S. 54). Bildung definiert sich damit nicht nur aus dem Nachgehen, sondern dem Eindämmen und Leiten des Sammeltriebs, was bereits auf die zwiespältige Haltung gegenüber dieser Praxis verweist: Wird das Sammeln aktuell innerhalb der Pädagogik als Möglichkeit einer „ästhetischen Alphabetisierung" gesehen, mittels derer Kinder „mit ihrer Umwelt in Austausch treten können, noch bevor sie differenzierte kognitive und sprachliche Kompetenzen" haben (Duncker 2018, S. 15), wurde es traditionell als große Gefahr für Kinder gewertet.

Besonders die Reformpädagogin Maria Montessori, die äußerst prominent für eine Autonomisierung kindlicher Entwicklung eintrat, warnte vor der kindlichen „Sammelwut": Noch 1950 in ihrem Werk *Il segreto dell'infanzia* (dt.: *Kinder sind anders*) spricht sie vom Sammeln als „seelische[r] Anomalie", die zu „Besitztrieb" führe (Montessori, 1987, S. 168). Das ihrer Meinung nach wesenhaft ordnungsliebende und bescheidene Kind würde hier äußerst bedrohlich auf Abwege gebracht und in seiner natürlichen Bildung zu einem mündigen Bürger gestört. Denn mit dem Sammeln kämen vor allem Gier, das Auftrumpfen-Wollen gegenüber anderen sowie Maßlosigkeit zum Zug.

Montessori spricht damit eine Pathologisierung des Sammelns an, welche ebenfalls mit Anbruch der Moderne in der Psychoanalyse forciert wurde: Sigmund Freud, der alle erwachsenen Neurosen aus dem kindlichen Seelenleben ableitet, versteht die Sammelleidenschaft als zwanghaften Ersatzmechanismus. In einem Brief an Wilhelm Fließ beschreibt er 1895 den erotischen Hintergrund dieser Tätigkeit: „Wenn [...] der Hagestolz Tabakdosen sammelt, so substituiert [er] sein Bedürfnis nach – zahlreichen Eroberungen. Jeder Sammler ist ein substituierter Don Juan Tenorio", der sich über die angeeigneten Gegenstände die ihm fehlende Lust verschaffe (Freud, 1962, S. 101).

In Freuds Studie zur Analerotik ist der Sammel- und Besitztrieb ferner eine präödipale kindliche Lust, und zwar den Kot zurückzuhalten (Freud, [1908] 2000). Doch erst Ernest Jones spricht explizit von dem regressiven Charakter dieser Aktivität:

> „Alle Sammler sind Analerotiker und die gesammelten Gegenstände fast durchwegs typische Kotsymbole: z. B. Geld, [...] Marken, Eier, Schmetterlinge – die beiden letzteren sind Symbole für Kinder – Bücher, ja selbst wertlose Dinge, wie Stecknadeln, alte Zeitungen und ähnliches". (Jones, 1919, S. 85)

Die dazugehörige Lust am Auffinden und Ausgraben käme ebenfalls aus der analen Phase des Kindes, in der das inzestuöse Verlangen nach „unterirdischen Gängen, Höhlen und [...] der Erforschung des Leibes der Mutter Erde" dominiere (Jones, 1919, S. 85). Sammeln wird demensprechend als Sublimation der infantilen Angst vor dem Verlust der Fäkalien wie dem Vergnügen, sie zu behalten, bewertet.

Gleichzeitig betont Jones, dass dieser Trieb „bei Kustoden von Museen und Bibliotheken von hohem Werte" sei: Hier führe er zu jener „große[n] Zuneigung [...und] hingebende[r] Sorgfalt" (Jones, 1919, S. 85), die umfassende Sammlungen prägten und sie für Außenstehende erst zu Bildungsstätten machten. Die Dualität des Sammelns, die auch für die Gegenwart relevant ist, zeigt sich in Jones' Ausführungen sehr deutlich: Einerseits gilt es als affektgesteuerter, zu

Habsucht und Geiz sowie Unordnung und Schmutz verführender Trieb; andererseits als (museale) Kulturtechnik, die Ordnung in die Fülle der Welt bringt, soziale Kontakte fördert und Wissen ebenso generiert wie weitergibt.

Heutzutage wird in der psychoanalytischen Forschung vor allem die pathologische Seite des Sammelns betont, besonders in seiner extremsten Form: dem Messie-Syndrom. Hier ist die/der Sammler*in zahlreicher Gegenstände nicht mehr fähig, diese zu ordnen – weder durch eine selektierende Beschaffung noch durch eine geregelte Aufbewahrung. Diese graduell unterschiedlich ausgeprägten „Hoarding Disorders" seien die Folge fehlgeleiteter primärer Objektbeziehungen und Verlusttraumata: „Collecting frequently represents the attempt to fix self and world again when they have become unstuck, [...it] offers a way to console oneself for being left, give narcissistic validation and calm tempestuous emotions" (Subkowski, 2006, S. 387). Auch hier gilt das Sammeln folglich als Ersatzleistung aufgrund von fehlenden oder mit Angst behafteten sozialen Kontakten sowie als Versuch, die erschreckende Vergänglichkeit der Welt und des Ichs aufzuhalten. Besonders der Philosoph Jean Baudrillard betont, dass jedes Sammeln den neurotischen Akt darstelle, durch serielle Anhäufung von Dingen den diachronen Zeitablauf zu unterbrechen (Baudrillard, 1991, S. 110).

Dagegen steht, vor allem mit Ludwig Duncker et al. (2014), die gegenwärtige Erziehungswissenschaft, die mit dem Sammeln eine maximal positiv besetzte „bildende und identitätsstiftende Tätigkeit" (S. 19) anvisiert. Statt fehlgeleiteter (prä-)ödipaler Prozesse werden in den von vielen Kindern autonom angelegten Sammlungen *Wege zur ästhetischen Bildung* vermutet, die anstelle von Schrift und Zahl auf Leiblichkeit und einer „interaktiven Auseinandersetzung mit der Umwelt" fußten (Duncker, 2018, S. 15). Mit ihren Stein-, Tier-, aber auch Barbie- und Yu-Gi-Oh!-Archiven würden Jungen und Mädchen Konzentration und Ordnungssinn, Sorgfalt sowie strategisches Geschick lernen. Zudem stärkten die Tausch- und Beschaffungswege die soziale Interaktion mit Gleichaltrigen und häufig auch im Familienkreis, da über die Lieblingsobjekte viel gesprochen oder mit ihnen gespielt werden kann.

Kindliche Sammler*innen werden hier keineswegs als sich selbst isolierende, geizige oder prahlende Analcharaktere beschrieben. Stattdessen würden oft kommerziell wertlose Sammlungen geschaffen, die kein klares Ziel verfolgen: „[...] Steine, Muscheln und Vogelfedern sind nicht auf Vollständigkeit angelegt. Deshalb sind sie auch offen für überraschende Funde, sie sind nicht berechenbar in ihrer Entfaltung und den Wegen ihrer Weiterentwicklung durch die Kinder" (Duncker et al., 2014, S. 21). Deutlich wird die von Montessori noch abgesprochene Möglichkeit der Autonomie und Selbstverwirklichung für Kinder, die Duncker in seinem Buch *Wenn Kinder sammeln* anhand 31 realer Depots verdeutlicht.

So spielt Lara (10), leidenschaftliche Sammlerin von Briefmarken, Schnee-kugeln, Schleich-Figuren, Barbies, Schlümpfen, Steinen, Muscheln und Hai-fischzähnen – mit erwachsenen Maßstäben gemessen also ein Messie – oft mit Schleich und Stein zugleich oder verteilt erst alle Schlümpfe und dann alle Bar-bies in ihrem Zimmer (Duncker et al., 2014, S. 133). Ihre Interessen wechseln ebenso wie ihre Sammlungen und deren Bezüge. Andere Kinder haben den größten Genuss in dem langen, ausführlichen Betrachten einzelner Gegenstände: So wie Niklas (9), der aus dem Betasten der Steine ein Gesellschaftsspiel macht: „Wer zum Beispiel die Augen verbunden hat, irgendeiner, derjenige muss immer erraten, welcher Stein das war" (Duncker et al., 2014, S. 103). Das Ziel dieser Sammlungen besteht also nicht in einem „Display" oder krampfhaften Horten, sondern in der Möglichkeit des Hervorholens und Versteckens sowie des Fan-tasiespiels.

Damit wird das freie Erkunden und Ertasten sowie Kombinieren der Dinge dieser Welt erprobt. Duncker spricht von Sammlungen daher auch als „Kulturen der Kindheit" (Duncker et al., 2014, S. 20), die gleich dem Spiel als ein Bereich angesehen werden müssen, in dem das Kind selbst „kulturell vermittelte als auch Kultur vermittelnde Handlungsweise[n]" (Tesan, 2011, S. 11) erlerne. Die Frage ist nun, ob sich diese sinn- und identitätsstiftende Tätigkeit auch in wesentlich abstrakteren Wunderkammern einholen lässt: wie zum Beispiel dem Spielan-gebot für Kinder im Netz.

1.3 Digitales Sammeln im Netz

Noch immer besteht das Netz für Kinder, wie viele medienpädagogische Un-tersuchungen betonen, zu einem Großteil aus von Konzernen etablierten An-geboten (u. a. Dander et al., 2020), die auch ohne kostenpflichtige Inhalte nicht frei von Verwertungslogik (etwa durch frühe Kund*innenbindung) sind. Einer der größten Anbieter ist TOGGO, der Kinder-Fernsehsender von Super-RTL, der auf seiner Website mit kostenlosen Flash-Spielen und Videos wirbt. Hier werden Mädchen wie Jungen neben viel Werbung bereits auf der Home-Seite von ihren Lieblingsstars empfangen: u. a. Barbie und Ninjago von Lego. Ähnlich wie zu Beginn des Privatfernsehens Mitte der 1980er Jahre herrscht im Kinderweb of-fensichtlich immer noch „unregulierter Wildwuchs", wenn es um redaktionelle und werbende Inhalte geht (Feil et al., 2004, S. 59). Interessanterweise bestehen die daraus entwickelten Spiele hauptsächlich aus der Praxis des Sammelns und Tauschens.

Bei Barbie kann das Kind zum Beispiel eine ganze Traumvilla von den Wänden bis zu den Möbeln einrichten, indem es Herzen, Diamanten und andere Kostbarkeiten über ein Geschicklichkeitsspiel ergattert. Hierfür müssen die begehrten Gegenstände in verschiedenen Anordnungen sortiert werden, sodass Dreier-, Vierer- oder Fünferreihen entstehen. Das grundlegende Prinzip des Sammelns, Vorrat anschaffen und arrangieren, bildet also die Grundlage beider Spielebenen. Dabei besteht die Steigerung des Spiels darin, immer mehr Herzen, Diamanten oder Sterne einzusammeln, über den immer gleichen Spielablauf und Mausklick – nur die Anschaffungsmöglichkeiten im Barbiehaus variieren.

Bei den Ninjagos muss man statt Herzen und Diamanten sogenannte „Profipunkte" sammeln, um ein schnelleres Auto oder eine neue Rennstrecke freizuschalten. Auf diesen Strecken können wiederum leuchtende Kreisel eingesammelt werden, die dem Fahrzeug einen „Boost" oder Schild verleihen. Alle Spiele auf dieser Website bestehen also aus der Praxis des (Ein-)Sammelns, Hortens und Tauschens – mit deutlich ökonomischer Tendenz. Diese wird auch in der Forschung von einem „ästhetischen" Sammeln unterschieden: „Ökonomisches Sammeln ist akkumulierend. Ästhetisches Sammeln dagegen ist differenzierend" (Sommer, 2011, S. 45). Die ökonomische „Vernichtungslogik" ist für Manfred Sommer deswegen auch nur eine unzureichende Variante des Sammelns, die Verzehr und Verbrauch statt Erhaltung und Sinnstiftung lehrt (Sommer, 2011, S. 45). Während bei TOGGO und auch auf anderen Online-Spielplattformen (u. a. www.spielaffe.de) Gegenstände nur angehäuft werden, um diese einzutauschen, zeigen die realen Depots der Kinder, wie wichtig die Aufbewahrung und Chance der immer wieder neuen Sortierung ist.

Bei den Websites gibt der extrem einfache, limitierte Aufbau jedoch vor, wie die Dinge einzusammeln oder zu kombinieren sind. Die Spielabläufe sind durchgehend linear und können oft nur durch einen bestimmten Maus- oder Tastenklick vollzogen werden. Sie regen damit weder zur Kreativität noch zur Eigenständigkeit an. Das Ziel ist klar vorgegeben: neue Rennstrecken oder Möbel zu ergattern, je nach Geschlecht. Dies liegt natürlich auch an der kostenfreien Verfügbarkeit, doch stellen gerade diese Angebote auf dem digitalen Markt für Kinder das am breitesten rezipierte Angebot dar und müssen dementsprechend auf ihre bildenden und identitätsstiftenden Potenziale hinterfragt werden. Viele medienpädagogische Studien betonen diese Notwendigkeit gerade vor dem Hintergrund der Entstehung des Netzes: Trotzdem es „aus einem Mischverhältnis von Grundlagen- und militärnaher Forschung [hervorgegangen sei], ist seine Weiterentwicklung grundlegend durch kapitalistische Produktions- und Reproduktionsverhältnisse geprägt" (Dander et al., 2020, S. 28). Aus diesem Grund müsse sowohl bei der Etablierung als auch Analyse digitalisierter Angebote die „kapitalistische Verwertungslogik" (Dander et al., 2020, S. 28) mitgedacht werden.

Im Bereich der Gratisspiele, die hier sehr selektiv auf einen der größten Anbieter reduziert wurden, ist das Ergebnis äußerst ernüchternd. Wovor Freud und Montessori warnten, wird im Netz eindeutig angefacht: Die leuchtenden, „plin-

genden" und vor allem aus Fandoms der Kinder stammenden Dinge fördern den
„Besitztrieb" und lassen durch die grelle Ästhetik und immer gleichen Spielabläufe haptisch und visuell geradezu eine „Sammelwut" entstehen. Trotz der für
die *Kultur der Digitalität* (Stalder, 2016) immer wieder hervorgehobenen Eigenschaften wie freie Vernetzbarkeit, Kollaboration und Vergemeinschaftung im
World Wide Web, zielen diese Angebote für Kinder hauptsächlich auf ein ein-
sames Horten, zum Kauf verführendes Ansammeln und insgesamt stark regu-
lierten Gebrauch der Medien.

Das Sammeln wird daher als große Gefahr des Internets für Kinder gesehen.
Besonders auf Elternforen und digitalen Ratgebern wird neben dem Cyber-
mobbing sowie dem Kontakt mit Pornographie, Rassismus und Gewalt vor allem
vor der Sammelfunktion des World Wide Web gewarnt: Das Netz, das alles
anbieten und gleichzeitig speichern kann, außerdem zum Austausch mit jedem
Menschen und sogar Dingen anrege, wirke auf das Kind extrem zerstreuend und
überfordernd (u.a. www.saferinternet.at/zielgruppen/eltern). Darüber hinaus
führe es dazu, dass die Kinder immer mehr – Input, Likes oder Points – wollten,
was vor allem im Social Net zu Schwierigkeiten führt. Hier sind es die für jeden
sichtbaren Herzen, Smileys und Likes, die ergattert werden müssen und abermals
auf die Sammlung als Selbstvermarktungsinstrument verweisen. Fehlen diese,
kann die Lücke in den virtuellen Sammlungen auch im realen Leben zu großen
Schwierigkeiten führen: Die Kinder fühlen sich ungeliebt, im schlimmsten Fall
gemobbt, und die sozialen Plattformen werden daher von Eltern und Päda-
gog*innen mit großer Sorge betrachtet (u.a. https://www.schau-hin.info/soziale
-netzwerke, 10.1.2022). Auch hier scheint das Sammeln seines eigentlich kreativen, kulturellen Kerns enthoben und wird stattdessen zu einer reinen Tätigkeit
des Hortens, Akkumulierens und Tauschens.

Zu fragen wäre daher, wie und wo tentative, subversive Elemente des Sammelns im Bereich der Medienangebote für Kinder zu finden sind. Denn was bei
den realen Sammlungen der Kinder auffällt, ist neben der „Lust am Anhäufen"
die ebenso große Lust am Umsortieren und Spielen mit den Depots – teilweise
sogar bis zu ihrer Auflösung: „Kinder verabschieden sich damit […] von einer
Phase ihres Aufwachsens und beginnen einen neuen Abschnitt ihres Lebens"
(Duncker et al., 2014, S. 151). Ästhetisches Sammeln ist also im Gegensatz zum
ökonomischen mit Trennungs- und Abschiedsriten verbunden, die wiederum
bildende Transformationsprozesse in Gang setzen. Während diese im Netz zu
fehlen scheinen, geben derzeit populäre Materialsammlungen wie digitale Fan-
Wikis und motivgeschichtliche Archive, wie etwa die Traumsammlungen in der
Kinder- und Jugendliteratur (auf die später Bezug genommen wird) trotz ihrer
Verwertungslogik mehr Raum für ein individuelles und zum Teil auch medien-
kritisches Erkunden.

2. Serielles Sammeln im Kontext populärer Jugendliteratur

Im Bereich der Kinder- und Jugendliteratur werden auf den ersten Blick v. a. Bilderbücher, aufgrund ihrer über den Text hinausgehenden Gestaltung als bildende Kunst, zu potenziellen Sammelobjekten. Diese Art des Sammelns fokussiert das objektzentrierte Begriffsverständnis. Es besteht ein enger Bezug zwischen dem Buch oder dem zu einer erzählten Welt gehörigen Merchandiseprodukt als Sammelobjekt und immateriellen Erfahrungen im Rahmen literarischer Kommunikation rund um Texte bzw. Bücher.

Ernst Seibert hält in Bezug auf das erwachsene Sammeln von (Kinder-)Büchern fest: „Das Kinderbuch als Großgattung bzw. Sparte kann im besten Sinne des Wortes als Gesamtkunstwerk verstanden werden […]. Zumeist ist nicht Kinderliteratur, sondern das Kinderbuch mit seinen Illustrationen Gegenstand des Sammlerinteresses" (Seibert, 2008, S. 26). Daher legt er nahe, dass unter Sammler*innen Jugendbücher nicht hoch im Kurs stehen. Diese Perspektive soll hier ausgeweitet werden, indem gezeigt wird, inwiefern Jugendbücher aus dem Bereich der Populärkultur durchaus „sammelnswerte" Objekt sind und wie von ihnen ausgehend Sammeltätigkeit initiiert werden kann. Als Veranschaulichungsbeispiel dient Material rund um die amerikanische Jugendbuchautorin Holly Black.

Denise Wilde (2015) spricht zwar vom Sammeln als „lebensumspannende[r] Tätigkeit" (S. 64), „[m]it der Pubertät scheint sich das Interesse für das Sammeln jedoch zumeist bzw. zunächst zu ändern. An die Stelle des Sammelns von alltäglichen Objekten tritt vielfach das Sammeln von Materialien aus dem Bereich der Popkultur (z. B. von Musikbands)" (Wilde, 2015, S. 65). Oder, so ist hier zu ergänzen, der populären Jugendliteratur.

Auf der einen Seite steht das materielle Buch selbst im Zentrum. Die von ihm transportierte Narration kann in unterschiedliche „Kleider" gehüllt werden, also in verschiedenen Editionen vorliegen. Diese Praxis des Buchmarkts bedient sich dabei der Grundsatzsäulen des seriellen Erzählens, „Wiederholung" und „Variation" nach Umberto Ecos Ausführungen (1990). Diese sind für den Aufbau von Sammlungen essenziell, wenn unterschiedliche künstlerische Umsetzungen derselben Kategorie von Objekt zusammengetragen werden. Veränderliche Elemente mit Blick auf „das Buch" sind dabei vor allem Einbandgestaltung, Illustration und „Bonusmaterial". Zu letzterem zählen ergänzte Inhalte wie im Lektoratsprozess Gekürztes, das nun doch abgedruckt wird, Interviews mit den Künstler*innen oder ein Auszug aus dem Text, der als nächstes in einer Serie erscheinen wird. Im Fall von Autor*innen populärer Jugendliteratur werden mitunter vor der Veröffentlichung eines neuen Werkes Listen oder Gegenüberstellungen von Editionen auf deren Websites oder Social Media-Kanälen veröffentlicht, die zeigen, welche Editionen welcher Vertriebsplattformen welches Bonusmaterial beinhalten.

2.1 Sondereditionen und Signaturen

Eine eher minimalistische Form stellt die Sonderedition der Buchhandelskette Waterstones von Holly Blacks *How the King of Elfhame Learned to Hate Stories* dar. Sie hebt sich von der Standardausgabe primär durch die Farbgestaltung ab, und ist markiert mit dem Hinweis: „W[aterstones] EXCLUSIVE" (https://www. waterstones.com, 10. 1. 2022). Als Zusatzinformation steht im Beschreibungstext: „includes a black cover and sixteen extra pages of Rovina Cai's art, from original sketches through the draft stages to final artwork that isn't in the book, with discussion by Holly Black. A standard edition is available here" (https://www.wa terstones.com, 10. 1. 2022). Sehr häufig wird die Markierung als Sonderedition auch durch eine gänzlich andere Einbandgestaltung und nicht selten durch Sticker am physischen Buch vorgenommen.

Bei bereits veröffentlichten Texten bieten u. a. Erscheinungsjubiläen oder das Herausbringen von Taschenbuchausgaben mögliche Anlässe, um Neuauflagen mit veränderter Ausstattung auf den Markt zu bringen. Neben dem sehr deutlichen kommerziellen Interesse treiben diese Inhalte den Weltenbau voran und stehen häufig im Kontext von seriellen Erzählungen. Dabei ist auch zu bedenken, dass jene Ausgaben häufig in „Wartezeiten" zwischen Teilen einer Serie publiziert werden. Somit ist eine der Aufgaben dieser Inhalte im Handlungssystem Literatur, Anlass für Anschlusskommunikation als Teil der sozialen Ebene von Lektüreprozessen zu bieten (Rosebrock & Nix, 2014, S. 15). Damit sind sie relevant für das Sammeln als soziale Praxis.

Das gerade gebrachte Beispiel von Waterstones ist mit „sold out. Unfortunately, we don't expect to receive any further stock" (https://www.waterstone s.com, 10. 1. 2022) kommentiert. Da diese Editionen sehr oft schnell vergriffen sind, transportieren sie die Aura seltener, sammelnswerter Objekte. Zudem verweist Holly Blacks Website für signierte Bücher auf eine bestimmte Buchhandlung. Bei der Auflistung ihrer Werke im entsprechenden Webshop findet sich neben einigen der Vermerk „not in stock – hard to find" (https://www.odys seybks.com/holly-black-books, 10. 1. 2022). Auch so können Texte einen Raritätsstatus und damit Sammelwert erhalten.

Im Kontext des materiellen Buches nimmt das signierte Exemplar einen besonderen Platz ein. Aus der Allgemeinliteratur ist dieses Phänomen hinlänglich bekannt und kann auf Jugendliteratur übertragen werden. Der Autor Burkhard Spinnen (2016) spricht in *Das Buch. Eine Hommage* an, dass „die Signatur das Massenprodukt Buch zurück in das Unikat" (S. 61) verwandelt. Spinnen spricht primär von der Bibliothekssignatur, aber auf die Unterschrift oder die Unterschrift in Kombination mit persönlicher Widmung an individuelle Leser*innen trifft die Beobachtung genauso zu.

Plattformen wie *Good choice reading. Virtual signings* vertreiben signierte Exemplare ausgewählter populärer Jugendliteratur. Da diese Angebote exklusiv *vor* dem Erscheinungsdatum angesetzt sind, sind sie klar an ein spezialisiertes Publikum gerichtet. Diese Strategie scheint aufzugehen, da die Edition üblicher Weise zum Zeitpunkt der Publikation bereits vergriffen ist. Eine Unterscheidung zwischen „unterschrieben" und „unterschrieben und gewidmet" sendet graduell abgestufte Exklusivitätssignale; die gewünschte Widmung ist im Bestellprozess in ein Feld einzutragen. Sie steht für eine symbolische Verbindung, die ein Autogramm zwischen individuellen Leser*innen und Autor*innen herstellen kann. Ferner wird bei manchen dieser Angebote die Unterschrift gestempelt oder ein *book plate* beigelegt. Das Exlibris wird hier umgedeutet und zeigt nicht mehr die Besitzverhältnisse des vorliegenden Buches, sondern die Urheber*innenschaftsverhältnisse bzw. Besitzverhältnisse des Inhalts der Texte, also des geistigen Eigentums an. Das Sammelobjekt wird dem Subjekt einverleibt.

Donald Horton und Richard Wohl (2001) sprechen im Kontext von Massenkommunikationsmedien von parasozialer Interaktion, einer Illusion persönlichen Kontaktes, eines Sich-Verbunden-Fühlens über große Distanz hinweg mit Personen des öffentlichen Lebens, die einem eigentlich fremd sind. Diese Beobachtung lässt sich auf den Besitz eines signierten Buches übertragen. So kann es im Kontext mit persönlichen Begegnungen stehen oder in Zeiten der Pandemie mit Online-Events, in deren Ticketpreis der Versand eines signierten Buches inkludiert ist. Hier besteht die Möglichkeit, dass die Sammeltätigkeit zwischen analog und digital changiert und dass mit dem Sammelobjekt das „Sammeln von Erinnerungen oder Erlebnissen" (Wilde, 2015, S. 13) stark verbunden wird. Auch ein ökonomischer Aspekt spielt hier eine Rolle, da für das Buch ebenso wie häufig für Eintritt bezahlt wird und das Handlungssystem Literatur nicht ohne wirtschaftliche Seite gedacht werden kann. In diesem Zusammenhang wird später darauf eingegangen, dass literarische Trauminszenierungen in fantastischer Jugendliteratur keineswegs frei von ökonomischen Logiken sind.

2.2   Unpacking Videos und Merchandisingprodukte

Eine Option zur Präsentation von Sonderausgaben als Sammelobjekte sind Unpacking-Videos, die Anika Ullmann (2016) in ihrem Artikel „Das Bücherregal als Ort der Selbstinszenierung" untersucht. Die oft nach Farbe oder Format zusammengestellten Bücherregale sind hier Kulisse von BookTuber*innen und gleichzeitig Ausstellungsort ihrer Sammlungen. „Vermittelt und gefeiert wird eine Atmosphäre, ein Lebensstil, in der das Medium Buch einen exponierten Status einnimmt, zugleich Lustobjekt und vertrauter Begleiter ist" (Ullmann, 2016, S. 2).

Der Fokus solcher Videos liegt einerseits auf Konsum und Materialität des Buches, dessen Einbandgestaltung und illustrierte Ausstattung oft hervorgehoben wird. Gleichzeitig wird das ökonomische Kapital auch durch soziales und kulturelles ergänzt, wenn über Buchvorstellungen literarisches Wissen demonstriert und vermittelt wird. Beobachtungen zu Sammlungen im Bereich populärer Jugendliteratur schließen also an die identitätsstiftende Funktion an, die bereits für kindliche Sammelaktivitäten hervorgehoben wurde. Jedoch scheint diese Praxis von den gänzlich arbiträren Sammlungen der Kleinen dadurch unterschieden, dass sie Geld kostet, auch wenn das für BookTuber*innen oft nicht zutrifft, da sie vielfach zu Werbezwecken Zusendungen erhalten. Wertet man diese als „Bezahlung," sticht der ökonomische Aspekt hier nochmals deutlicher heraus.

Unpacking-Videos müssen nicht ausschließlich auf das singuläre Buch ausgerichtet sein, sondern beschäftigen sich auch oft mit Bücherboxen. Diese enthalten neben dem Werk, und vielleicht einem gedruckten Autor*innenbrief auch des Öfteren „bookish goodies". Es besteht ein enger Bezug zwischen dem Buch oder dem zu einer erzählten Welt gehörigen Merchandiseprodukt als Sammelobjekt und immateriellen Erfahrungen im Rahmen literarischer Kommunikation rund um Texte bzw. Bücher. Grob lassen sich Merchandise-Produkte, die nicht an Filmadaptionen gebunden sind, sondern rein im Buchkontext stehen, nach eigenen Beobachtungen in folgende Kategorien einteilen: Zum einen (1) Utensilien für das Lesen und Schreiben (Lesezeichen, Stifte etc.), daneben (2) den Leseprozess atmosphärisch Begleitendes, das großteils parallel zum Buch „konsumiert" werden kann (etwa Tee, Naschwerk etc.), oder (3) jegliche Art von Produkt mit Textzitaten (etwa Tassen, Kleidungsstücke etc.) und letztlich (4) von den Texten inspirierte Objekte, die nach Beschreibung in den Narrationen entwickelt werden (etwa bestimmte Nahrungsmittel). Diese Kategorien können natürlich nicht trennscharf voneinander abgegrenzt werden, etwa wäre der Schokofrosch im Kontext der *Harry Potter*-Serie konsumierbar (2) und ist eine Süßigkeit, die in den Romanen beschrieben wird (4).

Für Holly Blacks Erzählwelten gibt es eine Vielzahl an Merchandiseprodukten, beispielsweise mit Zitaten versehene Tassen, bedruckte Stofftaschen, Kerzen und „Plushies", kleine Stofffiguren nach dem Vorbild ihrer Figuren, etwa Jude und Cardan aus der *The Folk of the Air*-Trilogie. Sie verweist auf ihrer Website explizit auf mehrere Anbieter (https://blackholly.com/for-readers/merchandise/, 10.1. 2022). Diese von Texten inspirierten Objekte ordnet Henry Jenkins in seiner Herangehensweise an transmediales Erzählen dem Charakteristikum der „Extractability" zu, die der Immersion gegenübersteht (henryjenkins.org, 10.1.

2022). Beide Konzepte beschreiben das Verhältnis von Lesenden und erzählter Welt im Alltag. Auf die Sammeltätigkeit übertragen gilt abermals eine Gleichzeitigkeit von Objektsammlung und Erfahrungssammlung.

2.3   Zwischen realem und virtuellem Sammeln

„Special Editions" können an der Schwelle zwischen Digitalität und Sammelobjekt stehen. Sie sind einerseits in ihrer Materialität an das physische Objekt Buch gebunden. Sie erhalten aber durch Bonusmaterial-Inhalte, wie die oben erwähnten Interviews oder geschriebene aber letztendlich nicht inkludierte Textpassagen, exklusive Inhalte, bezogen auf die Standardversion des Buches; diese werden aber üblicher Weise (entweder von den Autor*innen selbst oder von Leser*innen) über das World Wide Web zur Verfügung gestellt. Diese Verfügbarkeit, die oft ohne große zeitliche Verzögerung vonstattengeht, ergibt sich primär aus einem Zusammenwirken der Leser*innengemeinschaft, die im Sinne von Henry Jenkins „Convergence Culture" Inhalte als „knowledge community" (Jenkins, 2006, S. 28) zusammenträgt.

Ein anschauliches Beispiel hierfür sind auch Wikis: über die Plattform Fandom.com können nach dem Vorbild von Wikipedia zusammengestellte Wissenswelten zu bestimmten Erzählwelten abgerufen werden, die fast ausschließlich seriell orientiert sind; etwa *Harry Potter* oder *The Folk of the Air*. Ein solches Datensammeln lässt sich mit Duncker als „interessegeleitete Tätigkeit" (Duncker, 2018, S. 96) des Sammelns verstehen, die von Fans als Spezialist*innen zu einem erzählten Universum betrieben wird. Die digitalen Einträge, deren Verfasser*innen auf den Wiki-Seiten nachvollziehbar sind, können durchaus als „Lebensspuren" (Duncker, 2018, S. 101) mit biographischer Relevanz verstanden werden. Schließlich lässt aktive Beteiligung an einer solchen digitalen Sammlung auf die Relevanz des Lesens für die Verfasser*innen schließen. Figuren, Gegenstände und Handlungsstränge werden in vernetzten Beiträgen beschrieben, was immer wieder auch implizite Interpretationsansätze beinhaltet (https://the-folk -of-the-air.fandom.com/wiki/Elfhame, 10.1.2022). Die seriellen Erzählungen werden so zu digitalen Wunderkammern, in denen eine literarische Welt bestaunt werden kann. Bildung als Aspekt steht kaum im Vordergrund, aber in Fangemeinschaften als Gemeinschaften von Sammler*innen findet „eine kommunikative Wissensgenese und ein Wissensaustausch [statt], die sich aus der Beschäftigung der Sammler/-innen mit den Objekten, einem Wissen über das Gesammelte sowie einem Wissen um die Bedeutung des Gesammelten speisen." (Wilde, 2015, S. 15) Weltaneignung durch Sammeltätigkeit ist hier einerseits die Aneignung der erzählten Welt, aber auch im Sinne literarischer Kompetenz das Reflektieren der extratextuellen Realität anhand der erzählten Wirklichkeit.

3.   Traumarchive in der jüngeren kinder- und jugendliterarischen Fantastik

In der historischen Kinderliteratur lassen sich kindliche Träume häufig als Platzhalter für die kindliche Fantasietätigkeit lesen. Träumen betont die Opposition von kindlicher Fantasie und erwachsener Rationalität, wie schon in E.T.A. Hoffmanns *Nußknacker und Mausekönig* (1816), oder aber Lewis Carrolls *Alice's Adventures in Wonderland* (1865), den Pionieren kinderliterarischer Trauminszenierungen und der kinderliterarischen Fantastik. Diese Eigenschaft weisen auch aktuelle fantastische Traumerzählungen auf, wobei in diesen – wie sich noch zeigen wird – dem Aspekt des Sammelns eine bedeutsame Funktion zukommt. Zudem werden die kinderliterarischen Träume nicht mehr nur darauf reduziert, fantastische Ereignisse innerhalb der erzählten Wirklichkeit zu legitimieren, wie etwa in den *Alice*-Texten.

Zudem weisen Träume und Medien eine gemeinsame Schnittmenge auf. So gleicht die sinnliche, vornehmlich visuelle Erfahrung von Traumerlebnissen dem Konsum von Medieninhalten, was etwa am Beispiel der auffälligen Parallelen von Kinobesuchen und Traumaktivitäten bereits wissenschaftlich untersucht und belegt wurde (Stelte, 2018, S. 142–144.). Auch lässt sich Träumen ein gewisser Konstruktionscharakter attestieren, da diese sich gemäß Freud aus einer Melange von Tagesresten, also kürzlich Erlebtem, der Einschlafsituation und -haltung, sowie im Wachen unterdrückten Wünschen und Trieben speisen (Freud, 2005, S. 38f.). Diese komplexen Konstrukte sind eng mit der Persönlichkeit der Träumenden verbunden und können als Bausteine der als fragmentarisch verstandenen modernen Identität aufgefasst werden. Überdies weisen Träume nicht nur Bezüge zum Medium und zur modernen Identität auf, sondern auch zur Mediennutzung, die – insbesondere in Social-Media-Kanälen – darauf ausgerichtet ist, auch das höchst Private zu teilen (Ernst, 2012, S. 313). Während die individuellen visuellen Erlebnisse des Traumes innerhalb der außerliterarischen Realität nur dann zum Gegenstand der Betrachtung und zur Grundlage einer Kommunikation mit Anderen werden, wenn sie nach dem Aufwachen schriftlich fixiert oder verbal veräußert wurden (Alt, 2002, S. 19), ermöglicht es die fantastische Literatur den Figuren, diese Erlebnisse im Sinne eines Multi-Player-Spiels gemeinsam zu erfahren. Das kollektive Traumerlebnis ist nicht nur in Kerstin Giers *Silber*-Trilogie (2013–2015) das handlungstragende Motiv, auch in anderen fantastischen Texten wird das gemeinsame Träumen und das Eintauchen in fremde Träume leitmotivisch inszeniert. So kann der 12jährige *Traumspringer* Leo in Alex Rühles gleichnamigem Roman (2019) mühelos in die Träume anderer Figuren gleiten und der 13-jährige Protagonist Frederic aus Antonia Michaelis' *Die Nacht der gefangenen Träume* (2008) in die Traumsammlung seines Schuldirektors eintauchen und Gespräche mit den personifizierten Träumen seiner Mitschüler*innen und Lehrkräfte führen. In Ralf Isaus *Das Geheimnis der versteinerten Träume* (2011) werden Träume von jugendlichen, besonders begabten Träumenden künstlich erzeugt, modifiziert und gemäß den individuellen Wünschen zahlungskräftiger Kund*innen sogar vermarktet. Der Slogan der literarischen Traumfabrik, „Schlafen war gestern, heute ist YourDream" (Isau, 2011, S. 24), verspricht individualisierte Traumerlebnisse, die mit persönlichen Bildern der Kund*innen verknüpft werden und auf eine „Dream-Cap" heruntergeladen werden können. Auch in Rühles *Traumspringer* werden Träume aus ökonomischen Gründen gesammelt. Diese aktuellen literarischen Trauminszenierungen erweisen sich demnach keineswegs als frei von ökonomischen Logiken. Sie sind an die aktuellen Lebenswelten der jugendlichen Zielgruppe angepasst und erweitern die tradierte Verwendung des Traummotivs als Legitimierung fantastischer Ereignisse, um einen zum Medium avancierten literarischen Traum, der als Mittel der Gesellschafts- und insbesondere Medienkritik Verwendung findet.

Die gemeinsame Schnittmenge von literarischen Träumen und Medien bzw. Mediennutzung wird hier besonders deutlich. Dem Aspekt des Sammelns als mediale Praxis kommt in diesem Zusammenhang eine besondere Bedeutung zu, wie sich noch zeigen wird. Bei den Sammelpraktiken, die in *Traumspringer, Die Nacht der gefangenen Träume* und *Die Traummaschine* geschildert werden, geht es demnach nicht um eine harmlose jugendliche Freizeitaktivität, die eine ausgeprägte Leidenschaft für bestimmte Gegenstände zum Ausdruck bringt, sondern um antagonistische Aktivitäten, die den Selbstfindungsprozess der Figuren maßgeblich beeinflussen und mitunter sogar bedrohen. Diese drei Romane erfüllen auch Kriterien des Adoleszenzromans; wobei die klassischen Kategorien dieser Textsorte dadurch erweitert werden, dass die moderne jugendliche Identität als fragmentarisch wahrgenommen bzw. als solche inszeniert wird. Die literarischen Träume der kindlichen und jugendlichen Figuren können als ein Baustein dieser fragmentarischen, fluiden modernen Identität aufgefasst werden. Gleichzeitig wird das Handeln im Traum als mediales Handeln inszeniert, das Analogien zum virtuellen Spiel aufweist und zur Aneignung von spezifischen Fähigkeiten beiträgt. So lassen die aktuellen literarischen Darstellungen das Träumen als mediale Kompetenz in einem surrealen Raum erscheinen und betonen die enge Verknüpfung des individuellen Traummaterials mit der adoleszenten Persönlichkeit.

3.1   Psychoanalytische Deutung fantastischer Traumarchive

Die in den berücksichtigten fantastischen Erzählungen geschilderten Sammelaktivitäten lassen sich der Kategorie des immateriellen Sammelns von Erlebnissen und Erinnerungen zuordnen (Wilde, 2015, S. 13). Die Motivation für diese
Praktiken ist ebenso individuell und wandelbar wie die mit den Träumen verbundenen Erinnerungen und (mitunter traumatischen) Erlebnisse der Figuren.
So verfolgt der Schuldirektor Bruhns in *Die Nacht der gefangenen Träume* mit
seiner Traumsammlung zunächst eine ganz persönliche Bewältigungs- bzw.
Verdrängungsstrategie. Doch nachdem es ihm gelungen ist, eine Maschine zu
entwickeln, mit der er sich seiner persönlichen Angstträume entledigt, in welchen er mit dem rigorosen Leistungsdruck von Seiten seines Vaters konfrontiert
wird, verändert sich seine Persönlichkeit maßgeblich, was erst am Ende des
Romans aufgedeckt wird. Ohne die stetige nächtliche Konfrontation mit seinen
Kindheitsängsten und Minderwertigkeitskomplexen, übernimmt er Eigenschaften seines Vaters und beschließt, auch seine Schüler*innenschaft ihrer
Träume zu berauben, um sie zu gehorsamen Zöglingen zu modifizieren. Der 13-
jährige Protagonist Frederic entgeht diesen nächtlichen Überfällen, da er aufgrund des Verlusts seiner Mutter Stacheln am ganzen Körper trägt. Diese kann
nur seine Freundin Änna sehen, nachdem er sie mit einer „Vitamin A-Tinktur"
versorgt hat, die ihm eine alte Dame gegeben hat, die sich als der Traumsammlung entflohener personifizierter Traum entpuppt.

Die Motivation für die Traumsammlung des Direktors scheint demnach
durchaus mit einer Obsession im Freud'schen Sinne vergleichbar (Freud, 1962,
S. 101). Auch kann die Figur als Neurotiker gelesen werden, wobei Bruhns keineswegs einen libidinösen Fetisch gegenüber seiner Traumsammlung entwickelt, sondern auf deren endgültige Vernichtung sinnt. Frederic erkennt, dass er
den Direktor mit seinen Angstträumen konfrontieren muss, um den Kreis zu
durchbrechen und die Vernichtung der Träume zu verhindern. Sofern man die
verbannten Angstträume als Schatten im Jung'schen Sinne liest, d. h. als unerwünschte und womöglich abgespaltene Anteile der Persönlichkeit, böte sich eine
tiefenpsychologische Deutung unter Zuhilfenahme des Jung'schen Individua-
tionsmodells an (Jung, 1968). Erstaunlicherweise kreist dieser jugendliterarische
Text nicht um die bedrohte und schließlich gelingende Individuation des Protagonisten, sondern um die Aussöhnung mit und Integration von als negativ
empfundenen Persönlichkeitsanteilen einer erwachsenen Figur. Die erfolgreiche
Läuterung wird dadurch markiert, dass sich der Direktor als Erzähler der Geschichte zu erkennen gibt.

Dass sich psychoanalytische und tiefenpsychologische Lesarten anbieten,
wenn es um Traumdarstellungen geht, sollte nicht verwundern. Auch in den
anderen Erzählungen werden diese nahegelegt, nicht nur da es um Träume – den

„Königsweg zum Unbewussten" im Freud'schen Sinne – geht, sondern auch, weil das Motiv des geraubten Traumes häufig mit anderen fundamentalen Verlusterfahrungen verknüpft ist. Die Traumsammlungen sind folglich Ersatzleistungen, wie in der gegenwärtigen Psychoanalyse festgehalten. Sie dienen dem Zweck, Verlust und Vergänglichkeit einzudämmen und das Ich zu stärken.

Die emotionalen Schmerzen, die Frederic durch den Tod seiner Mutter erleidet, sind als Stacheln auf seinem Körper lesbar bzw. für andere sichtbar. Auch in Carolyn Comans *Die Traum-Maschine* (2011) geht es nicht nur um die Überwachung und Sammlung fremden Traummaterials, sondern auch um den Verlust der kleinen Schwester der Protagonistin Hope, die von den Eltern am Straßenrand ausgesetzt wird. Hope wird infolgedessen von den Eltern befohlen, die Existenz ihrer kleinen Schwester zu vergessen, an die sie sich folglich nur noch in ihren Träumen erinnern kann. Diese werden von Mitarbeitenden der „Traum-Bank" überwacht, gesammelt und erforscht. Im Schlaf- bzw. Traumlabor der Traum-Bank gelingt es Hope schließlich, die verlorene Schwester wiederzufinden. Die Motivation der Mitarbeitenden der Traum-Bank für ihre Sammlung von Träumen entspricht, ganz im Gegensatz zu den bereits geschilderten Absichten des Schuldirektors in *Die Nacht der gefangenen Träume*, den Überlegungen Wildes zum Sammeln von materiellen Gegenständen, da sich auch hier „eine kommunikative Wissensgenese und ein Wissensaustausch [vollziehen], die sich aus der Beschäftigung der Sammler*innen mit den Objekten, einem Wissen über das Gesammelte sowie einem Wissen um die Bedeutung des Gesammelten speisen" (Wilde, 2015, S. 15). Hier dominiert dementsprechend die Absicht der Wissensaneignung. Der Aspekt der Wissenschaftlichkeit wird überdies durch den Einsatz von Technik bzw. Maschinen unterstrichen. Diese Technisierung verleiht den Texten einen gewissen Science-Fiction-Charakter, lässt sich jedoch auch auf aktuelle außerliterarische Forschungsprojekte beziehen, in denen die Kommunikation mit Schlafenden und zwischen Schlafenden erforscht wird. (Oldis, 2018, S. 356f.).

Im letzten Beispiel, Alex Rühles *Traumspringer,* werden die als sammlungswürdige Medien begriffenen Träume mit mythologischen Konnotationen des Traums und Träumens verbunden. Der 12-jährige Protagonist Leon trifft in einem Traum auf drei uralte Schwestern, die unter seiner Schule unzählige in Gläsern konservierte Träume sammeln. „Was macht ihr hier?" (Rühle, 2019, S. 111), fragt Leon, woraufhin die drei Schwestern antworten: „Sammeln, sammeln, sammeln," (Rühle, 2019, S. 111), „Jede Nacht?" fragt er wieder. „Aber ja. Aber jaaa." (Rühle, 2019, S. 111) lautet die Antwort. Die hier geschilderte Sammelwut (das Traum-Depot unter Leons Schule ist nur eines von vielen) ist weder mit kompensatorischen Absichten noch mit dem Motiv der Wissensaneignung verbunden; angespielt wird hier zunächst auf die griechische Mythologie. Schließlich bittet Morpheus, der griechische Gott der Träume, höchst selbst den begabten Traumspringer Leon um Hilfe, da sein Bruder Krato, ein Dämon, Träume aus seiner Traumsammlung entwendet. Während Morpheus, dem griechischen Mythos entsprechend, Leon zunächst in Fledermausgestalt begegnet, handelt es sich bei Krato um keinen der im Mythos genannten, mit ihm verwandten Traumdämonen. Diese Figur erweist sich als von aktuellen gesellschaftlichen Bildern geprägt. Sein Interesse an den Traumarchiven, die die drei Schwestern um Morpheus sammeln, weil sie diese für besonders wertvoll und erhaltenswert erachten, ist primär ökonomisch motiviert. Er finanziert ein neuartiges Smartphone-Spiel, das die Spielenden mit individuellen Angsttraumszenarien konfrontiert, um sie final mit einem ganz persönlichen Wunschtraum zu belohnen. „Alle zehn Level kriegt jeder Spieler seinen persönlichen Glückstraum. Aber Angst und Schrecken verkaufen sich viel besser als Glück und Zufriedenheit. Deshalb brauche ich für das Spiel die tiefsten, dunkelsten Ängste meiner Schläfer" (Rühle, 2019, S. 224f.), erklärt Krato. Er entführt Menschen, um in einem geheimen Schlaflabor Angst- und Wunschträume zu produzieren und für sein Spiel nutzbar zu machen, indem er die Traum-Gläser zu Smartphone-Displays verarbeitet. Bei einer Werbeveranstaltung für das Smartphone-Spiel heißt es: „Sie werden nicht mehr wissen, wo die Wirklichkeit aufhört und das Spiel anfängt. Wie in Ihren intensivsten Träumen in der Nacht." (Rühle, 2019, S. 152) So gelangt insbesondere anhand dieses Beispiels der Bezug zu aktuellen Medienpraktiken der zeitgenössischen jugendlichen Leserschaft zur Darstellung, da der Traum und das (virtuelle) Spielen enggeführt werden.

3.2   Zum „Wesen" der materialisierten und mitunter personifizierten Träume

Der Umstand, dass die materialisierten Träume in Bibliotheks-ähnlichen Archiven gelagert und konserviert werden, macht den erzählten Traum mit Büchern und deren Archivierung vergleichbar. Die wissenschaftlichen Ausführungen zur literarischen Darstellung von Bibliotheken als Inszenierung von Wissensbeständen (Rieger, 2002, S. 19), aber auch „des narrativen Vergessens" (Hölter, 2008, S. 81) lässt sich folglich auf die hier in den Blick genommenen Traumarchive übertragen. Das fragile und flüchtige Traummaterial erweist sich als ebenso schützenswert und vergänglich wie die zwischen den Buchdeckeln konservierten Narrationen. Auch wenn die in den Blick genommenen Traumarchive Ähnlichkeiten aufweisen, wird das hier konservierte Material ganz unterschiedlich inszeniert. So kann sich Frederic in *Die Nacht der gefangenen Träume* mit personifizierten Träumen austauschen und diese sogar um Hilfe bitten. Auch haben die Träume hier Namen und können wachsen, wenn sie ungestört sind, aber auch schrumpfen, wenn sie mit einer autoritären Stimme aus einem Tonband konfrontiert werden. Einigen gelingt die Flucht aus der Gefangenschaft und sie beginnen ein Leben unter den Menschen, wie etwa Frederics ältere Nachbarin, die ihn mit „Vitamin A" versorgt. Erstaunlicherweise können die Träume auch in Hungerstreik treten und sterben (Michaelis, 2014, S. 233).

Im Unterschied hierzu werden die Traumgegenstände der Sammlung in *Traumspringer* lediglich als pulsierendes milchiges Licht (Rühle, 2019, S. 125) geschildert, das in Gläsern konserviert wird. Wenn die Gläser poliert werden, kann die bzw. der Betrachtende den jeweiligen Traum am Grund des Glases sehen (Rühle, 2019, S. 110). Inspiriert haben könnte Rühle dazu Roald Dahls Erzählung *Sophiechen und der Riese* (1982), da auch hier von einer in Gläsern archivierten Traumsammlung die Rede ist. Diese als „Traumothek" bezeichnete Sammlung dient dem Zweck der Archivierung, aber auch der Kombination, da verschiedene Träume auf Wunsch vermischt werden können, um einen „Wunschtraum" zu erzeugen, den der gute Riese auf Sophies Wunsch hin der Königin einhaucht. So erfährt diese von der Existenz gefährlicher Menschenfresserriesen und lässt diese unschädlich machen (Steinlein, 2008, S. 82).

In *Traumspringer* erfahren Träume keine Personifizierung, allerdings werden sie als Handlungsort viel relevanter als in den anderen Texten, da es Leon nur im Traum gelingt, die Machenschaften Kratos zu vereiteln; nicht nur, weil Morpheus ihn darum bittet, seinem Bruder Einhalt zu gebieten, sondern auch, weil er ein ganz persönliches Anliegen damit verbindet, denn die kleine Schwester seines Freundes wurde entführt und befindet sich nun unter den Schlafenden im Labor. Auch hier werden die antagonistischen Sammelaktivitäten demnach mit persönlichen Verlusterfahrungen und existenziellen Ängsten der jugendlichen Figuren verbunden.

Was die Motivation für diese fantastische Traumsammlung betrifft, werden zwei höchst unterschiedliche Absichten deutlich. Morpheus erweist sich als Wächter vergessener Träume im antiken, mythologischen Sinne, während die obsessiven Sammelaktivitäten seines Bruders Krato primär ökonomisch geleitet sind. So betont die Schwester Ombra, dass er vor allem „Geld. Ruhm. Den ganzen Unsinn, hinter dem die Menschheit herjagt" (Steinlein, 2008, S. 82), anstrebe. Deutlich wird an dieser Stelle, dass die geschilderten Sammelaktivitäten auch eine gesellschaftskritische Dimension aufweisen.

3.3   Zum Zweck der literarischen Traumarchive

So mannigfaltig die geschilderte Motivation für die jeweilige Traumsammlung in den berücksichtigten fantastischen Texten ausfällt, ist doch ein gemeinsamer Kern mit der Absicht, Träume zu konservieren und mitunter zu erforschen, verbunden: unterstreichen doch sämtliche Sammlungen die besondere Wertigkeit des konservierten Gegenstandes bzw. Mediums. Die Sammler*innen und

Wächter*innen der literarischen Träume bringen dies auf unterschiedliche Weise zum Ausdruck.

> „[I]ch weiß, dass ihr Menschen eure Träume dringend braucht. Ihr habt keine Ahnung, wie wichtig sie für euch sind. Weil ihr sie tagsüber vergesst. Dabei ist es, als hätte jeder von euch einen Schatz unter seinem Haus liegen. So was wie eure heimliche Fußbodenheizung. Die ist unsichtbar. Aber ihr wärmt euch trotzdem daran. Genauso wärmt sich euer Leben auch an euren Träumen." (Rühle, 2019, S. 162)

Der Schuldirektor Bruhns, der in Michaelis' *Die Nacht der gefangenen Träume* die Träume der Schüler*innenschaft und der Lehrkräfte absaugt und diese durch Pudding ersetzt, erklärt dieses Bemühen damit, dass Träume „der Nährboden für eigene Ideen" (Michaelis, 2014, S.192) seien. „Wenn er sie stiehlt, [folgert Frederic] hat er lauter brave Kinder" (Michaelis, 2014, S.192), die nur noch von Pudding träumen. Die ihrer Träume beraubten Figuren werden als willen- und fantasielose Wesen dargestellt. Hier offenbart sich die bereits angesprochene Betonung der Opposition von kindlicher Fantasie und erwachsener Rationalität, die in Traumerzählungen noch immer präsent ist.

Durch die Sammelaktivitäten der Antagonisten und die hiermit verbundene Gesellschafts- bzw. Medienkritik wird zu Reflexionen über den Wert von Träumen innerhalb einer mediatisierten Kultur angeregt. Auf der Textebene wird der mit den Träumen verbundene Nutzen sowohl auf ihre kathartische Funktion im Sinne Jungs (1968, S. 50) bezogen, aber auch die Gefahr angesprochen, diese ideellen Wertgegenstände zu missbrauchen und zu kommerzialisieren. Auch hierin kommt die mit den geschilderten Sammelaktivitäten verbundene Medienkritik zum Ausdruck, mit der an die Ausführungen zur „Gefahr" der „Sammelwut" und dem „Besitztrieb" erinnert sei. Während sich dieser Effekt ausschließlich am Beispiel der erwachsenen Antagonisten beobachten lässt, wird die Leserschaft durch das Schicksal der jugendlichen Figuren dazu angeregt, über die identitätsbildende und kreative Funktion der Sammlungsgegenstände bzw. -medien zu reflektieren.

4. Fazit

Die verschiedenen analogen und abstrakten Wunderkammern von Kindern und Jugendlichen lassen sich somit hinsichtlich ihrer sozialen Verflechtungen und Erkenntnismöglichkeiten als wichtige Komponenten für die Gestaltung des (medialen) Lebens beschreiben: Neben der Erkenntnistätigkeit mit Analyse- und Reflexionsmomenten ist die ästhetische Komponente mit der Artikulation von sinnlichen und magischen Bedeutungsgehalten, von Gefühlen, Träumen und Wünschen von Bedeutung. Ästhetisches Empfinden und Kreativität eröffnen

Räume der Fantasie. Sie schaffen einen Zugang zu neuen Welten, in denen der Pragmatismus einer auf der einen Seite stehenden objektiven, rationalen (Welt-) Ordnung und auf der anderen Seite stehenden subjektiven Sinnbildung überwunden wird. Eine vieldimensionale und variantenreiche, gegenständliche, soziale und symbolisch geprägte Wirklichkeit tritt zutage. Im Gegensatz zu den in den Blick genommenen digitalen Spielangeboten für Kinder weisen die realen wie erzählten Bucharchive eine ästhetische Akzentuierung auf, die das breite Spektrum literarischer Inszenierungen sowohl realer als auch fiktiver Sammlungsgegenstände veranschaulicht.

Primärmedien

Black, H. (2020). *How the King of Elfhame Learned to Hate Stories.* Little, Brown Books for Young Readers.

Black, H. (2018). *The Cruel Prince: The Folk of the Air 1.* Little, Brown Books for Young Readers.

Black, H. (2019). *The Wicked King: The Folk of the Air 2.* Little, Brown Books for Young Readers.

Black, H. (2019). *Queen of Nothing: The Folk of the Air 3.* Little, Brown Books for Young Readers.

Carroll, L. (1992). *Alice's Adventures in Wonderland.* William Morrow.

Coman, C. (2011). *Die Traum-Maschine.* (K. Kreuzer, Übersetzung). Dressler.

Dahl, R. (2016). *Sophiechen und der Riese.* (A. Quidam, Übersetzung). Rowohlt.

Gier, K. (2013). *Silber: Das erste Buch der Träume.* Fischer.

Gier, K. (2014). *Silber: Das zweite Buch der Träume.* Fischer.

Gier, K. (2015). *Silber: Das dritte Buch der Träume.* Fischer.

Hoffmann, E. T. A. (2006). *Nussknacker und Mausekönig.* Reclam.

Isau, R. (2011). *Das Geheimnis der versteinerten Träume.* cbj.

Michaelis, A. (2014). *Die Nacht der gefangenen Träume* (3. Auflage). Oetinger.

Rühle, A. (2019). *Traumspringer.* dtv.

Sekundärliteratur

Alt, P. (2002). *Der Schlaf der Vernunf: Literatur und Traum in der Kulturgeschichte der Neuzeit.* C.H.Beck.

Baudrillard, J. (1991). *Das System der Dinge: Über unser Verhältnis zu den alltäglichen Gegenständen.* Campus.

Beßler, G. (2012). *Wunderkammern – Weltmodelle von der Renaissance bis zur Kunst der Gegenwart.* Reimer.

Black, H. (n.d.). *Merchandise.* https://blackholly.com/for-readers/merchandise.

Dander, V., Bettinger, P., Ferraro, E., Leineweber, C. & Rummler, K. (Hrsg.). (2020). *Digitalisierung – Subjekt – Bildung: Kritische Betrachtungen der digitalen Transformation*. Barbara Budrich.

Duncker, L. (2018). *Wege zur ästhetischen Bildung: Anthropologische Grundlegung und schulpädagogische Orientierungen*. kopaed.

Duncker, L., Hahn, & K., Heyd, C. (2014). *Wenn Kinder sammeln: Begegnungen in der Welt der Dinge*. Klett.

Duncker, L., Frohberg, & M., Zierfuss, M. (1999). Sammeln als ästhetische Praxis des Kindes: Eine Befragung Leipziger Grundschulkinder. In N. Neuß (Hrsg.), *Ästhetik der Kinder: Interdisziplinäre Beiträge zur ästhetischen Erfahrung von Kindern* (S. 63–82). Gemeinschaftswerk der Evang. Publizistik.

Eco, U. (1990). Serialität im Universum der Kunst und der Massenmedien. In U. Eco (Ed.), *Im Labyrinth der Vernunft. Texte über Kunst und Zeichen* (S. 301–324). Reclam.

Ernst, T. (2012). Wer hat Angst vor Goethes Page Rank? In M. Beilein, S. Winko, & C. Stockinger (Hrsg.), *Kanon, Wertung und Vermittlung. Literatur in der Wissensgesellschaft* (S. 313–319). De Gruyter.

Fandom. (n.d.). Elfhame. The Folk of the air. https://the-folk-of-the-air.fandom.com/wiki/Elfhame.

Feil C., Decker, R., & Gieger C. (2004). *Wie entdecken Kinder das Internet? Beobachtungen bei 5- bis 12-jährigen Kindern*. Verlag für Sozialwissenschaften.

Freud, S. (1962). *Aus den Anfängen der Psychoanalyse. Briefe an Wilhelm Fließ: Abhandlungen und Notizen aus den Jahren 1887–1902*. Fischer.

Freud, S. (2000). Charakter und Analerotik. In S. Freud (Hrsg.), *Studienausgabe: Zwang, Paranoia, Perversion* (S. 25–30). Fischer.

Freud, S. (2005). *Die Traumdeutung* (12. Auflage). Fischer.

Hoins, K., & v. Mallinkrodt, F. (2015). Macht. Wissen, Teilhabe. Koordinaten zur Einführung. In K. Hoins & F. v. Mallinkrodt (Hrsg.), *Macht. Wissen. Teilhabe. Sammlungsinstitutionen im 21. Jahrhundert* (S. 9–20). transcript.

Hölter, A. (2008). Amnesien auf dem Zauberberg und anderswo: Überlegungen zu einer Poetik des narrativen Vergessens. In F. Bolln, S. Elpers, & S. Scheid (Hrsg.), *Europäische Memoiren. Mémoires européen* (S. 81–108). Vandenhoeck und Ruprecht unipress.

Horton, D., & Wohl, R. (2001). Massenkommunikation und parasoziale Interaktion: Beobachtungen zur Intimität über Distanz. In R. Adelmann (Hrsg.), *Grundlagentexte zur Fernsehwissenschaft. Theorie – Geschichte – Analyse* (S. 74–103). UVK-Verl.-Ges.

Jenkins, H. (2006). *Convergence Culture: Where Old and New Media Collide*. New York University Press.

Jenkins, H. (2009, 9.12.). *Revenge of the Origami Unicorn: The Remaining Four Principles of Transmedia Storytelling*. http://henryjenkins.org/blog/2009/12/revenge_of_the_origami_unicorn.html.

Jones, E. (1919). Über analerotische Charakterzüge. *Internationale Zeitschrift für Psychoanalyse, 5*(2), 69–92.

Jung, C. G. (1968). *Der Mensch und seine Symbole*. Olten.

Montessori, M. (1999 [1952]). *Kinder sind anders*. dtv.

Odyssey Bookshop (n.d.). Holly Black Books. https://www.odysseybks.com/holly-black-books.

Oldis, D. (2018). Die neuen coolen Medien der Träume. In A. Krovoza & C. Walde (Hrsg.), *Traum und Schlaf: Ein interdisziplinäres Handbuch* (S. 350–362). Büchner.

Pomian, K. (1994). Sammlungen – eine historische Typologie. In A. Grote (Hrsg.), *Macrocosmos in Microcosmo. Die Welt in der Stube. Zur Geschichte des Sammelns 1450 bis 1800* (S. 107–26). Springer.

Rieger, D. (2002). *Imaginäre Bibliotheken: Bücherwelten in der Literatur.* Fink.

Rosebrock, D., & Nix, D. (2014). *Grundlagen der Lesedidaktik und der systematischen schulischen Leseförderung* (7. Auflage). Schneider Verlag Hohengehren.

Saferinternet.at. Das Internet sicher nutzen! Europäische Union (Digital Europe (DEP)), Bundesministerium für Bildung, Wissenschaft und Forschung, Bundeskanzleramt, Bundesministerium für Digitalisierung und Wirtschaftsstandort, A1, Facebook. Retrieved January 17, 2023, from: www.saferinternet.at

SCHAU HIN! Was Dein Kind mit Medien macht. Bundesministeriums für Familie, Senioren, Frauen und Jugend, der öffentlich-rechtlichen Sender Das Erste und ZDF sowie des AOK-Bundesverbands. Retrieved January 17, 2023, from: https://www.schau-hin.info/soziale-netzwerke.

Seibert, E. (2008). *Themen, Stoffe und Motive in der Literatur für Kinder und Jugendliche.* Facultas.

Sommer, M. (2011). Eine Phänomenologie des Sammelns und des Sammlers. In H. Jocks (Hrsg.), *KUNSTFORUM international: Die heilige Macht der Sammler II. 211* (Oktober-November 2011), 38-49.

Spinnen, B. (2016). *Das Buch: Eine Hommage.* Schöffling.

Stalder, F. (2016). *Kultur der Digitalität.* Suhrkamp.

Steinlein, R. (2008). „eigentlich sind es nur Träume." Der Traum als Motiv und Narrativ in märchenhaft-phantastischer Kinderliteratur von E. T. A. Hoffmann bis Paul Maar. *Zeitschrift für Germanistik, 18*(1), 72–86. http://www.jstor.org/stable/23978587.

Stelte, I. (2018). Film. In A. Krovoza & C. Walde (Hrsg.), *Traum und Schlaf: Ein interdisziplinäres Handbuch* (S. 142–152). Metzler.

Ströer Media Brands GmbH. (n.d). SpieleAffe, https://www.spielaffe.de/.

Subkowski, P. (2006). On the psychodynamics of collecting. *The International Journal of Psychoanalysis, 87* (2), 383-401.

Tesan, H. (2011). Vom Sammeln. Gesammelte Aspekte einer Kulturtechnik. In M. Strobel & A. Dippel (Hrsg.), *Die Kunst des Sammelns: Phänomene des Ordnens, Archivierens und Präsentierens* (S. 11–20). Kunstvilla.

Ullmann, A. (2016). Das Bücherregal als Ort der Selbstinszenierung. *Buch & Maus, 3,* 2–4.

Waterstones. (n.d.). How the king of elfhame learned to hate stories. www.waterstones.com/book/how-the-king-of-elfhame-learned-to-hate-stories/holly-black/rovina-cai/97814 71410482.

Wilde, D. (2015). *Dinge sammeln: Annäherungen an eine Kulturtechnik.* transkript.

Suzana Jovicic

"I can see it in your eyes – you will become a gardener" – An ethnographic approach to the limits of empowerment through digital literacy among marginalised youth in Vienna

Abstract

As digitalisation seeps into homes, offices, and factories, disadvantaged youth are often portrayed as the losers of the digital transformation in the widespread representations of digital literacy and digital empowerment. Various studies indicate that young people with limited socio-economic resources and lower formal education are generally less able to use digital technologies strategically and productively for educational and professional purposes. Similarly, the Austrian digital curriculum presents digital literacy as a means to enable students to access "promising occupational fields". However, if their ideological underpinnings remain unquestioned, such benevolent measures may reinforce the implicit notion that young people are responsible for freeing themselves from professional constraints by applying digital skills that are considered productive and efficient in their leisure time. Building on the author's ethnographic research in youth centres, schools, and youth coaching facilities in Vienna between 2018 and 2022, this contribution complicates the story of seemingly deficient digital practices of young people negotiating unemployment, fragmented biographies, poverty, discrimination, a stratified school system, and limited career choices. It is argued that digital literacy comes in many forms and is interwoven with profound socio-political and economic exclusions of the "invisible children" (Lemish, 2021) of the Global North; exclusions that are neither caused by a lack of digital literacy alone nor can they be solved by "proficient" and "productive" digital practices that would seem strangely out of place.

Während die Digitalisierung in Lebens- und Arbeitswelten Einzug hält, werden benachteiligte Jugendliche in den "digital empowerment" Narrativen häufig als Verlierer*innen des digitalen Wandels dargestellt. Dabei stellen diverse Studien fest, dass junge Menschen mit begrenzten sozioökonomischen Ressourcen und geringer formaler Bildung tendenziell weniger in der Lage sind, digitale Technologien strategisch und produktiv für Bildungs- und Berufszwecke zu nutzen. Auch das österreichische digitale Curriculum (2018) präsentiert digitale Kompetenzen als Mittel, um Schüler*innen den Zugang zu "vielversprechenden Berufsfeldern" zu ermöglichen. Wenn ihre ideologischen Grundlagen jedoch unhinterfragt bleiben, können solche Maßnahmen die impliziten Annahmen verstärken, dass junge Menschen dafür verantwortlich sind sich "aus der Armut zu googeln", indem sie digitale Fähigkeiten, die als produktiv gelten, in ihrer Freizeit anwenden. Aufbauend auf der ethnografischen Feldforschung der Autorin in Wiener Jugendzentren, Schulen und

Jugendcoaching-Einrichtungen zwischen 2018 und 2022 verkompliziert dieser Beitrag das Narrativ der scheinbar defizitären digitalen Praktiken junger Menschen im Kontext von Arbeitslosigkeit, fragmentierten Biografien, Armut, Diskriminierung, stratifiziertem Schulsystem und begrenzten Berufswahlmöglichkeiten. Es wird argumentiert, dass digitale Kompetenz viele Formen hat und mit tiefgreifenden sozio-politischen und ökonomischen Exklusionen der "unsichtbaren Kinder" (Lemish, 2021) verwoben ist; Exklusionen, die weder durch einen Mangel an digitaler Kompetenz allein verursacht werden noch durch "produktive" digitale Praktiken gelöst werden können.

1.   Introduction

A few days before starting his apprenticeship as a gardener in Vienna, the 16-year-old Can[1] explained his choice:

> I can only be gardener or carpenter. I would rather be a carpenter, but you need math for that. And my teacher said to me, 'I can see it in your eyes – you're going to be a gardener'. My brother is also a gardener. Actually, I wanted to be an electrical engineer. I can do many things, I can even fix my own smartphone. But for that, I need math and a HTL [high school with a technical focus], so I can't do that. (Fieldnotes, 05.06.2019)

Can, like many visitors to the Viennese youth centers where I conducted ethnographic fieldwork in 2019[2] (Jovicic, 2020), faced a limited range of blue-collar occupations. The choice was often constrained by the young visitors' fragmented biographies, poverty, lack of role models, and discrimination – and had even become naturalised in their eyes, leaving seemingly no escape from predetermined career paths. In discourses about the digital literacy of marginalised groups, young people like Can are usually seen as the losers of digital transformation, as digitalisation moves into homes, offices, and factories. Indeed, some visitors had little or no access to computers or the Internet at home, or to institutionalised digital literacy trainings. However, as Can's situation demonstrates, the story behind this exclusion is more complicated than it seems at first glance. Can's informal knowledge of the inner workings of the smartphone was of little value to the formal institutions (be it school or future employers) that sanctioned his failure to adhere to their standards. At the same time, the dream of becoming an engineer was hindered by much more than digital literacy programmes could teach. Building on ethnographic material from fieldwork in two

---

1   All names have been changed and certain biographical details omitted or changed to preserve anonymity.

2   The author would like to thank the interlocutors, the supervisors of this work, as well as the reviewers and editors of this article for their contributions. This work was supported by the Austrian Academy of Sciences within the framework of the DOC-team and the Post-DocTrack scholarships.

Viennese youth centers, this chapter asks how underacknowledged forms of digital literacy are intertwined with profound socio-political and economic exclusions of the "invisible children" (Lemish, 2021). In the process, the over-optimistic narratives that attribute empowering outcomes of digital literacy programs to marginalised youth are scrutinised and embedded in anthropological and ethnographic research on the politics of the digital divide and literacy in different sociocultural contexts and within developmental frameworks.

2. Digital literacy

Given the high penetration of digital infrastructures in Vienna, Austria, the majority of youth aged 11–18 are likely to access the Internet daily (Statista, 2019). Moreover, following the emergence of new players in the market (such as affordable smartphones from China), the term "digital divide," which used to describe access inequalities, does not do justice to the complexity of digital exclusions that can no longer be divided into "haves" and "have-nots" (Scheerder et al., 2017). However, despite recent developments in the context of digital divide debates, frameworks may still rely on problematic dichotomies when underlying premises are rarely scrutinised. Before discussing such dichotomies, I will first present a brief historical overview of digital divide discourses, followed by the ethnographic case study.

2.1. The history of digital divide discourses

The initial idea of the "digital divide," which Scheerder et al. (2017) have called "the first level of the digital divide," emerged when the promise of the Internet's universal and democratic inclusivity met the persistent reality of digital exclusions around the world. On a global scale, the idea of ICT4D (Information and Communications Technologies for Development), which rely on technologies to address global inequalities and ideally eradicate poverty through access to information, began to show cracks (Ginsburg, 2008; Mazzarella, 2010). What was inflated into a "beautiful balloon" (Mazzarella, 2010, p. 785) was followed by a period of disillusionment in which the premises of ICT4D were criticized for emphasizing individualistic solutions to structural problems, thus leaving the poor to google their way out of poverty, as anthropologists have argued (Ginsburg, 2008; Mazzarella, 2010; Poggiali, 2016).

In the context of what Scheerder et al. (2017) call the "second-level digital divide," scholars in the early 2000s pointed out that ever-widening access to digital technologies required better approaches to describing digital inequalities beyond simple dichotomies. Rather than simply having or lacking access, the ways in which digital technologies were used also became the focus of scholarly attention. Rather than automatically using the technologies to obtain information, users also enjoyed the benefits of the new technologies or simply engaged in mundane communication, rather than spectacularly embracing the information age as ICT4D proponents imagined (Slater & Kwami, 2005). As Archambault has argued, the relevant information that her interlocutors in Uganda gathered with the new cell phones concerned mainly information about romantic infidelity rather than information about politics or economics (2011). In Mazzarella's (2010) study, Internet cafes in rural India originally attracted young men interested in pornography, while owning such a café in the early years of the Internet was less useful from a business perspective than for increasing the owner's "marriageability". Mere access to the Internet and information does not mean that users are suddenly able to lift themselves out of poverty, as the promise of ICT4D once implied (Donner, 2015; Hargittai, 2002; Livingstone & Blum-Ross, 2020; Mercer, 2006; Miller et al., 2021; van Dijk, 2017). In response to the assumptions behind ICT4D, anthropologists in particular have focused on the appropriation of digital technologies and media around the world, emphasising that they mostly lead to social reproduction rather than transformative change (Archambault, 2011; Horst & Miller, 2020; Vokes, 2018), and social media are also changed by the world, rather than the world only being changed by social media (Miller et al., 2016).

In the "third-level digital divide," (Scheerder et al., 2017) therefore, the micropolitics of the multiple digital divide are increasingly brought to the fore (Donner, 2015; van Dijk, 2017). Not only do digital technologies and infrastructures not automatically provide a ladder of social mobility, they can also reinforce global labour relations as users from the global South take on repetitive tasks in gaming, online platforms contribute to the fragmentation of labour within the platform economy and exacerbate neoliberal labour relations, gender and racial biases become embedded in seemingly neutral technologies, and technological waste ends up polluting the environment in areas not in the limelight of high-income countries.

2.2. Digital Literacy for Career Development

Despite these emerging multifaceted perspectives on different and situated forms of the digital divide, the ideological assumptions underlying contemporary approaches to digital literacy are not always challenged. Certain digital practices are sometimes still uncritically emphasized as valuable, empowering, worthy of encouragement, and attributed to the "information elite," while the working class remain linked to "entertainment" (Eichmann, 2000). For example, in their book "The App Generation", scholars Gardner and Davies (2013) highlight how young people use their apps in an "app-enabled" or "app-dependent" manner. Within this framework, practices perceived as productive, such as creative engagement with apps, inevitably appear as superior and empowering, while "passive" consumption of content emerges as a symptom of dependency and ultimately deficiency. The characterisation of digital practices as "toxic" in popular discourses of digital detoxification, such as the Silicon Valley-based initiative "Time Well Spent," imply that time is "well spent" only when it conforms to the habits of the cosmopolitan middle class in the U.S. and days are filled with mindfulness (Baym et al., 2020). Thus, well-intentioned attempts to highlight the digital exclusion of socioeconomically disadvantaged users may ultimately carry the undertone of a moral judgment that views certain digital practices associated with the working class or the seemingly addicted youth as problematic and a waste of time (Jovicic, 2020), while the pro-efficient, critical, and active users seem like ideal citizens. Not only does the time seem not spent "well", but it also appears to be a missed opportunity for professional development. Much of the literature on digital literacies concludes that

> people with higher education are significantly using the advanced applications of digital media for capital-enhancing goals relating to work, career, and study while people with lower education are using the simple applications of entertainment, commerce, and messaging (van Dijk, 2017, p. 8).

In a study conducted in Austria (Ikrath & Speckmayr, 2016), the authors came to a similar conclusion: disadvantaged youth are more likely to engage in "passive" activities, while their peers appear more active when it comes to posting content, using ad blockers or creating websites. They are also more likely to lack computers at home and therefore are less likely to use their devices for tasks related to school or work. In other words, young people with low levels of formal education are less likely to use digital media actively, confidently, and "to achieve their own goals at school or work" (2016, p. 18). The authors conclude that disadvantaged youth are left behind in terms of digital literacy and should therefore be targeted with digital literacy interventions (Ikrath & Speckmayr, 2016). This emphasis on the value of work- and career-related activities can be found in the national "Digitales Curriculum" introduced as guidelines for Austrian schools in 2018. The document outlines digital competencies necessary to use the Internet as a productive resource:

> As part of basic digital education, students are taught all the skills they need in order to use technologies consciously, productively, and reflectively for their own further de-

velopment or to gain a foothold in promising occupational fields. (Schule.at, 2018) [translated by the author]

As these studies and recommendations demonstrate, already disadvantaged young people also tend to experience exclusion in the digital sphere, while structural inequalities are reproduced – a dynamic I have encountered in my own ethnographic research. However, an uncritical emphasis on "productivity" and active engagement risks individualising structural problems that run much deeper than the ability to post a tweet, as anthropologists researching digital technology use in the Global South have long warned. It also implies that learning to use digital technologies critically, competently, and confidently increases the chances of a "promising occupational field" – an assumption that clearly did not aid Can in his professional aspirations, despite his ability to fix smartphones. Such a view can thus shift blame onto the shoulders of marginalised youth who seem a YouTube tutorial away from mastering social mobility.

Tackling the challenges of digital inequalities is certainly necessary and urgent, as the COVID-19 pandemic has clearly demonstrated. In fact, my own work includes digital literacy projects (e. g., Göbl et al., 2021). My aim is not to question the necessity of digital literacy programs and digital literacy building per se. As Mazzarella (2010) notes, functional problems sometimes need functional solutions, without the need to politicise this as myopic solutionism. It does not suffice, to speak with Mazzarella, to overlay abstract neoliberal critique over policies that seemingly distract from structural issues. Instead, what is needed is a dense and socioculturally differentiated exploration of the complexity of digital inequality, beyond the Global North-South divide and beyond the distinction between empowering and passive practices, so that implicit premises of discourses on digital literacy can be questioned based on ethnographic complexity. From an anthropological perspective, this means that the underlying explanatory models need to be continuously examined:

> future ethnographic attention should focus not only on how new media technologies generate novel social relations or economic opportunities at the margins but also on how they produce new explanatory models that both precipitate and conceal relations of inequality. (Poggiali, 2016, p. 406)

The following discussion of examples from my ethnographic fieldwork contributes contextual data to prevailing assumptions within digital literacy discourses regarding the career-advancing impact of related policies – not to dismiss them, but to challenge the underlying explanatory models that may be well-intentioned but may also further marginalise those they are intended to benefit. Digital literacy programs in all their diversity can benefit from better addressing the realities of "invisible children" (Lemish, 2021) by understanding what their seemingly problematic practices actually mean in a given context (Nemer, 2016;

Omari, 2018). The holistic, "non-digital-centric" (Pink et al., 2016) approach of the research presented here unravels how survival and stagnation in the present, rather than digital empowerment and self-optimisation towards a future, shape everyday life amid poverty, discrimination, and unemployment – a context in which digital inequalities are pressing and persistent, but digital literacy alone is not necessarily the key to social mobility and career advancement.

3.   Ethnographic case study

Can was one of many young people I encountered in youth centers during my weekly visits between January and November 2019, where I hung out in the afternoons to get a sense of their mundane digital activities. Barely noticeable practices such as fleeting scrolls, swipes and snaps were at the center of my research, as I explored what non-eventful, seemingly meaningless practices can unravel about young people's intimate relationship to their smartphones, especially in marginalised contexts. My main research site, the youth centers, offer free, living-room-like recreational spaces equipped with posters, books, board games and, more recently, computers or PlayStations. They are often located near larger public housing projects ("Gemeindebau") and therefore tend to attract visitors who have fewer resources to pursue other forms of structured leisure activities. Although the centres offer activities and spaces exclusively for girls, the gender imbalance remains considerable – a fact that affected my own research, as most of my interviewees were male. The youth center staff do not only manage the space, but also create lasting relationships and provide advice on work, life, and educational issues, mediate between peers and within families, and sometimes even accompany them to court appointments.

During the fieldwork, I conducted unstructured ethnographic interviews with the visitors and asked them questions about their everyday life in general and about digital technologies in particular. During the conversations, I noted down quotes and then transcribed the conversations and observations from memory and coded/analysed them according to constructivist grounded theory (Charmaz, 2014). Often, the topics included challenges in school or apprenticeship, questions of citizenship, asylum and foreignness, or relationships with peers and family. Over time, however, a chronic sense of boredom and frustration became palpable during the long afternoon-to-evening sessions, due to the sometimes-longstanding search for an apprenticeship or a permanent job after partaking in government apprenticeship programs, which Can was also just about to start. These programs, aimed to fulfil the "apprenticeship guarantee" (Ausbildungs-garantie) are called "ÜBA – Überbetriebliche Lehrausbildung," and are designed to train young people who cannot find a place in a private company and provide them with a government-funded apprenticeship and a daily structure that keeps them off the streets. However, these programs have been tainted with the stigma of failure, as the local newspaper Falter put it, calling it "second-hand apprenticeships and collection points for young people with baggage" (Goldenberg, 2020) [translated by the author]. A youth center staff member described such measures as "cosmetic" as they usually delay unemployment rather than address the underlying problems of neoliberal work structures, in which there are few options for disadvantaged youth, apart from low-paid work. For those whose place on the social mobility ladder is determined early on by their early choice of school in a country where the school system tends to reproduce social inequalities more than in other PISA participating countries (Nimmervoll, 2019), foreign-sounding names, limited language skills, or poor academic performance can leave young people with few employment options, such as non-unionized precarious contracts on construction sites, in the cab industry, delivery services, or other forms of underpaid manual labour.

In the centers, digital technologies, be they omnipresent smartphones, one of the few archaic computers, or a PlayStation, served to create opportunities for socialising and gaming, but also to make the chronic boredom amid prolonged unemployment more bearable. These technologies enabled the celebration of small successes and losing oneself in role-playing games in an environment where the prevailing feeling was that there was no chance of even finding a job, let alone a desirable career as an electrical engineer, game designer or car mechanic. Hanging out at youth centers or parks (see also, Mayer, 2011) and doing "nonsense," as some of the young people phrased it when asked about their daily activities on- and offline, was not an opportunity for empowerment but often a frustrating rollercoaster ride of hopes and failures amid endless rejections. Most of the mundane digital practices I observed had little in common with career-enhancing activities toward the promising career fields mentioned in the "Digitales Curriculum," not necessarily because the visitors lacked the appropriate skills, but because such activities made little sense. Yet, as I have argued elsewhere, seemingly "passive" activities were essential for actively participating in social life, whether through mobile gaming, sending regular Snaps, or window shopping on Instagram – to keep moving while other aspects of coming-of-age stagnated (Jovicic, 2020). If digital technologies played a relevant role in vocational activities, it was mostly in unexpected ways, as Faro's story demonstrates.

3.1. Performing busyness with digital technologies

I met 18-year-old Faro during one of his rare visits to the youth center after he asked for assistance in writing job applications. His family owned a shared computer, and he sometimes used it to play video games, but he had little experience writing documents in word processing software. Therefore, he occasionally visited the center to access the computer and seek help from the staff. Faro has lived in Austria with his mother and a brother since moving from Ghana as a child. At the time of his visit, he had just completed his apprenticeship as a façade builder and was looking for a job. As I was to find out, however, writing an application served less the purpose of actually finding a job and more to please the employment agency, which grants social benefits in return for proof of regular applications. As we searched for job application templates on the youth center's computer, I noticed his palpable frustration with the task. When asked why, Faro explained, "Because I hate my job. I don't like doing it, it sucks [...]. My mother pushed me to find an apprenticeship, and this is what I could get." As we proceeded with a draft, I noticed that his written language skills and grammar were barely adequate for an application, while he was also unsure of the typical application structure. Moreover, when I instructed him to copy and paste the template we had found, it became obvious that the folder structure and the logic behind it also made little sense to him – an activity so embedded in my daily life that it caught me by surprise. The amusement he expressed at the mediocre speed of my writing was another reminder that creating an application is not intuitive, but requires a whole range of skills, many of which have little to do with digital technologies. When we reached the "computer skills" part on his CV, he explained that he did not have any – despite his experience with video games that he obviously had, but had not considered as valuable.

After we completed the first draft of the application, we needed to send it to the appropriate companies. However, his frustration grew as I asked him where he would like to work: "I don't know what I want to do. They told me to send it somewhere, so I will send it somewhere," Faro replied absentmindedly as we googled construction companies. Another half hour passed as we continued to send reluctant applications into the ether, immersing ourselves in a busyness that led nowhere. Faro, stuck with unwanted applications, saw neither a way back nor a way forward. His fragmented biography, poor academic performance, and his criminal record condensed into a sense of frustration with the overall situation in which owning a computer or even learning to write an application meant little more than satisfying state institutions. In Austria, people with only a compulsory education or apprenticeship diploma or those without Austrian citizenship are more likely to be affected by unemployment, a chronic condition that has been gravely exacerbated by the economic impact of the pandemic (Arbeitsmarktservice, 2021; Integrationsfonds, 2020). The lack of jobs and apprenticeships particularly affects marginalised youth, who already face prejudice in the labour market (Goldenberg, 2020). As the stories of my interlocutors imply, these disadvantages can lead to spending several years in limbo and sending out endless job applications. As one of the staff members explained, negative attributions sometimes make it impossible for individuals to escape the bad reputation attributed to foreign citizenship of youth who were often born in Austria. In such cases, the staff member said, he advises them to keep "fighting," to keep writing to companies and asking if they can work for free, and then fighting their way up (Fieldnotes, 23.01.2019). However, given the sometimes family-related and sociocultural pressures to become a man and raise a family at a certain age, and the notion of unpaid or low-paying work with few prospects, the mental effort it takes to "fight" towards an unclear goal can be overwhelming. Moreover, as a staff member remarked, even when he manages to help an individual to find an apprenticeship, it is a bittersweet success, as for every position, "there are 199 others who did not make it" (Fieldnotes, 29.09.2019).

For youth like Faro, active engagement in career advancement meant keeping his head above water from a present position of stagnation rather than developing strategies for impossible futures. On the one hand, the employment agency demanded the performance of constantly applying for jobs; on the other hand, it also reinforced his exclusion from jobs that could foster more enthusiasm. The employment agency (AMS) recently implemented an algorithmic system to more efficiently allocate (re)training programs to those most likely to benefit. Particularly vulnerable individuals, such as the long-term unemployed or those with criminal records, are therefore less likely to receive such offers (ITA, 2021). Certainly, Faro would have benefited from digital competencies, but a well-structured, shiny Word document would not have distracted from underlying issues such as a criminal record. Moreover, proficiently writing a digital application without the support of youth center staff, who can provide continuous encouragement, would have been useful but superficial in terms of one's career if implicit knowledge about negotiating institutions and social mobility cannot be provided by role models elsewhere.

3.2.   Googling for social mobility

Arnel, 17, was a charismatic young man with a broad smile. If you could not see him because he was around the corner playing table tennis as the reigning champion, you could hear him telling everyone who wanted to listen about his latest adventures. Arnel was popular with both his peers and the staff, and had a keen eye for potentially expensive items. His parents had moved to Austria from

Bosnia and Herzegovina when he was a toddler and were now both working in low-paying jobs, while his father had a habit of occasionally borrowing money from him. Having graduated from middle school two years earlier, he was unsure what to do next and realised he had little time left to apply for a high school. Together with his mother, Arnel turned to the Google search engine to find a "good" school that would secure his future employment and would accept him despite his grades. The school with a vocational focus that he eventually landed at was a private school that promised a range of educational options: from service to office management, the possibilities they saw seemed enticing, as did the fact that he did not have to choose a vocational focus right away. Impressed by the school's online presence, he and his mother visited the principal, a middle-aged lady, who was very taken with Arnel according to his account and told his mother that she had "never seen such a well-mannered young man." Even before seeing his grades, the principal promised him a place.

The new school was not only geographically far from his home district, but also socially. The first thing Arnel noticed was that "there is a whole sea of Austrians, hardly any foreigners." He illustrated his observation with a picture of the class he kept on his smartphone: "Look, there are 25 people, and they're all Schwabos[3], except for four. And you know how Austrians are" (Fieldnotes, 02.10. 2019). He explained his discomfort with examples of perceived differences, including clothing styles or disparaging comments towards "foreigners," which ultimately led him to adjust to fit in: "I used to go to school in Adidas clothes and wear a cap, now I wear jeans and a sweater." His attempt to smooth over the differences, however, was not only the result of his careful observations, but also of direct pressure and bullying after he attended school for a while wearing the same jacket: "There was a group of girls in class who got on my nerves. They were like, 'Oh, so you only have one jacket?'" (Fieldnotes, 30.01.2019). Although he dismissed them as "bitchy," he proceeded to hide his gold chain under his sweater and reserve his Adidas clothes for leisure time. The comments of some classmates who openly identified with the right-wing FPÖ party (Freiheitliche Partei Österreichs) were harder to ignore. These included jokes about "shitty foreigners" and "Jugos" that made him want to punch a classmate once: "But I restrained myself, of course. I know if I do that, I'll get suspended. And I also know that they can't go too far and cross the line because I have a good relationship with the teachers and the principal. I can always go and complain and then they will be in trouble" (Fieldnotes, 02.10.2019). Both his astute ability to observe and negotiate differences and his well-cultivated relationship with adults enabled him to juggle the hopes and constraints of social mobility.

---

3 A widespread term for Germans and Austrians in former Yugoslav countries.

However, the promise of social mobility sparked by the private school's online presence soon reached its limits. One day, Arnel visited the youth center visibly upset. Recently, he realised that to qualify for a job as an office worker, which promised better working conditions and earnings than the job as a waiter he had tried during an internship, he would have had to take a completely different path when he entered school, namely one leading to the Matura (high school diploma that qualifies for further education or certain apprenticeships). Now, he had the choice of either staying in his educational track and completing it in one year, thus accepting the disappointment of not being able to increase his chances of a more promising career, or starting over on the other educational track leading to the Matura and committing to three more years of schooling. For Arnel, now 18, and his family, paying three more years of tuition and delaying his opportunities to earn money was not an option. As Arnel told us what he had just learned, I and other staff members expressed a sense of disbelief as we collectively made our way to the computer and searched the school's website. Buried in the complicated explanations about the different trajectories was the somewhat obscure information that Arnel was right and that there was little he could do at this point. Despite all the personal and collective efforts and seemingly easy access to information, googling a "good" school at the time when Arnel "didn't know what the Matura was, what it meant, and how to get there" (Fieldnotes, 02.10.2019) was a task that had little chance of success without a deeper understanding of complex institutions or the invisible rules of the social mobility game.

3.3. Informal structures

The limited understanding of how to collect certificates and navigate official institutions, be they schools, employment agencies, or other government agencies, is exacerbated when those institutions disorientate rather than help navigate through haphazard search engine optimisation of private schools or negligence by overburdened government agencies. On one occasion, JJ, who was 17 at the time, discussed his situation with us. After moving back and forth between Austria and Turkey several times, JJ did not know what to do in terms of further schooling or vocational training. According to JJ, the case worker at the employment agency rejected his application for benefits and told him to "go study something." However, the agency failed to tell him that in order to "study something," he needed a high school diploma equivalent, which he did not have. In addition, JJ, while stating that "university is good" and that he would like to attend it, especially since the state advised him to do so, had only a vague idea about what a university was. Unsure what to do, JJ looked for work, "You know, not working is not good," he said, "Working is good. A Turkish woman called me and said she could help me find a job at a temp agency" (Fieldnotes, 09. 10. 2019). Reliance on informal networks rather than institutionalised channels or digital platforms was a common occurrence, not only because digital platforms made little sense in this context, but also because personal networks could provide access to otherwise unattainable positions such as tram drivers or car mechanics – frequently mentioned but rarely achieved dream jobs for many of the young men. For example, Mirko, a 17-year-old truck mechanic, explained why he was one of the lucky ones: "I got the job just because my uncle is a truck owner and was an important customer there, so they hired me. It's a very good company, there are no foreigners. Austrians are great, but sometimes I wish there were more foreigners" (Fieldnotes, 23. 10. 2019). Seemingly out of place, Mirko wished for the familiarity that Arnel also traded for the chance of social mobility in a private school, where he suddenly faced a "sea of Austrians" and saw his gold chain, initially a sign of belonging, turn into a signifier of exclusion.

The low probability of outplaying the odds was even lower when teachers saw students' seemingly predetermined vocations in their eyes, as in Can's case. Here, a principally welcome piece of advice in an uncertain time of transition morphs into another layer of social reproduction, as Bourdieu et al. (Bourdieu et al., 1971) have argued. Yet, as Paul Willis (1977) has pointed out in his ethnographic research among working-class "lads" in 1970s Britain, the decision to fail and rebel against institutions can be seen as an act of agency. Indeed, after just a few weeks of working as a gardener in the government-funded program that trains young people for a year, after which they either must leave or are selected for an actual apprenticeship, Can was suspended after an argument with his instructor: "I told her I didn't want to keep working as a slave for €300 a month." His rebellion came at the price of suspension, but he also told it as a "success story" to his nodding peers at the youth center, perhaps to unburden himself (Mayer, 2011, p. 174) or to re-establish himself as an active participant in his biography that seemed pre-determined.

In these cases, informal trajectories, whether informal networks or learning to fix a smartphone outside the stratified school system, were essential for the youth to establishing themselves in an environment of state institutions that seemed indifferent at best or required young people to continuously perform busyness, a repetitive act that solidified their failure to find a desired job. Finding a job that offered them an immediate salary sometimes seemed irresistible, coming from a space of limited financial resources. There was an even greater urgency to use those resources carefully when inviting a girl out on a date or paying the bill in the shisha bar, rather than investing longer in education and further burdening the family for the sake of an uncertain future. Here, career advancement is not about planning for the future, but about stabilising oneself against the background of disorientating challenges and making the present meaningful as quickly and efficiently as possible. Accordingly, smartphones and computers are not used to plan a future that manifests itself in a polished and self-optimized LinkedIn profile, but to pass the time and make the present more bearable instead.

3.4.   (In)visibility

Online spaces thus become a mirror of constraints and desirable goods and professions that remain unattainable even if one knows how to post a tweet or a YouTube video (see also Schlechter, forthcoming). Moreover, the decision not to post anything and become "active" may not be due to the missing know-how, but because digital spaces are highly public and visible (Miller et al., 2016) and therefore to be avoided if one does not want to stand out, as Arnel tried to do when he changed his clothes to avoid being noticed for the wrong reasons. When I first met 17-year-old Arno, who sometimes DJ-ed at youth centre parties, he explained that he was a music producer. When asked if his music was on You-Tube, he responded with a statement I often encountered in various forms: "No, I wouldn't dare. There are so many haters on YouTube" (Fieldnotes, 08.02.2019). Visibility, after all, is a decision that is not straightforward, especially for those used to having their otherness sanctioned, whether online or offline. As scholars within migration studies have noted, the politics of visibility mean that othered and marginalised groups like "migrants" often remain invisible as individual actors within media and popular discourses, while their collective visibility contributes to their "othering" as a dangerous group (Bischoff, 2018; Steffen, 2016).

In addition, visibility must be negotiated against the widespread mistrust of institutions, be it the employment office or the police. On one of my early visits to the youth centers, I asked a group of young men if anyone would agree to an interview – to no avail. After several attempts to understand the reasons for this reluctance, they claimed that a few of them knew "someone who had told something" to the staff and who then had been subsequently searched by the anti-terror police because of suspicious "Islamist" activities. Moreover, as the staff subsequently explained, some associate the term "interview" with negatively connoted state institutions and questioning during the asylum process – a situation in which visibility becomes potentially problematic; in which one is quickly associated with danger and criminality, as young working-class men have historically been "out of place" in urban Vienna and beyond (Jovicic, 2020; van den Berg & O'Neill, 2017). As Omari's (2018) ethnographic research in the Brazilian favelas demonstrated, visibility in the form of smartphone ownership or posting content on social media may be ridden with risk in environments in which, in this case, drug gangs were fearful of their images being posted online and threatened those who were active online.

Sometimes, however, the potentially dangerous and invisible informal spheres can become a source of subversive digital literacy that is rarely identified as such in digital literacy surveys. During my fieldwork, a group of young men, some of whom had insecure status as asylum seekers, were involved in a case involving the theft of credit card data. After finding the payment data on the "dark web," they used it several times for small amounts and were eventually caught. What they did not realise at that moment was that the consequences of petty crimes committed out of youthful adventurism are compounded for those in legal limbo – asylum seekers whose status was about to change for the worse in exchange for a questionable price. After all, the stolen money was spent mostly on candy and crisps at the local supermarket. Playing around with subversive forms of digital literacy, whether online or offline, therefore carries a different weight for those already under the scrutiny of the state. As anthropologists have noted in a variety of contexts, access to information online is not by default "useful" in the sense of digital literacy ideals of empowerment (Archambault, 2011; Horst & Miller, 2020; Slater & Kwami, 2005), but also in the sense of rebellious empowerment of disenfranchised youth.

4. Conclusion

In December of 2020, a group of young people wrote an open letter to Austrian politicians, together with the Hirschstetten Youth Center:

> Finding an apprenticeship was not easy even before the Corona crisis. Now it is even harder. Many young people lose their apprenticeship or don't get one in the first place (…). Others have to share a computer and a room with their siblings. Some even have to organise the technology for learning at home (laptop, appropriate Internet connection,..). (Bogdan et al., 2020) [translated by the author]

The issues raised here clearly crystallised during my fieldwork a year earlier and were exacerbated during the COVID-19 pandemic. The digital divide has probably never been more precarious than during a period in which many young people lacked access to computers to write applications or participate in online classes, could not rely on the support of trusted institutions, and had to share limited devices and work space with siblings and parents (Goldenberg, 2020; Tóth et al., 2020). The fact that many scholars have moved away from writing about the digital divide in terms of mere access does not mean it no longer exists or that other needs necessarily come first, even among young people in the Global North. As Mazzarella writes,

No one will contest, presumably, that food, power, and health care are baseline requirements for human thriving. But the insistence that computers come later, as it were,
nevertheless also works to perpetuate the assumption that the appropriateness of a
technology should be evaluated in terms of a hierarchy of needs that can be known in
advance. (2010, p. 797)

However, what moving away from "first-level digital divide" narratives does
mean, is that the stories told around the digital divide need to be complicated,
rather than simply re-defined in terms of deficits that further marginalise those
already on the periphery, whose reliance on informal, invisible, and subversive
digital practices is critical to participating at all in the world around them in ways
meaningful to them, even if it is through buying crisps. Such a complicating
endeavour, however, is not meant to romanticise young people's activities and
agency, but to emphasise the everyday, diverse realities and small, barely noticed
practices (Pyyry & Tani, 2016) that unfold in diverse contexts. As human geog-
rapher Massey has influentially argued in relation to poststructuralist debates,
global and neoliberal structures are sometimes juxtaposed with romantic figures
of resistance in "the streets," imagined as dark backyards. "But resistance to
what?" asks Massey (2005). Neither do the young people mentioned here desire to
become agents of resistance to inequality, nor do they intend to appropriate
"enabling" (Gardner & Davis, 2013) technologies.

In debates on digital empowerment, hopes for social change are projected
primarily onto young people, whose personal growth in the West is linked to
expectations of discovering agency and becoming "agents of social change."
(Durham, 2008, p. 168). In the context of marginalised youth, these expectations
lead to a scholarly emphasis on resistance and rebellion (Durham, 2008), while in
the context of literacy overall, education is often presented as a "liberating force"
(Froerer, 2012). As Livingstone and Blum-Ross (2020) write, reliance on digital
literacy programs often stems from the parents' desperation to hold on to
seemingly easy promises when structural problems cannot be solved, promises
that, however, are ultimately disappointed. With the advent of digital technologies, narratives within the digital literacy frameworks that ascribe competence and modernity to those efficiently appropriating contemporary forms of
digital technologies, also associate others with the past, much like the colonial
approaches to technology saw the colonisers as proficient masters of technology
(Slama & Munro, 2015). However, as Frederiksen notes while drawing on Durham's work, an overemphasis on resistance tends to "overshadow the cases where
people don't really care about what's going on" (2017, p. 17).

The pandemic has not only unearthed the extent of digital divides but has also
brought home to those who have easy access to commercialised leisure activities
that the Internet is not only an idealized source of productivity, but sometimes
the only access to leisure when other options are limited. For many young people,

for whom hanging out in parks and malls or window shopping on Instagram is entangled with chronic boredom, this is a constant rather than a temporary reality. In contrast to the Western construct of adolescents as individuals in "becoming," the lived reality often consists of simply "being" (Stodulka, 2013) and making sense of adverse circumstances. Moreover, as Payal Arora (see also, Arora, 2019) has pointed out, the Internet serves as the "leisure economy of the poor." While "Westerners" tend to assume that poverty is "a compelling reason for the poor to choose work over play when they go online," ethnographic research shows that in many cases "play dominates work and leisure overtakes work" (Economist, 2019). Or as Mazzarella has phrased it, developmental digital literacy programs frequently assume that the rural poor are "motivated by functional utility" while the consuming middle classes are "driven by the pursuit of pleasure" (2010, p. 788). In the context of fragmented biographies, poverty, and exclusion from commercial spaces and labour markets, then, seemingly mindless scrolling through Instagram feeds does not represent a deficient practice to be exchanged for an active and seemingly empowering one, but rather a strategy of immediate survival here and now, not in some abstract future where one is anyway destined to become something one does not want to be. Here, mere access to computers without a multi-layered support system does not guarantee success in applications; googled information about schools can only be interpreted with an implicit knowledge of institutions; coveted jobs can be obtained through informal networks; and "active" visibility is not necessarily desirable for those for whom visibility can also mean exclusion and risk. Failure to optimise LinkedIn profiles or skilfully use social media as arenas of social performance and career advancement is not simply a symptom of a lack of digital literacy – rather, doing so would seem oddly out of place.

References

Arbeitsmarktservice, A. (2021). *Arbeitsmarktdaten im Kontext von Bildungsabschlüssen. Arbeitsmarktservice Österreich, Arbeitsmarktforschung und Berufsinformation.* https://www.ams.at/arbeitsmarktdaten-und-medien/arbeitsmarkt-daten-und-arbeitsmarkt-forschung/berichte-und-auswertungen.

Archambault, J. S. (2011). Breaking up 'because of the phone' and the transformative potential of information in Southern Mozambique. *New media & society, 13*(3), 444–456. https://doi.org/10.1177/1461444810393906.

Arora, P. (2019). The Leisure Divide. In *The Next Billion Users* (pp. 6–30). Harvard University Press.

Baym, N. K., Wagman, K. B., & Persaud, C. J. (2020). Mindfully scrolling: Rethinking Facebook after time deactivated. *Social Media+ Society, 6*(2). https://doi.org/10.1177/2056305120919105.

Bischoff, C. (2018). Migration and the Regime of the Gaze. A Critical Perspective on Concepts and Practices of Visibility and Visualization. In D. Bachmann-Medick & J. Kuggele (Eds.), *Migration. Changing Concepts, Critical Approaches.* Walter de Gruyter.

Bogdan, Tatjana, Vanessa, Alexandra, Maria, Bojan, Dejan, Amina, Kevin, Sarra, Kristina, David, Franziska, A., David, Gabriela, Dejam, Katarina, Natasa, Emmanuel, . . . Marina. (2020). *Bogdan und Tatjana machen sich stark.* Der Verein Wiener Jugendzentren. https://www.jugendzentren.at/wer-wir-sind-was-wir-tun/newsarchiv/bodgan-und-tatjana-machen-sich-stark/.

Bourdieu, P., Passeron, J.-C., & Hartig, I. (1971). *Die Illusion der Chancengleichheit: Untersuchungen zur Soziologie des Bildungswesens am Beispiel Frankreichs.* Klett.

Charmaz, K. (2014). *Constructing grounded theory.* SAGE Publications Ltd.

Donner, J. (2015). *After access: Inclusion, development, and a more mobile Internet.* MIT press.

Durham, D. (2008). New horizons: Youth at the millennium. *Anthropological quarterly, 81* (4), 945–957.

Economist, T. (2019, 08.06.2019). How the pursuit of leisure drives internet use. *The Economist* https://www.economist.com/briefing/2019/06/08/how-the-pursuit-of-leisure-drives-internet-use.

Eichmann, H. (2000). *Medienlebensstile zwischen Informationselite und Unterhaltungsproletariat* (Vol. 5). Peter Lang.

Frederiksen, M. D. (2017). Joyful pessimism: Marginality, disengagement, and the doing of nothing. *Focaal, 2017*(78), 9–22.

Froerer, P. (2012). Learning, Livelihoods, and Social Mobility: Valuing Girls' Education in Central India. *Anthropology & Education Quarterly, 43*(4), 344–357.

Gardner, H., & Davis, K. (2013). *The app generation: How today's youth navigate identity, intimacy, and imagination in a digital world.* Yale University Press.

Ginsburg, F. (2008). Rethinking the digital age. In *The media and social theory* (pp. 141–158). Routledge.

Göbl, B. H., Dayana, Jovicic, S., & Kriglstein, S. H., Helmut. (2021). *OutSmart! Evaluation of a Serious Game and its Conversational Interface for Reflective Social Media Use* GAME-ON®'2021, Aveiro.

Goldenberg, A. W., Birgit. (2020, 02.06.2020). Verloren im Lockdown. *Falter.* https://www.falter.at/zeitung/20200602/verloren-im-lockdown?fbclid=IwAR3bVHHvZLJaV4Kyby_cAJSBMVzjVJViP_bfVF-Hd39c0BNXr1P4IbTSX2k.

Hargittai, E. (2002). Second-level digital divide: Differences in people's online skills. *First monday, 7*(4).

Horst, H. A., & Miller, D. (2020). *The cell phone: An anthropology of communication.* Routledge.

Ikrath, P., & Speckmayr, A. (2016). *Digitale Kompetenzen für eine digitalisierte Lebenswelt: Eine Jugendstudie der AK Wien, durchgeführt vom Institut für Jugendkulturforschung.* http://emedien.arbeiterkammer.at/viewer/resolver?urn=urn:nbn:at:at-akw:g-850522.

Integrationsfonds, Ö. Ö. (2020). *10 Jahre Statistisches Jahrbuch: Zahlen, Daten und Fakten zu Integration* https://www.integrationsfonds.at/newsbeitrag/10-jahre-statistisches-jahrbuch-des-oeif-zahlen-daten-und-fakten-zu-integration-6966.

ITA. (2021). *Wie fair ist der AMS-Algorithmus?* Institut für Technikfolgen-Abschätzung. https://epub.oeaw.ac.at/ita/ita-dossiers/ita-dossier052.pdf.

Jovicic, S. (2020). Scrolling and the In-Between Spaces of Boredom: Marginalized Youths on the Periphery of Vienna. *Ethos, 48*(4), 498–516. https://doi.org/10.1111/etho.12294.

Lemish, D. (2021, 30.03.2021). *Six reflections on children and media research: A personal scholarly journey.* Youth, Media, Life 2021, Online.

Livingstone, S., & Blum-Ross, A. (2020). *Parenting for a digital future: how hopes and fears about technology shape children's lives.* Oxford University Press.

Massey, D. (2005). *For space.* Sage.

Mayer, D. (2011). *Park Youth in Vienna: A Contribution to Urban Anthropology.* LIT Verlag Münster.

Mazzarella, W. (2010). Beautiful balloon: The digital divide and the charisma of new media in India. *American Ethnologist, 37*(4), 783–804. http://www-jstor-org.uaccess.univie.ac.at/stable/40890788.

Mercer, C. (2006). Telecentres and transformations: Modernizing Tanzania through the Internet. *African Affairs, 105*(419), 243–264.

Miller, D., Costa, E., Haynes, N., McDonald, T., Nicolescu, R., Sinanan, J., Spyer, J., Venkatraman, S., & Wang, X. (2016). *How the world changed social media.* UCL Press.

Miller, D., Rabho, L. A., Awondo, P., de Vries, M., Duque, M., Garvey, P., Haapio-Kirk, L., Hawkins, C., Otaegui, A., & Walton, S. (2021). *The Global Smartphone: Beyond a Youth Technology.* UCL Press. https://discovery.ucl.ac.uk/id/eprint/10126930/.

Nemer, D. (2016). Online favela: The use of social media by the marginalized in Brazil. *Information technology for development, 22*(3), 364–379.

Nimmervoll, L. (2019, 03.12.2019). Pisa-Studie: Österreichs Schüler werden in Naturwissenschaften schlechter. *Der Standard.* https://www.derstandard.at/story/2000111780205/pisa-studie-oesterreichs-schueler-werden-in-naturwissenschaften-schlechter.

Omari, J. (2018). Digital Access amongst the Marginalized: Democracy and Internet Governance in Rio de Janeiro. *PoLAR, 41*, 277.

Pink, S., Horst, H., Postill, J., Hjorth, L., Lewis, T., & Tacchi, J. (2016). *Digital ethnography: Principles and practice.* Sage.

Poggiali, L. (2016). Seeing (from) Digital Peripheries: Technology and Transparency in Kenya's Silicon Savannah. *Cultural Anthropology, 31*(3), 387–411.

Pyyry, N., & Tani, S. (2016). Young Peoples Play With Urban Public Space: Geographies of Hanging Out. In B. Evans, J. Horton, & T. Skelton (Eds.), *Play and Recreation, Health and Wellbeing* (pp. 193–210). Springer Singapore. https://doi.org/10.1007/978-981-4585-51-4_8.

Scheerder, A., Van Deursen, A., & Van Dijk, J. (2017). Determinants of Internet skills, uses and outcomes. A systematic review of the second-and third-level digital divide. *Telematics and informatics, 34*(8), 1607–1624.

Schlechter, M. (forthcoming). *Sozialbindungen von Jugendlichen zwischen schulischen Regeln und digital-medialer Kommunikation. Eine lebensweltanalytisch-digital-ethnographische Erkundung des Kommunikationszeitraums Schule im Wandel.* Doctoral Thesis. University of Vienna].

Schule.at. (2018). *Lehrplan Digitale Grundbildung – einfach erklärt* Retrieved from https://themen.schule.at/themen/lehrplan-digitale-grundbildung.

Slama, M., & Munro, J. (Eds.). (2015). *From 'stone-age' to 'real-time': Exploring Papuan Temporalities, Mobilities and Religiosities.* ANU Press.

Slater, D., & Kwami, J. (2005). Embeddedness and escape: Internet and mobile use as poverty reduction strategies in Ghana. *Information Society Research Group (ISRG) report.*

Statista. (2019). *Wie lange bist Du pro Tag ca. im Internet aktiv?* https://de.statista.com/stati stik/daten/studie/1037042/umfrage/taegliche-internet-nutzungszeit-bei-jugendlichen-in-oesterreich/.

Steffen, K. (2016). *Mediating Mobility : Visual Anthropology in the Age of Migration* [Book]. WallFlower Press. https://search.ebscohost.com/login.aspx?direct=true&db=nlebk&AN=1232735&site=ehost-live.

Stodulka, T. (2013). *Coming of Age on the Streets of Java: A Life Course Perspective on Coping with Stigma and Marginality.* Freie Universität Berlin.

Tóth, B., Motter, M., & Horaczek, N. (2020, 17.11.2020). Chaos macht Schule. *Falter.* https://www.falter.at/zeitung/20201117/chaos-macht-schule.

van den Berg, M., & O'Neill, B. (2017). Introduction: Rethinking the class politics of boredom. *Focaal, 2017*(78), 1–8.

van Dijk, J. A. (2017). Digital divide: Impact of access. *The international encyclopedia of media effects,* 1–11.

Vokes, R. (2018). Before the call: Mobile phones, exchange relations, and social change in south-western Uganda. *Ethnos, 83*(2), 274–290.

Willis, P. (1977). *Learning to labor: How working class kids get working class jobs.* Saxon House.

3. Perception and emotion

Julia Sonnleitner

Kindheitsmedien – Jugendmedien. Medienartefakte als biografische Objekte

Abstract

Dieser Beitrag befasst sich damit, wie Medien der Kindheit und Jugend in späteren Lebensphasen neu bewertet werden. Einem semiotischen Medienbegriff folgend, untersuche ich, wie Dinge, die im Alltagsverständnis nicht als Medien gelten würden, zur Mediation eingesetzt werden. Das soziolinguistische Erkenntnisinteresse dieses Beitrags an Medien ergibt sich aus der Frage, wie diese aus Sicht von Sprecher*innen auf das Spracherleben (Busch, 2017), die emotional-leibliche Dimension von Sprache, wirken. Die Soziolinguistik setzt sich zunehmend damit auseinander, wie Sprache durch die materielle Welt mediiert ist (Barker, 2019; Karrebaek, 2017; Mpendukana & Stroud, 2020; Pennycook & Otsuji, 2017; Spitzmüller, 2018; Wells, 2020). Der Beitrag präsentiert erste Ergebnisse eines Forschungsprojekts, bei dem das Spracherleben von Menschen, die als Kinder vor dem Krieg in Jugoslawien geflohen sind, untersucht wurde. Der Ergebnisteil illustriert anhand von zwei biografischen Objekten aus der Kindheits- und Jugendzeit der Interviewpartner*innen, wie Dinge in unterschiedlichen Lebensabschnitten zur Kommunikation eingesetzt werden. Ich argumentiere, dass diese Objekte aufgrund geteilter Medienpraxis Vergemeinschaftung herstellen und zur kommunikativen Handlungsfähigkeit beitragen.

This chapter deals with the changing significance and value of media artefacts during a life time. Adapting a semiotic understanding of media, I explore how objects that would not commonly count as media gain a mediating character. My sociolinguistic interest in media springs from a focus on the lived experience of language (Busch, 2017), understood as the corporeal-emotional dimension of language, and how it is intertwined with mediation. In sociolinguistics, languages' mediation through materiality is increasingly discussed (Barker, 2019; Karrebaek, 2017; Mpendukana & Stroud, 2020; Spitzmüller, 2018; Wells, 2020). In this contribution, I focus on the entanglement of language and media biographies. Preliminary results from a research project that explored the lived experience of language among people who fled the war in Ex-Yugoslavia as children will be discussed. Two biographic objects from my interview partners' youth illustrate how things act as media in different phases of life. I argue that these objects create sociability (*Vergemeinschaftung*) due to shared media practice and engender communicative agency.

1.   Einleitung

Medien, die wir als Kinder oder Jugendliche benutzt haben, wurden vielleicht ausgesondert oder weggeworfen, vielleicht aber auch aufgehoben und wiedergefunden. Sicher hat sich aber verändert, wie wir diese Medien retrospektiv wahrnehmen und welche Praxis damit verbunden ist. Wenn ein Kinderbuch beispielsweise nicht mehr zum Vorlesen gebraucht wird, wenn die Kinder es gar nicht mehr lesen oder sogar verstehen können, dann wird es vielleicht trotzdem aufgehoben, verwahrt oder ausgestellt. Dieser Beitrag behandelt die Neubewertung von Medien der Kindheit und Jugend in Biografien von Menschen, welche transnationale Mobilität aufgrund von Krieg und Vertreibung erfahren haben.

In der Soziolinguistik der Medien wurde transnationale (Im-)Mobilität vor allem dahingehend untersucht, wie Menschen vor und nach der Verlagerung ihres Lebensschwerpunktes an einen anderen Ort mit ihren früheren Netzwerken in Kontakt bleiben (Madianou & Miller, 2013; Palviainen, 2020), sich mit der Diaspora am neuen Wohnort vernetzen (Eisenlohr, 2006; Halilović, 2013) oder wie sich die Kommunikation sowohl in lokalen als auch translokalen Netzwerken gestaltet (Lexander & Androutsopoulos, 2019; Palviainen & Kedra, 2020). Ein Aspekt, der bisher allerdings weniger Beachtung fand, ist die Frage, wie Medienartefakte in unterschiedlichen Lebensphasen immer wieder neu bewertet werden und zur Vergemeinschaftung (Hepp, Berg & Roitsch, 2014) beitragen.

Die hier vorgestellten Ergebnisse sind Teil des Projektes *Language in Motion*[1], in dem Sprachbiografien und Medienbiografien von Menschen untersucht wurden, die als Kinder oder Jugendliche in den 1990er Jahren im Zuge des Krieges in Jugoslawien vertrieben wurden und ihren Lebensmittelpunkt nach Österreich verlagerten. Projektziel ist, mit dem Konzept von Spracherleben (Busch 2017), dem ein phänomenologischer Zugang zu Sprache zugrunde liegt, zu untersuchen, wie Medien aus Sicht der Sprecher*innen die kommunikative Handlungsfähigkeit erweitern oder möglicherweise einschränken. Dieser Beitrag behandelt einen Teilaspekt, nämlich wie bestimmte Medienobjekte mit dem Spracherleben eines Lebensabschnitts in Zusammenhang stehen. Mein zentrales Interesse gilt daher dem biografischen Zusammenhang von Spracherleben und Medien.

Der gewählte biografisch-analytische Rahmen untersucht die historischen und sozialen Konfigurationen, in die das Spracherleben und Medienhandeln eingebettet sind. Welche Potentialitäten der Handlungsermächtigung erwachsen

1 Das Projekt (Laufzeit 2020–2023, Institut für Sprachwissenschaft der Universität Wien, Leiterin und Durchführende Julia Sonnleitner, Website https://languageinmotion.univie.ac.at/) wird aus Mitteln des Austrian Science Fund (FWF): T 1148-G gefördert und wurde mit Jürgen Spitzmüller eingereicht. Mein besonderer Dank gilt allen Interviewpartner*innen, die sich auf die Teilnahme eingelassen und damit die Forschung ermöglicht haben.

aus diesen Konfigurationen? Ich möchte damit nicht nur auf den Lebensabschnitt der Flucht und des Ankommens fokussieren, sondern untersuchen, wie Spracherleben und Medien als Möglichkeiten zur Vergemeinschaftung wahrgenommen werden. Damit schließe ich mich Ayşe Çağlar (2018) an, wenn sie schreibt:

> „Such a radical contemporaneousness will allow us to see migrants and non-migrants through a common analytical lens so we can study how all residents of a place (migrant or not) build their lives within the configuration of social forces given at a historical conjuncture" (Çağlar, 2018, S. 30).

So werden auch Medien und Sprachen in ihrer lebensweltlichen Eingebundenheit (Schütz & Luckmann, 2017 [1975]) untersucht. Damit sind in dem Fall die mit der Lebenswelt verbundenen typischen Aktivitäten und Institutionen (beispielsweise die Schule) gemeint sowie der spezifische Lebensort mit seiner materiellen und sprachlichen Welt, seinen Möglichkeiten und Bedingungen, wie sie von den Subjekten vorgefunden und aufgegriffen werden. Die biografische Perspektive nimmt die diachrone Veränderung dieser Raum-Zeit-Konstellationen in den Blick: Wie verändert sich die Bewertung von Medien und die Medienpraxis, wenn Menschen in andere Lebensphasen übertreten?

Der Beitrag ist in vier Teile gegliedert. Im ersten Teil werden die zentralen Konzepte vorgestellt, nämlich Spracherleben, ein semiotischer Medienbegriff und die Diskussion um biografische Objekte. Der zweite Teil behandelt das Forschungsdesign, das aus einem mehrstufigen, kooperativen Verfahren besteht. Im Ergebniskapitel werden zwei Beispiele vorgelegt, die aus dem biografischen Abschnitt der Kindheit bzw. der Schulzeit zweier Interviewpartner*innen stammen. Anhand dieser zwei Medienartefakte analysiere ich, wie sich ihre zugeschriebene Medialität sowohl in Hinblick auf Vergemeinschaftung als auch auf das Spracherleben verändert. Abschließend werden die Ergebnisse dahingehend zusammengefasst, wie die vorgestellten biografischen Objekte in verschiedenen biografischen Phasen als Medien fungieren.

2.   Konzepte

2.1   Spracherleben

Der zentrale Erkenntnisbereich dieser Arbeit, Spracherleben, nimmt die körperliche und emotionale Dimension von Sprache in den Blick. Im Sprachenrepertoire, der Gesamtheit der zur Verfügung stehenden kommunikativen Mittel, haben sich frühere kommunikative Situationen als Erfahrungen von kommunikativer Handlungsmacht oder Unbehagen aufgrund von Abwertung und

Ausgrenzung von Sprecher*innen abgelagert. Diese früheren Erfahrungen kommen in Einstellungen von Sprecher*innen gegenüber Teilen ihres Sprachenrepertoires zum Ausdruck. Buschs Arbeit (z. B. 2015; 2016a; 2016b; 2016c) rückt jene historischen und biografischen Übergänge in den Mittelpunkt, wenn Sprecher*innen merken, dass ihr bisheriges Sprachenrepertoire in einer neuen Situation nicht mehr angemessen ist, dass sie aufgrund ihres Sprechens abgewertet oder ausgegrenzt werden, beispielsweise aufgrund von transnationaler Migration und Flucht oder aufgrund von politischen Umbrüchen.

Dem Konzept Spracherleben liegt ein phänomenologischer Zugang zugrunde, der Sprache (nach Merleau-Ponty, 2012) als Geste der Hinwendung zum anderen begreift und sich entlang dieser drei Achsen entfaltet (Busch, 2017): Selbstwahrnehmung/Fremdwahrnehmung, Macht/Ohnmacht und Inklusion/Exklusion.

- *Selbstwahrnehmung/Fremdwahrnehmung:* diese Achse wird in sprachbiografischen Darstellungen meist dann thematisiert, wenn die Selbstwahrnehmung von Sprecher*innen, wenn sie neue kommunikative Räume betreten, nicht mit dem übereinstimmt, wie ihre Rede in der Fremdwahrnehmung registriert wird;
- die Dimension *Macht/Ohnmacht* bedeutet, wie Sprecher*innen ihre kommunikativen Ressourcen gegenüber bestimmten Sprachregimes (raumgebundene Sprachideologien) einschätzen und tatsächlich einzusetzen vermögen (oder nicht);
- die dritte Achse lenkt die Aufmerksamkeit darauf, dass Sprecher*innen aufgrund ihres sprachlichen Repertoires Erfahrungen von sozialer *Inklusion* und *Exklusion* machen.

Die Soziolinguistik setzt sich zunehmend damit auseinander, wie Sprache durch die materielle Welt mediiert ist (Barker, 2019;; Karrebaek, 2017; Mpendukana & Stroud, 2020; Pennycook & Otsuji, 2017; Spitzmüller, 2018; Wells, 2020). Diese Diskussion möchte ich dahingehend aufgreifen, wie Dinge aufgrund ihrer Eingebundenheit in die Kommunikation zu Medien werden und damit die kommunikative Handlungsfähigkeit erweitern (oder möglicherweise einschränken). Wenn also, aus einer phänomenologischen Perspektive, Sprache eine Geste der Hinwendung zum anderen ist, ist Materialität die Bedingung dieser Geste. Medien sind demnach als Dinge zu verstehen, die als notwendig wahrgenommen werden, um eine Hinwendung zum anderen zu ermöglichen, erschweren oder verunmöglichen. Die biografische Methodologie ermöglicht es, Spracherleben und die Koppelung von Spracherleben an Medien aus einer Subjektperspektive zu erforschen.

2.2   Ein semiotischer Medienbegriff

Sprachliche Zeichen brauchen, um in Erscheinung zu treten, eine Form von Materialität, die als ihr Medium fungiert (Schneider, 2008). Sie kann so unterschiedlich sein wie Schallwellen, Papier, ein Display, Körper oder Stein. Diese materielle Bedingung sprachlicher Zeichen wird jedoch von Sprecher*innen in unterschiedlichen Graden als solche wahrgenommen. Oft fällt die Materialität der Botschaft erst dann auf, wenn es zu Konflikten kommt (z. B. Gershons Studie über das als falsch empfundene Medium für den Kommunikationsakt des Schlussmachens; Gershon, 2010a), wenn die Kommunikation missglückt oder wenn aufgrund historischer Umbrüche oder technologischen Wandels Medien neu bewertet werden, etwa im Falle von Remediation (Bolter & Grusin, 1999; z. B. die Bedeutung von Briefen vor und nach der Einführung der E-Mail-Kommunikation). Die technischen Möglichkeiten eines Mediums sagen außerdem noch nichts über die tatsächliche Medienpraxis aus. Vielmehr ist Medienpraxis davon geprägt, welche Vorstellungen Akteure davon haben, wie Medien zu nutzen sind (Hoklas & Lepa, 2015). Aus diesen Gründen ist „Medien", so Couldry (2008) kein analytisch produktiver Begriff, denn er wird den unterschiedlichen Graden von Komplexität kommunikativer Prozesse nicht gerecht. Er schlägt stattdessen „Mediation" und „Mediatisierung" vor.

Ich lehne mich im Folgenden an einen semiotischen Medienbegriff an, um Prozesse der Mediation zu verstehen. Nach Scollon sind Mittel der Mediation (mediational means): „any semiotic object used to mediate social action" (2001, S. 7). Medien sind demnach potenziell alle Objekte, wenn sie 1. semiotisch sind und 2. soziales Handeln mediieren. Das heißt, dass sich nach dieser Definition die Frage, was ein Medium sein kann, auch auf Dinge erstreckt, die wir im Alltagsverständnis nicht als Medien bezeichnen würden, und alle möglichen als semiotisch wahrgenommene Objekte miteinschließt. Ein zentraler Aspekt dieser Definition, den Agha (2011) noch weiter ausarbeitete, ist, dass Objekte und Materialität nicht per se zeichenhaft sind, sondern als zeichenhaft wahrgenommen werden müssen. Agha versteht unter „Mediation" die materiellen und semiotischen Bedingungen jeder kommunikativen Handlung. Kommunikation setzt immer Zeichenhaftigkeit und Materialität voraus, wobei Vorstellungen von potenziell zeichenhafter Materialität historisch und lokal spezifisch sind (vgl. *Semiotic Ideologies;* Keane, 2003): „Social life has a mediated character whenever persons are linked to each other through speech and other perceivable signs in participation frameworks of communicative activity" (Agha, 2011, S. 163). Kommunikative Handlungen sind immer durch zeichenhafte Materialität mediiert. Nach diesem Medienverständnis geht es also darum zu untersuchen, was aus Perspektive sozialer Akteuere die sozialen, materiellen und semiotischen Bedingungen von Mediation sind.

Eine solche Perspektive nimmt auch das Konzept der Medialität (Spitzmüller, 2014) ein. In Abgrenzung zu verbreiteten Vorstellungen von Medien, die sie als technische Werkzeuge, Transportmittel oder soziale Institutionen verstehen, ist Medialität ein interpretatives Phänomen. Es nimmt in den Blick, was Sprecher*innen unter einem Medium verstehen und was es bewirkt (Medialitätserwartungen), in welchem Grad ein Medium als mediiert wahrgenommen wird (Medialitätswahrnehmung) und welche Werte und Eigenschaften mit einem Medium verbunden werden (Medialitätszuschreibungen) (Spitzmüller, 2014). Auch das verwandte Konzept der Medienideologien (*media ideologies*, Gershon, 2010b) unterstreicht, unter Berufung auf Keanes *semiotic ideologies* (2003), die Bedeutung der Materialität sprachlicher Zeichen. Gleichzeitig ist Materialität, der Bedeutung zugeschrieben wird, nicht einfach verfügbar, erkenntlich und offen zur Interpretation. Die Zeichenhaftigkeit von Materialität ist immer Teil einer diskursiven Erschaffung (Spitzmüller, 2018). Einerseits ist Materialität also die Voraussetzung für die Wahrnehmbarkeit von Zeichen, andererseits wird Materialität erst zum Zeichen, wenn sie als solches wahrgenommen und interpretiert wird. Ob und wie Materialität als bedeutsam wahrgenommen wird, erschließt sich uns aus der sozialen Praxis (zu der auch die diskursive Praxis gezählt wird).

2.3   Biografische Objekte als Mittel mediatisierter Vergemeinschaftung

Bei den Medien, die in diesem Beitrag vorgestellt werden, handelt es sich um Dinge, die alle Schwellen zwischen Lebensabschnitten in privaten Archiven überdauert haben. Ihre Geschichte ist eng mit der Biografie der Menschen verwoben, die sie produziert, gesammelt, verwahrt, im Rahmen des Projekts erforscht und für das Interview hervorgeholt haben. Ich spreche daher, in Anlehnung an Kopytoff (1986), der den Begriff „kulturelle Biografie der Dinge" einführte, von biografischen Objekten. Dinge besitzen demnach nicht nur *eine* Funktion und Bedeutung, die immer gleich bleibt, sondern durchlaufen aufgrund von gesellschaftlichen Veränderungen und Brüchen verschiedene Phasen, in denen ihnen jeweils eine andere Bedeutsamkeit und Wertigkeit zugeschrieben wird. Dinge können in einer anderen Phase ihres Lebens ihre bisherige Wirkung gänzlich verlieren oder eine neue akkumulieren. Daher ist eine zentrale Perspektive, wie sich mit der Zirkulation von Dingen in Raum und Zeit ihr *regime of value* (Appadurai, 1986), ihre Wertigkeitshierarchie ändert. Joy (2009) untersucht, wie Dinge in verschiedenen Phasen einerseits soziale Beziehungen herstellen und andererseits, wie soziale Gefüge die Produktion von Dingen ermöglichen. Sie beruft sich dabei auf Gell (1998), nach dem menschliche Handlungsmacht (agency) auf Dinge ausgelagert und über sie mediiert werden kann und zweitens auf Strathern (1988), nach der Handlungsmacht nicht aus dem

Individuum erwächst (als etwas, das das Individuum per se besitzen würde), sondern aus der Einbettung der Person in soziale Netzwerke und materielle Kultur (*distributed personhood*). Dinge haben also nicht nur eine Biografie aufgrund ihrer Einbindung in menschliche Lebenszusammenhänge, sondern auch umgekehrt, weil sich die menschliche Biografie in Dingen ablagert und auf sie auslagert.

Biografische Objekte werden also in verschiedenen Lebensabschnitten zur Mediation eingesetzt. Sie stellen nach Joy (2009, siehe Absatz oben) soziale Beziehungen her, was Hepp, Berg und Roitsch (2014) mit dem Begriff der „mediatisierten Vergemeinschaftung" erfassen. Unter „mediatisierter Vergemeinschaftung" wird die subjektive Wahrnehmung eines Zusammengehörigkeitsgefühls verstanden, das durch geteilte Medienpraxis entsteht. Sie lehnen sich dabei an Webers Begriff der Vergemeinschaftung an, der schreibt: „Eine solche gefühlte Zusammengehörigkeit betrifft dann Vergemeinschaftung, wenn sie handlungsleitend für Menschen ist, indem diese ‚auf Grund dieses Gefühls ihr Verhalten irgendwie *aneinander orientieren* (Weber 1972, S. 22, Herv. i. O.)'" (Hepp, Berg & Roitsch, 2014, S. 52). Das bedeutet, dass sich die Mitglieder einer Gruppe nicht qua Kategorie (z. B. als Familienmitglied, als Freund*in) als solche konstituieren, sondern durch ein subjektives Zusammengehörigkeitsgefühl einerseits und durch geteilte Medienpraxis andererseits. Der Begriff Vergemeinschaftung betont den aktiven Zusammenschluss, die Praktiken, die damit verbunden sind, dass Gruppenzugehörigkeit entsteht. Mediatisierte Vergemeinschaftung trete nach Hepp, Berg und Roitsch (2014) bei Jugendlichen nicht etwa nur oder verstärkt dort auf, wo eine lokale Vergemeinschaftung verunmöglicht ist, sondern gerade innerhalb jener Gruppen, in denen sich ihre Lebenswelt entfaltet. Die Autor*innen kommen zu dem Schluss, dass sich Mediatisierung sowohl in Bezug auf ortsübergreifende als auch auf lokale Vergemeinschaftung beobachten lässt.

3.   Das Forschungsdesign des Projekts *Language in Motion*

Im Projekt *Language in Motion*, bei dem bisher vier Interviewpartner*innen in je drei Sessions interviewt wurden, wurde ein mehrstufiges, kooperatives Forschungsdesign verfolgt: Die Interviewpartner*innen wurden in die erste, grobe Analyse des sprachenbiografischen Interviews miteinbezogen und wählten während der selbstständigen Forschungsphase, welches Thema und/oder welche Lebensphase ihrer Biografie sie weiter untersuchen wollten. Das sprachbiografische Interview wurde anhand eines Sprachenportraits erhoben: die Teilnehmer*innen wurden aufgefordert, jene Sprechweisen einzuzeichnen, die in ihrem Leben eine Rolle spielen. Es dient als Basis für die darauffolgende Beschreibung des Portaits. Die Interviews wurden auf Deutsch geführt mit gelegentlichen

Wörtern oder Phrasen auf Bosnisch/Kroatisch/Serbisch. Nachdem das Kriterium für die Teilnahme die Erfahrung der Flucht als Kind vor dem Krieg in Ex-Jugoslawien ist, war davon auszugehen, dass die Personen schwierige oder möglicherweise sogar traumatisierende Erlebnisse erfahren hatten. Die Interviewführung war deswegen darauf ausgelegt, weder im sprachbiografischen Interview noch in einer anderen Erzählaufforderung nach bestimmten biografischen Abschnitten zu fragen, sondern den Interviewpartner*innen selbst zu überlassen, über welche Lebensphase sie zu einem bestimmten Thema erzählen wollten. Damit erfragte ich dezidiert nicht „die" Biografie, als chronologische Abfolge von der Geburt bis zur Gegenwart, sondern zielte darauf ab, „kleine Geschichten" (*small stories*; Georgakopoulou, 2015) zu erheben. Diese kleinen Geschichten erlauben es, zueinander in Widerspruch zu stehen, ohne in den übergeordneten Sinn eines großen Ganzen eingeordnet werden zu müssen.

4.   Analysebeispiele

4.1   Vorbemerkung

Geleitet von diesen theoretischen Überlegungen arbeite ich in der Analyse heraus, wie biografische Objekte zur Mediation eingesetzt werden. Die Aufmerksamkeit wird erstens darauf gerichtet, wie Dinge im sozialen Gefüge eines Lebensabschnitts zur Mediation eingesetzt werden. Die Interviewpartner*innen rekonstruieren im Rückblick die Medienpraxis rund um diese biografischen Objekte und wie sich diese in späteren Lebensphasen veränderte. Zweitens arbeite ich heraus, in welchem Wechselspiel Spracherleben und Medien stehen. Entlang der Achsen des Spracherlebens, vor allem Inklusion und Exklusion, Handlungsmacht und Ohnmacht wird deutlich, wie die analysierten Medien Vergemeinschaftung durch geteilte Medienpraxis (Hepp, Berg & Roitsch, 2014) bewirken. Die beiden angeführten Beispiele stammen aus Interviews mit Personen, die in der 2. Hälfte der 1980er Jahre geboren sind.

4.2   *Beispiel 1*: Medien als Prozess der Vergemeinschaftung

Wenn man bedenkt, dass Deutsch für die meisten Interviewpartner*innen, als sie nach Österreich kamen, noch nicht Teil ihres sprachlichen Repertoires war, könnte man erwarten, dass die Erfahrung, an einen Ort zu kommen und sich (noch) nicht verständigen zu können, seinen Niederschlag in den Darstellungen des Spracherlebens findet. Diese Erfahrung nimmt allerdings bei den meisten Interviews nur einen marginalen Platz ein. Das erzählerische Hauptaugenmerk liegt beim eigenen Vermögen, diesen Zustand in kurzer Zeit überwunden zu haben. Den Achsen des Spracherlebens (Busch, 2017) entsprechend, steht in der erzählten Schulzeit also nicht die Ohnmacht, sondern die Erlangung kommunikativer Handlungsmacht im Zentrum sowie die Bedingungen und Strategien, die dazu geführt haben. Dieses Beispiel stellt Ergebnisse aus der Forschung einer Interviewpartnerin (Alja M.[2]) vor, bei denen es um materielle und institutionelle Bedingungen für kommunikative Handlungsmacht im biografischen Abschnitt der Schulzeit geht.

Alja M. kommt in einer Gemeinde im heutigen Bosnien zur Welt, wo sie auch ihre Kindheit und die ersten zwei Jahre ihrer Volksschulzeit verbringt. Als sie acht Jahre alt ist, verlagert die Familie den Lebensmittelpunkt aufgrund des Krieges nach Österreich. Ab diesem Zeitpunkt geht sie in einer Gemeinde in Osttirol zur Schule. Die Zeit an diesem Ort stellt im Interview einen Lebensabschnitt dar, der mit der Schule als einer zentralen Institution in Zusammenhang steht. Die Schule ist der Sozialisations- und Kommunikationsraum, der den größten erzählerischen Stellenwert innerhalb dieses biografischen Abschnitts (zwischen acht und 18 Jahren) einnimmt. Alja bewertet die Schule mit den Schreibanlässen und dem sozialen Gefüge einerseits und die Bibliothek andererseits rückblickend als wichtige Ressourcen für ihr Sprachenlernen und ihre kommunikative Handlungsfähigkeit.

In diesem Zitat begründet Alja ihre Entscheidung für ein bestimmtes Medium als Forschungsobjekt, das ich anhand ihrer Reflexionen dazu im Folgenden untersuchen werde:

> „AM: Ja, ich hab mir grad gedacht eben so es wär lustig zu schauen: wie schauen die Schularbeiten aus ahm vom Sprachlichen her, wie schauen aber diese Heftln aus, weil ich glaub das Verspielte is in den Heftln und die Schularbeiten sind halt das Reglementierende, Seriöse." (1w_2)

Das Medium, auf das sich Alja M. hier bezieht, ist ein Schulheft, in das sie mit Freund*innen gemeinsam Einträge machte. Im Verlauf des Interviews kristallisiert sich die Praxis rund um dieses Heft heraus. Es ist für Einträge einer bestimmten Personengruppe bestimmt, nämlich vier Freundinnen, und nur diese Gruppe darf in das Heft eintragen und die Einträge lesen. Die Einträge beziehen sich auf Ereignisse und Anekdoten des Schulalltags. Die Schreibpraxis ist zum Teil dialogisch, wenn jemand aus der Gruppe einen Eintrag macht und die anderen diesen Eintrag kommentieren, was zum Teil auch multimodal durch Zeichnungen geschieht. Andere Einträge wiederum sind nur von einer Autorin und stellen, als kleine Situationserzählungen, Dialoge aus dem Alltag dar mit ihren Charakteren, Redeweisen und sozialen Typen. In diesen kleinen Erzäh-

---

2 Die Namen wurden pseudonymisiert.

lungen findet sich die Vielsprachigkeit der Schule gerahmt und autorisiert von einer der vier Autorinnen wieder. In dieses Heft werden also kontinuierlich Einträge gemacht, es füllt sich sukzessiv mit Text und Zeichnungen und hier wird gesammelt, was von den vier Autorinnen als wert empfunden wird, aufgehoben zu werden. In vielerlei Hinsicht fungiert das Heft damit als Sammlung oder als Album, und damit haben wir es mit einer „latent enzyklopädischen, wenn auch zugleich ostentativ fragmentarischen Darstellung von Welt" (Schmitz-Emans, 2020, S. 557f.) zu tun.

Das Heft kann auch als Archiv verstanden werden, womit im Sinne Derridas gemeint ist, es als Ort einer Sammlung für potenziellen späteren Gebrauch zu verstehen. Ich leite das aus folgendem Zitat ab, bei dem Alja M. über die Medienpraxis in Zusammenhang mit diesem Heft reflektiert:

> „AM: Es waren, glaub ich, drei, vier von uns beteiligt // I: Ja // und man konnte schon auch als Externe sagen, schreibt's es rein, weil vielleicht brauchen wir es auch für die Maturazeitung oder so // I: Ah //, die es dann übrigens nie gegeben hat. Also, es war schon die Idee dahinter, dass man irgendwie so eine Sammlung macht an Kuriositäten, die so in der Schule passieren, aber es ist jetzt nicht durch die ganze Klasse gegangen. Wir haben aber sehr wohl eben Inhalte von der ganzen Klasse aufgenommen." (1w_3)

Im Heft werden Alltagsgeschehnisse der Schulwelt gesammelt, um sie potenziell später zu verwenden. In diesem Ausschnitt tritt die Maturazeitung als mögliches Medium hervor, in dem ausgewählte Einträge des Schulhefts später publiziert werden könnten. Allerdings ist die Maturazeitung nicht notwendigerweise der zentrale Beweggrund für die Eintragungen, sondern das grundsätzliche Anlegen einer solchen Sammlung und ihre potenziellen Verwendungen. Die Einträge könnten auf diese Weise zu einem späteren Zeitpunkt als Elemente eines Archivs verwendet werden. Derrida begreift das Archiv als einen Ort der Sammlung, die mögliche zukünftige Verwendungen schon im Blick hat. Allerdings entziehen sich die zukünftigen Verwendungen eines Archivs und der in ihm gesammelten Objekte der gegenwärtigen Kenntnis:

> „In einem rätselhaften Sinn, der sich *vielleicht* (vielleicht, denn aufgrund wesentlicher Gründe darf hier nichts als sicher gelten) aufklären wird, ist die Frage des Archivs, wiederholen wir es, nicht eine Frage der Vergangenheit. [...]. Es ist eine Frage von Zukunft, die Frage der Zukunft selbst, die Frage einer Antwort, eines Versprechens und einer Verantwortung für morgen. Wenn wir wissen wollen, was das Archiv bedeutet haben wird, so werden wir es nur in zukünftigen Zeiten wissen. Vielleicht. Nicht morgen, sondern in zukünftigen Zeiten, sogleich oder vielleicht niemals. Eine gespenstische Messianizität beeinflusst den Begriff Archiv und bindet ihn, wie die Religion, wie die Geschichte, wie die Wissenschaft selbst, an eine ganz eigenartige Erfahrung des Versprechens." (Derrida 1996, S. 44, kursiv i. O.).

Das Archiv hat somit eine zweifache Ausrichtung: Es weist sowohl in die Vergangenheit als auch in die Zukunft. Diese Potenzialität des Archivs ist es, die im Fall des Schulheftes zum Tragen kommt: Das Anlegen und Eintragen in das Schulheft hat schon die Zukunft in ihrem Horizont. Das Projekt einer Maturazeitung ist nur eine, wenn auch besonders naheliegende, Verwendung, gleichzeitig ist die Sammlung nicht umsonst, wenn diese Maturazeitung nie zustande kommt, denn das Heft als Archiv könnte zu späterer Zeit andere, noch unbekannte Verwendungen haben. Gleichzeitig soll hier jedoch auch nicht der „Nutzen" dieses Mediums überbewertet werden, denn was am Heft nach Aljas Erkenntnissen zentral war, auch ohne zukünftige Verwendung, war die Medienpraxis selbst: das Spiel mit Sprache und Prozesse der Vergemeinschaftung.

Das Heft, so wie es im Interview in Erscheinung tritt, steht in Zusammenhang mit der körperlichen und emotionalen Dimension von Sprache. Wie Alja im zweiten Interview vorankündigt, tritt im kollektiven Tagebuch das Verspielte der Sprache in den Vordergrund, während in den Schularbeiten Sprache als das „Reglementierende, Seriöse" in Erscheinung tritt („ich glaub das Verspielte is in den Heftln und die Schularbeiten sind halt das Reglementierende, Seriöse" 1w_2). Die Medialität des Hefts erlaubt das Spiel mit Sprache, die Freude am Formulieren, an der Repräsentation verschiedener Stimmen, Sprachen und Diskurse. Das korreliert auch mit Aljas visueller Gestaltung des Sprachenportraits, in dem sie sich umgeben von Wasser darstellt und für das Deutsch-Sprechen die Metapher „wie der Fisch im Wasser" findet.

Ein weiterer Aspekt dieses Mediums ist seine Wirkung auf Prozesse der Vergemeinschaftung (Hepp, Berg & Roitsch, 2014). Die Institutionalisierung des Hefts, das durch eine bestimmte Handlungspraxis entsteht (wer darf hineinschreiben, was schreibt man hinein, wie schreibt man es), bewirkt ein Wir-Gefühl und vice versa materialisiert das Objekt dieses Wir-Gefühl. Es stellt mediatisierte Vergemeinschaftung her (Hepp, Berg & Roitsch, 2014), was bedeutet, dass sich die Mitglieder der Gruppe zwar durchaus auch lokal, ohne Medium, als Freundinnengruppe formieren. Allerdings verfestigt das Medienobjekt und die Praxis, die damit verbunden ist, diese Gruppe und konstituiert sie möglicherweise durch diese trennscharfen Grenzen (wir – Externe) erst. Jedenfalls lässt es die Grenzen zwischen innen und außen stärker hervortreten.

Nach dem Ende der Schulzeit bekommt Alja eine Kopie dieses Hefts, die sie in einer Plastikschachtel in ihrer Wohnung aufbewahrt und vor allem bei Umzügen hervorholt und liest (1w_3). Aus diesem privaten Archiv wird es auch für dieses Interview herausgeholt, um damit Medienpraktiken, Spracherleben und Prozesse der Vergemeinschaftung zur Schulzeit zur Sprache zu bringen.

4.3   *Beispiel 2:* Zeigen und Schweigen: der doppelte Index von Medien

An diesem Beispiel wird deutlich, dass Medien bzw. Objekte nicht notwendigerweise Sprache in ihrer denotativen Funktion kommunizieren, sondern
gleichzeitig auf einen Inhalt verweisen und über ihn schweigen können. Luka K.
wurde in einer Gemeinde in Slawonien im heutigen Kroatien geboren. Als er zwei
Jahre alt war, begann der Krieg, zwei Jahre später flüchtete die Familie nach
Österreich. Zwei Jahre lang versuchten sie, in Österreich eine Aufenthaltsbewilligung zu bekommen und wurden immer wieder abgeschoben, bis sie schlussendlich eine dauerhafte Aufenthaltsgenehmigung in einer Gemeinde in Oberösterreich erhielten.

Als Luka das Sprachenportrait zeichnet, schraffiert er Kroatisch rot in den
oberen Teil des Torsos. Im Laufe des Interviews stellt sich dieser Teil seines
Repertoires, den er zunächst als Kroatisch bezeichnet, als komplexes Gebilde
heraus, das im Laufe seiner Biografie öfters geändert und angepasst wurde. Als
Luka das Portrait beschreibt, identifiziert er retrospektiv drei Phasen, die dieser
Teil seines Repertoires durchlaufen hat. Erstens das slawonische Kroatisch vor
dem Krieg, das er als Konglomerat verschiedener regionaler Einflüsse und
zeitlicher Schichten beschreibt, zweitens das Standardkroatisch ab Ende der
1990er Jahre, das von seinem Vater eingefordert wurde und schlussendlich die an
einer Stelle als „Serbo-Kroatisch" bezeichnete Sprache, die er aktuell mit seiner
Frau spricht.

Vom heutigen Standpunkt aus gesehen stellt sich die Sprache seiner Kindheit
als ein Gebilde vieler verschiedener Elemente dar, und zwar gerade deswegen,
weil sie zu einem späteren Zeitpunkt, Luka lokalisiert es Ende der 1990er Jahre,
Ziel von nationalistischer Sprachbereinigung wird. Diese Zäsur der bis dahin
gesprochenen Sprache findet statt, als Luka schon in einer Gemeinde in Oberösterreich zur Schule geht und Deutsch erlernt hat. In der zweiten Hälfte der
1990er Jahre kommt eine größere Zahl geflüchteter Kinder aus serbischen Regionen Bosniens und aus Serbien an seine Schule. Er übersetzt zwischen den
Kindern und der Lehrerin und freundet sich mit einigen an. Sein Vater verbietet
ihm allerdings aufgrund seiner politischen Position, sich mit den Kindern außerhalb der Schule zu treffen und als serbisch registrierte Wörter zu verwenden:
„es war eben nicht gewünscht // I: Ja.// und da kam eben so dieser Cut und
seitdem war eben Serbisch für mich als Sprache nicht mehr relevant in dem
Sinne" (2m_1). Mit Ende der 1990er Jahre geht eine Veränderung der bisherigen,
im täglichen Leben der Familie gebrauchten Sprache vor sich. Die Veränderung
ist bedingt durch die politischen Ereignisse im ehemaligen Jugoslawien und der
politischen „Lösung" des Konflikts durch die Aufteilung in ethnisch-territorial
definierte Regionen (im Fall Bosniens) und Nationalstaaten. Die Nationenbil-
dung war eng verwoben mit der Herausarbeitung nationalstaatlicher Standard-

sprachen in Abgrenzung zum bisherigen Standard und Linguonym Serbokroatisch (Greenberg, 2008). Diese makropolitische Situation findet ihren Niederschlag in der Familiensprachpolitik, bei der die bisher gesprochene Sprache der Familie auf Betreiben Lukas Vaters immer mehr zugunsten einer kroatischnationalistischen Sprachideologie zensuriert wird. Sie geht aber auch mit dem Verbot von Kontakten zu serbischen Kindern einher und dem Einfluss dieser auf Lukas Sprachenrepertoire. Die Sprache der Kindheit, die Luka als regionale Sprache darstellt, in der sich Elemente aus vielen anderen Sprachen und Redeweisen mischen, wird ab der Zäsur (im Interview „der Cut", „die Abzweigung") dem kroatisch-nationalistischen „(R)einheitsgebot" (Thoma, 2018) unterstellt. Die Familie lernt ab diesem Zeitpunkt, bestimmte Elemente, die als serbisch registriert werden, aus ihrem Repertoire zu verdrängen. Auf der Mikroebene der Familiensprache vollzieht sich also, was Bachtin die zentripetalen Kräfte nennt – eine Bewegung in Richtung der Vereinheitlichung des Wortes (Bachtin, 1979 [1975], S. 163f.) oder, im Sinne von Irvine und Gal (2000), eine Tendenz der Ausdifferenzierung.

In der Erzählung zu seinem Sprachenportrait nimmt Luka öfters Stellung zu dieser Familiensprachpolitik der Teilung von Sprache und Bevölkerung in Serb*innen und Kroat*innen, die von seinem Vater betrieben wurde, nämlich indem er sie immer ablehnte. Er traf sich weiterhin im Untergrund mit dem serbischen Freund aus der Schule und heiratete später eine serbische Frau. In seiner aktuellen Lebenssituation sind deswegen wieder als serbisch identifizierte Wörter, die von seinem Vater verboten wurden, Teil seiner Alltagskommunikation. Die Teilung in Nationalsprachen ist zwar nicht reversibel und Wörter werden der einen und der anderen Sprache zugeteilt, gleichzeitig ist die „Mischung" dieser Sprachen in der Kommunikation mit seiner Frau, wenn auch registriert, so doch „erlaubt" und seine Sprache nähert sich, wie er beschreibt, damit teilweise wieder jenem Slawonisch der Kindheit an: „[zeigt auf das Sprachenportrait, auf die rote Stelle, die er als Kroatisch bezeichnet], es ist nicht mehr ganz kroatisch, es ist eigentlich schon serbokroatisch geworden, weil einfach eben natürlich durch meine Frau ich auch / ist einfach das Serbische auch mehr reingekommen und früher auch schon immer Teil gewesen // I: Mhm.// und jetzt auch wieder adaptiert worden." (2m_3)

Das Objekt, das Luka im abschließenden Interview vorstellt, würde in den meisten, technisch definierten Vorstellungen nicht als Medium gelten, denn es handelt sich um Babyschuhe. In der folgenden Analyse arbeite ich anhand Lukas Darstellung heraus, wie dieses Objekt als Medium in verschiedenen Lebensphasen auftritt: erstens, im biografischen Abschnitt der jugoslawischen Zeit vor dem Krieg, als die Schuhe produziert wurden; zweitens die Zeit der Ausstellung des Objektes im Familienschrein; und drittens, der Platz dieses Objekts zum Zeitpunkt des Interviews. Abschließend werde ich die Schuhe als Medium sowohl von Weitergabe von Erinnerung als auch von Schweigen darüber mit dem Spracherleben in Beziehung setzen.

Das Ergebnis von Lukas Forschung ist, dass das Beispiel der Babyschuhe zeigt, wie Objekte in verschiedenen historischen und biografischen Abschnitten ihre Wirkmacht (Gell, 1998) entfalten. Er zeichnet ihre kommunikative Wirkung in verschiedenen Lebensabschnitten nach, um damit ihren aktuellen Stellenwert zu verdeutlichen. Zum ersten Abschnitt, dem Produktionskontext, ist zu sagen, dass die Familie vor der Flucht in einer Nachbarstadt von Vukovar wohnte. Lukas Mutter arbeitete in einer Fabrik in Vukovar, wo eine Schuhmarke hergestellt wurde, die in ganz Jugoslawien populär war. Zum Anlass der Geburt ihres Sohnes produziere sie in dieser Fabrik eigenhändig Babyschuhe. Diese Schuhe hat Luka nach wie vor und sie befinden sich jetzt im Zimmer seines Sohnes. Der folgende Ausschnitt stammt aus den ersten Minuten des Interviews, in denen Luka erzählt, was die Ergebnisse seiner Forschung waren.

> „LK: Und das, ich weiß nicht wieso, weil das [die Babyschuhe] hängt immer schon im Zimmer vom Kleinen, aber eben seit ich die Aufgabe habe mir Objekte mit einem anderen Bezug anzuschauen, // I: Mhm // hat mich das öfters in den Bann gezogen. Auch traurig gestimmt, // I: Ja // aber hauptsächlich so dieses, sie [Lukas Mutter] hat eben damals in Vukovar gearbeitet, in Vukovar ist schwierig gewesen alles, // I: Ja // dann eben diese Schuhe und dann die ganze Situation, weil ich eben von meiner Kindheit fast nichts weiß. Also, das ist so ein bisschen ein / Familiengeheimnis, würde ich nicht sagen, // I: Mhm // aber es wird eben nicht drüber gesprochen" (2m_3).

Aus der zitierten Stelle geht hervor, dass die Schuhe erstens auf die Kindheit verweisen. Sie sind das einzige Objekt, das aus der Zeit der Kindheit noch existiert:

> „LK: [...] das ist eigentlich das Einzige, was ich habe aus meiner Kindheit. // I: Mhm! // Also ich hab sonst · absolut nichts, also keine Spielsachen, keine Kleidung gar nichts, weil es halt durch die ständigen Umzüge und was auch immer, · irgendwann einmal verloren gegangen ist // I: Ja // <((langsam, deutlich)) außer die Schuhe.> Das ist das Einzige, · was ich halt noch hab aus meiner Kindheit." (2m_3)

Die Schuhe haben alle Umzüge, Ortswechsel und Schwellen der Biografie überstanden und stellen jetzt die einzige materielle Manifestation der Kindheit dar. Das Objekt verweist auf eine Zeit-Raum-Konfiguration, die es heute nicht mehr gibt: die jugoslawische Schuhfabrik, in der eine *der* bekanntesten Marken Jugoslawiens hergestellt wurde und diese Ära bildet im Rückblick, mit allem, was sich danach ereignet hat, einen Kontrast. So wie die Sprache zu diesem Zeitpunkt noch nicht getrennt war, war auch der Staat, die Menschen, die Schuhfabrik eine pan-jugoslawische, ungeteilt. Insofern korreliert dieses symbolisch aufgeladene Objekt mit dem oben beschriebenen Spracherleben im Lebensabschnitt der Kindheit. Die Schuhfabrik und die Sprache gehören beide zu einem Davor, einer

Zeit vor dem Krieg und der Teilung. Im Gegensatz zur späteren, nationalistischen Aufteilung in verschiedene Standardsprachen (und der Gewalt des Krieges, die dieser Aufteilung vorangig), erscheint die Sprache der Kindheit im Rückblick als eine vielsprachige, in der sprachliche Differenzen Regionen, Klassen, Zeiten bezeichnen aber noch kein Schibboleth zwischen nationalistischen Zugehörigkeiten (Busch & Spitzmüller, 2021). Die retrospektive Erinnerung dieses Spracherlebens (und der Schuhfabrik als Zeichen dieser Ära) ist als „Sehnsucht nach der Sprache davor" (Busch, 2010, S. 71) zu verstehen und zwar genau aus der Logik ihrer späteren gewaltsamen Teilung.

Die Schuhe sind ein materielles Zeugnis der Kindheit, gleichzeitig jedoch verweisen sie auf ein Schweigen. Schweigen ist nicht das Gegenteil von Sprache, sondern hat auch eine kommunikative Funktion und ist bedeutsam (Jaworski, 1993). So kann Schweigen die Funktion haben, den Kommunikationskanal offen zu halten und Ambiguität beizubehalten (nicht zu vereindeutigen) (Jaworksi, 1993, S. 48). Die Schuhe verstecken und offenbaren gleichermaßen. Auch das ist Teil des Spracherlebens, das sich in der Weitergabe einerseits des Objekts und andererseits des Schweigens über diese Zeit manifestiert. Das Schweigen, so deutet Luka mit dem Verweis auf die Zerstörung und Kriegsverbrechen in Vukovar an („in Vukovar ist schwierig gewesen alles"), hat seinen Ursprung in den historischen Ereignissen – dem Erleben von Krieg, Flucht, dem unsicheren rechtlichen Zwischenstadium bis zur Aufenthaltsbewilligung und dem Aufbau einer neuen Existenz. Auch im Interview sind die Schuhe ein Medium, um die Kindheit zur Sprache zu bringen *und* das Schweigen darüber, aber auch das eigene Erleben dieses Schweigens und worin es begründet ist. Luka beschreibt diesen doppelten Verweis der Schuhe auf die Kindheitszeit und das Schweigen über diese Zeit aufgrund der gewaltsamen Ereignisse mit dem Gefühl des Traurig-seins und gleichzeitig in-den-Bann-gezogen-Seins („in den Bann gezogen [...] auch traurig gestimmt").

Als die Familie schlussendlich eine Aufenthaltsbewilligung in der Gemeinde in Oberösterreich bekommt, werden die Babyschuhe gemeinsam mit einer kleinen Bronzestatue, die sein Bruder zur Geburt bekommen hat, und einer Kappe seines Großvaters ausgestellt. Luka nennt den Ort, an dem die drei Objekte ab dann in einer Gemeinschaft wohnen, den „Familienschrein" (2m_3), wobei die Objekte jeweils ihn (Babyschuhe), seinen Bruder (Bronzestatue) und seine Mutter (Kappe des Großvaters) repräsentieren. Alle drei verweisen auf die Zeit, über die nicht gesprochen wird, die aber ihre geteilte biografische Erfahrung darstellt. Sie wirken als Medien der Vergemeinschaftung bzw. sind materieller Teil des „doing family" (Schier & Jurczyk, 2007). Die Gemeinschaft dieser Objekte ist im Gegensatz zum Archiv aus dem vorigen Beispiel ausgestellt, sie sind Teil des häuslichen Alltagsbildes und erinnern an die Zusammengehörigkeit der drei Personen, die sie repräsentieren (wobei der Vater hier nicht repräsentiert wird).

Auch in der Gegenwart sind die Schuhe ausgestellt. Sie hängen jetzt im Zimmer seines Sohnes und können damit wiederum als ein Medium der Weitergabe von Erinnerung (bzw. Schweigen) an die nächste Generation verstanden werden.

5. Schlussfolgerungen

Die besprochenen Beispiele zeichnen die Verwobenheit von Spracherleben und Medien in ihrem jeweiligen lebensweltlichen Zusammenhang nach. Im ersten Beispiel bewirkt das gemeinsam geführte Heft die Vergemeinschaftung einer Gruppe von Freundinnen zur Zeit seiner Entstehung. Das Heft war gemäß der damaligen Praxis ein Prozess der Einschreibung, in den die Vielsprachigkeit der Schulwelt mit ihren Redeweisen, sozialen Typen und Diskursen Eingang fand und von den vier beteiligten Personen autorisiert wurde. Seine Medialität (Spitzmüller, 2014) ermöglicht sprachliche Praktiken des Spiels, der Ironie und der Distanzierung. Nach der Schulzeit wird das Heft kopiert, den Beteiligten geschenkt und befindet sich ab diesem Zeitpunkt im privaten Archiv, aus dem es zum Anlass des Interviews wieder hervorgeholt wird. Hier dient es wiederum als Medium, um sich zu erinnern und über diese Vergangenheit zu sprechen.

Die Babyschuhe aus dem zweiten Beispiel, das Produkt einer jugoslawischen Fabrik, korrelieren mit der präbabylonischen Phantasie einer „Sprache davor" (Busch, 2010), einer Zeit vor der gewaltsamen Teilung durch den Krieg, die auch in der Familiensprachpolitik ihren Niederschlag fand. Dieses biografische Objekt verweist sowohl auf einen bestimmten Lebensabschnitt mit seinen historischen Ereignissen und das Schweigen darüber. Erstens erinnert es an die Zeit vor dem Krieg, zweitens an den Krieg und die Vertreibung und drittens an die Zeit des dauerhaften Aufenthalts in Österreich, in der diese Schuhe, in der Gemeinschaft mit anderen Objekten, im Familienschrein ausgestellt wurden. Die Babyschuhe bewirken Vergemeinschaftung bestimmter Familienmitglieder durch die Praxis des Schenkens und späteren Ausstellens. Sie kommunizieren sowohl die Erinnerung an eine vergangene historische Zeit und ihr gewaltsames Ende als auch die Weitergabe der Erinnerung an die nächste Generation. Alle diese Phasen in der Biografie dieses Objekts verschwanden im Laufe der Zeit allerdings nie ganz, sondern haben sich, wie Schichten eines Palimpsests, im Objekt abgelagert. In den Beispielen wird offenbar, dass für das Spracherleben, neben der körperlichen und emotionalen Dimension, auch die materielle Dimension von Bedeutung ist: jene Materialität, mit der Zeichen in Erscheinung treten, wird aus einer Subjektperspektive bedeutsam.

Mit diesen Beispielen argumentiere ich, dass Dinge, die im Alltagsverständnis und nach technischen Medienauffassungen nicht als Medien gelten würden, doch zur Mediation eingesetzt werden. Soziales Handeln und Kommunikation sind, wie die Interviewpartner*innen reflektieren, durch die materielle Welt mediiert (Agha, 2011). Diese Dinge als biografische Objekte zu betrachten zeigt, dass die Objekte in den Beispielen nicht in allen Lebensphasen ein- und dieselbe Mediation bewirken oder einmal ein Medium sind und dann nicht mehr, sondern dass diese Dinge in verschiedenen Lebensabschnitten und zu verschiedenen historischen Zeiten Unterschiedliches kommunizieren. Die biografische Perspektive lässt zu, Medien und Sprachen als eingebettet in den jeweiligen lebensweltlichen Zusammenhang zu untersuchen. Das ermöglicht, den Fokus auf die Schwellen zwischen den Lebensabschnitten zu lenken, nämlich wie sich Spracherleben als auch Mediation (gemeinsam mit der Subjektivität der Person) aufgrund des Übertritts verändert. Dieser Beitrag fügt der Diskussion um *youth, media, life* hinzu, wie biografische Objekte der Kindheit und Jugend in unterschiedlichen Abschnitten der Biografie eine neue Bedeutsamkeit erlangen und zur Mediation eingesetzt werden.

Anmerkung zur Transkription

.	kurze Turn-interne Pause, Zögern
..	längere Turn-interne Pause
...	lange Turn-interne Pause

(())	Kommentare zu Modulation und non-/paraverbale Aktivitäten in der Sequenz, die durch < > gekennzeichnet ist, z.B. <((langsam, deutlich)) außer die Schuhe.>
/	Änderung der Syntax
//	Aktivitäten aktiven Zuhörens der Interviewerin, die keinen eigenen Turn indizieren, z.B. //I: Mhm.//
nichts	(Unterstreichung) Betonung eines Wortes oder einer Silbe

Referenzen

Agha, A. (2011). Meet mediatization. *Language and Communication, 31*(3), 163–170. https://doi.org/10.1016/j.langcom.2011.03.006.

Appadurai, A. (Ed.). (1986). *The social life of things: Commodities in cultural perspective.* Cambridge University Press.

Bachtin, M. (1979 [1975]). Das Wort im Roman. In R. Grübel (Hrsg.), *Die Ästhetik des Wortes* (S. 154–300). Suhrkamp.

Barker, M. (2019). Intersubjective traps over tricks on the Kazakhstani puppet stage: Animation as dicentization. *Journal of Linguistic Anthropology, 29*(3), 375–396. https://doi.org/10.1111/jola.12227.

Bolter, J., & Grusin, R. (1999). *Remediation. Understanding new media.* MIT Press.

Busch, B. (2010). Die Macht präbabylonischer Phantasien. Ressourcenorientiertes sprachbiografisches Arbeiten. *Zeitschrift Literaturwissenschaft und Linguistik LiLi, 40,* 58–82. https://doi.org/10.1007/BF03379844.

Busch, B. (2015). „Without language, everything is chaos and confusion...". Corporal-emotional linguistic experience and the linguistic repertoire. In U. Lüdtke (Ed.), *Emotion in language. Theory, research, application* (pp. 273–288). Benjamins. https://doi.org /10.1075/ceb.10.14bus.

Busch, B. (2016a). Biographic approaches to research in multilingual settings: Exploring linguistic repertoires. In M. Martin-Jones & D. Martin (Eds.), *Researching multilingualism. Critical and ethnographic perspectives* (pp. 46–59). Routledge. https://doi.org /10.4324/9781315405346.

Busch, B. (2016b). Heteroglossia of survival: To have one's voice heard, to develop a voice worth hearing. *Working Papers in Urban Language and Literacies, 188,* 1–12. https://wp ull.org/wp-content/uploads/2022/04/WP188_Busch_2016_Heteroglossia_of_surviv.pdf.

Busch, B. (2016c). Regaining a place from which to speak and to be heard: In search of a response to the ,violence of voicelessness'. *Stellenbosch Papers in Linguistics Plus, 49,* 317–330. https://doi.org/10.5842/49-0-675.

Busch, B. (2017). Expanding the notion of the linguistic repertoire: On the concept of *Spracherleben* – the lived experience of language. *Applied Linguistics, 38*(3), 340–358. https://doi.org/10.1093/applin/amv030.

Busch, B., & Spitzmüller, J. (2021). Indexical borders: The sociolinguistic scales of the shibboleth. *International Journal of the Sociology of Language, 272,* 127–152. https:// doi.org/10.1515/ijsl-2020-0095.

Çağlar, A. (2018). Chronotopes of migration scholarship: Challenges of contemporaneity and historical conjuncture. In P. Barber & W. Lem (Eds.), *Migration, temporality, and capitalism. Entangled mobilities across global spaces* (pp. 21–42). Palgrave MacMillan. https://doi.org/10.1007/978-3-319-72781-3_2.

Couldry, N. (2008). Mediatization or mediation? Alternative understandings of the emergent space of digital storytelling. *New Media & Society, 10*(3), 373–391. https://doi.org /10.1177/1461444808089414.

Derrida, J. (1997). *Dem Archiv verschrieben: Mal d'archive.* Brinkmann + Bose.

Eisenlohr, P. (2006). *Little India: Diaspora, time, and ethnolinguistic belonging in Hindu Mauritius.* University of California Press. https://doi.org/10.1525/j.ctt1ppkdj.

Gell, A. (1998). *Art and agency: An anthropological theory.* Clarendon Press.

Georgakopoulou, A. (2015). Small stories research. Methods – analysis – outreach. In A. De Fina, & A. Georgakopoulou (Eds.), *The Handbook of Narrative Analysis* (pp. 255–271). Wiley Blackwell.

Gershon, I. (2010a). *The Breakup 2.0. Disconnecting over New Media.* Cornell University Press. https://www-degruyter-com.uaccess.univie.ac.at/document/doi/10.7591/978080 1458637/html.

Gershon, I. (2010b). Media ideologies. An introduction. *Journal of Linguistic Anthropology, 20*(2), 283–293. https://doi.org/10.1111/j.1548-1395.2010.01070.x.

Greenberg, R. (2008). *Language and identity in the Balkans: Serbo-Croatian and its disintegration.* Oxford University Press.

Halilović, H. (2013). Bosnian Austrians: Accidental migrants in trans-local and cyber spaces. *Journal of Refugee Studies, 26*(4), 524–540. https://doi.org/10.1093/jrs/fet002.

Hepp A., Berg, M., & Roitsch, C. (2014). *Mediatisierte Welten der Vergemeinschaftung. Kommunikative Vernetzung und das Gemeinschaftsleben junger Menschen.* Springer VS. https://link-springer-com.uaccess.univie.ac.at/book/10.1007/978-3-658-02425-3.

Hoklas, A.-K., & Lepa, S. (2015). Welchen Beitrag „leistet" die Materialität der Medien zum soziokulturellen Wandel? In F. Krotz, C. Despotović, & M.-M. Kruse (Hrsg.), *Mediatisierung als Metaprozess. Transformationen, Formen der Entwicklung und Generierung von Neuem* (S. 281–302). Springer VS.

Irvine, J., & Gal, S. (2000), Language ideology and linguistic differentiation. In Kroskrity, P. (Ed.), *Regimes of language: Ideologies, polities, and identities* (pp. 35–84). School of American Research Press.

Jaworski, A. (1993). *The power of silence: Social and pragmatic perspectives.* Sage.

Joy, J. (2009). Reinvigorating object biography: Reproducing the drama of object lives. *World Archaeology, 41*(4), 540–56. https://doi.org/10.1080/00438240903345530.

Karrebaek, M. (2017). Thai veggies and hair removal products: space, objects and language in an urban greengrocery. *Social Semiotics, 27*(4), 451–473. https://doi.org/10.1080/10 350330.2017.1334394.

Keane, W. (2003). Semiotics and the social analysis of material things. *Language and Communication, 23*, 409–425. https://doi.org/10.1016/S0271–5309(03)00010-7.

Kopytoff, I. (1986). The cultural biography of things: commoditisation as process. In A. Appadurai (Ed.), *The social life of things: Commodities in cultural perspective* (pp. 64–91). Cambridge University Press.

Lexander, K., & Androutsopoulos, J. (2019). Working with mediagrams: A methodology for collaborative research on mediational repertoires in multilingual families. *Journal of Multilingual and Multicultural Development*, 1–18. https://doi.org/10.1080/01434632.2 019.1667363.

Madianou, M., & Miller, D. (2013). Polymedia: Towards a new theory of digital media in interpersonal communication. *International Journal of Cultural Studies, 16*, 169–187. https://doi.org/10.1177/1367877912452486.

Merleau-Ponty, M. (2012). *Phenomenology of perception.* (Donald Landes, Trans.). Routledge. (Original work published 1945)

Mpendukana, S., & Stroud, C. (2020). Of monkeys, shacks, and loos. Changing times, changing places. In A. Peck, C. Stroud, & Q. Williams (Eds.), *Making sense of people and place in linguistic landscape* (pp. 183–200). Bloomsbury.

Palviainen, A. (2020). Video calls as a nexus of practice in multilingual translocal families. *Zeitschrift für interkulturellen Fremdsprachenunterricht, 25*(1), 85–108. https://zif.tujo urnals.ulb.tu-darmstadt.de/article/id/3222/.

Palviainen, A., & Kedra, J. (2020). What's in a family app? Making sense of digitally mediated communication with multilingual families. *Journal of Multilingual Theories and Practices, 1*(1), 89–111. https://doi.org/10.1558/jmtp.15363.

Pennycook, A., & Otsuji, E. (2017). Fish, phone cards and semiotic assemblages in two Bangladeshi shops in Sydney and Tokyo. *Social Semiotics, 27*(4), 434–450. https://doi.o rg/10.1080/10350330.2017.1334391.

Schier, M., & Jurczyk, K. (2007). „Familie als Herstellungsleistung" in Zeiten der Entgrenzung. *Aus Politik und Zeitgeschichte. Beilage zur Wochenzeitung DAS PARLAMENT, 34/2007*, 10–17. https://www.bpb.de/shop/zeitschriften/apuz/30290/familie-als -herstellungsleistung-in-zeiten-der-entgrenzung/.

Schmitz-Emans, M. (2020). Album und Scrapbook. In M. Schmitz-Emans. (Hrsg.), *Literatur, Buchgestaltung und Buchkunst* (S. 549–561). De Gruyter.

Schneider, J. (2008). *Spielräume der Medialität. Linguistische Gegenstandskonstitution aus medientheoretischer und pragmatischer Perspektive.* De Gruyter. https://www-degruyter-com.uaccess.univie.ac.at/document/doi/10.1515/9783110206012/html.

Schütz, A., & Luckmann, T. (2017) [1975]. *Strukturen der Lebenswelt.* UVK.

Scollon, R. (2001). *Mediated discourse: The Nexus of Practice.* Routledge.

Spitzmüller, J. (2014). Commentary: Mediality, mediatization and sociolinguistic change. In J. Androutsopoulos (Ed.), *Mediatization and sociolinguistic change* (pp. 361–367). De Gruyter.

Spitzmüller, J. (2018). Multimodalität und Materialität im Diskurs. In I. Warnke (Hrsg.), *Handbuch Diskurs* (S. 521–540). De Gruyter.

Strathern, M. (1988). *The gender of the gift.* University of California Press.

Thoma, N. (2018). *Sprachbiographien in der Migrationsgesellschaft.* Transcript. https://www.transcript-verlag.de/978-3-8376-4301-5/sprachbiographien-in-der-migrationsgesellschaft/.

Wells, N. (2020). Language and transgenerational identity in Valparaíso's Italian community: Methodological and theoretical reflexions. In C. Mar-Molinero (Ed.), *Researching language in superdiverse urban contexts: Exploring methodological and theoretical concepts* (pp. 131–158). Multilingual Matters.

Moritz Meister / Thomas Slunecko

„Mali" – Dispositivanalyse einer Social Media Kampagne der deutschen Bundeswehr

Abstract

Im Herbst 2017 veröffentlichte die deutsche Bundeswehr auf YouTube, Instagram, Snapchat und Facebook die Social Media-Serie ‚Mali'. In 29 Episoden der in ‚Echtzeit' erzählten Serie sind acht Soldat*innen zu sehen: von der deutschen Kaserne bis in den westafrikanischen Auslandseinsatz und zurück begleitet eine Kamera die Protagonist*innen, oft filmen sie sich und einander auch selbst – etwa in einem engen Panzerfahrzeug sitzend. Parallel dazu wurden täglich Snaps und Instagram-Beiträge gepostet, ein Chatbot sendete Neuigkeiten aus dem Alltag und von Einsätzen per Direktnachricht an interessierte Facebook-User*innen.

Unsere Analyse bedient sich des Dispositivbegriffs, um dem multimedialen, plattformübergreifenden und interaktiven Charakter von ‚Mali' gerecht zu werden. Indem die diskursive Ebene um eine materiell-technologische Dimension erweitert wird, lassen sich Subjektivierungsformen rekonstruieren und gesellschaftlich-politische Problemstellungen identifizieren, auf die das Phänomen ‚Mali' reagiert und die es seinerseits transportiert. Insbesondere analysieren wir die vermeintliche Echtzeit der Serie als Aufmerksamkeits- und Affizierungsmittel, die visuelle Rahmung des Einsatzes als abenteuerliche Selbsterfahrung in einer unpolitisch-dekontextualisierten Außenwelt sowie die trichterartige Struktur, welche User*innen zur potenziellen Rekrutierung bei der Bundeswehr hinführt. Einen besonderen Platz nimmt die Analyse einer Episode ein, in welcher der Tod zweier Soldaten nach einem Hubschrauberabsturz be- und verhandelt wird. Kulturpsychologische Überlegungen zum Verhältnis von Social Media, Krieg/Militär und (Rahmungs-)Macht schließen den Beitrag ab.

In autumn 2017, the German Bundeswehr launched the social media series ‚Mali' on YouTube, Instagram, Snapchat and Facebook. In 29 episodes of the series narrated in ‚real time', eight soldiers can be seen: from the German barracks to the West African mission abroad and back, a camera accompanies the protagonists, who also often film themselves and one another – for example, sitting in a cramped armoured vehicle. In parallel, snaps and Instagram posts were uploaded daily, and a chatbot sent messages about everyday life and several operations to interested Facebook users.

Our analysis employs the concept of the dispositif to account for the multimedia, cross-platform, and interactive characteristics of ‚Mali'. By adding a material-technological dimension to the discursive level, we can reconstruct forms of subjectivation and identify socio-political problems which the phenomenon ‚Mali' reacts to, and which it in turn transports.

In particular, we analyse the seemingly real-time nature of the series as a means of attention and affect, the visual framing of the mission as an adventurous self-experience in a non-political, de-contextualised outside world, as well as the funnel-like structure that leads users to a potential recruitment by the Bundeswehr. A special focus lies on the analysis of an episode in which the death of two soldiers after a helicopter crash is addressed and negotiated. The contribution concludes with cultural-psychological reflections on the relationship between social media, war/military and (framing) power.

1 Einstieg ins Material

„Mali" ist eine Social Media-Serie der deutschen Bundeswehr. Im Oktober 2017 erschienen, jeden Montag bis Donnerstag immer um 17 Uhr, insgesamt 29 Episoden auf *YouTube* (Bundeswehr Exclusive, 2017b). Darin sind acht Soldat*innen während ihres UN-Auslandseinsatzes in Westafrika zu sehen. Im Stil von Reality-TV bzw. Video-Blog Formaten begleitet eine Kamera die Protagonist*innen in ihrem Alltag, oft filmen sie sich und einander auch selbst – etwa, wenn sie in engen Panzerfahrzeugen sitzen. Die Handlung beginnt in der deutschen Kaserne und erstreckt sich über Abreise und erste Tage im Basiscamp, Exkursionen in die naheliegende Stadt Gao und eine Aufklärungsfahrt durch die Wüste, Übungen auf der Schießbahn und für den Häuserkampf, einen Sandsturm, die Ablöse durch neue Soldat*innen bis schließlich zur Heimreise. Es gibt keinen fiktiven Gesamt-Plot, aber durchaus Dramatik und „Cliffhanger", z. B. als wichtige Diesel-Lieferungen ausfallen oder ein Panzerfahrzeug im Wüstensand stecken bleibt. Ergänzend wurden diverse Special-Videos zu besonderen Themen, z. B. Fitness im Camp, Sanitätsausbildung, beteiligte Berufsgruppen oder auch ein „Frauen Power Special" veröffentlicht. Die Gesamtlänge des Videomaterials beträgt ca. fünf Stunden.

Mali ist jedoch nicht nur eine YouTube-, sondern dezidiert eine Social Media-Serie. Im Vorfeld, parallel und nachträglich zur Veröffentlichung der einzelnen Folgen, wurden die Plattformen *Instagram, Facebook, Snapchat* (Abb. 1 & 2) und der Musikstreaming-Dienst *Spotify* bespielt[1]. Gemeinsam mit YouTube zählten diese laut der jahresaktuellen JIM-Studie (2017, S. 34f.) zu den beliebtesten Internetangeboten und wichtigsten Apps der 12–19 Jährigen in Deutschland.[2] Alle

---

1 Unsere Primärquellen sind die Präsenz von Mali auf YouTube (Bundeswehr Exclusive, 2017b), Instagram (@bundeswehrexclusive, o. J.), Facebook (Bundeswehr Exclusive, o. J.) und Spotify (Bundeswehr Exclusive, 2017a); alle zuletzt gesichtet am 20. 02. 2023. Die empirische Erhebung begann noch während des Erscheinungszeitraums im November 2017 und dauerte bis Juni 2018 an.
2 Diesen Hinweis verdanken wir Viktoria Flasche.

Inhalte sind über die Plattformen hinweg verlinkt und beziehen sich aufeinander, es werden aber jeweils unterschiedliche Bilder, Videoschnipsel oder Songs gepostet. Hinzu kam ein automatisierter *Chatbot* für den Facebook Messenger, welcher nach einmaliger Aktivierung per Direktnachricht täglich Neuigkeiten aus dem Geschehen in Mali sendet. Während die Serie lief, war dieser der meist genutzte deutschsprachige Chatbot (politik&kommunikation, 2019).

Bundeswehr Exclusive
24. November 2017 · ⊙

Der nächste Einsatz im Dunkeln kommt bestimmt, Kamerad. Also bereite dich gut vor und leg das Nachtsichtgerät an. Wo du deine Ausrüstung her bekommst? Einmal hier entlang und über den Link die exklusive Bundeswehr Lense auf Snapchat freischalten: http://bit.ly/BWSnapchatLense

Abbildung 1. Titelbild zu „Mali"   Abbildung 2. Snapchat-Lense „Nachtsichtgerät"

Finanziert wurden Produktion und Promotion Malis vom deutschen Verteidigungsministerium. Die Serie ist Teil der Social Media-Marke *Bundeswehr Exclusive*, die in diversen Kampagnen für die Bundeswehr als Arbeitgeber, d. h. die Rekrutierung von Nachwuchs-Soldat*innen, wirbt. Vorgänger Malis ist die weniger aufwendig produzierte Serie *Die Rekruten* von 2016, in der nicht ein realer Einsatz, sondern die Grundausbildung zu sehen ist. Gefilmt und geschnitten wurde Mali von der Reality-TV Produktionsfirma *Spin TV*, beworben durch die Marketingagentur *Castenow Communications*. Die Gesamtkosten beliefen sich auf 6,4 Millionen Euro, wovon zwei Millionen für die Produktion – das Videomaterial wurde drei Monate lang im Sommer 2017 gedreht – und 4,4 Millionen Euro für Werbung – deutschlandweite Kinospots, eine flächendeckende Plakatkampagne, Übertragung der Chatbot-Nachrichten in U-Bahnstationen, sowie Social Media selbst – ausgegeben wurden (Pfannenmüller, 2017).

Der Auslandseinsatz der Bundeswehr an sich steht hier zwar nicht im Analyse-Fokus, sollte jedoch als wesentliche Hintergrundinformation kurz vergegenwärtigt werden. Wieso ist die Bundeswehr in Mali? Der westafrikanische Staat zählt zu den ärmsten Ländern der Welt; Lebenserwartung und Durchschnittsalter sind extrem niedrig. Mit dem „arabischen Frühling" und dem Zusammenbruch Libyens wird die gesamte Sahelzone mit Waffen und Söldner*innen überschwemmt (Gänsler, 2021). Im trockenen Norden Malis, der die doppelte Fläche Deutschlands umfasst, aber durch die Sahara geprägt und von Touareg-Nomaden bewohnt ist, beginnen daraufhin erste Kämpfe. 2012 putscht die malische Armee. Unter bürgerkriegsähnlichen Zuständen setzen sich (z. T. islamistisch-) „terroristische" Gruppierungen im Norden fest. Das durch seine koloniale Vergangenheit verstrickte Frankreich startet 2013 eine Militärmission, um diese zu vertreiben (Cold-Ravnkilde et al., 2017). Zusätzlich beginnt im selben Jahr die UN-Operation MINUSMA, die mit 281 getöteten Blauhelmsoldat*innen (Stand: 20.02.2023) als gefährlichster laufender UN-Einsatz weltweit gilt.[3] Jüngere Schlagzeilen aus Mali berichten von einem Selbstmordanschlag, 180 Kilometer vom Camp in Gao entfernt, bei dem zwölf deutsche Soldaten teils schwer verwundet wurden (Szymanski, 2021). Nach wiederholten Putschs des malischen Militärs kündigt Frankreich im Sommer 2021 an, seine Militärmission zu beenden und sich weitgehend aus Mali zurück zu ziehen. Ein Jahr später ist die Frage, wer die zentrale Rolle Frankreichs, insbesondere bei der Sicherung des Militärflughafens in Gao, ersetzen könnte, offen – zumal die aktuelle malische Regierung dezidiert gegen die UN-Mission arbeitet (Johnson, 2022).

2   Methodologie: Dispositivanalyse

2.1   Der Dispositiv-Begriff

Wie lässt sich eine Social Media-Kampagne wie Mali kulturpsychologisch untersuchen? Kann sie dokumentarisch, tiefenhermeneutisch oder gar ideologiekritisch interpretiert werden? Lässt sie sich diskursanalytisch untersuchen? Wie ergiebig wären Bildanalysen des Instagram-Materials oder Videoanalysen der YouTube-Folgen? Unsere methodologische und forschungspraktische Abwä-

---

3 Die Abkürzung rührt aus dem franz. *Mission multidimensionnelle intégrée des Nations Unies pour la stabilisation au Mali*. Tagesaktuelle Informationen liefern die United Nations (o. J.). Die traurige Zahl der getöteten UN-Soldat*innen wuchs im Zuge unserer Beschäftigung mit Mali laufend an: Im Februar 2018 waren es 146, im Juli 2018 169, im März 2021 237. Die Todesopfer stammen überwiegend aus umliegenden afrikanischen Staaten.

gung sah zwar den potentiellen Ertrag jeder dieser Herangehensweisen, doch gleichzeitig würde keine das Phänomen in seiner Gänze zu fassen bekommen, d. h. in seiner multimedialen Erscheinungsform, technologisch vermittelten Interaktivität (insbesondere durch den Chatbot), plattformübergreifenden Vernetzung und nicht zuletzt gesellschaftspolitischen Relevanz.

Produktiv verbinden lassen sich die genannten Dimensionen hingegen über das von Foucault stammende Dispositiv-Konzept, mit dem die Ebene des Diskursiven (d. h. des Gesagten oder Geschriebenen, also sprachlich Vermittelten) um eine materiell-technische Dimension erweitert wird. Auch wenn argumentiert wurde, dass „das Wort ‚Dispositiv' als Terminus technicus für Foucaults Denkstrategie von entscheidender Bedeutung ist" (Agamben, 2008, S. 7), sind Foucaults eigene Äußerungen dazu rar. Es ist vor allem folgender Ausschnitt aus einem Gespräch Foucaults mit Jacques-Alain Miller, der immer wieder zitiert wird:

> „Was ich unter diesem Titel [Dispositiv] festzumachen versuche ist erstens ein entschieden heterogenes Ensemble, das Diskurse, Institutionen, architekturale Einrichtungen, reglementierende Entscheidungen, Gesetze, administrative Maßnahmen, wissenschaftliche Aussagen, philosophische, moralische oder philanthropische Lehrsätze, kurz: Gesagtes ebenso wie Ungesagtes umfasst. Soweit die Elemente des Dispositivs. Das Dispositiv selbst ist das Netz, das zwischen diesen Elementen geknüpft werden kann. Zweitens möchte ich in dem Dispositiv gerade die Natur der Verbindung deutlich machen, die zwischen diesen heterogenen Elementen sich herstellen kann. […] Drittens verstehe ich unter Dispositiv eine Art von […] Formation, deren Hauptfunktion zu einem gegebenen historischen Zeitpunkt darin bestanden hat, auf einen Notstand (urgence) zu antworten. Das Dispositiv hat also vorwiegend strategische Funktion." (Foucault, 1978, S. 119f.)

Auch wenn diese Erläuterungen auf den ersten Blick wenig systematisch wirken, stecken darin wesentliche Bedeutungsebenen des Dispositiv-Begriffs: wir haben es mit einem dezidiert *heterogenen Ensemble* zu tun, das eben nicht nur Diskurse, sondern auch noch viele weitere sozio-technische Elemente beinhaltet; diese verhalten sich nicht unabhängig voneinander, sondern bilden ein *Netz*; die so entstandene Formation reagiert auf einen jeweils historisch kontingenten *Notstand (urgence)*. Im Folgenden soll jede dieser drei Eigenschaften näher erläutert werden.

Dispositive als heterogene Ensembles. „Institutionen, Architektur, Gesetze usw. entstehen als Teil diskursiver sozialer Praxen, sind aber nicht auf den Diskurs reduzierbar" (Schaupp, 2019, S. 228). Um materielle Formationen analytisch dingfest machen zu können, ist der Diskursbegriff allein nicht ausreichend; er bedarf einer Ergänzung. Doch wie verhalten sich Diskurse und Dispositive zueinander? Unseres Erachtens bringen sie sich wechselseitig hervor. Dispositive bauen auf Diskurse auf, d. h. auf „Problematisierungen, Zielsetzungen und […]

Rationalitäten" (Bröckling & Peter, 2017, S. 284); und Diskurse werden wiederum von (medialen, technischen, infrastrukturellen) Dispositiven getragen. Damit ergeben sich nicht zuletzt für einen machtkritischen Forschungszugang neue Ansatzpunkte, denn „[w]enn Denkweisen wirksam sein, sich als Weisen des Regierens materialisieren sollen, müssen sie praktisch und das heißt auch technisch werden" (Bröckling & Krasmann, 2010, S. 25).

Dispositive als Netze. Als „heterogene soziotechnische Ensembles" lässt sich die „Handlungsmacht" von Dispositiven „nicht auf einzelne Elemente (Menschen, Dinge, Zeichen oder Apparaturen) zurückrechnen" (Seier, 2019, S. 223). Als Ganzes jedoch haben Dispositive durchaus eine „handlungsstrukturierende Funktion" (Schaupp, 2019, S. 228), die umso machtvoller ist, je enger und dichter die einzelnen Elemente bzw. Ebenen miteinander verknüpft sind. Denn dann verschränken sich Macht und Wissen, Selbst-, Fremd- und Weltverhältnisse auf eine je spezifische Art und Weise, die das Feld menschlichen Handelns, Denkens und Fühlens – nicht nur restriktiv, sondern auch produktiv – absteckt.

Dispositiv und urgence. Giorgio Agamben arbeitet aus Wörterbuch-Definitionen zum französischen „dispositif" drei umgangssprachliche Bedeutungen heraus (2008, S. 16): eine juristische – als *entscheidender* Teil eines Urteils oder Gesetzes, der „disponiert, das heißt anordnet"; eine technische – als „Weise, in der die Teile einer Maschine oder eines Mechanismus angeordnet sind"; und sogar (in Anbetracht unseres Materials erscheint das nicht ohne Ironie) eine dezidiert militärische – als „Gesamtheit der zur Ausführung eines Planes angeordneten Maßnahmen". Es geht in allen drei Fällen um spezifische *A*nordnungen auf etwas hin, um „Praktiken und Mechanismen […], die das Ziel haben, einer Dringlichkeit zu begegnen und einen mehr oder weniger unmittelbaren Effekt zu erzielen" (Agamben, 2008, S. 17). Dispositiven geht „ein Problem oder Konflikt voraus […], den sie performativ bearbeiten, wiederholen und verschieben" (Seier, 2019, S. 228). In ihrer Untersuchung „wird rückblickend gefragt, auf welches Problem das Netzwerk als strategische Anordnung reagiert" (Seier, 2019, S. 228).

Dispositiv und Subjekt. Bis hierhin wurden drei Bestimmungsstücke des Dispositivbegriffes erläutert, die unmittelbar an das Foucault'sche Schlüsselzitat anknüpfen. Eine wesentliche Frage wurde dabei jedoch noch nicht beleuchtet: Welche Rolle nimmt menschliche Subjektivität in den beschriebenen Geflechten von Materie, Wissen und Macht ein? Wie konstituiert sich ein Selbst in Dispositiven? In Anknüpfung an Foucault sind Autor*innen wie Rose (1996, 1999), Bröckling et al. (2000) oder Butler (2001) dieser Frage nachgegangen. Mit „Subjektivierung" wurde dazu ein Begriff gefunden, der den Prozess beschreiben soll, qua Dispositive(n) „in einer bestimmten Weise als Subjekt angesprochen zu werden, sich selbst als ein Subjekt zu begreifen und im Sinne dieses Selbst-Verständnisses an sich zu arbeiten" (Bröckling & Krasmann, 2010, S. 29). Dispositive bringen also die ihnen entsprechenden Subjekte hervor. Ohne solche würden sie nicht „als Regierungsdispositiv[e] funktionieren," – Regierung hier im weiten Foucault'schen Sinn einer machtvollen Lenkung – „sondern sich darauf beschränken […], bloße Gewaltanwendung zu sein." (Agamben, 2008, S. 24) Dispositive umfassen also individuelle wie kollektive „Selbstbilder und Rollenmodelle" (Bröckling & Peter, 2017, S. 284), d.h. explizite oder implizite Anrufungen, die sich überkreuzen und überlagern, konkurrieren oder verstärken können. Es gilt zu fragen, „wie Menschen sich selbst deuten und wahrnehmen sowie […] über welche Praktiken diese Selbstwahrnehmung und -deutung befördert wird" (Caborn Wengler et al., 2013, S. 12).

2.2 Mediale Mikro-Dispositive

Die Rezeptionsgeschichte des Dispositiv-Begriffs entlang der bisher skizzierten Bedeutungsdimensionen ist vielfältig: Von der Philosophie (Deleuze, 1991; Agamben, 2008) über die Sozial- (Bührmann & Schneider, 2012; Caborn Wengler et al., 2013) und Wirtschaftswissenschaften (Diaz-Bone & Hartz, 2017) reicht sie bis hin zu den Medienwissenschaften, wo der Dispositiv-Begriff insbesondere auf das Fernseh-Format in Anschlag gebracht wurde (Stauff, 2005; Gnosa, 2018; Seier, 2019). Wir möchten das Dispositiv-Konzept hier einen Schritt weiter zur Erforschung gegenwärtiger digital-medialer Konstellationen zuspitzen. Unseres Erachtens eignet es sich hierfür hervorragend, da sich mit ihm die weltbildende Funktion von Medien (Slunecko, 2008; Slunecko & Bösel, 2022) ebenso anerkennen wie analysieren lässt. In Medien-Dispositiven bilden sich „machtvolle, weil wahrnehmungs- und handlungsrelevante Wirklichkeitsdefinitionen" (Bührmann & Schneider, 2012, S. 12). Dabei gilt es für Forscher*innen, „die spezifische, darin gleichsam materialisiert zum Ausdruck kommende Mensch-Maschine-Konstellation zu charakterisieren und bezüglich ihrer wirklichkeitsformierenden Wirkungen und Effekte auf die Nutzenden (und Produzierenden) zu deuten" (Bührmann & Schneider, 2012, S. 13).

Hierbei ist eine analytische Unterscheidung zwischen Mikro- und Makro-Dispositiven gewinnbringend (Meinhof, 2018; Schaupp, 2019). Mikro-Dispositive sind „konkrete Maschinen" (Deleuze, 1996, S. 15), die sich relativ präzise technologisch, situativ und temporal eingrenzen lassen. Sie kommen „in bestimmten gesellschaftlichen Teilbereichen zur Geltung" (Seier 2019, S. 53). Makro-Dispositive hingegen sind breiter und abstrakter. In den Medienwissenschaften wären solche Makro-Konzepte z.B. die Informationsgesellschaft, die Gesellschaft des Spektakels, die Plattformgesellschaft, die Generation „YouTube" o.ä. (Seier, 2019, S. 55), in den Sozialwissenschaften der Digital-, der kybernetische- oder der Überwachungskapitalismus (Zuboff, 2018), das Metrische Wir (Mau, 2017), das

Unternehmerische Selbst (Bröckling, 2007) oder die Kontrollgesellschaft (Deleuze, 1993). So instruktiv derartige Gesellschaftsdiagnosen sein mögen, wollen wir
sie nicht apriori unterstellen, sondern ggf. aus unserem Untersuchungsgegen-
stand „bottom-up" herauspräparieren. Unser Ziel ist jedenfalls die „Rekon-
struktion" eines diskursiv-materiellen „Kraftfeldes", das keineswegs homogen
und widerspruchsfrei sein muss (Bröckling & Peter, 2017, S. 284).

Mit Seier (2019, S. 15) gesprochen möchte diese Arbeit also ein Verständnis
von Mali entwickeln, „das es erlaubt, angesichts sich vielfältig überlagernder
kultureller, sozialer, technischer und ästhetischer Gefüge, spezifische Mediendispositive so zu isolieren, dass sie zugleich auch in ihrer Verknüpfung zu anderen Gefügen/Dispositiven (Arbeitsformen, Geschlechterverhältnisse, Körper-
kulturen u.v.m.) sichtbar bleiben". Diese Vielschichtigkeit hat Konsequenzen für
die Frage „nach den subjektivitätsgenerierenden Effekten von Medien" (Seier,
2019, S. 49), denn es wird nicht etwa nur ein Fernseh-Subjekt von einem Insta-
gram-Subjekt abgelöst, „sondern es sind vor allem heterogene mediale Konstellationen, die in den Blick geraten. Unterschiedliche Medien werden gleichzeitig bedient, parallel zu Fernsehsendungen wird im Internet gebloggt und in
Chat-Foren diskutiert" (Seier, 2019, S. 49). Mali stellt eben dafür ein Parade-
beispiel dar, wobei die Nutzung verschiedener Plattformen von den Ma-
cher*innen sogar schon vorweggenommen ist.

2.3   Dispositivanalyse als Forschungsstil

Konkrete methodologische Übersetzungsversuche des Dispositiv-Konzepts sind
bislang eher rar. Am einschlägigsten ist ein Band von Andrea Bührmann und
Werner Schneider (2012). Darin schlagen die Autor*innen vier Leitfragen vor.
Diese richten sich nach den/dem:
- *diskursiven Praktiken*: Was wird wie gesagt, was nicht?
- *Subjektivierungen*: Wie werden die Betroffenen adressiert? Welche Annahmen
  stecken implizit oder explizit in den Anrufungen und Interaktionsaufforde-
  rungen?
- *Objektivationen*: Wie kommen Technologie, Design, Struktur, Verlinkung,
  Interaktionsmöglichkeiten zum Einsatz?
- *gesellschaftlichen Kontext*: Auf welche soziale Umbruchsituation, welchen
  aktuellen „Notstand" (urgence) reagiert das untersuchte (Mikro-)Dispositiv?

Die Leitfragen bieten Orientierung und Analyse-Perspektiven, sollen aber, so
empfehlen es Bührmann und Schneider, nicht als fixes Template verstanden
werden, das es „abzuarbeiten" gelte und in welches sich das empirische Material
zwingend einfügen lassen müsse, sondern eher als ein „Forschungsstil" (2012,

S. 75). Diese Betonung methodischer und forschungspraktischer Flexibilität haben wir uns zu Herzen genommen, um die Dispositivanalyse weiterzuentwickeln und zeitgemäß zu halten: Denn die digital-technologische Durchdringung der Lebenswelt auf (fast) allen Ebenen, insbesondere via Smartphones, steckte, als Bührmann und Schneider ihre Dispositivanalyse entwickelt haben, quasi noch in Kinderschuhen.[4] Mit den digital-medialen Mikro-Dispositiven – seien es Apps, smarte Wearables oder eben Social Media-Serien – hat sich die Natur des Forschungsgegenstandes verändert.

Digitale User-Interfaces erfordern unser Mitwirken: Tippen und Wischen, die Fingerspitze auf den Sensor drücken, Einloggen, Liken, Teilen, Freigeben, Senden, Bestätigen, Synchronisieren, usw. All die Interaktionsangebote und Handlungsaufforderungen, zusammenfassbar im englischen Begriff *Affordances*, die sich uns im digitalen Raum bieten, sind kaum passiv rezipierbar, sondern überwiegend aktiv erfahrbar. Ein markantes Beispiel aus Mali: Wenn man z. B. nicht aktiv auf Nachrichten des Chatbots reagiert, tut sich dort weiter nichts. Die Anforderungen eines digitalen Dispositivs kann man als User*in oder Follower*in nur bedingt (meist um den Preis des Ausschlusses) abweisen oder umgehen. Auch die zeitliche Organisation der Social-Media Serie erfordert eine entsprechende, synchronisiert-aktive Teilhabe am virtuellen Geschehen.

Diese unausweichliche Aufforderung zum Mitmachen mag zum Teil den besonderen Sog einer tendenziell immersiven „user experience" (in den Worten der Human-Computer-Interaction Forschung) erklären, die gleichsam nach den User*innen greift und sie gezielt affiziert. Dieser phänomenologische Gesamtcharakter ginge verloren, würden wir das Dispositiv fein säuberlich in Einzelaspekte seziert vor uns legen. Forscher*innen müssen demzufolge bei der Analyse eines digital-medialen Dispositivs „tief in den Fluss des Geschehens ein[] tauchen" (Wacquant, 2014, S. 98), anstatt in sicherer methodologischer Distanz zu verharren (Devereux, 1984). So erscheint uns ein (auto-)ethnographischer Forschungszugang dem Gegenstand angemessen, nämlich „den sachkundigen und empfindsamen Organismus der Beobachter*in als zentrales Untersuchungswerkzeug einzusetzen" (Wacquant, 2014, S. 97) – ein Motiv, das insbesondere für die Wiener Kulturpsychologie (Bösel, 2017; Slunecko, 2017, 2020), aber auch für andere zeitgenössische methodologische Überlegungen in den Sozialwissenschaften (Breuer et al., 2019) charakteristisch ist und sich in jüngster Zeit für die Analyse von Apps bewährt hat (Slunecko & Chlouba, 2021; Meister & Slunecko, 2021; Meister, 2022).

---

4 Das erste *iPhone* erschien Ende 2007, Apps folgten daraufhin. Smart-Watches und ähnliche Wearables kamen im Lauf der 2010er-Jahre auf den Markt. *Instagram* ging 2010 online, *Snapchat* 2011.

Der*die Forscher*in generiert also analysierbares Material durch aktive Teilnahme. Das konkrete Arbeitsvorgehen besteht in einem kontrollierten Eintauchen und Durchlaufen bzw. Durchklicken des Untersuchungsgegenstandes. Ein bestimmtes Erkenntnisinteresse und möglichst konkrete (aber nicht unabänderliche) Forschungsfragen sollten zuvor bereits expliziert worden sein. Feldnotizen in einem Forschungstagebuch dienen der Dokumentation und Reflexion eigener Irritationen, Assoziationen, Interpretationsfährten und affektiver Resonanzen. Darüber hinaus ist auch eine systematische Erfassung der z. T. flüchtigen digitalen Inhalte, z. B. durch Screenshots, unabdingbar. Erfahrungsgemäß wird es hierbei schnell herausfordernd, einen Überblick zu behalten. Mali hat uns mit einer ausufernden Fülle an potenziell interessantem Material konfrontiert. Visualisierungen und Skizzen der digitalen Struktur des Dispositivs haben sich hier als hilfreich erwiesen. Auch Parameter wie Aufruf-Zahlen und User*innen-Kommentare können – je nach Erkenntnisinteresse – auf Relevanz hinweisen. In Mali traf dies auf die Folge „Das größte Opfer" (s. unten) zu, in der beide überdurchschnittlich hoch ausfielen.

Die Forscher*innen beginnen also einen (auto-)ethnographischen Bericht, während sie sich im Feld bewegen, ähnlich dem Versuch, im Laufen eine Landkarte oder einen Lageplan zu erstellen. Für Mali mit seinem umfangreichen Videomaterial haben wir dazu etwa auch eine tabellarische Übersicht aller Episoden erstellt und darin die Inhalte der Folgen kurz paraphrasiert. Beides, Aufzeichnungen des Materials sowie der eigenen Resonanzen, sollten möglichst zueinander in Bezug gesetzt werden. Diese „Rohdaten" können später, sowohl in Interpretationsgruppen (etwa in Seminaren oder Kolloquien) als auch während des individuellen Schreibprozesses, tiefgehender interpretiert, synthetisiert und mit bestehender Literatur in Beziehung gesetzt werden.

3   Empirische Analyse

3.1   „Sei hautnah mit dabei!" – Mali als virtuelles Echtzeit-Erlebnis (Video-Beschreibung *Bist du bereit? Offizieller Trailer* vom 09. 10. 2017)

Um die obige Arbeitsdefinition unseres Gegenstandes weiter zu spezifizieren: Mali ist eine *interaktive* Social Media-Serie. Einen nicht unwesentlichen Teil des Erzählstranges erfährt man als Rezipient*in nur, wenn man den zugehörigen Chatbot für den Facebook Messenger aktiviert hat und regelmäßig mit diesem „chattet".

Der Chatbot „holt die Zielgruppe mit zwei bis drei Echtzeitnachrichten am Tag ab und zieht sie eng in das Geschehen in Mali hinein – anfangs über Protagonist*innen-Steckbriefe, später mit Handy-Filmen aus dem Wüstencamp, GIFs, oder Echtzeit-Bildern [sic!] wie beispielsweise dem Abschießen einer Leuchtrakete" – so ein Marketing-Branchenmagazin (Pfannenmüller, 2017). Man darf sich den Chatbot jedoch nicht wie einen Menschen vorstellen, mit dem man einfach frei hin- und herschreiben könnte. Die Interaktionsmöglichkeit beschränkt sich nämlich auf vorgegebene, standardisierte Befehle, die man als Buttons antippen muss, wie hier z. B. „Ich bin bereit" (Abb. 3). Indem das Design des Chatbots diese, und nur diese, technische „affordance" stellt – anbietet und sogleich auffordert, auf diese Weise mit ihm zu interagieren, – manifestiert sich auch ein spezifisches Rollenverhältnis. Als User*in des Bots bewegt man sich v. a. (passiv) in den vorgezeichneten Bahnen standardisierter Antworten, muss aber dennoch (aktiv) mittippen. Nur so reagiert der Bot unmittelbar, während er bei freien Texteingaben nur anbieten kann, diese an menschliche Mitarbeiter*innen weiterzuleiten.

So deutlich der Roboter-Charakter (von da kommt ja die Kurzform „-bot") dieser Technologie bei einem solchen „Ausbrechen" aus vorprogrammierten Interaktionsbahnen wird, so ist es andererseits bemerkenswert, wie „menschlich" das Chat-Erlebnis, hält man sich strikt an die Antwortbuttons, wirkt. Dafür sorgt der Duktus der Bot-Nachrichten, die oft mit Emojis und kleinen Witzen gespickt sind. Aber auch die Interface-Ebene stützt die Illusion eines schreibenden Gegenübers: Denn nachdem man einen Antwortbutton angetippt hat, erscheint die Antwort des Bots nicht etwa unmittelbar, sondern erst nach ein paar Sekunden Verzögerung, in der eine Reihe von Punkten („…") zu sehen ist, die sich wellenartig bewegen. In gängigen Messenger-Apps bedeutet dies üblicherweise, dass das Gegenüber gerade tippt. „Bleib dran, warte kurz, gleich kommt was", verheißen die tänzelnden Punkte. Sie überbrücken die kurzen Wartezeiten, die zwischen menschlichen Chatpartnern unvermeidlich entstehen. Doch in diesem Fall sitzt da niemand, der eine Nachrichten erst mühsam eingeben müsste. Der effiziente und schnelle Algorithmus hinter dem Bot bleibt dadurch hinter einem langsam-menschlichen Imago verborgen.

Dieses vermeintlich menschliche Gegenüber legt zeitweise durchaus einen militärisch-strammen Tonfall an, der sich in Großbuchstaben und Ausrufezeichen manifestiert: „ACHTUNG, Kamerad!" Wer gibt hier eigentlich wem Befehle? – lässt sich an dieser Stelle fragen. Man wird vom Chatbot adressiert, als ob er einem militärische Kommandos geben könnte. Zwar ist dem*der User*in ein Antworten und Reagieren möglich, aber nur mittels vorgegebener Templates. In Kontrast zu dem Bild eines*einer selbstbestimmt lenkenden Technik-Nutzer*in hinter dem Bildschirm, werden hier implizit militärische Kommunikationsformen eingeübt, in denen man sich am unteren Ende der Befehlskette befindet.

Ein (forschungspraktischer) Zugang zu diesem Material ist voraussetzungsvoll und folgenreich. Im Gegensatz zu den YouTube- oder Instagram-Inhalten sind die Nachrichten nicht öffentlich einsehbar, sondern nur im direkten „Chat" erfahrbar: Nicht nur ein eigenes Facebook-Profil ist notwendig (mit der Aktivierung geht auch eine datenschutzrechtliche Einwilligung in die Auswertung des User*innen-Profils durch Bundeswehr Exclusive einher); der Chat-Prozess ist auch zeitlich flüchtig. Denn der Chatbot schreibt einem nicht selten „proaktiv" und mit den neu erschienenen Nachrichten laufen alte Antwort-Möglichkeiten ab. Wenn man nichts verpassen möchte – ein ähnliches Prinzip liegt der Snapchat-App zugrunde – muss man regelmäßig, am besten mehrmals täglich, seinen Messenger öffnen. Das Geschehen in Mali, so die Suggestion, geht ja auch weiter. Dadurch gewinnt Mali als Mikro-Dispositiv einen besonderen „Zug", der auch den (Forschungs-)Alltag unweigerlich mitgestaltet. Das ist durchaus beabsichtigt, denn mittels Chatbot solle, so Dirk Feldhaus, Verantwortlicher für Personalwerbung der Bundeswehr, der Eindruck entstehen, „als wenn ein Freund vor Ort dabei wäre und einen [sic!] den Tag über Nachrichten teilt und das ist nochmal ein ganz anderes Erlebnis, um wirklich nah an dem Einsatz dabei zu sein" (zit. nach Schildbach, 2017).

Abbildung 3. Konversation mit dem Chatbot. Anonymisierter Screenshot aus https://pbs.twimg.com/media/DLdDL5vWsAAmgOh?format=jpg&name=medium (abgerufen am 15.03. 2021)

Abbildung 4. ‚Alarm im Camp' – Chatbot-Nachricht. Facebook-Posting vom 19.10.2017

Die Rede von der „Echtzeit", in der alles veröffentlicht wird, ist in Mali diskursiv markant. Abb. 4 zeigt so eine Nachricht des Chatbots, der nachts um halb eins warnt: „Alarm im Camp". Solche aufregenden Informationsschnipsel, jeweils im Präsens formuliert, oft auch in Form kurzer Videos, erhalten Follower*innen rund um die Uhr. Sind sie also Teil eines Geschehens, das so 1:1 (nur ein paar Tausend Kilometer entfernt) stattfindet? Unter den Rezipient*innen Malis scheint gerade die Alarm-Nachricht für einige Verwirrung gesorgt zu haben, denn das Social-Media-Team sah sich am selben Tag zu einem erklärenden Instagram-Posting veranlasst (@bundeswehrexclusive, 2017a). Dort heißt es vorweg, dass alle Soldat*innen inzwischen wohlbehalten zuhause sind. Der Begriff „Echtzeit" wird hier umgedeutet, insofern er nur bezeichnen soll, dass Ereignisse *zu der gleichen Uhrzeit* gepostet werden, wie sie geschehen sind – aber sehr wohl um Tage zeitlich versetzt, gerafft und geschnitten.

Welche diskursive Funktion erfüllt diese „Echtzeit"? Sie suggeriert erstmal Nähe, ein ungefiltertes „Dabei-Sein" bei den authentischen Erlebnissen der Soldat*innen. Kollektive Affektschwingungen können so synchronisiert werden (Slunecko, 2008, S. 175). Es entsteht ein leicht schauriger Spannungsbogen, der Aufmerksamkeit fesselt: Es könnte ja wirklich etwas passieren und die Follower*innen bekommen es sofort, als erste, mit. Gleichzeitig bleiben die veröffentlichten Inhalte genau plan- und kontrollierbar; so wurde z.B. militärisch relevantes Kartenmaterial, das immer wieder im Hintergrund sichtbar ist, vor der Veröffentlichung mit einem Blurring-Filter überdeckt.

Auf eine der forschungsleitenden Fragen – wie adressiert Mali den*die Rezipient*in? – lässt sich zwischenzeitlich ein Antwortversuch formulieren: Während man sich im Social-Media-Universum von Mali bewegt, nimmt man (pseudo-)synchron an den Ereignissen im Einsatzgebiet teil; wird dabei immer als „Kamerad" angesprochen und gleichsam selbst zum Soldaten (so normalisiert sich etwa auch der Anblick von Waffen und die Anrede in militärischen Rängen). Das alles kann man niederschwellig und unterhaltsam auf sich einwirken lassen, ohne Komfort und Sicherheit der heimischen Couch opfern zu müssen – zumindest so lange, bis man real bei der Bundeswehr anheuert.

3.2   „Spannender, als den ganzen Tag nur Memes gucken" –
       Mali als außerweltliches Abenteuer

Die folgenden analytischen Beobachtungen schwenken zwischen Viskurs, also der filmischen Machart der Serie, und Diskurs, womit alles sprachliche Material in und um Mali anvisiert wird. Die erkenntnisleitenden Fragen lauten: Was wird gesagt, was bleibt ungesagt? Was wird *wie* filmisch dargestellt, und wie nicht? Was ist (nicht) sagbar? Und: was ist zu sagen (normative Aussageforderungen bzw. -verbote)? (Bührmann & Schneider, 2012, S. 97). Der vorliegende Beitrag kann weder eine umfassende Diskurs-, noch eine Videoanalyse zu Mali liefern, möchte aber auf markante Punkte im Material hinweisen.

Der rotbraune Wüstensand prägt das Erscheinungsbild Malis wohl am auffälligsten (s. oben: Abb. 1). Dieser oder ähnliche Farbtöne finden sich einerseits tatsächlich in vielen Aufnahmen vor Ort, wurden aber auch in der nachträglichen Aufbereitung der Serie, insbesondere in Intro und Logo, hervorgehoben und so zum markanten visuellen Merkmal, das Mali-Content auch über verschieden Plattformen hinweg unmittelbar erkennbar macht. Besonders in Folge 7: „Festgefahren in der Wüste" könnte man fast meinen, Mali spiele nicht auf dieser Erde, sondern auf dem Mars. Tatsächlich erinnert das Motiv der endlosen roten Wüste an den Film *Der Marsianer* (2015).[5] Die schwer bewaffneten Soldat*innen auf Ausfahrt erscheinen in Mali wie Science-Fiction-Figuren auf einem Wüstenplaneten, wie sie jüngst in *Dune* (2021) zu sehen waren. Beim Überlebenskampf technologisch hochgerüsteter Menschen in der lebensfeindlichen Umgebung eines außerirdischen Planeten mitzufiebern scheint einen Nerv unserer Zeit zu treffen, wie z. B. der Publikumserfolg von *Avatar* (2009) bezeugt.

Doch der mediale Referenzrahmen Malis berührt nicht nur Hollywood-Filmproduktionen, sondern auch die Gaming-Industrie. Jene gedeiht seit den 00er Jahren in so prächtiger Wahlverwandtschaft mit dem Militär, dass Expert*innen der Science & Technology Studies von einem „Military-Entertainment Complex" sprechen (Lenoir & Caldwell, 2018). Auch Mali weist einige Ähnlichkeiten mit der Ästhetik gängiger Action, Ego-Shooter und Adventure-Videospiele auf.[6] Diesen Eindruck verstärkt der brachiale Sound. Wuchtige Bässe, hohe Vocals, Dissonanzen und ein schneller Takt wirken „aufputschend" (der Soundtrack wurde auf einer eigenen Spotify-Playlist zum Nachhören veröffentlicht).

Doch bei allen Affinitäten ist in Mali eben auch etwas anders, als man es aus Hollywood-Blockbustern oder auch Ego-Shootern kennt. Häufig filmen sich die Protagonist*innen mit der Handkamera selbst, oft in engen Räumen, während professionelle Kameraleute abwesend sind und sie nebenher andere Dinge tun. In diesen Szenen ist Mali ganz dem Social Media Format verhaftet, wie ein Video-Blog oder „Follow Me Around". Als Zuseher*in ist man sehr nah an den Darsteller*innen, und diese sind offenkundig Laien, also keine Schauspieler*innen, und damit auch eine Stufe näher an uns Zuseher*innen. Der häufige Perspektivwechsel aus Selbst-Filmen und (bewegten, da aus einem Fahrzeug gefilmten) Landschaftsansichten erzeugt Lebendigkeit.

---

5 Diesen Hinweis verdanken wir Stefan Hampl.
6 Konkret enthält z. B. eine Szene im „Offiziellen Kinospot" bei 00:24 beachtliche visuelle Parallelen mit dem Beginn der Mission „Operation Swordbreaker" aus *Battlefield 3*.

Die gefilmten bzw. sich selbst filmenden Soldat*innen sprechen zu und für uns Zuschauer*innen, während die Einheimischen Kulisse bzw. Statisten darstellen, z. B. als niedliche Kinder, die in die Kamera lächeln oder versuchen, heimlich leere Patronenhülsen von der Schiessbahn zu sammeln (Folge 26). In den Vordergrund rücken Einheimische kurzzeitig, wenn sie eine potentielle Bedrohung darstellen: „Der Typ da hat ne AK auf dem Rücken" (Folge 4, 00:05–00:08; gemeint ist ein Kalaschnikow-Sturmgewehr). Während einer Ausfahrt durch das nächtliche Gao filmt die Kamera in Nachtsicht-Optik aus dem Inneren eines gepanzerten Fahrzeugs die ortsansässigen Menschen, was unwillkürlich an eine Art „Safari" erinnert. Während zwischen den lokal Anwesenden durch Panzerglas, Rollen- und Kulturunterschiede oder Sprachbarrieren Distanz herrscht, die sich im Blick der Kamera widerspiegelt, sind die Protagonist*innen uns, im heimischen Wohnzimmer, dank medialer Vermittlung, äußerst nahe.

Wie Mali hingegen *nicht* aussieht: Wie in den Nachrichten. Mit herkömmlichen journalistischen Bildern von Militäreinsätzen hat Mali kaum Gemeinsamkeiten – weder mit pompösen Militärparaden (eine Ausnahme gibt es in der Folge 25: „Das größte Opfer", dazu unten mehr) noch mit verwackelten Mitschnitten unmittelbarer Kampfhandlungen. Überspitzt könnte man formulieren: Mali-Schauen fühlt sich eher so an, als ob der Lieblings-Influencer in einem außerweltlichen Abenteuer unterwegs wäre, denn wie die tägliche Nachrichtensendung, die von den Grausamkeiten der Welt berichtet.

Spezifisch für einen bestimmten Diskurs ist nicht nur, was wie gesagt wird, sondern auch das jeweils Ungesagte. In Mali sucht man klassische, nationalistische Militärrhetorik („Vaterland", „Pflicht", „Feinde") vergebens. Überhaupt ist das Ausbleiben eines Feindes, ja zumindest temporären Gegners, auffällig: Wir sehen Panzerfäuste, aber keine Panzer, auf die zu schießen wäre. Hierin unterscheidet sich Mali von früherer Militärpropaganda, die lange Zeit genau darauf abzielte, ein möglichst anschauliches Feindbild zu konstruieren, um nach diesem Schema Angst und Aggression zu mobilisieren. Zwar ist in Mali gelegentlich vage von „Islamisten", „Aufständischen" oder „Touareg" die Rede, doch bleibt das eher ein abstraktes Füllwort für etwas, das weder gezeigt noch genauer beschrieben wird, geschweige denn politisch oder historisch verortet. Der Feind ist unsichtbar, die Gefahr jedoch in jeder Minute – insbesondere, wenn sich die Protagonist*innen schwer gepanzert außerhalb des Camps begeben – spürbar.

Doch wenn es kein Vaterland und auch kein anderes „höheres Ziel" gibt, für das zu sterben sich lohnen würde, wozu dann das eigene Leben riskieren? Diese Frage formuliert ein konkretes Handlungsproblem, auf das das Mikro-Dispositiv Mali reagieren musste. Wie tut es das? Unter anderem, indem es die Soldat*innen selbst zu Wort kommen lässt: „Ja, war 'ne gute Zeit. […] War 'ne coole Erfahrung, 'ne spaßige Zeit. War'n halt auch scheiss Zeiten dabei, ne. Aber, würd's halt immer wieder machen", resümiert Oberfeldwebel Johnny, gerade wieder in

Deutschland (Folge 29, 09:30–09:37). An anderer Stelle, nach einem simulierten Häuserkampf-Manöver mit Kampfhund, sagt Oberfeldwebel Kai: „Es war halt 'ne mega geile Erfahrung" (Folge 24, 04:17–04:18).

Mehr als jede Pflicht, Verantwortung oder Ehre sind es Spaß und die subjektive Erfahrung, die als Maßstab angelegt werden, was angesichts des adoleszenten Alters der Protagonist*innen fast klingt, als ob der Auslandseinsatz als „gap-year" nach der Schulzeit fungieren könnte. Um diese Deutung besser einordnen zu können, sind Studien zur Entstehung der westlichen Kriegskultur hilfreich, wie sie der israelische Militärhistoriker Yuval Noah Harari (2008) vorlegte. Auf der Grundlage von Tagebüchern, die im und um das Schlachtfeld herum verfasst wurden, konnte Harari zeigen, dass der Krieg für die Kombattanten selbst erst ab dem 19. Jahrhundert – Tolstois *Krieg und Frieden* von 1865 kann hier als Orientierungsmarke dienen – die Bedeutung einer *ultimativen Erfahrung* einnahm. In dieser ultimativen Erfahrung offenbart sich eine zu Friedenszeiten nur latente Wahrheit, sei es als Desillusionierung oder als positive Erleuchtung. Seit dem 2. Weltkrieg hat sich die Kriegskultur endgültig hin zum Individuum und weg von überindividuellen, „höheren" Narrativen verschoben – und damit auch die mediale Aufbereitung und (halb-)fiktionale Unterhaltungsindustrie rund herum. Vor diesem historischen Hintergrund zeichnet sich die Einbettung, aber auch das spezifisch Neue und Besondere an Mali ab. Der Auslandseinsatz wird zwar primär individuell gedeutet, er führt aber auch nicht zu Desillusionierung oder Erleuchtung – in akutes Kampfgeschehen waren die deutschen Soldat*innen in Mali ja auch nicht verwickelt. Vielmehr, so scheint es, soll er einfach Spaß machen, cool und aufregend sein. Doch was, wenn sich die Bedrohung realisiert, reales Grauen in den spaßigen Abenteuer-Kosmos einbricht?

3.3   Einbruch des Realen: „Das größte Opfer"

Am 26. Juli 2017, während der Dreharbeiten zu Mali, stürzte ein deutscher Tiger-Kampfhubschrauber in der Nähe des Camps der Protagonist*innen ab. Der mit Explosiv-Raketen bewaffnete Helikopter wurde völlig zerstört, beide Piloten starben auf der Stelle. Als Ursache konnte nachträglich eine technisch fehlerhafte Einstellung des Autopiloten rekonstruiert werden (Gebauer, 2018).

Episode 25, „Das größte Opfer", ist dem Absturz gewidmet. Die hier gezeigten Interviews wurden noch vor der Überstellung der Verstorbenen geführt, außerdem ist Videomaterial von der Fahrt zur Absturzstelle zu sehen. Kurz darauf wurden die Dreharbeiten für zwei Monate pausiert, später jedoch fortgesetzt. Obwohl zum Erscheinungsdatum im Oktober schon lange bekannt, wurde der Absturz in der Serie nie zuvor erwähnt, so dass es eine Art dramaturgischen

Überraschungsmoment gibt. Was passiert in dieser Folge? Schon in den ersten Sekunden wird deutlich, wie die Episode aus der Reihe fällt: es ist die einzige Folge, in der zu Beginn keine Musik ertönt und das Intro mit dem MALI-Schriftzug nicht eingeblendet wird. Auch fehlen in der Beschreibung die Links zu Chatbot und Spotify-Playlist. Stattdessen beginnt das Video mit einer nüchternen Texteinblendung, die das Datum des Absturzes nennt. Daraufhin sehen wir die bekannten Protagonist*innen in einem unbekannten Setting: Einzeln sitzend, auf einem Klapphocker vor dunklem Hintergrund, knie- bzw. brustaufwärts gefilmt, gut ausgeleuchtet (Abb. 5). Die Gefilmte*n blicken leicht links an der Kamera vorbei, auf eine*n unsichtbare*n Interviewer*in. Durch die stabile Kamera und gezielte Beleuchtung erscheinen diese Aufnahmen, in Kontrast zu den vorigen Folgen, nicht mehr amateurhaft-nah, sondern wie typische professionelle Fernseh-Interviews. Die einzelnen Sprecher*innen sind geschickt gegengeschnitten; das Erzählte folgt einer chronologischen Dramaturgie: Erst wird der Alltag zuvor geschildert (Sport, Mittagessen), dann der plötzliche Einschnitt durch die „furchtbare Meldung" über das Notfunkgerät (00:21–00:45).

Nun bedient sich die Episode eines interessanten dramaturgischen Mittels, um den Inhalt der angedeuteten dunklen Vorahnung zu konkretisieren. Verschiedene TV-Nachrichtensendungen werden zusammengeschnitten, in denen die Sprecher*innen nüchtern den Absturz vermelden. Dieses externe Material fungiert als „objektive" Referenz, als den Zuschauer*innen alltagsweltlich bekannte mediale Autorität: hier ist nichts (mehr) fiktional oder nachgestellt, was in Mali passiert, ist „echt".

Abbildung 5. Daniel im Interview-Setting. Folge 25, Standbild bei 00:24

Abbildung 6. Daniel im Panzerfahrzeug. Folge 25, Standbild bei 03:54

Das bezeugt auch Videomaterial, das in der Folge zu sehen ist und wohl tatsächlich vom Tag des Absturzes stammt: Wir sehen einen bekannten Protagonisten, Verbindungsoffizier Daniel, als Vorhut auf dem Weg zur Absturzstelle (Abb. 6). Er sitzt in einem fahrenden Panzerfahrzeug, filmt sich selbst und sagt:

> „Äh umso näher man jetz (.) der Absturzstelle äh kommt umso mehr äh umso nervöser wird man man weiß nich (.) was ein dort (.) fürn Bild erwartet [Schnitt] mein=man weiß es schon; natürlich; da wird n Hubschrauber in Trümmern liegen aber das is ja eh (1)

((verzieht den Mund)) keine schöne Erfahrung, die wir jetz machen werden (.)" (Folge 25, 03:27–03:42)

Daniel spricht schnell, fast hektisch. Obgleich im unpersönlichen „man" formuliert, ist die Szene intensiv und emotional berührend. Wir sehen einen Menschen in einer kritischen, ja existenziellen – und damit für den Krieg eigentlich charakteristischen – Situation. Im ganzen Mali-Kosmos wird in diesen Sätzen das unterschwellige, reale Grauen, das potenziell zu jedem Militäreinsatz dazu gehört, am stärksten spürbar. Werden wir Daniel nun bis zur Absturzstelle folgen und den zertrümmerten Helikopter, die Leichen der beiden Soldaten sehen? Nein, denn aus Daniels Funkgerät kommt ein Befehl: „Ähm die Jungs äh solln keine Fotos machen mit Handy nich mit gar nichts; kommen" (03:54–04:02). Daniel bestätigt das und wendet sich dann wieder zur Kamera:

> „Ich hab auch gra:d die Anweisung bekommen was absolut verständlich is das an der Absturzstelle wenn wir dort eintreffen keine Bilder gemacht werden ((schüttelt den Kopf)) es wird nich gefilmt; verständlicherweise ähm das geht niemanden was an (2) ja darum werde ich äh die Kamera dann zu gegebenem Zeitpunkt auch ausmachen" (04:10–04:25).

Mit einem Schnitt befinden wir uns nun wieder im Interview-Setting. Hauptmann Michael, mit Tränen in den Augen: „Da war nichts mehr (1) so wie es ma=war" (04:25–04:30). Auch wenn er die gefallenen Kameraden nicht persönlich gekannt habe, stehe er vor einer „Leere". Doch die Leerstelle wird bald mit professionellen Deutungen gefüllt: nun kommen ein Militärpfarrer und die Truppenpsychologin zu Wort. Letztere: „da wird sich das ganze Kontingent, dessen bewusst ((atmet laut ein)) dass einfach was passieren kann dass was Schlimmes passieren kann" (04:57–05:11). Was genau eigentlich Schlimmes passieren kann, bleibt unausgesprochen. Stattdessen orientiert sich die Truppenpsychologin am Kameradschaftsbegriff: „Un=ich hoffe (.) dass dieses Bewusstsein dazu beiträgt dass die Kameradschaft auch noch stärker werden kann in dem Kontingent" (06:24–06:34).

Abbildung 7. Särge und Spalier, vom Flugzeug-inneren aus. Folge 25, Standbild bei 09:17

Abbildung 8. Totale über den Flugplatz mit Helikoptern. Folge 25, Standbild bei 09:33

Den Abschluss der Episode bilden Aufnahmen der Trauerzeremonie, in der, so Hauptmann Michael, „wir (1) Spalier stehn werden durchs ganze Lager [Schnitt] so von sein Kameraden Abschied zu nehmen; die Ehre zu erweisen (1)" (06:38– 06:50). In unseren Recherchen durch Mali war dies die einzige Stelle, an der der Begriff „Ehre" aufgetaucht ist. Die militärische Zeremonie wirkt feierlich und ergreifend, der Eindruck wird durch tiefe, langsame Cello-Musik verstärkt. Es wird salutiert, die Verstorbenen erhalten Orden. Die Särge, von zwei großen Deutschland-Flaggen überdeckt, werden durch ein Spalier aus Soldat*innen, das bis in den Horizont reicht, über das Rollfeld getragen. Die Kamera fängt das Ganze in mehreren, monumental wirkenden Totalen und einer fast symmetrischen Aufnahme aus dem Inneren des Transportflugzeugs ein (Abb. 7). In der letzten Einstellung sieht man zwei Helikopter, die über den weiten, hellen Himmel fliegen (Abb. 8). Das Bild verblasst zu einem weißen Hintergrund. Darauf erscheint in schwarzer Schrift „IN GEDENKEN AN DIE BEIM ABSTURZ GETÖTETEN KAMERADEN" (09:44).

In „Das größte Opfer" lässt sich beobachten, wie ein Einbruch des Realen Risse im Spaß- und (Selbst-)Erfahrungsdiskurs von Mali zu hinterlassen droht, auf den reagiert werden muss. Dies geschieht auf mehreren Ebenen: Diskursiv durch einer Art Rückgriff auf traditionelle militärische Deutungsmuster, konkret Begriffe wie „Opfer" und „Ehre" (die sonst an keiner Stelle der Serie fallen) sowie durch den verstärkt forcierten Kameradschaftsbegriff[7], nicht zuletzt mittels professionell-psychologischer Unterstützung. Die Rede vom „Vaterland" wird hingegen von den Machern der Kampagne auch hier nicht verwendet; in den Kommentarspalten hingegen ist sie hoch virulent.[8] In der Darstellungsart der Episode (Viskurs) werden Mittel aus Kontexten aufgegriffen, die sich vom Gesamtstil der Serie unterscheiden: die Nachrichten-Ausschnitte, das Interview-Setting und die pompösen Total-Aufnahmen der Trauerzeremonie. Ergänzend erfährt das traumatische Ereignis des Absturzes spezifische diskursive Deutungen – als „furchtbare Meldung", „was Schlimmes", das passieren kann, oder „Opfer" zur Stärkung der Kameradschaft – und wird in Summe wieder so eingeholt, dass das Dispositiv Mali als Ganzes in seiner Funktion weitgehend unbeeinträchtigt bleibt. Jedenfalls erfolgreich war „Das größte Opfer" in der Social

---

7 Der Kameradschaftsbegriff ist sozial- bzw. militärhistorisch durchaus zu problematisieren, als „Leitbild einer Sozialkultur, die durch kommunikative Verdichtung im Inneren und Abschottung nach außen gekennzeichnet ist" (Kühne, 2006, S. 22). Im Kontrast zum Ideal eines eigenständig moralisch geleiteten Selbst war dieser für die Wehrmachts-Veteranenkultur der Nachkriegszeit zentral und wurde von der Unterhaltungsindustrie seither rege aufgegriffen (Kühne, 2006, S. 250).

8 Auf Instagram liest man z. B.: „Ihr habt gelobt dem deutschen Vaterland treu zu dienen und zu verteidigen. Diesen Schwur habt ihr Erfüllt!" (marc130700, 23. 11. 2017). Unter dem YouTube-Video kommentiert ein User namens GermanMilitaryPower: „Mein tiefstes Beileid. Mögen euch unsere Vorväter in Valhalla begrüßen."

Media-Währung „Aufmerksamkeit"; als Folge 25 von 29 hatte sie eine der höchsten Klickzahlen, und das, obwohl die Videoaufrufe zum Ende der Serie hin etwas abnahmen.

3.4   „Folge der Bundeswehr in den Einsatz" – Mali als Trichter

Doch was ist eigentlich die „Funktion" Malis? Nachdem es in den vorigen Abschnitten primär um relativ feine Muster im Diskurs und Viskurs der Serie ging, soll abschließend noch einmal „herausgezoomt" werden, um die Gesamtstruktur, den Aufbau, die Architektur des Dispositivs in den Blick zu rücken. Dabei liegt ein besonderer Fokus auf den Schnittstellen und Verlinkungen. Wie Seier (2019, S. 232) beobachtet, ist in Dispositiven „Handlungsmacht immer verteilt, sind Handlungen immer dislokal organisiert". D. h. Handlungen „können nie allein auf Diskurse oder auf Praktiken, Subjekte oder Artefakte zurückgeführt werden, sondern auf ihre Verknüpfung" (Seier, 2019, S. 232). Bei digitalen Forschungsgegenständen können solche *Links*, in einem ganz buchstäblich technischen Sinn, stark handlungsleitend sein.[9]

Vor diesem Hintergrund lässt sich auch die Beobachtung im Material einordnen, dass die vielen bespielten Plattformen extrem stark untereinander verlinkt sind und aufeinander verweisen: Unter jedem YouTube-Video stehen Links zum Facebook-, Instagram-, Spotify- und Snapchat-Kanal. Auch umgekehrt werden auf diesen Social Media-Seiten Teaser (kurze Videoschnipsel) veröffentlicht, die auf die YouTube-Videos neugierig machen sollen. Das heißt, dass man schon mit einem zufällig auf YouTube oder Instagram angeklickten Video sehr schnell in einen ganzen Kosmos hineingerät, der einen dann potentiell auf allen eigenen Plattformen begleitet. Möchte man nichts von Mali verpassen, muss man dem Kanal Bundeswehr Exclusive auf allen Plattformen folgen.

Es bleibt aber nicht nur bei unterhaltsamem und unverfänglichem Content. Mit dem Erscheinungsverlauf der Serie wurden zunehmend Inhalte gepostet, die Bezug zu einer Karriere bei der Bundeswehr haben, mit Inhalten wie „360 Stellen", „Kann man als Frau beim Bund Karriere machen?" und „Stelle uns Deine Fragen". Am 29. November 2017 schließlich, also nach der „Echtzeit"-Veröffentlichung, wurde der Mali-Chatbot eingestellt und stattdessen ein neuer Bot vorgestellt: der „Job-Bot". In dem entsprechenden Instagram-Posting heißt es:

---

9 Das zeigt sich nicht zuletzt daran, dass das gesamte Geschäftsmodell von Social Media Influencer, bei dem jährlich Millionen umgesetzt werden, wesentlich darauf basiert, dass personalisierte Links vom Influencer-Posting hin zum Online-Shop eines beworbenen Produkts führen (und Klick- bzw. Verkaufszahlen entsprechend rückführbar sind) (Nymoen & Schmitt, 2021).

„Kamerad, du interessierst dich für eine Karriere bei der @Bundeswehr? Dann möchten wir dir an dieser Stelle unseren neuen Kameraden #JobBot vorstellen. Er hat heute seinen Dienst angetreten und hält interessante Infos zum Thema „Karriere" für dich bereit und beantwortet dir deine Fragen." (@bundeswehrexclusive, 2017b)

In der Verwandlung von Chat- zu Job-Bot wird die Richtung des Dispositivs explizit sichtbar. Das eng gesponnene Netz Malis ist also, topographisch ge-sprochen, nicht einfach flach ausgebreitet – wenn auch diese breite Ausgangslage nützlich ist, um einen möglichst großen Teil des Zielpublikums „abzuholen". Wie in einem Trichter rutscht alles, was in die breite Öffnung geraten ist, nach innen; verengt sich hin zu einem schmalen Hals, der auf ein Ziel ausgerichtet ist: der Bewerbung bei der Bundeswehr (aus Sicht der User*innen) und der Rekrutierung neuer Soldat*innen (aus Sicht der Produzent*innen). Auf diesen Punkt hin kondensiert Mali.

4 Fazit & Ausblick

Die Frage, in welche Makro-Dispositive Mali eingebettet ist bzw. auf welche *urgence* es reagiert, lässt sich nicht mehr durch Detailanalysen beantworten. Vielmehr müssen wir versuchen, das Phänomen in einem größeren gesell-schaftspolitischen und historischen Kontext zu verorten.

Als Ausgangspunkt lässt sich festhalten: Die Bundeswehr sucht dringend Nachwuchs. Die allgemeine Wehrpflicht wurde in Deutschland 2011 abgeschafft, das Verteidigungs-Etat steigt seit 2015 – erstmal seit Ende des Kalten Krieges – jedoch kontinuierlich (*Trendwende Finanzen*, o. J.). Die Bundeswehr befindet sich also auf Wachstumskurs, wie die damalige Verteidigungsministerin von der Leyen 2016 verkündete: „Ein Vierteljahrhundert des Schrumpfens ist vorbei. Es ist Zeit für die Bundeswehr, wieder zu wachsen" (zit. nach Schulze, 2016).

Dabei konkurriert sie jedoch mit der Privatwirtschaft, unter deren Jobbe-schreibung keine lebensgefährlichen Militäreinsätze fallen, um Arbeitskräfte. Die geläufige Metapher für diese Konkurrenzsituation ist treffenderweise eine militaristische: *„war on talent"* (präziser müsste es wohl heißen: „war for talent"). Erschaffen wurde diese Phrase durch das Consulting-Unternehmen McKinsey[10], das schon 1998 in einem „advertorial" an Human Ressource Manager schrieb: „There is a war on talent, and it will intensify" (zit. nach Suzman, 2021). Auch dieser Kriegsschauplatz hat sich in den letzten Jahren verändert; „The new war for talent" findet heute wiederum vornehmlich im Digitalen statt (McKinsey,

---

10 Rückblickend wirkt es nachgerade ironisch, dass das Verteidigungsministerium unter von der Leyen ausgerechnet zu dieser Unternehmensberatung allzu enge Beziehungen pflegte, die als „Berateraffäre" öffentlich wurden (ZEIT ONLINE, 2020).

2015). Die zeitgemäße Lösung lautet folglich zielgruppenspezifische Online-Werbung, am besten dort, wo Jugendliche und junge Erwachsene die meiste Bildschirmzeit verbringen: auf YouTube, Instagram, Snapchat und Co. In diesem „Krieg" also kommt Mali zum Einsatz. Damit bewegt sich die Bundeswehr in „neues Terrain" und muss sich entsprechend kleiden bzw. (als professionelle Dienstleistung einer Agentur) kleiden lassen. Denn im (deutschsprachigen Mainstream-) Social Media herrscht ein Stil bzw. Habitus mit eigenen Diskursregeln, eigener Bildsprache, Darstellungskonventionen und Referenzen.

Der Auslandseinsatz in Mali bedeutet Abenteuer und persönliche Erfahrung, nicht nur für die Soldat*innen selbst, sondern auch für uns Zuseher*innen. Denn wir werden nicht nur zeitlich synchron (wenn auch gerade nicht „echtzeitlich" im konventionellen Wortsinn) über die neuesten Ereignisse auf dem Laufenden gehalten, und durch das emotionale Storytelling unterhalten, sondern sind immer auch indirekt in der Rede der Protagonist*innen adressiert, die „für uns" in Afrika sind und sich auch noch dabei filmen. Als außerweltliches, halb-virtuelles und apolitisches Abenteuer, an dem wir so bequem teilhaben können, erscheint es abwegig, das ganze Unterfangen hinsichtlich seiner Ursachen, des geopolitischen Kontexts, lokaler Effekte oder militärischer Erfolgsaussichten zu hinterfragen.

Die Episode „Das größte Opfer" nimmt eine Sonderstellung im Mali-Kosmos ein, insofern als die reale Gefährlichkeit des dargestellten Militäreinsatzes mit der virtuellen Abenteuer-Logik der Darstellungsweise zu kollidieren droht. Tatsächlich distanziert sich diese Folge, diskursiv wie audiovisuell, von dem sonst gängigen Social-Media-Stil und greift auf externes Material (Tagesschau-Ausschnitte), standardisierte Interview-Settings und streng geometrisch komponierte Großaufnahmen zurück. Die Rezipient*innen sind dadurch wieder mehr in der distanzierten Zuschauer*innen-Rolle, weniger „mittendrin dabei".

Als Social Media-Serie bildet Mali ein neuartiges Genre, bei dem plattformübergreifend ein Narrativ erzählt, ja eine ganze virtuelle Welt geschaffen wird, die möglichst eng auf die mediale Lebenswelt junger Menschen zugeschnitten ist. Wie sich, betrachtet man die Gesamt-Topographie Malis über den Ausstrahlungszeitraum hinweg, jedoch zeigt, weist diese Welt eine Krümmung, einen zentralen Sog hin zu dem vordefinierten Ziel auf, dass sich Follower*innen bei der Bundeswehr bewerben. Somit kann der anfängliche Aufruf des Chatbots, der Bundeswehr in den Einsatz zu folgen, durchaus wörtlich verstanden werden.

In dieser Funktion kann Mali, in den Augen des deutschen Verteidigungsministeriums, als erfolgreich bezeichnet werden: Die einzelnen YouTube-Folgen wurden im Schnitt etwa 500.000-mal angeklickt (Stand: Dezember 2021). Zwischen Start und Ende der Serie wurde die Bundeswehr-Karrierewebsite 60 % häufiger aufgerufen als zuvor. Auch die zuständige Telefon-Hotline wurde von 34 % mehr Personen angerufen als zuvor (Bundeswehr Personal, 2018). Dirk von

Holleben, ein Presse-Verantwortlicher der Bundeswehr, sagte dazu in einem Interview:

> „Jeder dritte junge Deutsche kennt die Serie. Wir haben es also geschafft, ein so schwieriges Thema wie den Auslandseinsatz in der jungen Zielgruppe authentisch und auf Augenhöhe näher zu bringen. Damit haben wir auch erreicht, die Bedenken gegen Auslandseinsätze ein Stück weit abzubauen." (zit. nach politik&kommunikation, 2019)

Eine tatsächlich erhöhte Rekrutierungsquote als kausale Folge der Kampagne nachzuweisen, ist hier weder zu leisten noch Ziel des dispositivanalytischen Vorgehens. Es lässt sich aber durchaus eine gesellschaftliche Reichweite und damit Relevanz nachweisen. Für den Erfolg des medialen Mikro-Dispositivs spricht auch, dass auf Mali zahlreiche Folgeformate erschienen sind: *Biwak, Die Springer, KSK, Survival, Die Rekrutinnen, Besatzung Bravo, Die Mission, Airteam* und jüngst *Semper talis.* Dabei zeigt sich im Lauf der Zeit eine Anpassungsfähigkeit im Feld: So wurde der Chatbot ab „Die Springer" vom Facebook-Messenger auf WhatsApp verlagert, die diesen als beliebteste Messenger-App verdrängt hat. Snapchat wurde hingegen bereits mit „Biwak" im Frühjahr 2018 nicht weiter bespielt.

Mali, als Mikro-Dispositiv verstanden, ist aber mehr als eine erfolgreiche Marketing-Masche. Es setzt für sein Funktionieren komplexe technologische Apparate (z. B. Smartphone oder Laptop), digitale Infrastrukturen (Social Media-Plattformen, Chatbots), Praktiken der Rezipient*innen (like, follow, share) und Wissensfelder (Militärkultur, Video-Gestaltung, digitales Marketing etc.) voraus. Aus diesen heterogenen Einheiten setzt sich Mali zusammen; es ist das Netz, das sich über und zwischen ihnen spannt. Unter global-medialer Perspektive fügt sich Mali in die Entwicklung einer „mediatisation of war", die mit dem Aufkommen digitaler Medien entschieden transformiert wird (Hoskins & O'Loughlin, 2010). In der heterogenen Medienlandschaft des 21. Jahrhunderts hat sich die Arena, wer wie über Militäreinsätze berichtet, entscheidend gewandelt (Kaempf, 2013). Während das Monopol über TV- und Rundfunk-Nachrichten lange Zeit praktisch in der Hand öffentlich-rechtlicher bzw. privater Institutionen lag, bietet die direkte Nutzung von Social Media-Kanälen, um eigene Inhalte zu streuen, den militärischen Akteuren selbst ganz neue Möglichkeiten: „Military social media sites collapse the gap between the military and the media, enabling militaries to become the media themselves" (Crilley, 2016, S. 62). Im Falle Malis hat sich die Bundeswehr Unterstützung und Know-How aus der Marketingbranche eingekauft, das ändert aber nichts an der Konstellation, dass nicht mehr eine unabhängige journalistische Instanz, sondern die Armee selbst die Berichterstattungs-Hoheit über ihren Einsatz besitzt.

Dass militärische Inhalte dabei nahtlos in den persönlichen Social Media-Feed einfließen, weckt bei Wissenschaftler*innen, die sich – in diesem Fall aus angloamerikanischer Perspektive – mit dem Phänomen befasst haben, offenbar Irritationen:

> „there is something strange about seeing videos of military operations in Afghanistan alongside photographs of my friend's cat and various status updates about the everyday goings on of family and friends." (Crilley, 2016, S. 63)

Mit der hier zur Sprache gebrachten Irritation sind wir zum Ausgangspunkt unserer Beschäftigung mit Mali zurückgekehrt. Kritisches Unbehagen markierte den Start unserer Forschungsbemühungen (und trieb sie laufend an). Etwas an Mali erschien uns so noch nicht dagewesen. Unser Anliegen war es, dieses neue Terrain etwas zu explizieren, für sozial-mediale und digital-technologische Umbruchmomente und die damit einhergehenden Machteffekte zu sensibilisieren. Letztlich soll dies zu einer kritischen Debatte der gesellschaftspolitischen – und angesichts des Alters der Zielgruppe Malis insbesondere auch bildungsrelevanten – Implikationen dieser Entwicklungen beitragen.

Abschließend soll auf Desiderate und Potentiale einer weiteren Erforschung des Materials hingewiesen werden. Bührmann und Schneider (2012, S. 12) betonen angesichts medialer Dispositive das „Zusammenspiel von technischer Apparatur, Medieninhalten sowie institutionellen Praktiken ihrer Produktion und vor allem ihrer Rezeption und Nutzung" (Przyborski & Slunecko, 2020). Vor allem die Rezeptions-Seite verspricht eine produktive Ergänzung unserer bisherigen Analysen, denn darin könnten potentiell praktische Aneignungsformen ans Licht treten. Diese könnten sich z.B. in Reaction-Videos, Reviews oder Parodien wiederum digital-medial äußern. Auch die Kommentar-Funktion stellt als öffentlicher Resonanzraum der Videos ein noch zu erschließendes Feld dar: „we can begin to make sense of an audience's active interpretation, consumption and usage of military social media sites through the comments they make" (Crilley, 2016, S. 62f.). Auch Gruppendiskussionen bzw. Interviews mit Follower*innen oder – zeitlich wäre das inzwischen möglich – Soldat*innen, die Mali gesehen und sich daraufhin der Bundeswehr verpflichtet haben, wären vielversprechend. Wir versprechen uns von derartigen Triangulierungen eines dispositivanalytischen Ansetzens mit Verfahren, die auf Rezeption von und/oder konkrete Handlungspraxis mit digitalen Dispositiven abzielen, ein hohes methodologisches Potential, das wir in Zukunft weiter ausloten wollen (Meister et al., in Vorbereitung).

5   Literatur

Agamben, G. (2008). *Was ist ein Dispositiv?* Diaphanes.

Bösel, B. (2017). „Von uns selbst schweigen wir" – noch immer? Präliminarien zu einer epistemologischen Bekenntnistheorie. In T. Slunecko, M. Wieser, & A. Przborski (Hrsg.), *Kulturpsychologie in Wien* (S. 55–75). Facultas.

Breuer, F., Muckel, P., & Dieris, B. (2019). *Reflexive Grounded Theory: Eine Einführung für die Forschungspraxis.* Springer Fachmedien.

Bröckling, U. (2007). *Das unternehmerische Selbst: Soziologie einer Subjektivierungsform.* Suhrkamp.

Bröckling, U., & Krasmann, S. (2010). Ni méthode, ni approche. In J. Angermüller & S. Van Dyk (Hrsg.), *Diskursanalyse meets Gouvernementalitätsforschung–Perspektiven auf das Verhältnis von Subjekt, Sprache, Macht und Wissen* (S. 23–43). Campus.

Bröckling, U., Krasmann, S., & Lemke, T. (Hrsg.). (2000). *Gouvernementalität der Gegenwart: Studien zur Ökonomisierung des Sozialen.* Suhrkamp.

Bröckling, U., & Peter, T. (2017). Das Dispositiv der Exzellenz. In R. Diaz-Bone & R. Hartz (Hrsg.), *Dispositiv und Ökonomie: Diskurs- und dispositivanalytische Perspektiven auf Märkte und Organisationen* (S. 283–303). Springer Fachmedien. https://doi.org/10.100 7/978-3-658-15842-2_11.

Bührmann, A. D., & Schneider, W. (2012). *Vom Diskurs zum Dispositiv: Eine Einführung in die Dispositivanalyse* (2., unveränd. Aufl.). transcript-Verlag.

Bundeswehr Exclusive. (o. J.). *Bundeswehr Exclusive* [Facebook page]. Facebook. https:// www.facebook.com/BundeswehrExclusive.

Bundeswehr Exclusive. (2017a, Oktober 18). *MALI SOUNDTRACK* [Music playlist]. Spotify. https://open.spotify.com/playlist/6higyFvlK9HioYE84b0vgp.

Bundeswehr Exclusive. (2017b, November 30). *MALI | Folge uns in den Einsatz | Alle Folgen* [Video playlist]. YouTube. https://www.youtube.com/playlist?list=PL0nyHde37tIZGqc sRjKLc0WkPwIQZdT4T.

Bundeswehr Personal. (2018, Juli 16). *Neue YouTube-Serie: „Die Springer – Mach den Sprung Deines Lebens".* presseportal.de. https://www.presseportal.de/pm/116137/4008 772.

@bundeswehrexclusive. (o. J.). *@bundeswehrexclusive* [User profile]. Instagram. https:// www.instagram.com/bundeswehrexclusive/.

@bundeswehrexclusive. (2017a, Oktober 19). *Was bedeutet eigentlich Echtzeit? Passiert das alles im MaliBot gerade wirklich? Diese und ähnliche Fragen wurden uns schon häufig gestellt.* [Photograph]. Instagram. https://www.instagram.com/p/BabjewzgEZb/.

@bundeswehrexclusive. (2017b, November 29). *Kamerad, du interessierst dich für eine Karriere bei der @Bundeswehr? Dann möchten wir dir an dieser Stelle unseren neuen Kameraden #JobBot vorstellen.* [Video]. Instagram. https://www.instagram.com/p/Bc FPdyZg7-3/.

Butler, J. (2001). *Psyche der Macht: Das Subjekt der Unterwerfung.* Suhrkamp.

Caborn Wengler, J., Hoffarth, B., & Kumięga, Ł. (2013). *Verortungen des Dispositiv-Begriffs: Analytische Einsätze Zu Raum, Bildung, Politik.* Springer Fachmedien.

Cold-Ravnkilde, S., Albrecht, P., & Haugegaard, R. (2017). Friction and Inequality among Peacekeepers in Mali. *The RUSI Journal, 162*(2), 34–42. https://doi.org/10.1080/030718 47.2017.1328810.

Crilley, R. (2016). Like and share forces: Making sense of military social media sites. In *Understanding Popular Culture and World Politics in the Digital Age*. Routledge.

Deleuze, G. (1991). Was ist ein Dispositiv? In F. Ewald & B. Waldenfels (Hrsg.), *Spiele der Wahrheit. Michel Foucaults Denken* (S. 153–162). Suhrkamp.

Deleuze, G. (1993). Postskriptum über die Kontrollgesellschaften. In G. Deleuze (Hrsg.), *Unterhandlungen. 1972–1990* (S. 254–262). Suhrkamp.

Deleuze, G. (1996). *Lust und Begehren*. Merve-Verlag.

Devereux, G. (1984). *Angst und Methode in den Verhaltenswissenschaften*. Suhrkamp.

Diaz-Bone, R., & Hartz, R. (Hrsg.). (2017). *Dispositiv und Ökonomie: Diskurs- und dispositivanalytische Perspektiven auf Märkte und Organisationen*. Springer Fachmedien.

Foucault, M. (1978). *Dispositive der Macht: Über Sexualität, Wissen und Wahrheit*. Merve-Verlag.

Gänsler, K. (2021). Schlechte Nachrichten aus dem Sahel. *Südwind Magazin, September-Oktober 2021*(9–10), 9–12. https://www.suedwind-magazin.at/schlechte-nachrichten-a us-dem-sahel/.

Gebauer, M. (2018, Dezember 12). *Mali: Bundeswehr sieht Schuld für „Tiger"-Absturz bei Airbus*. Der Spiegel. https://www.spiegel.de/politik/ausland/mali-toedlicher-tiger-abst urz-bundeswehr-sieht-die-schuld-bei-airbus-a-1243250.html.

Gnosa, T. (2018). *Im Dispositiv: Zur reziproken Genese von Wissen, Macht und Medien*. transcript Verlag.

Harari, Y. N. (2008). *The ultimate experience: Battlefield revelations and the making of modern war culture, 1450–2000*. Palgrave Macmillan.

Hoskins, A., & O'Loughlin, B. (2010). *War and media*. Polity Press.

JIM Jugend, Information, (Multi-) Media. (2017). Medienpädagogischer Forschungsverbund Südwest. https://www.schau-hin.info/fileadmin/content/Downloads/Sonstiges/J IM_2017.pdf.

Johnson, D. (2022, Juli 17). *Eskalation zwischen Mali und UNO: Bamako blockiert Blauhelme*. Die Tageszeitung: taz. https://taz.de/!5868931/.

Kaempf, S. (2013). The mediatisation of war in a transforming global media landscape. *Australian Journal of International Affairs, 67*(5), 586–604. https://doi.org/10.1080/10 357718.2013.817527.

Kühne, T. (2006). *Kameradschaft: Die Soldaten des nationalsozialistischen Krieges und das 20. Jahrhundert*. Vandenhoeck & Ruprecht.

Lenoir, T., & Caldwell, L. (2018). *The military-entertainment complex*. Harvard University Press.

Mau, S. (2017). *Das metrische Wir: Über die Quantifizierung des Sozialen*. Suhrkamp.

McKinsey. (2015, Oktober 1). *Discussions on digital: The new war for talent*. https:// www.mckinsey.com/capabilities/people-and-organizational-performance/our-insight s/discussions-on-digital-the-new-war-for-talent.

Meinhof, M. (2018). Mikrodispositive als Bindeglied zwischen ethnomethodologischer Videoanalyse und Dispositivanalyse. In C. Moritz & M. Corsten (Hrsg.), *Handbuch Qualitative Videoanalyse* (S. 167–180). Springer Fachmedien. https://doi.org/10.1007/ 978-3-658-15894-1_10.

Meister, M. (2022). Corporate Mood Tracking. Emotionale Selbstvermessung am Arbeitsplatz. *AugenBlick. Konstanzer Hefte zur Medienwissenschaft, 85*, 55–70.

Meister, M., Przborski, A., & Slunecko, T. (in Vorbereitung). *Vermessene Wissenschaft: Medientechnisches Handeln mit Forschungsinformationssystemen.*

Meister, M., & Slunecko, T. (2021). Digitale Dispositive psychischer Gesundheit. Eine Analyse der Resilienz-App ‚SuperBetter'. *ZQF–Zeitschrift für Qualitative Forschung, 22* (2), 242–265. https://doi.org/10.3224/zqf.v22i2.05.

Nymoen, O., & Schmitt, W. M. (2021). *Influencer: Die Ideologie der Werbekörper.* Suhrkamp.

Pfannenmüller, J. (2017, Oktober 10). *Bundeswehr-Social-TV: „Mali" folgt auf „Die Rekruten".* W&V. https://www.wuv.de/Archiv/Neue-Bundeswehr-Serie-%22Mali%22-folgt-auf-%22Die-Rekruten%22.

politik&kommunikation. (2019, Februar 19). *Wie die Bundeswehr mit einem Chatbot die Angst vor Auslandseinsätzen abbauen will.* https://www.politik-kommunikation.de/politik/wie-die-bundeswehr-mit-einem-chatbot-die-angst-vor-auslandseinsaetzen-abbauen-will/.

Przyborski, A., & Slunecko, T. (2020). Understanding Media Communication: On the Significance of Iconic Thinking for a Praxeological Model of Communication. *SAGE Open, 10*(3), 2158244020952064. https://doi.org/10.1177/2158244020952064.

Rose, N. (1996). *Inventing our Selves: Psychology, Power, and Personhood.* Cambridge University Press.

Rose, N. (1999). *Governing the soul: The shaping of the private self* (2. ed.). Free Association Books.

Schaupp, S. (2019). Die totale Evaluation: Skizze zu einer materialistischen Dispositivanalyse. In D. Rode & M. Stern (Hrsg.), *Self-Tracking, Selfies, Tinder und Co.* (S. 225–248). transcript Verlag. https://doi.org/10.14361/9783839439081-010.

Schildbach, L. (2017, Oktober 23). *Bundeswehr-Serie „Mali" – Abenteuer Krieg?* Deutschlandfunk. https://www.deutschlandfunk.de/bundeswehr-serie-mali-abenteuer-krieg-100.html.

Schulze, T. (2016, Mai 11). *Bundeswehr auf Wachstumskurs.* Die Tageszeitung: taz. https://taz.de/!5299609/.

Seier, A. (2019). *Mikropolitik der Medien.* Kulturverlag Kadmos.

Slunecko, T. (2008). *Von der Konstruktion zur dynamischen Konstitution: Beobachtungen auf der eigenen Spur* (2., überarb. Aufl.). Facultas.

Slunecko, T. (2017). Beobachtungen auf der eigenen Spur. Bemerkungen zu einem für die Wiener kulturpsychologische Schule charakteristischen Motiv. In T. Slunecko, M. Wieser, & A. Przborski (Hrsg.), *Kulturpsychologie in Wien* (S. 27–54). Facultas.

Slunecko, T. (2020). Tracking One's Own Path – a Methodological Leitmotif of Cultural Psychology. *Integrative Psychological and Behavioral Science, 54*(1), 196–214. https://doi.org/10.1007/s12124-019-09479-2.

Slunecko, T., & Bösel, B. (2022). Das Unbehagen in der digitalen Zuwendung. Ein Gespräch. *AugenBlick. Konstanzer Hefte zur Medienwissenschaft, 85*, 127–137.

Slunecko, T., & Chlouba, L. (2021). Meditation in the age of its technological mimicry. A dispositif analysis of mindfulness applications. *International Review of Theoretical Psychologies, 11*, 63–77. https://doi.org/10.1007/s12124-019-09479-2.

Stauff, M. (2005). *Das neue Fernsehen: Machtanalyse, Gouvernementalität und digitale Medien*. LIT.

Suzman, J. (2021, Oktober 24). *How McKinsey & Co. Created „The War for Talent" in 1998 to propagate a „myth of brilliance"*. ThePrint. https://theprint.in/pageturner/excerpt/how-mckinsey-co-created-the-war-for-talent-in-1998-to-propagate-a-myth-of-brilliance/755705/.

Szymanski, M. (2021, Juni 27). *Anschlag in Mali: „Erhebliche Bedrohungslage"*. Süddeutsche.de. https://www.sueddeutsche.de/politik/mali-anschlag-kampfdrohnen-spd-1.5335104.

Trendwende Finanzen. (o. J.). Abgerufen 20. Februar 2023, von https://www.bundeswehr.de/de/ueber-die-bundeswehr/modernisierung-bundeswehr/verteidigungshaushalt-trendwende-finanzen.

United Nations. (o. J.). *MINUSMA*. United Nations Peacekeeping. Abgerufen 20. Februar 2023, von https://peacekeeping.un.org/en/mission/minusma.

Wacquant, L. (2014). Für eine Soziologie aus Fleisch und Blut. *sub\urban. zeitschrift für kritische stadtforschung*, *2*(3), 93–106. https://doi.org/10.36900/suburban.v2i3.151.

ZEIT ONLINE. (2020, Juni 23). *Berateraffäre: Opposition macht Ursula von der Leyen mitverantwortlich*. Die Zeit. https://www.zeit.de/politik/deutschland/2020-06/berateraffaere-ursula-von-der-leyen-verteidigungsministerium.

Zuboff, S. (2018). *Das Zeitalter des Überwachungskapitalismus*. Campus Verlag.

Claudia Kawai / Ulrich Ansorge

Rating pictures on different sides of the globe – A juxtaposition of Chinese and US American emotional evaluations

Abstract

Central constructs often differ between members of different cultures and nations. However, the internet allows for an exchange of content across national boundaries. Therefore, the internet could have a leveling effect on cultural differences. In the present study, we compared the meaning of emotions between China and the USA. We hypothesized that cross-nationally shared semantics might be a function of the ratio of the exposure to culture-specific versus culturally shared content. Therefore, we expected younger people, having grown up with the internet, to show more cultural commonalities than older people with a larger extent of pre-internet exposure to nationally specific content. To study this question, we analyzed emotion-related ratings (valence and arousal) of black-and-white silhouette pictures from two large samples of US Americans and Mainland Chinese nationals of different ages. While US Americans rated both very positive and very negative pictures as highly arousing, Chinese participants rated (only) very positive pictures as highly arousing, but very negative pictures as lowly arousing. Importantly, in line with a leveling influence of the internet, the younger age groups showed more similar valence-arousal patterns cross-nationally, with less agreement in the older groups.

Mitglieder unterschiedlicher Kulturen und Nationen fassen Begriffe oft unterschiedlich auf. Das Internet erlaubt hingegen den Austausch von Inhalten über nationale Grenzen hinweg. Daher könnte das Internet einen nivellierenden Effekt auf kulturelle Differenzen entfalten. In der vorliegenden Studie verglichen wir die Bedeutung von Emotionen zwischen China und den USA. Wir vermuteten, dass die über Nationen hinweg geteilte Bedeutung eine Folge des Verhältnisses sein könnte, in welchem Mitglieder der beiden Nationen kultur-spezifischen versus kultur-geteilten Inhalten ausgesetzt waren. Daher erwarteten wir, dass jüngere Personen, die mit dem Internet aufgewachsen sind, mehr kulturelle Übereinstimmungen zeigen als ältere Personen, die in der Vor-Internet-Zeit einem größeren Ausmaß national spezifischer Inhalte ausgesetzt waren. Um die Hypothese zu untersuchen, analysierten wir emotionsbezogene Einschätzungen (der Valenz und der Erregung) von schwarz-weißen Umrisszeichnungen in zwei großen Stichproben von US-Amerikaner*innen und Festland-Chines*innen unterschiedlichen Alters. Während sehr positive und sehr negative Bilder von Amerikaner*innen als hoch erregend eingeschätzt wurden, schätzten chinesische Versuchsteilnehmer*innen (nur) sehr positive Bilder als hoch erregend ein, sehr negative Bilder aber als wenig erregend. Von Relevanz für unsere

Forschungshypothese und im Einklang mit dem nivellierenden Einfluss des Internets zeigte sich in den jüngeren Altersgruppen ein über die Nationen hinweg ähnlicheres Valenz-Erregungs-Muster als unter den älteren Versuchsteilnehmer*innen.

A Study on Cross-Cultural Differences and Similarities in Emotional Evaluations

> "In its most general sense, globalization refers to a reduction of distance and difference across the globe. [...] In a material sense, people of different societies are growing closer to each other and getting to know each other better" (Zürn, 2003, p. 341 f.).

In the last decades of the 20th century, a number of scholars brought forward theories about how globalization might influence the cultures of the world, among them *cultural imperialism* (for review see, e. g., Hamm & Smandych, 2005; see also Sparks, 2012) and *cultural convergence theory* (Kincaid, 2002; Rogers & Kincaid, 1981). While the former theory postulates a predominantly unidirectional, culture-overriding influence and the latter hypothesizes a unified, global culture, both could result in a homogenization of concepts, values, and representations across nations. Shared media consumption is one outcome perpetuated by globalization, and both of the above theories consider media to be a major factor in terms of culture-influencing power (Gurevitch et al., 1982; Hjavard, 2008). For example, the dominance of a language such as English on the internet opens the door for cultural content from the English-speaking sphere (Pimienta et al., 2009) and English language-specific influences on individual cognition (e. g., Slobin, 2000). Now, towards the end of the first quarter of the 21st century, scholars are (still) interested in empirically assessing the predictions made decades ago. Some empirical findings emerged that speak for a global homogenization of media content, consumption and taste (Fu & Govindaraju, 2010; Song, 2018), including new media (e. g., Lee, 2007). In their analysis of box-office revenue development of Hollywood movies across 25 countries around the world, Fu and Govindaraju (2010) found evidence for a global taste assimilation towards American audiences: Within- and between-country homogeneity in movie taste increased significantly between the years 2002 and 2007.

One particularly interesting case study vis-à-vis Western influence and/or cultural homogenization is certainly China, considering the tension that arises from the trend of global flow of information in the digital age on the one hand, and the opposing, restricting force of governmental media censorship on the other (see, e. g., Song, 2018).

In the face of predictions for a homogenization in culture across language and nation boundaries, we wanted to investigate whether a trend of convergence might be observable in semantic evaluations. To this end, we examined the rating behavior for picture material between two countries – the United States of America and the People's Republic of China – in a cross-sectional study. We reasoned that media exposure in general and shared media consumption, in particular, is greater for younger individuals ("digital natives") than for older individuals (Auxier & Anderson, 2021; Kemp, 2020). Take the example of TikTok, a social medium used in different countries, including China, where it is labelled "Douyin" and comes with some restrictions, and the US. Of the over 2 billion users that have downloaded the app and consume more than 1 billion videos every day, the majority of its user base stems from younger age groups (10–19 years: 32.5%, 20–29 years: 29.5%, 30–39 years: 16.4%, 40–49 years: 13.9%, 50+ years: 7.1%; Baker, 2021).

If it is true that shared media consumption across cultures is in fact both, an outcome of globalization as well as a trigger for assimilation of cultures, then we would expect that the younger participants, with more mutual contact points, display more cross-cultural agreement across national and language boundaries than older participants.

For our test, we used a common semantic characteristic, present in different languages and cultures: Each and every concept carries emotion value(s), which can be characterized along a number (often two or three) of semantic dimensions. There are different systems to "break down" emotional content; we will follow the circumplex model of affect, which defines emotion in a two-dimensional valence-arousal space (Russell, 1980), with valence denoting a dimension with the poles of displeasure and pleasure and arousal denoting a dimension ranging from calmness to excitement.

Cross-national or -cultural studies comparing affective ratings to validate picture databases like IAPS (Lang et al., 1997) show mixed results. Generally, a high degree of similarity was found across a range of different countries for valence evaluations (e. g., Deák et al., 2010; Gong & Wang, 2016; Grühn & Scheibe, 2008; Verschuere et al., 2001). However, ratings for emotional arousal were often reported to diverge to a greater extent (e.g., Gong & Wang, 2016; Grühn & Scheibe, 2008; Kurdi et al., 2017). Pictures and their emotional meanings in terms of valence and arousal can vary for a number of reasons, such as idiosyncratic experiences that the viewer has made with a particular picture. However, humans acquire their semantic knowledge also via text and media reception and comprehension (e.g., Johnson-Laird, 2010; Kintsch & Van Dijk, 1987; Al-Maroof et al., 2021), opening the door for commonalities in how humans schematically organize their semantic knowledge (e.g., Komatsu, 1992; Rumelhart & Ortony, 1977).

1.　Method

We collected ratings of affective picture material from Chinese and US citizens across different age groups in an extensive online study, where participants gave their evaluations on the emotional valence or arousal for a series of images on a Likert-style scale. Below, we present some of the findings of interest that highlight differences and similarities within and between the rater groups. The data for the norming process was acquired from our Bicolor Affective Silhouettes and Shapes (BASS) database (see Kawai et al., 2021). Especially in cross-national research on cultural differences and similarities, silhouette pictures have the advantage of being "language-neutral" to a greater extent than words, since they do not differ regarding length, orthographic neighbors, etc. Moreover, they can be considered "culturally neutral" to a greater extent than photorealistic pictures are since silhouettes depict less idiosyncratic details than their photorealistic counterparts would, thus counteracting potential race- or culture-related biases, for instance, the cross-race effect (see, e.g., Malpass & Kravitz, 1969; or Young et al., 2012, for review).

1.1　Positionality statement

The authors wish to disclose their positionality as white researchers with Western backgrounds and acknowledge the possibility of unconscious biases at every stage of the research process.

1.2　Participants

The US data was collected as a representative sample, using Prolific (www.prolific.co), a crowdsourcing service that specializes in providing participants for qualitative and quantitative research studies. The Chinese data collection was managed by Dynata, a market research company (for more information, see Kawai et al., 2021).[1] After exclusions, data from a total of 777 US participants and 869 Chinese participants was analyzed.[2] The demographic data is summarized in Table 1.

1　Ethnicity was not collected in the Chinese rating and while the sample aimed at a representative distribution in gender and age, the older age brackets were severely underrepresented. Therefore, in the results section, we could not report reliable results for the oldest Chinese age group of 58 years and above.

2　Exclusion criteria pertained to demographic constraints (e. g., country of residence, being at least 18 years of age) and data quality measures (passing attention checks, providing confirmation codes). For details on the motivation for the exclusion criteria, see Kawai et al., 2021.

	US			China		
	N	Mean Valence Rating (SD)	Mean Arousal Rating (SD)	N	Mean Valence Rating (SD)	Mean Arousal Rating (SD)
Sex						
Female	402	5.70 (2.39)	5.00 (2.25)	419	5.49 (1.97)	5.25 (1.84)
Male	375	5.58 (2.17)	4.99 (2.28)	450	5.45 (1.94)	5.38 (1.82)
Sum	777			869		
Age						
18–27	138	5.41 (2.23)	4.85 (2.24)	186	5.42 (1.99)	5.23 (1.85)
28–37	147	5.55 (2.13)	4.90 (2.33)	419	5.48 (1.97)	5.38 (1.9)
38–47	132	5.66 (2.36)	5.04 (2.21)	176	5.47 (1.94)	5.32 (1.68)
48–57	134	5.70 (2.26)	4.96 (2.39)	74	5.50 (1.85)	5.20 (1.75)
58+	226	5.78 (2.37)	5.17 (2.16)	14	5.47 (1.78)	5.45 (1.74)
Ethnicity						
Asian	58					
Black	106					
Mixed	35					
Other	30					
White	548					

Table 1. Demographics of the included participants from the US and Chinese ratings with corresponding means and SD for valence and arousal.

1.3   Materials

The Bicolor Affective Silhouettes and Shapes (BASS) database consists of 583 black-on-white silhouette pictures, uniformly measuring 300 × 300 pixels (average file size 2.2 KB, range 0.43–5.88 KB). The images depict a wide range of content (including silhouettes of humans, animals, objects, and nature scenes) and was collected from various online sources with a particular focus on covering the breadth of the emotional valence (negative, neutral, positive) and arousal (low/calming, medium, high/exciting) dimensions. For some examples of the BASS images see Figure 1.

Figure 1. Example of five silhouettes taken from the BASS.

1.4   Procedure

Ratings for valence and arousal were given by two separate groups, whereby each participant only gave ratings on a single emotional dimension, for a subset of the silhouette database (ca. 145 pictures). Approximately half of the participants in each country group evaluated the valence of the material, and the other half evaluated the arousal. The rating study was completed in a web browser (e.g., Google Chrome, Firefox, etc.). Participants followed the link provided to them, which brought them to a web page, programmed with HTML/JavaScript. A rating trial started with the presentation of a picture on grey background (RGB: 128, 128, 128). After two seconds, the picture disappeared and was replaced by a nine-point Likert-style rating scale (arousal: labelled from *very low* to *very high*; valence: labelled from *very negative* to *very positive*). The terms valence and arousal were explained in the instructions before the task started. Valence was defined as the positivity/negativity of a picture, stating that: "Negative valence means that something is unpleasant or bad. Positive valence means that something is pleasant or good." Arousal was explained in the following terms: "Low arousal means that something is calm, tranquil or unexciting. High arousal means that something is intense, exciting or exhilarating."

2.   Results

The reliability of our data was assessed by generating 1,000 random split halves of our sample and calculating the Spearman-Brown reliability coefficient for the BASS silhouettes' mean ratings between these two halves. This procedure was done four times, separately for valence and arousal ratings per country group. Across both emotion dimensions and country groups, interrater reliability was extremely high, indicating a strong general agreement among raters (US valence: $\bar{R}_{val} = .986$; US arousal: $\bar{R}_{aro} = .921$; China valence: $\bar{R}_{val} = .980$; China arousal: $\bar{R}_{aro} = .921$).

2.1   Range of emotion ratings

US raters gave, on average, more extreme affective ratings than their Chinese counterparts for the same picture material. Comparing the mean ratings for the 583 silhouette pictures between the two countries showed a broad range of affective ratings on both dimensions for the US participants (valence mean ratings ranging from 1.11–8.35, overall $M = 5.64$, $SD = 1.76$; arousal mean ratings ranging from 2.51–7.23, overall $M = 5.00$, $SD = 1.02$), but a narrower range for the Chinese participants (valence mean ratings ranging from 1.47–7.84, overall $M = 5.46$, $SD = 1.37$; arousal mean ratings ranging from 3.65–6.75, overall $M = 5.31$, $SD = 0.64$).

2.2   Valence-arousal-relationship across the ages

The most notable difference in the ratings between the two countries emerged when the valence-arousal relationship for the stimulus material was compared. Since each of the 583 pictures has an average valence rating as well as an average arousal rating from the US group and from the Chinese group, we correlated the two average ratings (valence and arousal) separately for each country.

Generally, the US ratings were characterized by a u-shaped relationship between valence and arousal, expressing the tendency that medium-valence stimuli (e. g., emotionally "neutral") are simultaneously rated with low arousal values, with the arousal increasing (slightly asymmetrically) for more positive and more negative pictures. Thus, Pearson's correlation coefficient (measuring linear correlation) showed a weak, negative linear trend, with $r(581) = -.323$, 95% CI [−.394, −.248], $p < .001$. In contrast, ratings from the Chinese group were generally characterized by a strong positive linear correlation, with $r(581) = .805$, 95% CI [.774, .832], $p < .001$. These relationships are illustrated in Figures 2 A (for the US) and 2B (for China) below, where the mean valence rating for each silhouette picture is plotted against its corresponding mean arousal rating for the different age groups since age turned out to be a characterizing factor in our results. Figure 2A shows the u-shaped relationship for US participants with generally high agreement across age groups. Surprisingly, this was not the case for the Chinese sample (see Figure 2B): Younger Chinese participants showed a valence-arousal relationship that resembled the u-shape of the US group. However, with increasing age, the Chinese participants displayed an increasingly linear valence-arousal relationship, with negative pictures displaying low arousal values and increasingly positive pictures displaying increasingly higher arousal values. This means that (a) cross-cultural agreement between the US and China is higher in the younger than in the older age groups (see Figure 2, and Tables 2–3), and (b) intra-cultural agreement between younger and older participants was lower in the Chinese than in the US group (see Tables 3–4 for arousal ratings). While this trend is apparent for both emotion dimensions, cross- as well as intra-national agreement in the valence dimension was generally higher than for arousal.

	Valence Correlation [95% CI]	Arousal Correlation [95% CI]
Age		
18–27	.910 [.895, .923]	.530 [.469, .586]
28–37	.921 [.908, .933]	.219 [.140, .295]
38–47	.899 [.882, .913]	.170 [.090, .248]
48–57	.856 [.833, .876]	−.069 [−.150, .012]
58+ *	.689 [.644, .730]	.251 [.173, .326]

Table 2. US and Chinese valence and arousal rating correlations per age group.

	ch.18_27	ch.28_37	ch.38_47	ch.48_57
us.18_27	.5304	.1607	.0487	−.0464
us.28_37	.5535	.2191	.129	.0456
us.38_47	.5246	.2998	.1702	.0635
us.48_57	.4828	.1172	−.0068	−.0693

Table 3. Comparison of correlations in arousal ratings between age groups between countries.

	us.18_27	us.28_37	us.38_47	us.48_57		ch.18_27	ch.28_37	ch.38_47	ch.48_57
us.18_27	1				ch.18_27	1			
us.28_37	.8745	1			ch.28_37	.6289	1		
us.38_47	.7988	.8183	1		ch.38_47	.536	.764	1	
us.48_57	.8618	.8374	.8264	1	ch.48_57	.4808	.7173	.7293	1

Table 4. Comparison of correlations in arousal ratings between age groups within countries.

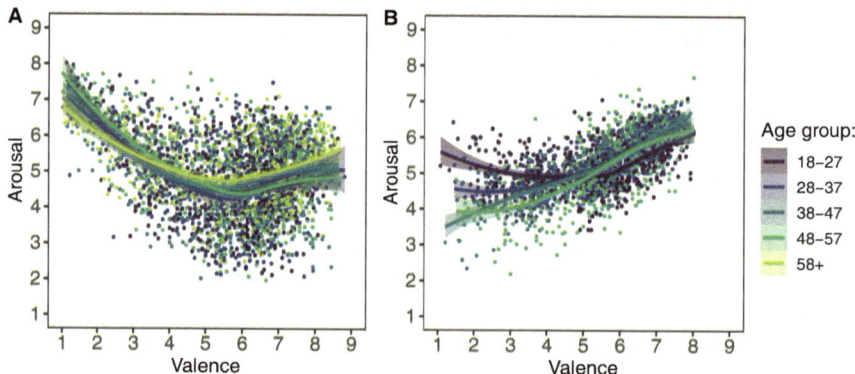

Figure 2. Valence-arousal-relationship for the BASS images across countries and age groups. Note: The oldest age group (58+) includes only 14 Chinese participants (cf. Table 1), and is therefore not displayed in the plot.

3.   Discussion

In our comparison of picture evaluations across large samples from the US and China, we found that valence ratings were highly similar between countries, which is in line with previous research using photographic material (e. g., Gong & Wang, 2016). However, Chinese participants used a narrower range of emotion ratings on both dimensions (valence, arousal) than US participants did, possibly as a result of a supposed preference for moderated affect expression in Chinese culture (also pertaining to the collectivism-individualism debate, see, e.g., Tjosvold & Sun, 2002; Tsai et al., 2007).

Age-related comparisons revealed an interesting pattern in terms of rating behavior in that the younger Chinese participants were more in accordance with the "Western" rating pattern and became increasingly dissimilar to the US ratings with increasing age. This would be in line with the hypothesis that the younger generations are affected to a greater extent by the leveling influence of shared media. This led to another important finding, namely the relatively strong generational difference effect within the Chinese sample (most evident in the arousal, and to a lesser extent also the valence dimension). While rating behavior within the US sample was fairly homogenous throughout the age brackets (in the form of a u-shaped relationship), the tendency of younger Chinese raters to attribute higher arousal values to negative stimuli than older Chinese raters was most predominant for the youngest group (18–27 years of age). Previous research on age effects in comparable studies (such as other picture stimulus norming procedures) cannot account for the data pattern we observed: Several studies investigating emotion regulation and aging found a stronger negative linear relationship between valence and arousal for older than younger participants (Grühn & Scheibe, 2008; Smith et al., 2005), in that negative pictures received more intense arousal ratings, linearly decreasing with increasing positivity – the inverse picture to our Chinese sample, and also different from the u-shape for the elderly US participants. However, these studies utilized different stimulus material, and despite the demonstrated validity of the BASS, response patterns might differ from those acquired with other picture databases. Notably, the rating behavior between the older age groups increasingly diverges between China and the US.

It is possible that the lower arousal ratings of the negative images among Chinese participants reflect some type of culture-specific ethics that has been widespread in China but is not as present in the West, such as an influence of Buddhism or of Confucianism (e.g., Lin & Ho, 2009). Both of these ethical frameworks emphasize an attitude that can be described as uninvolved or disinterested and, in a sense, calm regarding the negative emotions of pain and suffering (e. g., Ekman et al., 2005; Viràg, 2014). A generally low arousal among older Chinese participants regarding negative emotions might reflect both a regular exercising of a disinterested attitude, especially towards one's negative emotions, and the higher degree of importance assigned to these ethical (or even religious) attitudes by the older generation, rather than the younger Chinese participants (cf. Hu, 2017). However, whether the difference originates from emotion perception, conception, or evaluation is impossible to determine from our experiment.

Another possible explanation might be that our study was limited by sampling error and that the older Chinese participants confused emotional arousal with valence. As mentioned above, Dynata is a market research company, and their participant pool might not be as used to participating in behavioral studies as the user base we reached with Prolific for our US sample. Especially the older Chinese participants might be less accustomed than the Western participant pool to these kinds of rating procedures or the affective concepts "valence" and "arousal". This does not mean that elder Chinese participants deviated from a norm. Rather, our research was conducted based on methodologies developed in the West, and we simply cannot be sure that practice with the corresponding methodologies and concepts is as widespread in China as in the West. In light of this explanation, the found age differences in China would be more reflective of the semantics of scales developed in the West that are better understood by younger Chinese partic- ipants. In addition, valence might have been spared from these influences, as previous findings suggest that agreement on the arousal dimension is com- paratively lower than on valence, within and between cultures (Grühn & Scheibe, 2008; Kurdi et al., 2017).

A limitation of the study presented here is that emotion ratings are a rather indirect test of the effects of shared media consumption. Future studies should include a direct measure of media consumption (e. g., questionnaires, media diaries). Moreover, shared media consumption is but one feature brought about by globalization, which younger generations might have experienced to a dif- ferent degree than older generations. Younger participants might also have travelled more than older participants, or they might have participated in other, media-independent forms of intellectual exchange or entertainment which foster multilingualism or multiculturalism. In our study, we did not control for any of these factors.

Furthermore, while our data might suggest a unidirectional influence (from the US towards China), our measures are too coarse to make such assumptions (see the debate on cultural imperialism versus cultural consensus). Our study neither intends nor has the power to allow for drastic conclusions about a gen- erational shift in affective evaluations that have developed in the wake of glob- alization. Thus, further (also longitudinal) studies are highly desirable for an investigation of the globally relevant issue of the leveling out of conceptual semantic differences between nations or cultures. Additionally, a comparison between Mainland China and the US could be amended by including historically "Westernized" parts of China, like Hong Kong. Nevertheless, a leveling influence on semantic evaluations as an effect of common media exposure in the wake of globalization provides a parsimonious explanation of our data.

4.   Conclusion

Throughout the data, we observed the trend that international or intercultural agreement in affective ratings was highest among the younger age groups (18–37 years of age). Generally, with increasing age, the affective ratings given by the US and the Chinese groups diverged more from one another. This characteristic was more apparent in the arousal ratings, which overall displayed less agreement within and between country groups than valence. This is an interesting point in itself, suggesting that arousal might be a less clearly defined and fuzzier concept than emotional valence (see e.g., Kurdi et al., 2017; Lang et al., 1997). However, we want to point out that to the extent that content filters can gear the selective usage of global media, we should also see growing or novel rifts between cultures as a consequence of internet-based media usage in the future. As content filters are not only reflective of nation- or state-based censorship but also mirror algorithm-based preselection of newly presented content based on a user's past interests (e.g., DeVito, 2017), these heterogeneity-increasing media influences are likely to deepen existing differences between cultures within nations (e.g., Cahn & Carbone, 2010; Talhelm et al., 2014), besides the levelling influences of shared media cultures that we highlighted in the present article.

References

Al-Maroof, R., Ayoubi, K., Alhumaid, K., Aburayya, A., Alshurideh, M., Alfaisal, R., & Salloum, S. (2021). The acceptance of social media video for knowledge acquisition, sharing and application: A comparative study among YouTube users and TikTok users for medical purposes. *International Journal of Data and Network Science*, 197–214. https://doi.org/10.5267/j.ijdns.2021.6.013.

Auxier, B., & Anderson, M. (2021). Social media use in 2021. *Pew Research Center*. https://www.pewresearch.org/internet/wp-content/uploads/sites/9/2021/04/PI_2021.04.07_Social-Media-Use_FINAL.pdf.

Baker, A. (2021). TikTok demographics – age, country, gender & income. *ContentCareer*. 05 May 2021. https://contentcareer.com/blog/tiktok-demographics-age-country-gender-income/.

Cahn, N., & Carbone, J. (2010). *Red families versus blue families: Legal polarization and the creation of culture.* Oxford University Press.

Deák, A., Csenki, L., & Révész, G. (2010). Hungarian ratings for the International Affective Picture System (IAPS): A cross-cultural comparison. *Empirical Text and Culture Research, 4*(8), 90–101.

DeVito, M. A. (2017). From editors to algorithms: A values-based approach to understanding story selection in the Facebook news feed. *Digital Journalism, 5*(6), 753–773. https://doi.org/10.1080/21670811.2016.1178592.

Ekman, P., Davidson, R. J., Ricard, M., & Alan Wallace, B. (2005). Buddhist and psychological perspectives on emotions and well-being. *Current Directions in Psychological Science, 14*(2), 59–63. https://doi.org/10.1111/j.0963-7214.2005.00335.x.

Fu, W. W., & Govindaraju, A. (2010). Explaining global box-office tastes in Hollywood films: Homogenization of national audiences' movie selections. *Communication Research, 37*(2), 215–238. https://doi.org/10.1177/0093650209356396.

Gong, X., & Wang, D. (2016). Applicability of the International Affective Picture System in Chinese older adults: A validation study: Cross-cultural validity of the IAPS. *PsyCh Journal, 5*(2), 117–124. https://doi.org/10.1002/pchj.131.

Grühn, D., & Scheibe, S. (2008). Age-related differences in valence and arousal ratings of pictures from the International Affective Picture System (IAPS): Do ratings become more extreme with age? *Behavior Research Methods, 40*(2), 512–521. https://doi.org/10.3758/BRM.40.2.512.

Gurevitch, M., Bennett, T., Curran, J., & Woollacott, J. (Eds.). (1982). *Culture, society and the media.* Methuen.

Hjarvard, S. (2008). The mediatization of society: A theory of the media as agents of social and cultural change. *Nordicom Review, 29*(2), 105–134.

Hamm, B., & Smandych, R. (2005). *Cultural imperialism.* Broadview Press. https://doi.org/10.3138/9781442602090.

Hu, A. (2017). Changing perceived importance of religion in mainland China, 1990–2012: An age-period-cohort analysis. *Social Science Research, 66*, 264–278. https://doi.org/10.1016/j.ssresearch.2016.10.014.

Johnson-Laird, P. N. (2010). Mental models and language. In P. C. Hogan (Ed.), *Encyclopedia of language sciences.* Cambridge University Press.

Kawai, C., Lukács, G., & Ansorge, U. (2021). A new type of pictorial database: The Bicolor Affective Silhouettes and Shapes (BASS). *Behavior Research Methods.* https://doi.org/10.3758/s13428-021-01569-7.

Kemp, S. (2020, July 21). *More than half of the people on earth now use social media.* DataReportal. https://datareportal.com/reports/more-than-half-the-world-now-uses-social-media.

Kincaid, D. L. (2002). Drama, emotion, and cultural convergence. *Communication Theory, 12*(2), 136–152. https://doi.org/10.1111/j.1468-2885.2002.tb00263.x.

Kintsch, W., & van Dijk, T. A. (1978). Toward a model of text comprehension and production. *Psychological Review, 85*(5), 363–394. https://doi.org/10.1037/0033-295X.85.5.363.

Komatsu, L. K. (1992). Recent views of conceptual structure. *Psychological Bulletin, 112*(3), 500–526. https://doi.org/10.1037/0033-2909.112.3.500.

Kurdi, B., Lozano, S., & Banaji, M. R. (2017). Introducing the Open Affective Standardized Image Set (OASIS). *Behavior Research Methods*, *49*(2), 457–470. https://doi.org/10.375 8/s13428-016-0715-3.

Lang, P. J., Bradley, M. M., & Cuthbert, B. N. (1997). International Affective Picture System (IAPS): Technical manual and affective ratings. *NIMH Center for the Study of Emotion and Attention*, *1*, 39–58.

Lin, L.-H., & Ho, Y.-L. (2009). Confucian dynamism, culture and ethical changes in Chinese societies – a comparative study of China, Taiwan, and Hong Kong. *The International Journal of Human Resource Management*, *20*(11), 2402–2417. https://doi.org/10.1080/ 09585190903239757.

Malpass, R. S., & Kravitz, J. (1969). Recognition for faces of own and other race. *Journal of Personality and Social Psychology*, *13*(4), 330–334. https://doi.org/10.1037/h0028434.

Pimienta, D., Prado, D., & Blanco, Á. (2009). Twelve years of measuring linguistic diversity in the Internet: Balance and perspectives. https://www.ifap.ru/pr/2010/n100305c.pdf.

Rogers, E. M., & Kincaid, D. L. (1981). *Communication networks: Toward a new paradigm for research*. Free Press.

Rumelhart, D. E., & Ortony, A. (1977). The representation of knowledge in memory. In R. C. Anderson, R. J. Spiro, & W. E. Montague (Eds.), *Schooling and the acquisition of knowledge* (pp. 99–135). Erlbaum.

Russell, J. A. (1980). A circumplex model of affect. *Journal of Personality and Social Psychology*, *39*(6), 1161–1178. https://doi.org/10.1037/h0077714.

Slobin, D. I. (2000). Verbalized events: A dynamic approach to linguistics relativity and determinism. In S. Niemeier & R. Dirven (Eds.), *Evidence for linguistic relativity* (pp. 107–138). John Benjamins. https://doi.org/10.1075/cilt.198.10slo.

Smith, D. P., Hillman, C. H., & Duley, A. R. (2005). Influences of age on emotional reactivity during picture processing. *The Journals of Gerontology: Series B*, *60*(1), P49–P56. https://doi.org/10.1093/geronb/60.1.P49.

Song, X. (2018). Hollywood movies and China: Analysis of Hollywood globalization and relationship management in China's cinema market. *Global Media and China*, *3*(3), 177–194. https://doi.org/10.1177/2059436418805538.

Sparks, C. (2012). Media and cultural imperialism reconsidered. *Chinese Journal of Communication*, *5*(3), 281–299. https://doi.org/10.1080/17544750.2012.701417.

Talhelm, T., Zhang, X., Oishi, S., Shimin, C., Duan, D., Lan, X., & Kitayama, S. (2014). Large-scale psychological differences within China explained by rice versus wheat agriculture. *Science*, *344*(6184), 603–608. https://doi.org/10.1126/science.1246850.

Tjosvold, D., & Sun, H. F. (2002). Understanding conflict avoidance: Relationship, motivations, actions, and consequences. *International Journal of Conflict Management*, *13* (2), 142–164. https://doi.org/10.1108/eb022872.

Tsai, J. L., Miao, F. F., Seppala, E., Fung, H. H., & Yeung, D. Y. (2007). Influence and adjustment goals: Sources of cultural differences in ideal affect. *Journal of Personality and Social Psychology*, *92*(6), 1102–1117. https://doi.org/10.1037/0022-3514.92.6.1102.

Verschuere, B., Crombez, G., & Koster, E. (2001). The International Affective Picture System a Flemish validation study. *Psychologica Belgica*, *41*(4), 205. https://doi.org /10.5334/pb.981.

Virág C. (2014). Early Confucian perspectives on emotions. In V. Shen (Ed.), *Dao companion to classical Confucian philosophy. Dao companions to Chinese philosophy* (Vol 3, pp. 203–225). Springer. https://doi.org/10.1007/978-90-481-2936-2_9.

Young, S. G., Hugenberg, K., Bernstein, M. J., & Sacco, D. F. (2012). Perception and Motivation in Face Recognition: A critical review of theories of the cross-race effect. *Personality and Social Psychology Review, 16*(2), 116–142. https://doi.org/10.1177/108 8868311418987.

Zürn, M. (2003). Globalization and global governance: From societal to political denationalization. *European Review, 11*(3), 341–364. https://doi.org/10.1017/S10627987030 00322.

4. Crisis and critique

Barbara Katharina Reschenhofer

Placing displacement online: Examining the identifiability of informational content about flight for children on YouTube

Abstract

This study examines the multimodal presentation of informational content about flight for young viewers on YouTube. Thumbnails and other paratextual features, including tags and titles, of top-ranking search results were analyzed to evaluate the respective videos in terms of their findability on YouTube and their identifiability as child-friendly. The data for the analysis was collected using five search phrases, which produced eight highest-ranking results each. From a total of forty search results, the thumbnails and other paratextual features of the four most commonly cross-occurring search results were multimodally and qualitatively examined. Common multimodal strategies for thumbnail design were found to include conceptual images, a target group-oriented layout, and use of graduation. Both positive and negative framing were used amongst the top four thumbnails. Findings on metadata, such as tags or titles, revealed that most search results were either not effectively or at all tagged.

Diese Studie untersucht die multimodale Präsentation von kindgerechten Suchergebnissen zum Thema Flucht auf Youtube. Thumbnails und weitere Paratexte, wie beispielsweise Tags und Titel, von höchstgereihten Suchergebnissen wurden analysiert, um die jeweiligen Videos hinsichtlich ihrer Findbarkeit auf YouTube und ihrer Identifizierbarkeit als kindgerecht zu bewerten. Die Daten wurden durch die Eingabe von fünf mehrwortigen Suchbegriffen gesammelt, die jeweils acht höchstgereihte Suchergebnisse lieferten. Aus insgesamt vierzig Suchergebnissen wurden die Thumbnails sowie andere paratextuelle Merkmale der vier am häufigsten vorkommenden Suchergebnisse multimodal und qualitativ untersucht. Es wurde festgestellt, dass beliebte multimodale Strategien für das Thumbnail-Design konzeptionelle Bilder, ein zielgruppenorientiertes Layout und diverse Abstufungen in Form und Größe umfassten. In den vier analysierten Thumbnails wurde sowohl positives als auch negatives Framing angewandt. Eine kritische Evaluierung der Metadaten wie Tags oder Titel zeigte außerdem, dass die meisten Suchergebnisse entweder nicht effektiv oder gar nicht mit relevanten oder gezielten Schlagworten versehen waren.

1.   Introduction

Since the mid 2010's, the snowballing global interest in the topic of flight and displacement has manifested in growing media coverage of what has been commonly referred to as a "migration crisis" (Kurvet-Käosaar et al., 2019, p. 127). Refugee narratives are thus no longer predominantly found on traditional news channels but also in popular culture, whether this be in the form of a children's picturebook or a video clip on social media. However, with the growing range of content about flight come complex nuances which shape new multimodal genres. Whilst a picturebook written for young readers may be rather easily identifiable as such, an online video about flight may not be as unambiguously allocated to a specific target demographic. Freely accessible digital video content about flight for young viewers does not suggest child-friendliness via the same markers as picturebooks might – or does it? This chapter aims to investigate precisely such supposed markers which attempt to signify, to a potential viewer, that a video is indeed a child-friendly piece of informational content about refugees.

Though the objects of study are a narrow selection of YouTube videos, the pressing question enquires into the identifiability of informational content for children about flight and, thus, the actual videos themselves will not fully be taken into account. The videos' metadata, in fact, qualify as more relevant for the present study as they represent their respective videos' *digital paratexts* (see also Genette, 1997; Rodríguez-Ferrándiz, 2017; Burwell & Miller, 2016), and oftentimes act as the primary gatekeeper on algorithmic platforms, such as YouTube. Thumbnails, therefore, become key ingredients in marking a video as child-friendly, flight-related, and informational or educational. Of course, other metadata, such as the title, description box, and tags, also play a role in the findability of a video and its identifiability as child-friendly and will be considered as well, albeit in less detail. This study's definition of child-friendliness draws on rankings by the British Board of Film Classification (Green, 2011, p. 175; BBFC, 2022) as well as on Neumann and Herodotou's (2020) evaluation of online video content for young viewers. Child-friendly content should thus meet the requirements for the BBFC's classification "U Universal – Suitable for all" (BBFC, 2022), which marks films as appropriate for viewers as young as four years of age. These films are generally "set within a positive framework and should offer reassuring counter-balances to any violence, threat or horror" (BBFC, 2022). Child-friendly content thus does not necessarily have to be entirely positive, which, in the case of flight experiences would lead to a romanticizing or trivializing representation. The overall framework, however, should remain predominantly positively framed and reassuring to be credited with the label of child-friendliness.

The general methodology, which is elaborated on in the following section, follows a fairly straightforward approach of, first, deciding on a number of intuitive YouTube search phrases and then qualitatively analyzing the metadata of a narrowed-down pool of the generated search results. As social media algorithms are ever-changing and new content is being uploaded on a daily basis, it is important to note that the present study represents but a snapshot of online activity, which is likely affected by factors of geo-locality and temporality. For the present research, the objects of study were collected on a laptop device, located in Austria. The study was conducted in the early months of 2021.

2.   Methodology

To find, access, and then compile a short list of digital objects of study, a search engine, and a selection of keywords to search for had to be decided upon. YouTube.com was chosen as the former, and a list of five phrases was chosen for the latter. These key phrases included "what is a refugee", "who is a refugee", "refugee information for children", "refugee explained for kids", and "refugee explained". When attempting to simulate a range of five searches for child-appropriate content about flight, the most likely types of internet users for such a scenario had to be established. It was hypothesized that it might either be a child's guardian (of some sort) or the child themself to look up such content on YouTube. The phrases "refugee information for children" and "refugee explained for kids" were, thus, meant to simulate a guardian's video search, whilst "what is a refugee" and "who is a refugee" were meant to approximate what a young internet user may enter into the search bar. The fifth phrase, "refugee explained", could, arguably, easily be used by either an adult or youth, when trying to find educational or informational content about refugees.

Each key phrase produced its own set of eight highest-ranking videos, suggested by the YouTube algorithm. The five searches thus provided a pool of forty results (videos), wherein a number of videos appeared several times within this selection. To further narrow down the search results for the qualitative analysis, the final selections were based on the frequency of appearance. Across the five searches, a total of four videos appeared more than three times in the pool of forty search results:

- "What is a refugee?" by *Save the Children Australia* (henceforth labelled "A")
- "What does it mean to be a refugee? – Benedetta Berti und Evelien Borgman" by *TED-Ed* (henceforth labelled "B")
- "Who is a Refugee?" by *UNHCR Teaching About Refugees* (henceforth labelled "C")
- "Kids Meet A Refugee | Kids Meet | HiHo Kids" by *HiHo Kids* (henceforth labelled "D")

Figure 1: Sketch-recreations of the four top-ranking thumbnails. "What is a refugee?" (top left), "What does it mean to be a refugee?" (top right), "Kids Meet A Refugee" (bottom left), "Who is a Refugee?" (bottom right). The original artwork is not shown in this study, as the U.S. law of fair use does not apply to Austria, where this study was conducted (see Google 2022).

While figure 1 is a recreation of the four top-ranking thumbnails, figure 2, below, illustrates the appearance of the four most frequently appearing thumbnails (A, B, C, D). From said four top-ranking thumbnails, two (B, C) appeared a maximum of five times, one appeared four times (A), and another one appeared three times (D). The other search results, which have not been regarded in this study, appeared a maximum of twice, with the vast majority of them only appearing a single time throughout the five searches.

Although this chapter is concerned with the identifiability of YouTube content about refugees for children, the aspect of popularity needs to, briefly, be addressed as well. According to what is generally known about the YouTube algorithm, the more often a video is watched and the better it retains its viewers' unobstructed attention, the more often it will be suggested to a wider audience, thereby exponentially increasing the video's reach (see also Zhou et al., 2010). Furthermore, older videos will, naturally, have aggregated more views over time than more recently posted ones. These factors are only some of a number of multivariate reasons as to why a particular piece of content is favorably ranked on YouTube (Benson, 2017, p. 54).

One aspect of popularity, however, does find its place in the present study, as the factors leading to content being findable and identifiable as part of a specific genre also affect the video's clickability. A video's clickability is defined as its magnitude to persuade a user to click on and view it (see also Picone et al., 2019, p. 2023; Blom & Hansen, 2015). Elements which factor into this equation include the video's title, thumbnail, description box, and tags. Not only do they contribute to whether a video is clicked on, but these categories of metadata will also either help or deter a video from ranking high in a given search result.

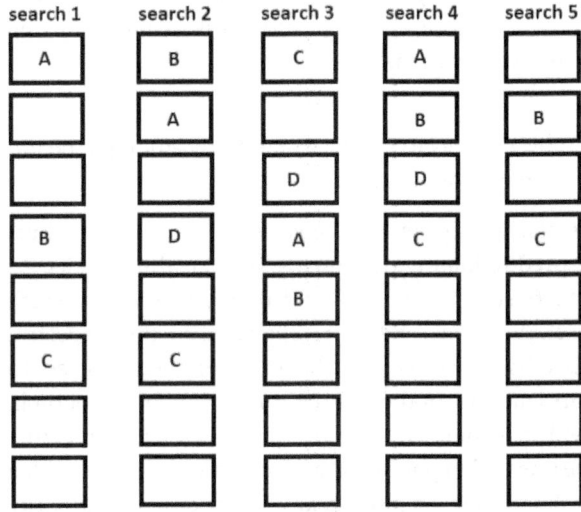

Figure 2: The four top-ranking thumbnails (A, B, C, D) as they appeared throughout the five searches. Search 1: "refugee explained for kids". Search 2:"refugee information for children". Search 3: "what is a refugee". Search 4: "who is a refugee". Search 5: "refugee explained".

3.   Research Questions

The main focus of this qualitative analysis of online content will lie on the thumbnails and their design, as they represent the most prominent, multimodal type of metadata. Whilst titles and tags certainly play a role in the identifiability of informational refugee videos for children, thumbnails visually appeal to beholders of all demographics, albeit to varying effects. Whilst tags are most often hidden from the average user, thumbnails are designed to be seen. Honing in on this aspect of visual appeal, this study hypothesizes that a popular strategy, when creating thumbnails for refugee-themed content for children, will be the use of illustrations rather than photographs in the video's thumbnails. This hypothesis gives rise to the following three research questions:

1. What is the ratio of photographic imagery to artistic illustrations amongst the top results' thumbnails, and what might this suggest?
2. Which multimodal strategies are used in the top search results and how effective are these in catching a child's or their guardian's attention?
3. In how far do the titles and tags suggest child-friendliness, and is this achieved successfully across the top search results?

4.   Findings

To summarize the findings, the three major research questions will first be answered concisely, before receiving more elaborate attention in the following
section named "Discussion and Implications".

**What is the ratio of photographic imagery to artistic illustrations amongst the top
results' thumbnails, and what might this suggest?**

Out of the forty initial results, twenty-seven videos used illustrations whilst
thirteen used photographs, predominantly of humans, in their thumbnails. As
mentioned previously, the forty search results do not represent forty different
videos. Across the five searches, various videos re-appeared in the respective
eight top-ranking search results. Nevertheless, the ratio of twenty-seven to
thirteen stands as a solid representation of the ratio of illustration to photograph,
as it demonstrates that the videos with illustrated thumbnails rank higher across
this study's searches than the ones using photographs. In each search, every video
counts as a vote for either illustration or photograph in an online popularity
contest, so to say. That being said, a channel's magnitude (measured in sub-
scribers and average views per video) as well as the considered video's age (i. e.,
how long it has been online) must also be taken into account when making
assumptions on popularity. This will be touched on in more detail in the final
section of this chapter.

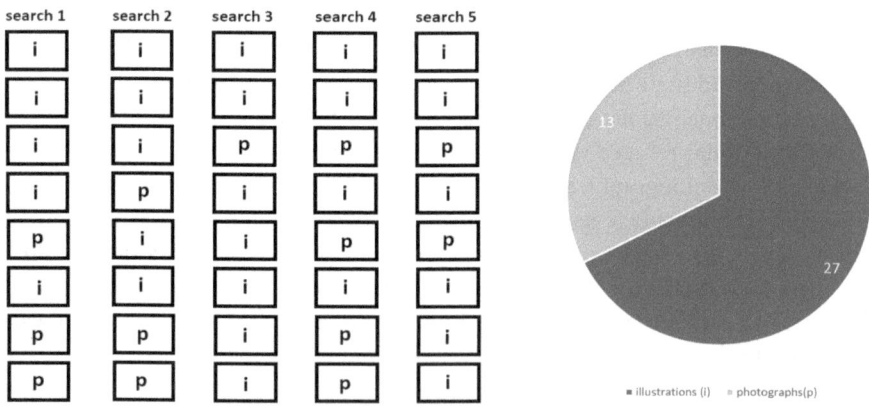

Figure 3: Thumbnails which used illustrations (i) and those which used photographs (p); pie chart
of the ratio of illustrations to photographs.

Which multimodal strategies are used in the top search results and how effective are these in catching a child's or their guardian's attention?

For the qualitative analysis of the multimodal thumbnails, Painter et al.'s (2013) terminology and framework was primarily consulted. Three main strategies could be identified as prominently used across the search results. These include Painter et al.'s (2013) conceptual images, i.e. illustrations which invite the beholder to ponder their oftentimes symbolic meaning (p. 56), a focus group-oriented layout, i.e. a grouped arrangement of salient elements, (p. 113), and graduation, i.e. variation in size and volume of salient elements (p. 44f.). Aside from these three metafunctional strategies of garnering the user's attention, positive as well as negative framing as described by Chang and Lee (2009) also appeared to be used quite strategically to construct affect in the thumbnails. With the term framing, scholars like Chang and Lee (2009) refer to the creation of positive, negative, or neutral moods or associations which are evoked through the design of a text or product. The four top-ranking thumbnails suggest that overt, visual tonality – whether this be optimistic or pessimistic – paired with a curation of carefully placed, salient images, makes for a reliable recipe when aiming to design a clickable thumbnail.

Figure 4: Sketch-recreations of the four, top-ranking thumbnails. Positively framed (top left), negatively framed (top right, bottom right), neutral to positively framed (bottom left). The original thumbnails also made use of colorization and saturation to contrast.

It must be noted here that Chang and Lee's (2009) use of the term *framing* is not at all synonymous with Painter et al.'s (2013). Whilst the former use the term to describe affective tone or nuance, the latter use it in a more literal sense, to refer to an image's outlining border. When using the term *framing*, this chapter exclusively refers to Chang and Lee's (2009) definition, as moods and associations evoked by multimodal texts stand at the center of this study rather than the texts' artistic designs as such.

Out of the four thumbnails in question, only two are, arguably, overtly marked as child-friendly by using predominantly positive framing as well as the depiction of children. "What is a refugee?" and "Kids Meet A Refugee" target a young audience by using thumbnails which simulate a child's drawing or feature a photograph of children, respectively. Furthermore, their metatext explicitly mentions *kids* or *children*. The two thumbnails are framed in neutral to wholly positive ways, which, again, reinforces the notion that they are safe for children to consume. Elements which contribute to a such positive framing include smiling individuals, bright colors, and a focus-group layout (see Painter et al., 2013, p. 111) which suggests togetherness of the depicted individuals rather than op-position between them.

"What does it mean to be a refugee?" and "Who is a refugee?" represent the two more negatively-framed thumbnails. Whilst the previously mentioned thumbnails, through their focus groups, suggest togetherness, "Who is a Refu-gee?" implies division by depicting a group of supposed refugees barred from crossing a border to the other side, where soldiers halt them from approaching. "What does it mean to be a refugee?" focuses less on division but more on isolation, as its only depicted figure is a black silhouette of a supposed refugee, standing on a barren and deserted landscape. Whilst the two negatively-framed thumbnails do, too, feature illustrations, these differ from the positively-framed images in one, major way: None of the depicted persons are either facing the beholder or have clearly visible facial expressions. The figures thereby become abstract stand-ins for human beings rather than individuals with whom the beholder might be able to connect. This is relevant in so far as research suggests that children respond particularly positively and strongly to – specifically pos-itive – facial expressions (Vesker et al., 2018, p. 424).

In how far do the titles and tags suggest child-friendliness, and is this achieved successfully across the top search results?

The findings regarding metadata on titles and tags are not as conclusive as those on thumbnails. However, they do give rise to two main implications. Firstly, many of the titles use concise questions rather than assertive statements, which is certainly inclusive of a younger audience, as short questions generally do not presuppose prior knowledge on a given topic, whereas specified titles might. Secondly, most of the videos' tags do not feature particularly specific keywords or relevant search phrases. Whilst some videos do emphasize child-friendly content through their tags, most of them use neither child- nor particularly adult-friendly tags in an effective or algorithm-conscious way. For instance, one video uses vague and general terms such as *war* or *hunger*, whilst another does not use any tags at all. Both the use of non-succinct keywords as well as the entire omission of tags represent missed opportunities for contributing to a video's findability as well as its identifiability as belonging to a specific genre (e.g., educational/informational child-friendly content about flight).

"Who is a Refugee?" does market itself as educational, especially as it is uploaded by the *UNHCR Teaching About Refugees* YouTube channel. Therefore, a case could be made for the UNHCR-affiliated video being easily mistaken for an educational video about flight for young viewers. Both "What does it mean to be a refugee?" and "Who is a refugee?" are, indeed, videos which use language which is more suited for mature audiences. Whilst the videos themselves consist of non-graphic, illustrative collages and cartoons, the at times more sophisticated vocabulary and complex topics covered, nevertheless, imply older target audiences.

This simulated YouTube search for child-friendly, informational YouTube content about refugees, therefore, reveals that there are, in fact, common strategies used by content creators to make such videos more findable and identifiable as belonging to a specific subgenre of content. However, a strategy for a clear, metatextual distinction between educational or informational material for adults versus that for children has yet to be developed. Whilst using terms like *children* or *kids* in the digital paratext to signpost child-friendliness is certainly helpful for users browsing the web, other terms, such as *educational*, become more ambiguous, as they do not specify a target demographic. As a result, the user is left to figuratively sieve through a variety of thumbnails with heterogenous target demographics, which all look quite similar to one another on the surface yet are definingly different in their actual audio-visual delivery.

Finally, it can be concluded that the disseminators of complex, socio-political, and moral issues, such as displacement, oftentimes opt for strategies to spread awareness by packaging informational content up in what can easily be mistaken for markers of child-friendliness. Using illustrations in thumbnails, for instance, is an all too popular strategy for visually conceptualizing complex subject matters, even for adults (Bounegru & Forceville, 2011, p. 220). Positive framing, whether it be of a thumbnail or a title, has thus been found to be a more or less reliable indicator of whether a highly complex and upsetting issue might be delivered in a way which is not too graphic nor unsettling for child viewers. As both adult as well as child demographics appear to be targeted using illustrated thumbnails, their framing is, ultimately, what appears to give the internet user an additional inkling as to whether the respective video might be suitable for younger viewers.

5.   Discussion and Implications

The summarized findings will now be discussed in more detail and with respect to their wider implications. Recounting the number of illustrations versus photographs in the forty preliminary results, the ratio translated to twenty-seven to thirteen (27:13), respectively. The following four videos appeared at least three times across the five searches. Three out of the four used illustrations in their thumbnails, whereas one used a photograph.

- "What is a refugee?" by *Save the Children Australia* (illustration)
- "What does it mean to be a refugee? – Benedetta Berti und Evelien Borgman" by *TED-Ed* (illustration)
- "Kids Meet A Refugee | Kids Meet | HiHo Kids" by *HiHo Kids* (photograph)
- "Who is a Refugee?" by *UNHCR Teaching About Refugees* (illustration)

These results suggest that illustrations are not just clicked on often but also that they are favored by the content creators who design them. Why might this be the case? What makes illustrations a more popular choice when it comes to disseminating information about flight? Rather apparent explanations could be that illustrations can be created child-friendly, in the sense that they can be designed to be less graphic or geopolitically specific than photographs may be. Simplifying and conceptualizing complex issues in a rather general illustration, without too much detail or many distractions, is a plausible strategy for visualizing flight for a young audience. Furthermore, illustrating gives the artist more freedom to frame a narrative as an optimistic story of hope (positive framing) or a dire tale of hardship (negative framing). As audio-visual child-friendly content, according to the BBFC (2022) or Neumann and Herodotou (2020, p. 4467), should be framed more positively rather than negatively, the artist can exploit their creative freedom and take these recommendations into consideration. This adds a rather important generic dimension to the otherwise content-focused label of child-friendliness discussed above.

5.1.   Multimodal strategies

The four top-ranking thumbnails demonstrate how three major multimodal strategies are employed to illustrate flight to a potentially younger audience. Again, borrowing terminology from Painter et al. (2013), the thumbnail images appear to be what the scholars refer to as "conceptual images" (p. 56). In the context of picturebooks, Painter et al. explain how conceptual images invite young readers to read "for significance" (2013, p. 56) rather than for plot or character recognition. This concept can directly be applied to YouTube thumbnails, as the latter, similarly to a page in a picturebook, convey a multimodal message, thought, or narrative within a single image. A key trait of a conceptual image, according to Painter et al., are static poses which slow down the overall reading process (2013, p. 56). Such images tend to be found in either the very beginning or the very end of a picturebook (Painter et al., 2013, p. 56). This, too, ties in with the fact that thumbnails often mark the beginning of a user's viewing experience. They are, so to say, the cover pages of the YouTube video.

The four thumbnails under consideration can all be read as conceptual images, which represent concepts rather than actions. The thumbnail of "What is a refugee?" is a vibrant, colorful illustration of diverse people, standing together, below a garland, spelling out *WELCOME*. The characters all stand together, statically, on what appears to be grass, joining hands and symbolizing unity and togetherness. It is left to the beholder to speculate whether any or which of the characters depicted are refugees. "What does it mean to be a refugee?" is almost the polar opposite. Here, the colors are colder and less saturated. There is only one character standing with their back toward the beholder. Barely any features can be made out, as only the character's black silhouette is depicted. Their long, black hair is swaying in the wind, as they stand on what seems to be a desolate and barren landscape. The font, too, is kept in grey and black, and in a rather eerie stylization. These two thumbnails represent conceptual images which, despite their almost diametrically opposing affective nuances, invite the beholder to pause and reflect in a similar manner. Both thumbnails feature static cartoon-style depictions of people with little detail or visual distraction around the characters. Both employ illustrations as well as verbiage to multimodally hint at what the overall tone of the video might be – this aspect of affective tone will be discussed in more detail in the section on *framing*. Regardless of affect, the two thumbnails correspond to Painter et al.'s (2013) characteristics of a still and pensive conceptual image.

The other two thumbnails, too, make use of Painter et al.'s (2013) conceptual image. The thumbnail of "Kids Meet A Refugee" shows a photograph of three children, each sitting on a plain chair. The background is left entirely bare, with only a white-to-grey gradient keeping it from being wholly blank. Just like in the previously discussed thumbnails, there are no other visual distractions present. The beholder is invited to pause and take in the image of the protagonist trio. Although the children's clothing and parts of the font in the image's verbiage are rather bright, the overall color scheme is not overwhelmingly bright or saturated. The conceptual image delivers the idea behind the title of the video quite matter-of-factly, without much affective manipulation. The thumbnail of "Who is a Refugee?" is, arguably, the least conceptual and most narrative of the four. Painter et al. point out that most picturebook pages will be less static and more narrative, i.e. depicting some sort of action (2013, p. 58). The thumbnail in question appears to be more dynamic than the previous three, yet still conceptual in its symbolic message. The image depicts a large group of people being separated from two soldiers by a barrier of sorts. The uniformed men gesticulate for the crowd to stop and not get closer. This notion of forced separation is additionally underlined by a traffic post, resembling a stop-sign, which is placed to the right of the image. Like the images before, this thumbnail features no further details which would distract the beholder. The background is kept in a monochromatic grey.

Graduation and layout are another two multimodal strategies, as mentioned in Painter et al.'s (2013) framework, which shape the conceptual images in the four thumbnails in question. Painter et al. distinguish between two major ways in which a focus group can be composed. On the one hand, a focus group can have a centrifocal composition, meaning that there is an overt center in an image. On the other hand, an image can have an iterating focus group, whereby elements of said group are either aligned or scattered, without a definitive center in the middle of the vector (2013, p. 111). Graduation then comes into play when the various elements of a focus group appear in different sizes.

As illustrated in the figure above, the bottom two thumbnails, "Kids Meet A Refugee" and "Who is a Refugee?", appear to follow the centrifocal focus group model. Whilst "Kids Meet A Refugee" features three children sitting alongside one another, the child in the middle is the overt center of the image. They are all the same size, yet one child assumes a central position in the beholder's eyes. The layout suggests that the child in the middle is, therefore, the refugee whom the other two children meet in the video. This is a prime example of how layout can inform the way a beholder understands an image.

Similarly, "Who is a Refugee?" features a centrifocal focus group by having two soldiers stand closer to the angle of the beholder, whilst a crowd in the distance is placed in the center of the image. The soldiers are therefore larger in size, whilst the group of less distinguishable characters is disappearingly small. Here, graduation comes into play to signify distance and separation between the soldiers and the crowd. This, too, informs the beholding experience and suggests that the crowd in the distance is a group of refugees, barred from crossing over to the soldiers' side. The two thumbnails thus employ both layout and graduation to not only describe the relationship between the characters (two children meet a third; two soldiers versus a group) but also to compositionally identify who the refugee is (the child in the center; the group of people in the center).

The thumbnail of "What is a refugee?" features an aligned, iterating focus group, as all the cartoon characters are lined up next to one another, without a definitive central figure marking the middle of the illustration (Painter et al., 2013, p. 111). The characters are also relatively equal in size, whereby the only difference in graduation is made on account of the age groups the characters are

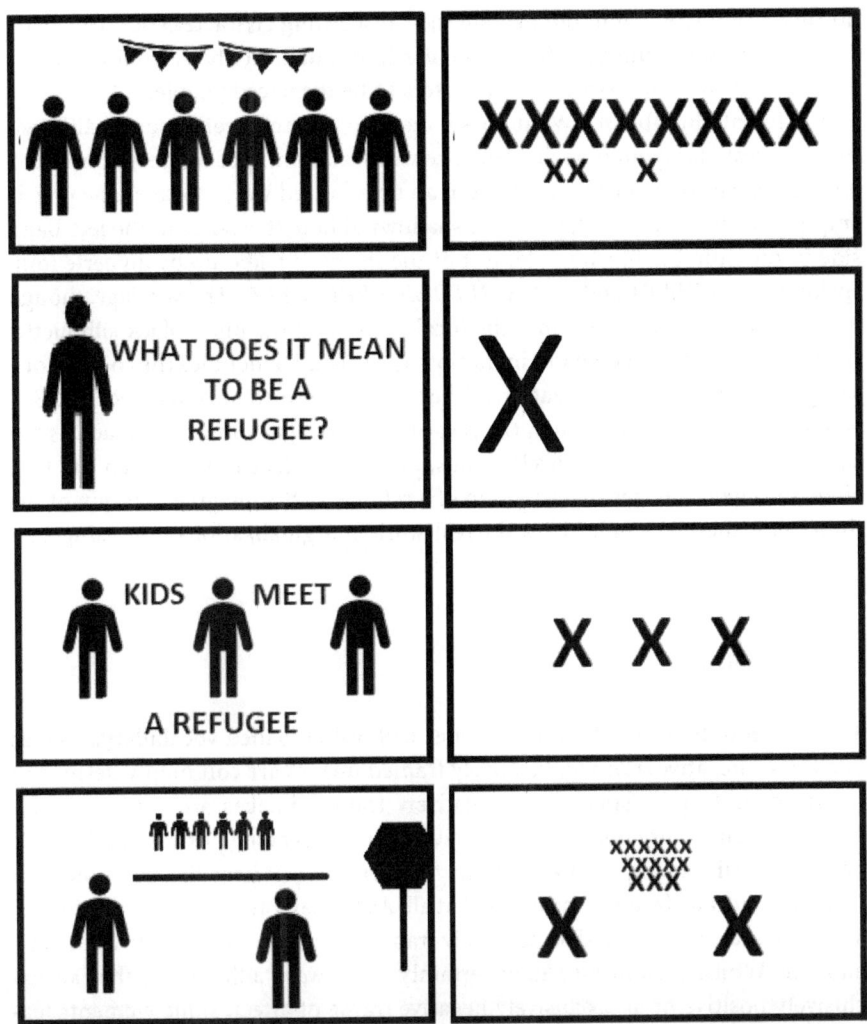

Figure 5: Thumbnail sketches (left column) and a simplification of their respective layouts (right column). "What is a refugee?" (top), "What does it mean to be a refugee?" (second to top), "Kids Meet A Refugee" (second to bottom), "Who is a Refugee?" (bottom).

meant to represent. The adult characters stand next to one another, joining hands, whilst the children are positioned slightly in front of some of the adults. One of the adult characters is also holding a small infant. Nevertheless, the image leaves a rather two-dimensional impression, each character appearing equal in significance to the overall illustration. The only details which give each character a sense of uniqueness are their respective hairstyles, complexion, and the colors of their clothes. However, because each character is so unique, this, in turn, lets no single character stand out despite their discerning characteristics. Diversity, so to say, becomes unity, in this particular thumbnail. Neither layout nor graduation single out any particular characters to be displaced people.

The fourth thumbnail, "What does it mean to be a refugee?", is quite different from the rest. Its layout is not as clearly centrifocal, compared to the first two. Yet, it does appear to be polarized, albeit in an unbalanced way, whereby one pole is empty (Painter et al., 2013, p.110). A shadowy silhouette stands at the left-hand side in the thumbnail, whilst the rest of the image is taken up by an eerie font, spelling out "*WHAT DOES IT MEAN TO BE A REFUGEE?*". The verbiage, though it is slightly off-center, becomes the focal point, and the pitch-black silhouette, with its long hair and gown put in motion by the wind, embodies the concept of a refugee, almost like a visualization of the capitalized word next to it. "*REFUGEE*" is written in a darker font than the rest of the verbiage – almost as black as the silhouette of the character itself – thus, drawing a clear link between the two. Here, the layout pushes the depiction of a refugee to the imagined margin of the thumbnail, thereby emphasizing the real-world marginalization of the refugees it represents.

5.2.   Framing

The notion of framing oftentimes comes with value-loaded vocabulary, such as positive or negative framing. Positively framed images are commonly defined as uplifting, and optimistic, whilst negatively framed images are connoted with pessimism and a dire outlook on whatever it is that is being portrayed (Chang & Lee, 2009). Discussing such a seemingly binary concept begs the question as to whether neutrally framed images exist at all. As humans are complex individuals, an image may be perceived as positively framed by one but negatively framed by another. Whilst illustrations may certainly not always adhere to either an exclusively positive or an exclusively negative frame of affect, some elements featured within an illustration can, indeed, carry highly symbolic meaning and loaded connotations. Chang and Lee (2009), for example, point to studies which suggest that negatively framed language, used by charitable organizations, is often more successful in terms of achieving donations. However, there are boundaries to the effectiveness of negative framing, as potential donors can also become resistant to a cause when they feel that their sympathy is being enforced. Nevertheless, research has demonstrated that negative framing is most successful at catching the audience's attention, which is, after all, the first step in getting an individual engaged for a cause (Chang & Lee, 2009).

This idea of framing verbal narratives can be applied to visuals as well. In fact, images will be processed more quickly by the beholder's brain and, thus, make the individual more susceptible to the first impression of an image, according to how it is framed (Longley & Nordström, 2018, p. 66). Images can act as moderators for the either positively, neutrally, or negatively framed content, meaning that they can inspire hope or shock the beholder, for instance.

In the context of charity work, for example, both strategies, i. e. positive as well as negative framing, have been found to trigger action within potential donors. Recent research draws on findings by scholars such as Smith and Berger (1996) and Isen (1993), which suggests that circumstances which evoke positive feelings in an individual will likely inspire said person to "maintain the positive feeling state" (Chang & Lee 2009, p. 2930). Choosing positively framed thumbnails for a video about refugees might, thus, motivate viewers to act in ways of support for the greater cause, whether that might take shape in the form of a donation or volunteer work. Alternatively, negative framing has been found to work in a similarly effective way, as it tends to employ less saturated colors or detail which might distract from the actual informational content (Zhou & Xue, 2019, p. 420). Referring back to research on children responding particularly strongly to positive facial expressions (Vesker et al., 2018), though, this might in turn suggest that children will be more receptive to positively framed YouTube thumbnails.

More aptly, in the context of YouTube, the phenomenon generally known as *clickbait* makes use of the widely known fact that potential viewers will feel particularly drawn to shocking images or headings. Moreover, eye-tracking studies have found that negatively framed visuals do in fact garner more attention than verbal information or logos might (Alonso Dos Santos et al., 2017, p. 346). This perhaps explains the proliferation of negatively framed thumbnails appearing across YouTube. Overall, though, it is important to point out that no singular type of framing can be deemed as ultimately the most efficient strategy. As viewers and consumers of media will differ in complexity on an individual level, different strategies of appealing to the audience will achieve different outcomes. Whilst some studies on charity work suggest that negative framing has been proven to be more successful at triggering action within donors and benefactors (Chang & Lee, 2009, p. 2913), others imply that the opposite can be true under certain circumstances, namely when "cold images" (Choi et al., 2016, p. 420), for instance, evoke negative feelings in the beholder, deferring them from donating (Choi et al., 2016, p. 425).

Although studies on charity work and their effect on potential benefactors are undoubtedly relevant to the discussion of images and affect, the present study is concerned with views, rather than monetary donations. Negative framing has, indeed, been found to grab an audience's attention, particularly in written form (Banks et al., 1995; Homer & Yoon 1992; Chang & Lee, 2009, p. 2913). Amongst a variety of responses in an audience, negatively framed messages often tend to disrupt the audience's expectations (Buda & Zhang, 2000; Chang & Lee, 2009,

p. 2913). It can be proposed that what works for verbal messages in writing may very well work similarly in multimodal forms of expression. Following this logic, a negatively framed thumbnail will, generally, reel in more views than a positively framed one. However, what must be kept in mind is that, oftentimes, a guardian will monitor or lead a child's internet use. In this case, an adult may be more prone to letting a young one watch a video whose thumbnail looks reassuring rather than unsettling.

5.3.   A note on titles, tags, and text

Aside from the main objects of study, namely the thumbnails, further metadata warrants a brief discussion as well. Whilst a video's title and description box text are openly visible to any YouTube user, the tags are hidden. This section will comment on the choice of verbiage within the overt and covert paratext, revealing successful and less effective strategies of making child-friendly refugee content findable and identifiable as such.

The examination of titles and description box texts calls for a simple qualitative analysis of verbal text, seeking to identify commonly chosen words as well as syntactical patterns or styles, which might, firstly, ensure comprehensibility to young audiences and secondly, explicitly signpost what demographic the videos might target. Three out of the four top-ranking videos of this study phrased their titles as questions, making the video content easy for both child and adult audiences to recognize as relevant to their search. It must be kept in mind that young users, as well as their guardians, might use precisely such questions (What is a refugee? Who is a refugee?) to search for content in the first place. A relevant and searchable title makes a YouTube video more findable, which lets it rank higher in the search results. The description boxes then act as supplements to provide additional information about the suitability of the content for certain demographics.

The analysis of the respective videos' tags followed a two-part approach: First, the browser extension *TubeBuddy* was used to make visible the keywords and phrases which each video had been tagged with. Second, the tags' relevancy was evaluated by entering flight-related terminology into the YouTube search bar and letting YouTube's predicted search complete the search. By comparing the predicted search results to the chosen tags, the latter could be assessed as making the videos either highly or poorly searchable. The top four videos' tags, as revealed by the extension *TubeBuddy*, did not, in fact, reflect commonly searched-for keywords. Many tags included less relevant words, such as names of non-profit organizations, instead of potentially searched-for phrases. Two ("What is a refugee?", "Who is a refugee?") of the four top-ranking videos, unfortunately, did not make use of the tag function at all. Tags to help users identify content as child-friendly, this study suggests, might have included "for children", "learning about refugees", or "child-friendly". Nevertheless, the fact that even poorly tagged videos were amongst the highest-ranking in this study shows that other metadata, such as thumbnails or titles, have an immensely large pull of their own. Here, it must be acknowledged that the source channel's popularity, too, plays a role in whether a video reels in enough views to let it rank higher in the algorithm.

6.   Conclusion

To conclude, a range of patterns in the design of video thumbnails could successfully be identified. Aside from choices of framing (either positive or negative), the thumbnails under consideration featured a clear preference for illustrations over photographs as well as a strategic employment of layout and graduation to construct characters and their relations to one another. Those thumbnails which were framed in a positive way were, in fact, used for videos targeted toward a younger audience, whilst the negatively framed thumbnails belonged to videos which appeared to have been created for older viewers. These findings suggest that the creators of such YouTube thumbnails of child-friendly content tend to have the young one's guardians in mind, as they might be more prone to selecting a positive image over an unsettling one. Positive, non-threatening on-screen behavior is amongst the criteria for age-appropriate content for children, as defined by Neumann and Herodotou (2020, p. 4467), who specifically evaluate YouTube content aimed at young audiences. In YouTube thumbnails, this would translate to the depiction of smiling persons holding hands rather than isolated, faceless figures. Although negatively framed thumbnails and clickbait headings appear to be no rarity on YouTube, the creators of child-friendly thumbnails appear to avoid reeling in young audiences with shock tactics.

Finally, this study deems the overall findability and identifiability of child-friendly informational content about refugees as insufficient. Firstly, most uploads, regardless of which demographic they target, appear to use illustrations in their thumbnail images. This can, simply put, lead to mature content being mistaken for child-friendly content. Secondly, the paratextual opportunities for marking content as child-friendly or flight-related were, too often, missed or insufficiently exploited. Simple steps, such as choosing relevant tags or adding information about the target demographic in the title or description box would, more effectively, help the multimodal packaging of a YouTube search result (i. e. video) be identifiable as either suitable or unsuitable by the user conducting the search.

7.　References

Primary

HiHo Kids. (27. September. 2018). Kids meet a refugee | Kids Meet | HiHo Kids. *YouTube.* https://www.youtube.com/watch?v=7GdDnbNpRNE&t=2s.
Save the Children Australia. (18. June. 2020). What is a refugee? *YouTube.* https://www.youtube.com/watch?v=CRk8eaW3X1Y&t=25s.
TED-Ed. (01. March. 2018). What does it mean to be a refugee? – Benedetta Berti and Evelien Borgman. *YouTube.* https://www.youtube.com/watch?v=25bwiSikRsI.
UNHCR teaching about refugees. (23. October. 2017). Who is a refugee? *YouTube.* https://www.youtube.com/watch?v=GvzZGplGbL8&t=58s.

Secondary

Alonso Dos Santos, M., Lobos, C. Muñoz, N., Romero, D., & Sanhueza, R. (2017). The influence of image valence on the attention paid to charity advertising. *Journal of Nonprofit & Public Sector Marketing, 29*, 346–63. https://doi.org/10.1080/10495142.2017.1326355.
Banks, S. M., Salovey, P., Greener, S., Rothman, A. J., Moyer, A., & Beauvais, J. (1995). The effects of message framing on mammography utilization. *Health Psychology, 14*, 178–184. https://doi.org/10.1037/0278-6133.14.2.178.
BBFC. (2022). Rating. Website. https://www.bbfc.co.uk/rating/u.
Benson, P. (2017). *The discourse of YouTube: Multimodal text in a global context.* Routledge. https://doi.org/10.4324/9781315646473.
Blom, J. N., & Hansen, K. R. (2015). Click bait: forward-reference as lure in online news headlines. *Journal of Pragmatics, 76*, 87–100. https://doi.org/10.1016/j.pragma.2014.11.010.
Bounegru, L., & Forceville, C. (2011). Metaphors in editorial cartoons representing the global financial crisis. *Visual Communication, 10*, 209–229. https://doi.org/10.1177/1470357211398446.
Buda, R., & Zhang, Y. (2000). Consumer product evaluation: The interactive effect of message framing, presentation order, and source credibility. *Journal of Product and Brand Management, 9*, 229–242. https://doi.org/10.1108/10610420010344022.
Burwell, C., & Miller, T. (2016). Let's play: Exploring literacy practices in an emerging videogame paratext. *E-Learning and Digital Media, 13*, 109–125. https://doi.org/10.1177/2042753016677858.
Chang, C., & Lee, Y. (2009). Framing charity advertising: influences of message framing, image valence, and temporal framing on a charitable appeal. *Journal of Applied Social Psychology, 39*, 2910–935. https://doi.org/10.1111/j.1559-1816.2009.00555.x.
Choi, J., Rangan, P., & Singh, S. N. (2016). Do cold images cause cold-heartedness? the impact of visual stimuli on the effectiveness of negative emotional charity appeals. *Journal of Advertising, 45*, 417–26. https://doi.org/10.1080/00913367.2016.1185982.

Genette, G. (1997). *Paratexts: thresholds of interpretation.* Translated by J. E. Lewin. Cambridge: Cambridge UP.

Google. (2022). *Fair use auf YouTube.* Website. https://support.google.com/youtube/answer/9783148?hl=de.

Green, J. (2011). Case study: Lilo & Stitch. (2002). In E. Lamberti (Ed.), *Behind the scenes at the BBFC: Film classification from the silver screen to the digital age* (pp. 275–277). Palgrave Macmillan.

Homer, P. M., & Yoon, S. (1992). Message framing and the interrelationships among ad-based feelings, affect, and cognition. *Journal of Advertising, 21,* 19–33. https://doi.org/10.1080/00913367.1992.10673357.

Isen, A. M. (1993). Positive affect and decision making. In M. Lewis & J. Haviland (Eds.), *Handbook of emotions* (pp. 413–435). Guilford.

Kurvet-Käosaar, L., Ojamaa, T., & Sakova, A. (2019). Situating narratives of migration and diaspora: An introduction. *Trames, 23,* 125–143. https://doi.org/10.3176/tr.2019.2.01.

Longley, A., & Nordström, T. (2018). Beyond clicks for causes: eEabling digital communications. In N. Garsten & I. Bruce (Eds.), *Communicating Causes* (pp. 57–70). Routledge. https://doi.org/10.4324/9781351022224.

Neumann, M. M., & Herodotou, C. (2020). Evaluating YouTube videos for young children. *Education and Information Technologies, 25,* 4459–4475. https://doi.org/10.1007/s10639-020-10183-7.

Painter, C., Martin, J. R., & Unsworth, L. (2013). *Reading visual narratives: Image analysis of children's picture books.* Equinox Publishing.

Picone, I., Kleut, J., Pavlíčková, T., Romic, B., Møller Hartley, J., & De Ridder, S. (2019). Small acts of engagement: Reconnecting productive audience practices with everyday agency. *New Media & Society, 21,* 2010–2028. https://doi.org/10.1177/1461444819837569.

Rodríguez-Ferrándiz, R. (2017). Paratextual activity: Updating the Genettian approach within the transmedia turn. *Communication & Society, 30,* 165–182. https://doi.org/10.15581/003.30.35800.

Smith, G. E., & Berger, P. D. (1996). The impact of direct marketing appeals on charitable marketing effectiveness. *Journal of the Academy of Marketing Science, 24,* 219–231. https://doi.org/10.1177/0092070396243003.

Vesker, M., Bahn, D., Degé, F., Kauschke, C., & Schwarzer, G. (2018). Perceiving arousal and valence in facial expressions: Differences between children and adults. *European Journal of Developmental Psychology, 15,* 411–425. https://doi.org/10.1080/17405629.2017.1287073.

Zhou, L., & Xue, F. (2019). Effects of color in disaster relief advertising and the mediating role of cognitive elaboration. *Journal of Nonprofit & Public Sector Marketing, 31,* 403–427. https://doi.org/10.1080/10495142.2018.1526750.

Zhou, R., Khemmerat, S., & Gao, L. (2010). The impact of YouTube recommendation system on video views. *Proceedings of the 10th ACM SIGCOMM Conference on Internet Measurement,* 404–410. https://doi.org/10.1145/1879141.1879193.

Susanne Blumesberger

Vielfalt unerwünscht in Österreich zwischen 1933 und 1945: Kinder- und Jugendmedien als Propagandainstrumente?[1]

Abstract
Während der Zeit des Nationalsozialismus wurden die Medien überwacht, gesteuert, zensuriert und gleichgeschaltet, davon waren Medien für Kinder und Jugendliche ebenfalls betroffen (Adam, 2010; Barbian, 2010). Es wurden Werke geschaffen und gefördert, die mehr oder weniger subtil ein einheitliches Menschenbild propagierten, denn Vielfalt war nicht erwünscht (Blumesberger, 2009; Blumesberger, 2000). Andere Medienerzeugnisse wurden ignoriert, verboten und schließlich auch verbrannt. Interessant ist, dass, wie wir aus späteren Berichten wissen, diese Werke zwar rezipiert wurden, jedoch zusätzlich beispielsweise auch unpolitische oder sogar widerständige Bücher zur Hand genommen wurden. Vielfalt ließ, bzw. lässt, sich also schwer unterdrücken. So schrieb Marcel Reich-Ranicki: „Wie immer meine Schulzeit war – ich habe nie mehr gelesen als in diesen Jahren. Die verbotene Literatur zu bekommen, war nicht schwierig. In den Bücherschränken meiner Verwandten standen die Romane und Erzählungen von Thomas und Heinrich Mann, von Arnold und Stefan Zweig, von Schnitzler, Werfel und Feuchtwanger" (Reich-Ranicki, 1992, S. 64f.). Auch auf der Seite der Urheber*innen lässt sich nur schwer eine Trennung zwischen angepasst und widerständig herstellen. Zu viele Graubereiche gab es, z. B. camouflierte Texte, in denen politische Bezüge versteckt waren, wie kontrafaschistische, propagandistische oder implizite Texte, die durch Enträumlichung und Entzeitlichung gekennzeichnet waren, deren direkter Bezug zur NS-Zeit verwischt war (Benner, 2015, S. 24).
Schlagwörter: *Kinderliteratur, Nationalsozialismus, Propaganda, Vielfalt*

During the National Socialist era, the media were monitored, controlled, censored and brought into line, and this also affected media for children and young adults (Adam, 2010; Barbian, 2010). Works were created and promoted that more or less subtly propagated a universal understanding of humankind because diversity was undesirable (Blumesberger, 2009; Blumesberger, 2000). Other media products were ignored, banned, and finally also burned. It is interesting that, as we know from later reports, these works were indeed read, but in addition, for example, non-political or even resistant books were also picked up. Diversity has always been difficult to suppress. Marcel Reich-Ranicki wrote about his

---

1 Der Beitrag basiert auf einem Langzeitprojekt zum Thema „Österreichische Kinder- und Jugendliteratur in den Jahren 1933 bis 1945".

school years that it was not difficult to get hold of forbidden literature because his relatives' bookcases contained novels and stories by Thomas and Heinrich Mann, Arnold and Stefan Zweig, Schnitzler, Werfel, and Feuchtwanger (Reich-Ranicki, 1992, S. 64f). On the side of the authors, too, it is difficult to make a distinction between conformist and resistant. There were too many grey areas, for example, camouflaged texts in which political references were hidden, such as counter-fascist, propagandist, or implicit texts that were characterized by a decontextualization of time and space, whose direct reference to the Nazi era was blurred (Benner, 2015, S. 24).

Keywords: *Children's literature, National Socialism, propaganda, diversity*

1.   Einleitung

Der Beitrag, der natürlich nur einen kleinen Ausschnitt des Gesamtprojekts beleuchten kann, beschäftigt sich vor allem mit der Frage, wie Propaganda in Kinder- und Jugendmedien funktioniert oder eben nicht funktioniert und welche Faktoren hier unterstützend oder hemmend wirken. Auch Erinnerungen von Zeitzeug*innen sollen berücksichtigt werden:

> Wer in jenen Jahren aufwuchs, dem wurde der Nationalsozialismus wie ein Sack über den Kopf gezogen. Die Lebensbedingungen mußten nicht einmal bewußt gelernt werden, sie wuchsen uns zu, wir wuchsen in sie hinein. Wir kannten nur die Welt, in der wir lebten, und wir hielten sie für normal. (Hensel, 1992, S. 117)

Anstöße durch Impulse von außen oder durch Lektüreerlebnisse konnten jedoch dazu führen, dass es zu einem Umdenken und zum Teil auch zu einem widerständigen Handeln kam: So erzählt Hensel weiter:

> Inzwischen war ich so weit, daß ich eigentlich nur noch verbotene Bücher lesen wollte. Sie brachten auch eine Art Jagdvergnügen, man mußte sie aufstöbern wie scheues Wild. Die Lektüre hing ab von den Zufälligkeiten der Beute. Ich fand sie in den Ramschkästen der Antiquare, in der Landesbibliothek im Darmstädter Schloß, in der zweiten Reihe der Bücherschränke von Bekannten. (Hensel, 1992, S. 118)

Der Fokus des Projekts liegt hauptsächlich auf vier Schwerpunkten, die in diesem Beitrag nur kurz angerissen werden können:

Um einen umfassenden Überblick zu erhalten, wäre es wichtig zu wissen, welche Werke in diesem Zeitraum von Autor*innen in Österreich und in diversen Exilländern publiziert, bzw. wieder aufgelegt wurden. Eine möglichst vollständige Auflistung aller Werke, die an Kinder oder Jugendliche adressiert oder mehrheitlich von ihnen gelesen wurden, wäre wünschenswert.

In einem weiteren Schritt wäre es hilfreich, ausgewählte Werke inhaltlich zu erschließen, denn damit ließen sich weitere Fragen klären. Interessant ist unter anderem, welche Intentionen in den Werken zu erkennen sind, bzw. ob es sich um eindeutig politisch engagierte Literatur handelt, um widerständige Texte, die sich gegen das faschistische Regime auflehnten, oder um bewusst neutral gehaltene Werke. Untersucht werden sollen auch jene Texte, die sich auf den ersten Blick keiner dieser Kategorien zuordnen lassen, sich bei näherer Betrachtung eventuell doch als bewusst eingesetzte Medien für oder gegen das Regime erweisen. Diese Fragen scheinen vor allem deshalb interessant zu sein, da bisher in der Forschung über Medien während der NS-Zeit die Beschäftigung mit kinder- oder jugendliterarischen Texten eher unterrepräsentiert ist und bei den bereits vorhandenen Studien meist auf bekanntere Werke bzw. Autor*innen fokussiert wird, eine Gesamtübersicht, die auch unbekanntere Autor*innen und Werke einschließt, jedoch noch aussteht (Blumesberger, 2020).

Für die Untersuchung einer Zeit, in der die Produktion von Literatur unterschiedlichen Reglementierungen unterworfen war, ist es unerlässlich, auch die jeweiligen Rahmenbedingungen für das Publizieren im angegebenen Zeitrahmen genauer zu betrachten. Deshalb scheint es für das Projekt sinnvoll, Literaturinstanzen und Verlage in Österreich, aber auch in den jeweiligen Exilländern, zu beleuchten sowie Zensurmaßnahmen und Förderungen, die den Literaturmarkt stark beeinflussten, zu berücksichtigen und miteinander in Beziehung zu bringen. Auch hier steht eine umfassende Studie für den Bereich Kinder- und Jugendliteratur in Österreich noch aus.

Um das Gesamtgefüge betrachten zu können, ist es außerdem sinnvoll, die Autor*innen und zum Teil auch die Übersetzer*innen selbst näher zu betrachten. Einige von ihnen waren politisch aktiv, unterstützten die Ziele des Nationalsozialismus und verbreiteten diese Werte auch in ihren Werken, wie beispielsweise Johanna Haarer[2] (Blumesberger, 2014; Haarer & Haarer, 2012) oder Karl Springenschmid[3], andere bekämpften den Faschismus und versuchten in ihren Büchern für junge Menschen antifaschistische Überzeugungen zu transportieren. Zu ihnen gehörten etwa Béla Balázs[4], Anna Maria Jokl[5] und Alex Wedding[6].

---

2 Johanna Haarer (1900–1988) leitete unter anderem das Referat der „Gausachbearbeiterin für rassenpolitische Fragen in der NS-Frauenschaft" (Blumesberger, 2014; Haarer & Haarer, 2012).

3 Karl Springenschmid (1897–1981) war bereits 1932 der damals noch illegalen NSDAP und des ebenfalls noch illegalen NS-Lehrerbundes beigetreten. Er war als Lehrer an verschiedenen Orten tätig und leitete schließlich zwischen 1938 und 1945 den NS-Lehrerbund in Salzburg. Er initiierte und leitete die Bücherverbrennung in Salzburg, schrieb zahlreiche Werke für Jugendliche mit nationalsozialistischer Tendenz, setzte sein Schreiben auch nach 1945 fort (Amir, 2020).

4 Béla Balázs (1884–1949) war als Filmkritiker, Schriftsteller, Regisseur und Drehbuchautor tätig. Er war ab 1918 Mitglied der Ungarischen Kommunistischen Partei, floh 1919 nach Wien, begründete die moderne Filmtheorie, lebte ab 1926 in Berlin, ab 1932 in Moskau, kehrte 1945 nach Budapest zurück. Er schuf wichtige proletarisch-revolutionäre Werke für Kinder.

5 Anna Maria Jokl wurde 1911 in Wien in einem jüdischen, assimilierten Elternhaus geboren. Sie war als Schriftstellerin, Psychotherapeutin und Journalistin tätig. Vor allem ihr mehrfach-

Zwischen diesen beiden Polen gibt es natürlich zahlreiche Abstufungen sowie Personen, die versuchten sich politisch möglichst neutral zu verhalten. Interessant dabei ist es nicht nur, die Karrieren der Autor*innen zwischen 1933 und 1945 zu betrachten, sondern auch die Zeit davor und danach in den Blick zu nehmen. Dadurch kann deutlich gemacht werden, welche Positionen die Schriftsteller*innen, auch eher unbekannte, jeweils innehatten, welche Werke sie vor, während und nach der Zeit des Nationalsozialismus publizieren konnten und wie sich ihre Karriere nach 1945 gestaltete.[7] (Blumesberger, 2020) Der erste Eindruck aus dem mehrjährigen Projekt ist, dass selbst stark belastete Personen, wie Karl Springenschmid, bereits einige Jahre nach dem 2. Weltkrieg erneut Werke auf den Markt bringen konnten.

Daraus ergeben sich zwei essenzielle Fragen, auf die ich im Folgenden im Überblick eingehen möchte: Einerseits ist zu überprüfen, inwieweit während der Zeit 1933 und 1945 publizistische Vielfalt unerwünscht war und wie diese Ideologie durchgesetzt wurde. Andererseits soll erforscht werden, wie Kinder- und Jugendmedien als Propagandainstrumente eingesetzt wurden.

2. Unterdrückung der Vielfalt

Zu den Maßnahmen gegen Autor*innen zählten etwa Schreibverbote aus politischen oder „rassischen" Gründen, das Drängen der Schriftsteller*innen in diverse Exilländer, Inhaftierungen und im schlimmsten Fall die Ermordung von unerwünschten Personen. Um Werke zu verbieten, wurden mehrere „Listen des unerwünschten Schrifttums" herausgegeben, Zensurmaßnahmen eingeführt, Publikationsverbote ausgesprochen, Papierzuteilungen gestoppt und Werke physisch vernichtet.

Mehrere Institutionen übten Zensur aus und griffen in die Werke ein. Das Einfügen von Propaganda war beispielsweise bei Lesebüchern eine häufig praktizierte Taktik, um die Kinder im Schulunterricht möglichst flächendeckend mit entsprechenden Werten indoktrinieren zu können. Zwischen Textbeispielen oder Gedichten von klassischen Autor*innen fanden sich nicht selten Reden, Sprüche oder Auszüge aus Büchern der nationalsozialistischen Elite, wie etwa

---

adressiertes Werk „Die Perlmutterfarbe" zeigt, wie früh Jokl die Gefahr des Faschismus erkannt hat (Blumesberger, 2014; Blumesberger et al., 2014).

6 Alex Wedding (1905–1966) wurde in Salzburg geboren, lebte ab 1925 in Berlin, war mit Franz Carl Weiskopf verheiratet, mit dem sie sich gemeinsam gegen die faschistische Kinderliteratur engagierte. Wedding gilt als Wegbereiterin der sozialistischen Kinder- und Jugendliteratur der DDR (Blumesberger & Seibert, 2007; Blumesberger, 2014).

7 Ein erster Schritt dazu wurde mit der Datenbank „Österreichische Kinder- und Jugendliteratur zwischen 1933 und 1945" gesetzt, die unter http://www.dbkjlf.at/ abrufbar ist.

Adolf Hitler oder Joseph Goebbels, bzw. wurden diese weit verbreiteten Werke durch Lesestücke von geförderten Autor*innen bereichert. Gleichzeitig wurden Textbeispiele unerwünschter Schriftsteller*innen nicht mehr abgedruckt; sie wurden nicht einmal mehr erwähnt. Ein beliebtes Mittel, um faschistische Ideen zu verbreiten war es, neuaufgelegte Publikationen mit entsprechenden Vorworten zu versehen. Ein Beispiel dafür ist *Hannerl in der Pilzstadt* (1941), wo die Autorin Annelies Umlauf-Lamatsch[8] in einem Vorwort auf die Wichtigkeit hinwies, die „Volksgemeinschaft" zu unterstützen und Pilze zu sammeln. Auch inhaltlich passte das sonst außerhalb des politischen Kontexts gelesene Märchenbuch durch den vehementen Hinweis, die giftigen Pilze auszurotten, gut in das Bild der damaligen Zeit.

Erwünschte Autor*innen wurden durch vielfältige Maßnahmen gefördert. So wurden Preise ausgeschrieben, Lesereisen organisiert, der schriftstellerische Nachwuchs gefördert und erfolgreiche, regimetreue Autor*innen vom Kriegsdienst befreit. Gut nachvollziehbar ist das beispielsweise bei Karl Springenschmid. Seine Publikationen und jene von anderen erwünschten Autor*innen wurden ausgezeichnet, erhielten finanzielle Unterstützung und wurden in Zeitungen und Zeitschriften abgedruckt. Außerdem wurden Papierkontingente zugeteilt, Ausstellungen und sonstige Bewerbungsaktionen organisiert.

Diese Maßnahmen waren jedoch weniger konzise und aufeinander abgestimmt, als man vorerst vermuten würde. Eine einheitliche Linie gab es schon deshalb nicht, weil sich unterschiedliche Stellen um das „gute Buch" bemühten. Darunter waren unter anderem:

- Die Abteilung Schrifttum im Reichsministerium für Volksaufklärung und Propaganda (RMVP), geleitet von Joseph Goebbels
- Die Reichsschrifttumskammer in der Reichskulturkammer
- Die Reichstelle für das Volksbüchereiwesen im Reichserziehungsministerium
- Die Parteiamtliche Prüfungskommission zum Schutze des NS-Schrifttums
- Das Amt Schrifttumspflege in der Dienststelle Alfred Rosenbergs
- Die Literaturabteilungen der Reichsjugendführung, des NS-Lehrerbundes
- Die Jugendschriftenstelle im Nationalsozialistischen Lehrerbund (siehe Barbian 2010)

Vor allem die Maßnahmen gegen unerwünschte Autorinnen waren vielfältig und an unterschiedlichen Lebensläufen sehr gut zu erkennen. Sie reichten von Schreibverboten, Ausschluss aus dem literarischen Leben, Enteignung, Gewalt,

---

8 Annelies-Umlauf-Lamatsch (1895–1962) war als Lehrerin und Schriftstellerin tätig. Während der NS-Zeit verbreitete sie nationalsozialistische Propaganda, dennoch erschienen ihre zahlreichen Märchenbücher auch nach 1945 weiter, wurden in viele Sprachen übersetzt und mehrmals neu aufgelegt (Blumesberger, 2001; Blumesberger, 2014).

bis zur Vertreibung und im schlimmsten Fall bis zur Ermordung. Als ein Beispiel soll hier die aus einer assimilierten jüdischen Wiener Familie stammende Psychoanalytikerin, Schriftstellerin und Übersetzerin Anna Maria Jokl genannt werden. (Jokl, 2011) Sie musste mehrmals fliehen, zunächst 1933 nach Prag und über Polen nach England. 1945 ging sie in die Schweiz, 1948 in die DDR und 1965 nach Jerusalem. Jokl gehörte zu den Schriftsteller*innen, die gegen Faschismus anschrieben. Das zeigt ihr 1937, nicht nur für Kinder, verfasstes Buch *Die Perlmutterfarbe. Ein Kinderroman für fast alle Leute*, das erstmals 1948 erschien. Sie hat darin anhand zweier Schulklassen weit vorausschauend beschrieben, wie Faschismus entsteht.

Auch Béla Balázs, Filmkritiker, Drehbuchautor und Schriftsteller, in Szeged, damals Österreich-Ungarn, geboren, kam 1919 nach Wien. Auch er war jüdischer Herkunft. Bereits 1918 war er Mitglied der Ungarischen Kommunistischen Partei, 1919 floh er nach Wien, 1926 übersiedelte er nach Berlin. Anfang der 30er Jahre wurde er nach Moskau eingeladen, um einen Film über die „Räte-Revolution" in Ungarn zu drehen. Als Jude und Kommunist konnte er 1933 nicht nach Deutschland zurückkehren. Erst 1945 war es ihm möglich, erneut in Budapest zu leben. Wie Jokl nutzte auch Balázs das Medium Kinderbuch, um auf den Faschismus aufmerksam zu machen. Eines seiner wichtigsten Kinderbücher, *Heinrich beginnt den Kampf*, erschien erstmals 1939 in Moskau. Der Protagonist Heinrich, der sechsjährige Sohn antifaschistischer Eltern, wird zunächst als begeisterter Nazi geschildert, auf den die Märsche großen Eindruck machen. Eines Tages wird sein Vater als Kommunist verhaftet und von der Polizei abgeholt. Schließlich gelingt es der Mutter, durch die Erzählung eines parabelhaften Märchens, ihn zu einem kleinen Widerstandskämpfer zu machen. Heinrich versteckt sogar einen Kommunisten im engen Zimmer, das er mit seinen Eltern bewohnt. Bei der Polizeiuntersuchung in diesem Raum wird sein geliebter Hund getötet. Schlussendlich kämpft er mit zahlreichen anderen Kindern gegen die so genannten „Pimpfe"[9], die das Begräbnis seines geliebten Haustieres stören wollen.

Die Maßnahmen gegen unerwünschte Werke waren ebenfalls vielfältig und uneinheitlich. Das Reichsministerium für Volksaufklärung und Propaganda (RMVP) gab 1940 eine „Liste der für Jugendliche und Büchereien ungeeigneten Druckschriften" heraus, die 1942 mit einem Nachtrag und 1943 in einer veränderten zweiten Auflage erschien. In der „Liste der für Jugendliche und Büchereien ungeeignete Druckschriften" von 1940 kann man auf Seite 3, §2 lesen:

> Die Reichsschrifttumskammer führt eine Liste solcher Bücher und Schriften, die ungeeignet sind, in die Hände Jugendlicher zu gelangen oder in Büchereien geführt zu werden.

---

9 Damit wurden in der NS-Zeit Mitglieder der Hitlerjugend bezeichnet.

Solche Schriften dürfen

1. nicht in Schaufenstern und allgemein zugänglichen Bücherständen öffentlich ausgelegt werden;
2. nicht durch Reisende, Bücherkarrenhändler, Ausstellungshändler und sonstige Händler ohne festen Verkaufsraum vertrieben werden;
3. nicht in Leihbüchereien, Volksbüchereien, Vereins-. Betriebs-, Werk-, Hotel-, Krankenhaus-, Schiffs- und ähnlichen Büchereien verliehen, vermietet, veräußert oder vorrätig gehalten werden;
4. nicht an Jugendliche unter achtzehn Jahren ausgehändigt werden.

Nach Auffassung der Nationalsozialist*innen hätten diese Werke möglichst lückenlos verschwinden sollen, was aber, wie wir unter anderem aus Zeitzeug*innenberichten, wie bereits oben von Marcel Reich-Ranicki, wissen, nicht wirklich gelang.

Subtiler war es, nationalsozialistisches Gedankengut in Schulbücher einzuschleusen, indem, wie ebenfalls bereits oben geschildert, beispielsweise in Lesebüchern zwischen Texten von klassischen Autor*innen auch Prosa oder Lyrik von nationalsozialistischen Autor*innen abgedruckt wurden. Ein weiterer Schritt war das Umtexten von Liedern, deren Text durch das gemeinsame Singen bei Festen und Gruppenabenden besonders lange im Gedächtnis blieben.

Andererseits wurden erwünschte Autor*innen stark gefördert. Zu den am besten verdienenden Autor*innen während der Zeit des Nationalsozialismus zählten Mirko Jelusich[10], Schlüsselperson der NS-Kulturpolitik in Österreich, Karl Springenschmid, und Johanna Haarer, Autorin von *Die deutsche Mutter und ihr erstes Kind*, einem Erziehungsratgeber, der leicht modifiziert bis in die 1980er Jahre immer wieder neu aufgelegt wurde, und das an Kinder adressierte Werk *Mutter, erzähl' von Adolf Hitler* (Benz, 2013; Söchtig, 2019). Auch die heute eher als „Märchenmutti" bekannte Autorin zahlreicher Kinderbücher, Annelies Umlauf-Lamatsch, publizierte 1939 *Ein Kinder-Festspiel zur Geburtstagsfeier unseres Führers und ein Märchen zur Maifeier* (Blumesberger, 2001).

Kinder- und Jugendbücher wurden also gezielt als Propagandainstrumente eingesetzt. Dafür wählte man mehrere Wege. Werke wurden beispielsweise zur verpflichtenden Schullektüre erklärt. Der Nationalsozialistische Lehrerbund

---

10 Mirko Jelusich (1886–1969) war unter anderem als Filmdramaturg, Zeitungsredakteur, Theaterkritiker und Bankbeamter tätig. Er gründete aus Antisemitismus den „Kampfbund für deutsche Kultur" und sprach sich schon sehr früh für den Anschluss an Deutschland aus. 1938 wurde er Direktor des Wiener Burgtheaters. Seine zahlreichen historischen Werke, die sich auch an Jugendliche richteten, waren weit verbreitet. Er zählte zu den Spitzenverdienern während des 3. Reiches. 1945 wurde er verhaftet, 1946 stand er auf der Liste der gesperrten Autoren des Unterrichtsministeriums. Er blieb seinen Ansichten auch später treu. (Sachslehner, 1985; Blumesberger, n.d.)

(NSLB) bemühte sich um die Kanonisierung der Klassenlesestoffe, wobei er hier, anders als das Reichsministerium für Wissenschaft, Erziehung und Volksbildung (RMWEV), sämtliche Literatur dazu zählte, die an Schulen angeboten wurden, also neben Schulbüchern, Büchern aus den Schulbibliotheken, billige Jugendschriftenreihen und Zeitschriften. Die preiswerten Jugendschriftenreihen sollten zeigen, dass man auch für wenig Geld gute Lektüre und nicht nur so genannte „Schundhefte" erwerben konnte. In der Zeitschrift *Jugendschriften-Warte* erschienen wiederholt Beiträge, die zur Kanonisierung der erwünschten Literatur beitragen sollten.

Erwünschte Bücher wurden in Empfehlungslisten beworben. „Das Buch der Jugend 1934/35" und „Das Buch der deutschen Jugend 1939/40" sind Beispiele dafür. Diese Listen wurden jährlich publiziert, umfassten zwischen 600 und 1200 Titel und wurden an Verleger*innen, Bibliothekar*innen, Buchhändler*innen, aber auch Eltern, Kinder und Jugendliche verteilt. Zusätzlich gab es auch thematisch ausgerichtete Listen empfehlenswerter Kinder- und Jugendliteratur, z. B. „Das Sachsenland in der Jugendschrift" (1934) oder Listen szenischer Texte, wie „Für Fest und Feier" (1935). Der NSLB gab von 1933 bis 1942 jährlich Jugendbuchverzeichnisse unter dem Titel „Das Jugendbuch im Dritten Reich", „Das Buch der Jugend", „Das Buch der deutschen Jugend" und „Das deutsche Jugendbuch" heraus. Aber da sich mehrere Instanzen eher unkoordiniert um das „gute Jugendbuch" bemühten und auch unterschiedliche Listen herausgegeben wurden, kann man von keiner einheitlichen Linie sprechen (Blumesberger, 2020).

Erwünschte, bzw. in Auftrag gegebene Bücher wurden in Zeitungen und Zeitschriften als besonders wertvoll beworben und sehr positiv rezensiert, Lesungen machten auf die Werke aufmerksam, (Schul-)bibliotheken wurden entsprechend ausgestattet, ebenso wie Buchhandlungen. Der NSLB wollte das „gute" Jugendbuch auch mit Jugendbuchausstellungen bewerben. Am 21.6.1938 wurde beispielsweise die Ausstellung unter dem Titel „NS-Schrifttum für die deutsche Schule" in Wien eröffnet. Ab 1934 wurden Veranstaltungen wie diese meist im Anschluss an die vom Reichsministerium für Volksaufklärung und Propaganda (RMVP) jeweils im Herbst durchgeführten „Woche des deutschen Buches" verrichtet. Auch Rundfunkübertragungen dazu fanden statt. Gleichzeitig wurde vom NSLB die Anordnung herausgegeben, dass in Schulen, Behörden, Parteilokalen, Organisationen und in Schaufenstern des Einzelhandels Plakate angebracht werden sollten, die den Titel „Das Buch – ein Schwert des Geistes" trugen. (Josting, 1995, S. 210)

Ab 1936 wurden unbekannte und bekannte Schriftsteller*innen aufgerufen, sich an den „Hilf mit!" und Hans-Schemm-Preisausschreiben zu beteiligen. Auch Kinder und Jugendliche wurden eingeladen, bei diversen Wettbewerben teilzunehmen, um den schriftstellerischen Nachwuchs zu fördern. Der NSLB regte zunächst an, dass die Kinder die in ihrer Heimat mündlich überlieferten Märchen, Sagen, Lieder und Sprüche schriftlich festhalten sollten. Nach Ausbruch des Krieges sollten sie ihre Kriegserlebnisse festhalten, war man doch davon überzeugt, dass dieser Krieg zu einem Sieg für Deutschland führen würde. Viele dieser Texte wurden in den vom NSLB herausgegebenen Schülerzeitschriften abgedruckt.

In den Jahren 1933 bis 1945 wurden insgesamt 107 periodische Literaturpreise und 13 Auszeichnungen vergeben. Zu den Preisen zählen beispielsweise der Nationalpreis für Film und Buch, der Goethe Preis, der Schillerpreis, der NSDAP-Preis für Wissenschaft und Kunst, der Hans-Schemm-Preis für das deutsche Jugendschrifttum, der Preis des Stabchefs der SA für Dichtung und Schrifttum und der „Hilf mit!"-Preis. Der Verlag Enßlin & Laiblin vergab ab 1942 für die vier besten Jugendbücher des Jahres Preise in der Höhe von 2.000, 1.000 und zweimal 500 RM und versprach, die Summe um jeweils 500 RM zu erhöhen, wenn es sich dabei um ein spezifisches Mädchenbuch handelte, da sich davon zu wenige am Markt befanden, die den Werten der NS-Politik entsprachen.

Die Reichsjugendführung organisierte für die Buchwoche 1940 für den 29. Oktober in 42 Städten Lesungen mit bekannten Schriftsteller*innen, darunter auch Mirko Jelusich. Sämtliche Gebiets- und Obergauführer wurden aufgefordert, an ihren Orten Dichterlesungen und Vortragsabende zu gestalten. Für die Auswahl der Künstler*innen musste die „Vorschlagsliste für Dichterlesungen" herangezogen werden, für die Buchauswahl hatte man sich am Verzeichnis „Jugend und Buch 1940" zu orientieren. (Josting, 1995, S. 215) Inwieweit jedoch Dichterlesungen den gewünschten Erfolg brachten, kann nur schwer beurteilt werden, bzw. wurde darüber auch im NSLB kontrovers diskutiert. Die Lesungen sollten keine Massenveranstaltungen sein und das Kind sollte das Buch bereits aus dem Unterricht kennen, außerdem durfte die Spannung nicht fehlen. Von der Reichsschrifttumsstelle wurde zwischen 1937 und 1942 eine „Vorschlagsliste für Dichterlesungen" herausgegeben, in der entsprechend geförderte Autor*innen genannt wurden. (Josting, 1995, S. 215)

Während der NS-Zeit galt auch der Rundfunk als wichtiges Propagandainstrument. Der Kinderfunk orientierte sich am Volksmärchengut (Seibert, 2020). Man sprach vom „Fernererbten, vom Denken und Fühlen des deutschen Volkes aus Jahrtausenden her" (Stenzel, 2008, S. 437). Jüngere Kinder wurden zum Basteln und Singen angeregt, ältere hörten den „Hitlerjugend-Funk". Die Hitlerjugend betreute eigene Radiosendungen und setzte sich mit dem Hörspiel auseinander.

Ebenso wurde der Film, der während der NS-Zeit ein beliebtes Medium war, entsprechend eingesetzt, um eine große Anzahl an Menschen beeinflussen zu können. Beliebt waren Märchenfilme, sehr bekannt der Jugendfilm *Hitlerjunge Quex* (1933) von Karl Aloys Schenzinger, der auf dem gleichnamigen Roman aus dem Jahr 1932 beruht und die Entwicklung eines fünfzehnjährigen Jungen, Heini Völker, zum Nationalsozialismus schildert. Aus einer kommunistischen Arbeiterfamilie stammend, wendet sich Heini den Nationalsozialisten zu, wird HJ-Führer und stirbt schließlich bei einem kommunistischen Anschlag. Das Buch wurde ab 12 Jahren empfohlen und sehr positiv rezensiert (Grenz, 1977, S. 127 f). „Jugendfilmstunden" sollten Kinder und Jugendliche an den Film heranführen und auf den späteren Kriegseinsatz vorbereiten, bzw. später zum Durchhalten motivieren.

Lieder hatten während der NS-Zeit eine sehr große Bedeutung, sie wurden auswendig gelernt und zu unterschiedlichen Anlässen gesungen, sowohl im privaten Kreis als auch bei offiziellen Gelegenheiten. Die Lieder wurden im Radio ausgestrahlt und erreichten somit fast flächendeckend alle Personen. Gudrun Wilcke erinnert sich, wie wirkungsvoll die Wiederholungen der Texte war:

> Die nationalsozialistischen Lieder, die wir jungen Mädchen während der Heimabende beigebracht bekamen, wurden vor allem beim Wandern, Marschieren und auf NS-Feiern gesungen. Manche von ihnen, Lieder mit gemäßigteren Texten, erweiterten auch unser familiäres Repertoire. Oft sang ich sie, wenn ich allein war. Die Lieder gaben mir Mut und Kraft. Sie enthielten alles, woran ich glaubte. Bücher und Lieder waren durchwärmt von der Liebe, der Hingabe zu meinem Land und seinem „Führer" Adolf Hitler. Auch wenn ich noch so schlechte Noten erhielt und noch so hässlich war – ich war eine Deutsche und eingebunden ins deutsche Volk, geborgen in ihm. Das war doch etwas! (Wilcke, 2005, S. 1)

Bekannt war *Wir Mädel singen. Liederbuch des BDM*, das 1937 im Georg Kallmeyer Verlag erschien. Auf 194 Seiten waren 248 Lieder abgedruckt. Thematisch waren die Lieder dem Jahreskreislauf angepasst, es fehlten jedoch christliche Lieder, der Bezug zur Kirche war von den Nationalsozialist*innen nicht gewünscht, sollte doch der „Führer" das Heil bringen.

Das Theater wurde von den Nationalsozialist*innen sehr kritisch beurteilt. Hitler brachte es in *Mein Kampf* mit ungezügelter Sexualität in Verbindung. „Schmutzige Instinkte", Marxismus, Pazifismus und Philosemitismus wurden damit assoziiert (Stollmann, 1987, S. 72). Wie auch in der Literatur kam es auch beim Theater zu „Säuberungen" des jüdischen Volkes und politisch Andersdenkenden, schließlich wurde es gleichgeschaltet und zum politischen Führungsmittel erklärt. Theaterdarbietungen wurden ab 1933 zu politischen Demonstrationen (Stollmann, 1987, S. 73). Insgesamt wurden im Theater fast ausschließlich historische Stoffe vorgetragen, deren Helden als Vorläufer der Nationalsozialisten dargestellt wurden.

Nationalsozialistische, faschistische und antisemitische Werte wurden mehr oder weniger subtil auch in Zeitungen und Zeitschriften für Kinder und Jugendliche weitergegeben. An Zeitschriften, die zwischen 1933 und 1945 erschienen, sind unter anderem zu nennen: *Schmetterling* (1926 bis 1941), *Der*

Papagei (1939–1941), *Der Teddybär* (1930–1934), *Dideldum* (1929–1941), *Jugendschriften-Warte* (1893–1944), *Hilf mit!* (1933–1945) und *Deutsche Jugendburg* (1933–1945). Tatjana Schruttke identifiziert 55 Zeitschriften, die zwischen 1924 und 1944 von der Hitler-Jugend im In- und Ausland veröffentlicht wurden (Schruttke, 1997, S. 39). Es gab aber auch konfessionelle Jugendzeitschriften, verlagseigene und allgemeine Jugendzeitschriften, sowie die illegale Jugendpresse der Widerstandsbewegung (Schruttke, 1997, S. 114f). Diese konnten sich zum Teil recht gut tarnen, viele von ihnen wurden jedoch nach der Machtergreifung der Nationalsozialist*innen bald eingestellt.

3. Widerstand gegen die Gleichschaltung der Kinder- und Jugendliteratur

Die Kinder- und Jugendliteratur zwischen 1933 und 1945 ist vielfältiger, als man auf den ersten Blick vermuten würde. Neben eindeutig propagandistischen Werken gab es jene, die subtilere Botschaften enthielten, sowohl für als auch gegen das herrschende System. Es gab aber auch eindeutig antifaschistische Gegenbeispiele, darunter Texte von Hermynia Zur Mühlen[11], Anna Maria Jokl, Marie Neurath[12] und Alex Wedding, um nur einige zu nennen.

Die zunächst überzeugte Kommunistin und spätere linke Katholikin Hermynia Zur Mühlen schuf beispielsweise mit *Was Peterchens Freunde erzählen* ein proletarisches Kindermärchen. Peter liegt mit einem gebrochenen Bein im Bett und ist tagsüber alleine in der ärmlichen Wohnung. Die Mutter muss schwer arbeiten. Damit Peter und damit auch die lesenden Kinder und eventuell auch die vorlesenden Erwachsenen verstehen, wer am wirtschaftlichen Elend der Arbeiter*innen schuld ist, lässt Zur Mühlen einzelne Gegenstände, wie beispielsweise ein Stück Kohle oder einen Teekessel von der Ungerechtigkeit und Ausbeutung erzählen. Durch ihre proletarischen Märchen zählt die Autorin zu den bekanntesten und bedeutendsten Kinderbuchautor*innen der proletarisch-revolutionären Literaturbewegung der Weimarer Republik. (Blumesberger & Thunecke,

---

11 Hermynia Zur Mühlen (1883–1951) wurde in Wien in eine adelige Familie geboren, rebellierte jedoch schon früh gegen ihre adelige Herkunft, setzte sich mit sozialen Problemen auseinander und wurde Kommunistin. Insgesamt übersetzte sie nahezu 150, meist sozialkritische, Werke russischer, französischer, englischer und amerikanischer Autor*innen (Blumesberger, 2014; Blumesberger & Thunecke, 2019).

12 Marie Neurath (1898–1986) studierte Mathematik und Physik in Göttingen und studierte an der Kunstschule. Sie kam mit Otto Neurath nach Wien und arbeitete mit ihm zusammen am Wiener Wirtschaftsmuseum, wo sie gemeinsam mit ihm Isotype (International System of Typographic Picture Education) entwickelte. Nach seinem Tod führte sie Otto Neuraths Arbeit fort und publizierte zahlreiche Sachbücher für Kinder (Blumesberger, 2014).

2019) Für sie hatte die Literatur diesen Auftrag zu erziehen. So sah sie auch in der Kinder- und Jugendliteratur das Potential, auf junge Leserinnen und Leser einwirken zu können und beschäftigte sich auch theoretisch mit Kinder- und Jugendliteratur. (Zur Mühlen, 1919) Marie Neurath setzte die Bemühungen ihres Mannes Otto Neurath, durch Piktogramme komplizierte Sachverhalte einfach darzustellen, in zahlreichen Kinderbüchern fort. Sie gab in ihren Werken Einblicke in U-Bahnstationen, ins Weltall und in das Innere von Gegenständen. Außerdem engagierte sie sich dafür, dass auch Personen, die nicht lesen konnten, mittels grafischer Aufbereitung Zugang zu Wissen erhielten. Schon während des Krieges beschäftigte sie sich mit einer möglichen „Re-Education" des Deutschen und stellten eine Sammlung von Texten zusammen, die in der Nachkriegszeit als Gegenpropaganda der nazistischen Ideologie wirken sollte. Alex Wedding schuf nicht nur selbst zahlreiche Kinderbücher, sondern beschäftigte sich auch theoretisch mit Kinder- und Jugendliteratur und rief gleichzeitig zum Kampf gegen faschistische Kinderliteratur und zum Schreiben antifaschistischer Texte auf. Sie gilt als Wegbereiterin der sozialistischen Kinder- und Jugendliteratur der DDR und trat stets für die Anerkennung der Kinder- und Jugendliteratur als Bestandteil der Nationalliteratur ein. In ihren Beiträgen, Aufsätzen und Rezensionen versuchte sie, die Kinder- und Jugendliteratur durch maßstabsetzende Kritik zu fördern, korrespondierte mit ihren Leser*innen und mit Literaturzirkeln und führte Gespräche zu Kinder- und Jugendbüchern. Außerdem setzte sie sich sehr für ihre Kolleg*innen und deren kinderliterarische Werke ein. Wedding thematisierte auch die Tatsache, dass Kinderliteratur oft nicht ernst genug genommen wurde:

> Das Gebiet der deutschen antifaschistischen Kinderliteratur ist außerordentlich vernachlässigt, ein Mißstand, der von uns Schriftstellern ernst genommen und abgestellt zu werden verdient. [...] Leider wird dieses Literaturgebiet oft und zu Unrecht von Kritikern und Schriftstellern als nicht zur Literatur gehörig angesehen. (Wedding, 1937, S. 50–52)

Antifaschistische Literatur konnte zumeist nur im Exil entstehen. Die Bedingungen für die Autor*innen waren in den Exilländern so unterschiedlich, dass von einer einheitlichen Exilliteratur nicht gesprochen werden kann. Die Tatsache, dass sich unter den in das Exil getriebenen Schriftsteller*innen auch viele befanden, die für Kinder- und Jugendliche schrieben, ist erst spät in die Forschung eingegangen. Auch die Kinder- und Jugendliteraturforschung hat diesen Bereich erst recht spät wahrgenommen (Blumesberger, 2018). Deshalb sind auch noch viele Fragen offen, beispielsweise welche Werke wirklich rezipiert wurden (Graf, 1997). Insgesamt ist zu sagen, dass im Exil eine Vielfalt an literarischen Formen und Themen in der Kinder- und Jugendliteratur entstand.

4. Fazit

Gudrun Wilcke, die selbst im NS-System aufwuchs, davon massiv beeinflusst wurde und später zahlreiche Kinder- und Jugendbücher darüber schrieb, meinte:

> Die NS-Schultexte, -Bücher, -Lieder haben uns, die wir damals Kinder, dann Jugendliche waren, jahrelang begleitet. Sie haben unsere Begeisterung für die nationalsozialistische Bewegung angefacht und geschürt. Nicht nur wir jungen Menschen, auch viele unserer Eltern haben damals nicht gemerkt, welche fatalen Wirkungen die Lektüre solcher Bücher auf uns hatten und wie verhängnisvoll NS-Liedertexte, verbunden mit ins Ohr gehenden Melodien, uns massiv ideologisch beeinflussten. Unter den Mitteln des NS-Staates, die junge Generation politisch zu verführen, waren sie wahrscheinlich das effektivste. (Wilcke, 2005, S. 13)

Die Aufarbeitung der österreichischen Kinder- und Jugendliteratur zwischen 1933 und 1945 umfasst also zahlreiche Aspekte, die miteinander zu betrachten sind. Um die Literaturlandschaft in den Jahren zwischen 1933 und 1945 zu verstehen und möglichst lückenlos darstellen zu können, dürfen auch die Kinder- und Jugendmedien nicht ausgespart werden. Das betrifft jene Werke, die zu dieser Zeit in Österreich verlegt, bzw. neu aufgelegt wurden, und auch all jene, die in diversen Exilländern erschienen sind. Beide Gruppen sind, was den Inhalt und ihre politische Ausrichtung betreffen, nicht homogen, sondern sehr divers. Bücher für Kinder dienten oft als Sprachrohr (Blumesberger, 2010) der Autor*innen, um beispielsweise vor dem Faschismus zu warnen, wie etwa Jokls „Die Perlmutterfarbe". Sie trugen im Gegensatz dazu aber auch nationalsozialistische Propaganda in Kinderzimmer, Schulen und Kindergärten oder versuchten bewusst, einen möglichst apolitischen Raum zu schaffen, in denen die Leser*innen sich erholen können sollten. Das war jedoch nicht so einfach, denn rasch war ein Text zu pazifistisch, zu kitschig oder propagierte Werte, die nicht mehr gelten sollten. Diese Vielfalt gilt es zu entdecken und wieder bewusst und sichtbar zu machen.

Primärliteratur

Balázs, B. (1939). *Heinrich beginnt den Kampf.* Verlagsgenossenschaft Ausländischer Arbeiter in der UdSSR.

Haarer, J. (1934). *Die deutsche Mutter und ihr erstes Kind.* Lehmann.

Haarer, J. (1939). *Johanna: Mutter, erzähl' von Adolf Hitler: Ein Buch zum Vorlesen, Nacherzählen und Selbstlesen für kleinere und größere Kinder.* Lehmann.

Jokl, A. M. (1948). *Die Perlmutterfarbe: Ein Kinderroman für fast alle Leute.* Dietz.

Jokl, A. M. (2011). *Aus sechs Leben.* Jüdischer Verlag im Suhrkamp Verlag.

Reichsministerium für Volksaufklärung und Propaganda Abteilung Schrifttum (Hrsg.). (1940). *Liste der für Jugendliche und Büchereien ungeeignete Druckschriften.* Verlag des Börsenvereins der Deutschen Buchhändler zu Leipzig.

Umlauf-Lamatsch, A. (1939). *Ein Kinder-Festspiel zur Geburtstagsfeier unseres Führers und ein Märchen zur Maifeier.* Deutscher Verlag für Jugend und Volk.

Umlauf-Lamatsch, A. (1941). *Hannerl in der Pilzstadt.* Deutscher Verlag für Jugend und Volk.

Wedding, A. (1937). Kinderliteratur. *Das Wort. Literarische Monatsschrift,* 4–5, 50–52.

Bund deutscher Mädel (Hrsg.). (1937). *Wir Mädel singen. Liederbuch des Bundes Deutscher Mädel.* Kallmeyer.

Zur Mühlen, H. (1919). Junge-Mädchen-Literatur. *Die Erde,* 14/15, 473–474.

Sekundärliteratur

Adam, C. (2010). *Lesen unter Hitler. Autoren, Bestseller, Leser im Dritten Reich.* Galiani.

Amir, C. M. (2020). *Karl Springenschmid (1897–1981): Wegbereiter nationalsozialistischer Ideologie und Vertreter deutschnationalen Gedankenguts auf Lebenszeit.* (Diplomarbeit). Universität Wien. https://utheses.univie.ac.at/detail/53913.

Barbian, Jan.-P. (2010). *Literaturpolitik im NS-Staat: Von der „Gleichschaltung" bis zum Ruin.* Fischer.

Benner, J. (2015). *Federkrieg. Kinder- und Jugendliteratur gegen den Nationalsozialismus 1933–1945.* Wallstein.

Benz, W. (2013). Mutter, erzähl' von Adolf Hitler! (Johanna Haarer, 1939). In W. Benz (Hrsg.), *Handbuch des Antisemitismus. Judenfeindschaft in Geschichte und Gegenwart. Band 6 Publikationen* (S. 466–468). Walter de Gruyter.

Blumesberger, S. (n.d.). *Datenbank Kinder- und Jugendliteraturforschung: Österreichische Kinder- und Jugendliteratur zwischen 1933 und 1945.* http://www.dbkjlf.at/.

Blumesberger, S. (2000). „Die Haare kraus, die Nasen krumm." Feindbilder in nationalsozialistischen Kinderbüchern. *Biblos. Beiträge zu Buch, Bibliothek und Schrift,* 2(49), 247–268.

Blumesberger, S. (2001). Anneliese Umlauf-Lamatsch: Märchenmutti oder Propagandaautorin? *Biblos. Beiträge zu Buch, Bibliothek und Schrift,* 2(50), 211–225.

Blumesberger, S. (2009). Von Giftpilzen, Trödeljakobs und Kartoffelkäfern – Antisemitische Hetze in Kinderbüchern während des Nationalsozialismus. *Medaon. Magazin für Jüdisches Leben in Forschung und Bildung,* 5, 2009. https://phaidra.univie.ac.at/o:48388.

Blumesberger, S. (2010). Kinderliteratur als geistiger Zufluchtsort und Sprachrohr in der Not? In G. Franciszek (Hrsg.). *Vielheit und Einheit der Germanistik weltweit. Akten des XII. internationalen Germanistenkongresses Warschau* (S. 245–249). Frankfurt am Main.

Blumesberger, S. (2014). *Handbuch der österreichischen Kinder- und Jugendbuchautorinnen.* Böhlau. https://hdl.handle.net/11353/10.368988.

Blumesberger, S. (2018). Kinder- und Jugendliteratur im Exil. Ein Überblick über die Jahre 1933–1945. In E. Adunka, P. Driessen Gruber, & S. Usaty (Hrsg.), *Exilforschung: Österreich. Leistungen, Defizite & Perspektiven* (S. 258–278). Mandelbaum.

Blumesberger, S. (2020). Facetten der politisch aufgeladenen Kinder- und Jugendliteratur in Österreich zwischen 1933 und 1945. In C. Roeder (Hrsg.), *Parole(n) – Politische Dimensionen von Kinder und Jugendmedien* (S. 79–91). J.B. Metzler.

Blumesberger, S., & Seibert, E. (Hrsg.). (2007). *Alex Wedding (1905–1966) und die proletarische Kinder- und Jugendliteratur.* Edition Praesens.

Blumesberger, S., Kümmerling-Meibauer, B., Mikota, J., & Seibert, E. (Hrsg.), (2014). *„Hieroglyphe der Epoche?" Zum Werk der österreichisch-jüdischen Autorin Anna Maria Jokl (1911–2001).* Praesens.

Blumesberger, S., & Thunecke J. (Hrsg.). (2019). *Die rote Gräfin. Leben und Werk Hermynia Zur Mühlens während der Zwischenkriegszeit (1919–1933).* Praesens.

Graf, W. (1997). *Lesen und Biographie. Eine empirische Fallstudie zur Lektüre der Hitlerjugendgeneration.* Francke.

Grenz, D. (1977). Entwicklung als Bekehrung und Wandlung. Zu einem Typus der nationalsozialistischen Jugendliteratur. In M. Lypp (Hrsg.), *Literatur für Kinder.* (S. 123–154). Vandenhoeck und Ruprecht,.

Haarer, J., & Haarer, G. (2012). *Die deutsche Mutter und ihr letztes Kind. Die Autobiografien der erfolgreichsten NS-Erziehungsexpertin und ihrer jüngsten Tochter.* Offizin.

Hensel, G. (1992). Der Sack überm Kopf. In M. Reich-Ranicki (Hrsg.), *Meine Schulzeit im Dritten Reich. Erinnerungen deutscher Schriftsteller* (3., erw. Auflage, S. 109–125). Deutscher Taschenbuch-Verlag.

Josting, P. (1995). *Der „Jugendschrifttums-Kampf" des Nationalsozialistischen Lehrerbundes.* Olms-Weidmann 1995.

Reich-Ranicki, M. (1992). Geliehene Jahre. In M. Reich-Ranicki (Hrsg.), *Meine Schulzeit im Dritten Reich. Erinnerungen deutscher Schriftsteller* (3., erw. Auflage, S. 50–66). Deutscher Taschenbuch-Verlag.

Sachslehner, J. (1985). *Führerwort und Führerblick. Mirko Jelusich. Zur Strategie eines Bestsellerautors in den Dreißiger Jahren.* Hain.

Schruttke, T. (1997). *Die Jugendpresse des Nationalsozialismus.* Böhlau.

Seibert, E. (2020). Mythisierung des Märchens als Propagandaliteratur in der NS-Zeit und ihre weitreichenden Folgen. *libri liberorum. Fachzeitschrift für Kinder- und Jugendliteraturforschung, 54/55,* 7–20.

Söchtig, B. (2019). Krumme Nasen, krauses Haar und ein verschlagener Charakter – Antisemitische Stereotype im NS-Kinderbuch Mutter, erzähl von Adolf Hitler! Von Johanna Haarer. In H. Hombrecher & C. Bräuer (Hrsg.), *Zeit Spiegel. Kinder- und Jugendliteratur der Jahre 1925 bis 1945* (S. 76–78). Wallstein.

Stenzel, G. (2008). Radio für Kinder- und Jugendliche. In R. Wild (Hrsg.), *Geschichte der deutschen Kinder- und Jugendliteratur* (3. Aufl.). J. B. Metzler.

Stollmann, R. (1987). Theater im Dritten Reich. In J. Thunecke (Hrsg.), *Leid der Worte. Panorama des literarischen Nationalsozialismus* (S. 72–89). Bouvier Herbert Grundmann.

Wilcke, G. (2005). *Die Kinder- und Jugendliteratur des Nationalsozialismus als Instrument ideologischer Beeinflussung. Liedertexte – Erzählungen und Romane – Schulbücher – Zeitschriften – Bühnenwerke.* Lang.

Dafna Lemish

Like post-cataract surgery: What came into focus about children and media research during the pandemic[1]

Abstract

During COVID I came to realize that many of the themes brewing in my recent writing about the state of media and children research became crystal clear. In this commentary I discuss six of these themes: the need to abandon the discourse of negativity; the need to focus on what and how children are using media – not just how much; the need to study disparities in the media landscape; the need to reject binary thinking in our field; the need to consider the context of our studies; and the need to bridge the scholarly and professional worlds.

Während COVID wurde mir bewusst, dass viele der Themen, die in meinen jüngsten Veröffentlichungen über den Stand der Kindermedienforschung brodelten, plötzlich ganz scharf hervortraten. In diesem Kommentar gehe ich auf sechs Themen und Desiderata ein: Wir müssen den Diskurs der Negativität verlassen; wir müssen uns darauf konzentrieren, welche Medien von Kindern wie genutzt werden – und nicht nur in welchem Umfang sie es tun; wir müssen Ungleichheiten in der Medienlandschaft untersuchen; wir müssen dem binären Denken in unserer Disziplin entgegentreten; wir müssen die Kontexte unserer Studien stärker berücksichtigen; und wir müssen eine Brücke zwischen der wissenschaftlichen und der beruflichen Welt bauen.

The COVID-19 crisis put much of my then on-going research on-hold: Studying parent-child interactions in public places while engaged with mobile phones was halted; plans for a second phase of studying the roles of grandparents in mediating their grandchildren's media use was postponed; and responses in my on-going interviews with immigrant academics about their concept of "home" took a dramatic turn. Instead, I found myself engaged with Nelly Elias (Israel) in a self-therapeutic study on parental humor on social media, which gave us many much-needed laughs. Continuing to follow what was happening in children's lives, I

---

[1] This article is reprinted with permission from Taylor & Francis, Ltd (https://www.tandfonline.com): Lemish, D. (2021). Like post-cataract surgery: What came into focus about children and media research during the Pandemic. *Journal of Children and Media*, *15*(1), 148–151.

joined an international initiative to study the role of media during the pandemic in 42 countries led by Maya Götz (Germany).

However, while busy with these studies, it seems my mind was actively engaged in another endeavor: I came to realize that many of the themes brewing in my recent writing about the state of media and children research became crystal clear. It took such a monumental crisis to give me the confidence to assert them in action-oriented language. Here they are for your consideration:

1.   Abandon the discourse of negativity

It is time to focus on a realistic view of the media's centrality in children's and our own lives. Doing so requires redirecting our field from the alarmist themes dominating public discourse as well as a significant portion of our scholarship about children's use of media. "Alarmist" discussion of too much "screen time" has focused on contributions of media use to societal ills, such as social alienation, growing anxiety and depression, substance abuse, obesity, and just plain idle waste of time. Proponents warn the public that media use displaces healthier, more essential activities needed for proper development and wellbeing, such as school-related assignments, outdoor activities, and social engagement.

The pandemic turned everything upside down. Suddenly "screen time" is involved in everything, and most certainly it is not a waste of time. It facilitates schooling; it provides existential information; it helps release tension and anxiety; it connects children to their family and friends; it allows parents the ability to get some work done at home. Even escapism doesn't sound like a bad word anymore. After all, don't we all seek some escapism from reality these days to remain sane and resilient?

2.   Focus on what and how – not just how much

So much of the discussion around "screen time" is focused on "how much." How many children own devices, from what age, how many hours and minutes they devote to it, how much they are using it at home and in public, how effective is parental mediation in cutting the time they spend with screens. The quantity of owning and viewing has been king in much of the public debate, but also significant portion of our research.

The pandemic reminds us of what some of us have been saying for years: It is not about the amount as much as it is about What is being accessed and How. Suddenly it has become legitimate for children (and adults) to be in front of screens most of their waking hours, and reflection focuses on what they are doing there: How effective is zoom teaching? Where can you find age-appropriate news for children? Would grandchildren sing "happy birthday" to grandma on Facetime? Can siblings work the puzzle online collaboratively? These have become so much more important questions than the reductive question "how long have children been in front of the screen."

3. Study disparities in the media landscape

As observed in two commentaries in this journal in 2019, by Amy Jordan and Kate Prendella in volume 13(2) on "The invisible children of media research" and my own farewell commentary "A room of our own" in volume 13(1), most media research focuses on white middle-class children from high-resource countries. Achieving a more socially just academia involves breaking through systematic structural obstacles.

We don't have to go far to recognize the severity of this disparity in our communities: students who do not have a computer and/or access to reliable internet to connect to school; children who live in poverty and those who are homeless; children of minoritized populations that have been hit more severely by both the health implications of the pandemic as well as by the economic devastation; children with disabilities or chronic diseases. They are right next door to our campuses, yet we know almost nothing about the role media have in their lives and how well – if at all – are they being served by them. At a time of deep racial and social reckoning, we need to do our share, in our research questions, our methods, and our engagement with the communities we are studying by developing, applying, and honing inclusion strategies. Such research demands particular care and willingness to apply participatory strategies with the communities studied that aim to build trust over time, such as listening and knowledge sharing.

4. Reject binary thinking in our field

Media scholarship relies too heavily on binary thinking, which has been deeply criticized by feminist theory (in which my own work has been grounded), among others. Such binarism thinks of children as fundamentally different from adults; distinguishes between media as leisure contents and activities at home versus those that are educational at school; contrasts play and learning; regards media use in the privacy of homes as distinct from those in public spaces.

The pandemic has challenged all of these and other binaries. School and home have collapsed into one, as did the private and the public. Suddenly adults and

children of all ages occupy the same space continuously and have to share resources and devices. Teachers and parents are desperate to find educational
activities that combine play and movement. Adults and children are experiencing
a similar sense of isolation and trauma and have limited opportunities to separate themselves into distinct worlds of "childhood" versus "adulthood." Even
some traditional gender role distinctions are being challenged when everyone is
restricted together to the same private space, exposed to each other's interests
and activities. Surely we realize, first hand, that binary thinking is restrictive and
blocks creativity.

5.   Consider context

Much audience-related scholarship examines children living in one particular
context – be it familial, social, geographical, or cultural. Yet, ecological scholars
of media use argue the need to think of the child as located amidst confluences of
layers of contexts – from the closest circle of the family to society-at-large, and
beyond to global culture.

The pandemic revealed the urgent need to invest more in cross-cultural
studies. Doing so will help us discern what is specific and unique to a particular
context and what is more of a universal nature in children's media uses. Our current
international study conducted in 42 countries, mentioned above, is driving this
point home in two particular types of comparisons. First, when we compare what
children knew about the pandemic and second, how they reacted to it. The
emergent findings could be explained as a function, for example, of the media
they had access to in their countries, public discourse they were embedded in,
educational policies and practices unique to their societies, and even the kind of
"fake news" that circulated in their social networks. While very few of us can
undertake a global comparative study, more modest feasible comparisons are highly
valuable as well: They require partners embedded in the cultures studied, an
openness for a non-judgmental appreciation of difference, a shared language, and
agreement on the principles of academic practices. In my experience, the understanding of our scholarly literature's comparative analyses afforded through cross-
cultural study reveals findings that stand the "test" of place and temporal variance
versus those prone to contextual variation.

6.   Bridge scholarly and professional worlds

Despite many calls over the years for more engaged scholarship, including conference- sessions devoted to this topic and the work of passionate individuals in our community, very little bridging is happening. As a result, our research is very slow to arrive in the hands of professionals who are creating content for children, policymakers who make decisions that impact them, or educators and parents who care for them day in and day out. At the same time, as scholars, we are missing so much by not learning from the immense experience of professionals who can sharpen our questions and understanding of children as well as bring very different perspectives to our scholarly endeavors.

The pandemic highlights this need, as well as a few exemplary collaborations between scholars and media professionals. The latter are investigating challenges experienced in remote-schooling; look into filling voids of age-appropriate informative content for children about the pandemic; exploring policy issues related to surveillance of children's intensified activities online. Bridging efforts are also advanced by organizations such as *Common Sense Media, Prix Jeunesse International, Scholars and Storytellers, The Center on Media and Child's health*, among others. Yet, much more engagement is needed on the part of scholars. Simply put, we are not involved enough. This may be because our institutions have been slow to value and reward engaged scholarship. Those of us who are more established and secure in our positions should be leading engagement and change efforts in this direction.

In closing, only time will tell if I need actual cataract surgery after spending so much time in zoom meetings during this surreal period. In the meanwhile, my metaphorical surgery made these themes strikingly clear to me. While none are new, they are now just more glaring. I wonder if you agree?

Short biographies of contributors / Kurzbiografien der Autor*innen

Ulrich Ansorge is a full professor of cognitive psychology (tenured) at the University of Vienna. He received his doctoral degree at the University of Bielefeld/ Germany in 2000. He mostly studies human vision and attention, using an experimental approach.

Mag. Dr. Susanne Blumesberger, MSc. Studium der Medien- und Kommunikationswissenschaft und Germanistik an der Universität Wien. Arbeitet als wissenschaftliche Bibliothekarin im Bereich Forschungsdatenmanagement an der Universität Wien. Von 1999–2014 Koordinatorin und Principal Investigator mehrerer wissenschaftlicher Forschungsprojekte am Institut für Wissenschaft und Kunst, Wien. Seit 2007 Repositorienmanagerin an der Universität Wien Seit 2016 Leiterin der Abteilung Repositorienmanagement PHAIDRA Services an der Universitätsbibliothek Wien. Seit 2007 Lehrbeauftragte für Kinder- und Jugendliteratur an der Universität Wien. Seit 2013 Vorsitzende der Österreichischen Gesellschaft für Kinder- und Jugendliteraturforschung. Forschungsschwerpunkte: Kinder- und Jugendliteraturforschung, Exilliteratur. Mitherausgeberin der Zeitschrift „libri liberorum", zahlreiche Fachbereiche in nationalen und internationalen Fachzeitschriften im Bereich Kinder- und Jugendliteraturforschung und Bibliothekswissenschaft. https://orcid.org/0000-0001-9018-623X.

Dr. Julia Boog-Kaminski arbeitet am IFK (Internationales Forschungszentrum Kulturwissenschaften), Wien, und forscht zurzeit an einer Habilitation über *Das Wissen des Kindes*, in der alternative Formen infantiler Welt- und Wissensaneignung in der Kinder- und Jugendliteratur, Philosophie und Psychoanalyse untersucht werden. Publikationen zum Thema: „Die Unordnung der Dinge. Wenn Kinder sammeln", in: AVENUE – Das Magazin für Wissenskultur, Nr. 7 (2019), einzusehen unter: https://avenue.jetzt/sammeln/sammelspiele/ „‚raufladen, was man will' – Gebloggte Metanarrativität in Flurin Jeckers Jugendroman Lanz (2017)", in: Anne-Rose Meyer (Hg.): Internet – Literatur – Twitteratur.

Erzählen und Lesen im Medienzeitalter. Perspektiven für Forschung und Unterricht, Berlin 2019, S. 85–105.

Rino Bosso is an independent researcher with a keen interest in the pragmatics of online intercultural communication. He has worked as a research fellow and lecturer in English for Specific Purposes at the University of Cagliari, Italy, and has recently completed a PhD on Virtual English as a Lingua Franca (VELF) communication at the University of Vienna, Austria. His most recent publications focus on the longitudinal investigation of informal learning processes enacted through naturally-occurring VELF exchanges. He has co-edited with Inmaculada Pineda the volume titled Virtual English as a Lingua Franca to be published by Routledge in 2023. https://orcid.org/0000-0001-6909-8526.

Valentin Dander, Dr. phil., ist Erziehungswissenschaftler und Medienpädagoge. Er ist Professor für Medienbildung und pädagogische Medienarbeit an der Hochschule Clara Hoffbauer in Potsdam und leitet den gleichnamigen dualen BA-Studiengang. Zu seinen Arbeitsschwerpunkten zählen u. a. medienpädagogische Bildungs- und Wissenschaftstheorie, politische Medienbildung, Daten- und Medienkritik sowie Macht- und Herrschaftskritik. Er ist Stand 2023 im Vorstand der DGfE-Sektion Medienpädagogik und Sprecher der Initiative Bildung und digitaler Kapitalismus. https://orcid.org/0000-0001-9978-8405.

Mag. Dr. Katharina Ghamarian-Krenn, BA is a senior lecturer at KPH Wien/ Krems, where she teaches language didactics and linguistics courses. She has trained as a secondary school teacher for English and German at the University of Vienna. Recently she is enrolled in the doctoral program of University Vienna, where she received the uni:docs scholarship for her doctoral project. Her research interests are mostly located in the area of Applied Linguistics with a specific focus on vocabulary and the concept of Extramural English. Yet, she is also involved in research projects related to the primary school curriculum in Austria.

Claudia Kawai obtained a Bachelor's degree in English & Scandinavian Studies from Humboldt University of Berlin and a Master's degree in Psycholinguistics from Bielefeld University. After a 2-year freelancing period in Tokyo, she became a DOC fellow of the Austrian Academy of Sciences at the Department of Cognition, Emotion, and Methods in Psychology of Vienna University, where she received her PhD for her work on cross-cultural investigations into implicit color-valence associations in 2021. She currently works at the Swiss Federal Laboratories for Materials Science and Technology, researching the physical and psychological effects of noise-induced stress and the restorative potential of green spaces. https://orcid.org/0000-0001-5149-6921.

Rodney H. Jones is Professor of Sociolinguistics at the University of Reading. He has published fourteen books and over one hundred journal articles and book *chapters,* including *Understanding Digital Literacies: A practical introduction,* 2nd edition (Routledge, 2021) and the *Routledge Handbook of Language and Creativity*(2015). He is particularly interested in the ways digital media are changing norms and practices around visibility, learning and community.

Suzana Jovicic is an ÖAW Post-DocTrack and ESPRIT Fellow (FWF) and lecturer at the Department of Social and Cultural Anthropology and the Centre for Teacher Education, University of Vienna. She completed her BA and PhD in Social and Cultural Anthropology (University of Vienna) and her MSc in Psychological and Psychiatric Anthropology (Brunel University) and was a visiting researcher at University College London and James Cook University Singapore. She specialises in digital, design and psychological anthropology, youth, as well as interdisciplinary and participatory research. She is convenor of the European Network for Psychological Anthropology and co-founder of the Digital Ethnography Initiative.

Dafna Lemish is a Distinguished Professor and Interim Dean at the School of Communication and Information at Rutgers University, the founding editor of the *Journal of Children and Media,* and a Fellow of the International Communication Association (ICA). She is the author and editor of numerous books and articles on children and media, including recently *The Routledge International Handbook of Children, Adolescents, and Media* (edited, 2022); *Children and Media Worldwide in a Time of a Pandemic* (co-edited with Götz, 2022); *Kakao-Talk and Facebook: Korean American youth constructing hybrid identities* (with Park, 2019); *Fear in Front of the Screen: Children's Fears, Nightmares and Thrills* (with Götz & Holler, 2019).

Dr. Sonja Loidl ist freie Literaturwissenschaftlerin, freie Mitarbeiterin der STUBE Studien- und Beratungsstelle für Kinder- und Jugendliteratur und externe Lehrende am Institut für Germanistik der Universität Wien. Dort hat sie von 2013 bis 2022 den fächerübergreifenden Bereich Kinder- und Jugendliteratur betreut. Ihre Forschungsschwerpunkte sind Phantastik, transmediales Erzählen in der Jugendliteratur und Autorschaftskonzepte.

Florian Mayrhofer is a university assistant and PhD candidate at the Department of Practical Theology at the Faculty for Catholic Theology at the University of Vienna and also working as a teacher. He studied Catholic Theology (Mag. theol.) and Teacher Education for Religious Education and French (Mag. theol.) at the University of Vienna, the Catholic University of Eichstätt-Ingolstadt and the

Université Catholique of Lyon. In his research he focuses on implications and challenges of digitalization for religious educational processes. His dissertation project examines anthropological and learning theory prerequisites of digital storytelling practices and storytelling in religious educational processes. Further research interests are cooperative models of Religious Education and interreligious learning and gender in Religious Education. Further information: https://t1p.de/ad6ya.

Moritz Meister is a PhD candidate at University of Vienna and teaches at the Department for Cognition, Emotion, and Methods in Psychology. Furthermore, he is working as research associate at Bertha von Suttner Private University St. Pölten. His work focuses on cultural psychology, dispositif analysis and qualitative research methods with a special emphasis on the investigation of apps/digital interfaces and users' practices with(in) them. Full list of research activities: https://www.suttneruni.at/portfolio/mmeister?en.

Lisza-Sophie Neumeier is an MEd (Teacher Education Programme for English and History) and MA (English Language and Linguistics) student at the University of Vienna. She has been working as a student assistant and communications officer for the research platform #YouthMediaLife since October 2020. Her latest publication is concerned with the translanguaging behaviors of teachers in Austrian upper-secondary CLIL and EFL classrooms. She is currently conducting research for her MEd thesis on informal language learning and foreign language enjoyment among young adults in Austria. Her contribution to this volume displays her research interest in social media discourse and genre analysis.

Viera Pirker is full professor for Religious Education and Media Didactics at Goethe University Frankfurt am Main since 2020. Her research focuses on Religious Education facing the Digital, Visual Religious Cultures, Identity and Plurality. The Development of Subject Didactics and Teachers' Professionalization mark other important topics of her work. She studied Catholic Theology at Tübingen University, Jewish Studies and Interreligious Dialogue at Hebrew University of Jerusalem and worked at the Institute of Religious Education, Catechetics and Didactics at Sankt Georgen Graduate School of Philosophy and Theology where she pursued her doctorate in 2012. 2016–2020 she was member of faculty at the Institute for Practical Theology, Department of Catholic Theology of Vienna University. Full list of research activities: https://tinygu.de/rpmd.

Susanne Reichl is professor of contemporary English literature at the Department of English and American Studies at the University of Vienna and head of the research platform #YouthMediaLife. Her research interests include time travel stories, children's and young adult literature and media, reading and the teaching of reading and literature, and the way that social media platforms create new book cultures and literary discourses. She is co-editor of the *CLELE journal* (Children's Literature in English Language Education).

Barbara Katharina Reschenhofer is pursuing her doctorate in the study of multimodal children's literature about flight at the University of Vienna, where she also obtained her MA in Anglophone Literatures & Cultures and her BA in English & American Studies. Her research interests include attachment narratives in poetry and prose, picturebook studies, ecocritical studies, and learning & teaching in Higher Education.

Iris Schäfer, Dr. phil., ist wissenschaftliche Mitarbeiterin am Institut für Jugendbuchforschung der Goethe-Universität Frankfurt am Main. Sie hat in Frankfurt und London Allgemeine und Vergleichende Literaturwissenschaft und Germanistik studiert und wurde im Jahr 2015 mit einer Arbeit zu Krankheitsdarstellungen in jugendliterarischen Texten um 1900 und um 2000 promoviert (erschienen 2016 unter dem Titel: Von der Hysterie zur Magersucht. Adoleszenz und Krankheit in Romanen und Erzählungen der Jahrhundert- und der Jahrtausendwende). Seit 2013 lehrt und forscht sie am Institut für Jugendbuchforschung; insbesondere zu psychoanalytischen Zugängen zu Kinder- und Jugendmedien, zu Traumdarstellungen sowie zur erzählten Mode.

Thomas Slunecko, tenured professor at the Department for Cognition, Emotion, and Methods in Psychology at University of Vienna; expert in qualitative research methodology; cultural psychologist interested in questions pertaining to the mediatization of the life world; studies in medicine, human biology, psychology and philosophy at University of Vienna 1981–1988; MSc in psychology 1988; Fulbright scholar at the California Institute for Integral Studies, San Francisco 1991/92; Dr. phil. (1995) and habilitation (2002) in psychology, University of Vienna; licensed as clinical psychologist and as psychotherapist; head of a Vienna-based independent research institute (www.ikus.cc); full member of the Austrian Psychotherapy Council. http://homepage.univie.ac.at/thomas.slunecko.

Ute Smit is professor of English Linguistics at the University of Vienna, Austria and vice head of the research platform #YouthMediaLife. Her applied linguistic research focuses mainly on English in, and around, education at the crossroads of classroom discourse, language policy, internationalisation, English as a lingua franca and multilingualism. She is presently involved in various international research projects and the chair of ICLHE (Integrating Content and Language in Higher Education). Her publications include monographs and edited volumes (published e.g. by Benjamins, De Gruyter, Palgrave), and numerous journal articles (e.g. in *Applied Linguistics, English for Specific Purposes, International Journal of Bilingualism and Bilingual Education, System, TESOL Quarterly*).

Julia Sonnleitner has a post-doc position in Applied Linguistics at the University of Vienna. In her current project, *Language in Motion*, she explores the impact of media and materiality on the lived experience of language. She was trained in linguistics, anthropology, and Slavonic Studies and holds a Ph.D in social and cultural anthropology. Her Ph.D dissertation on transmitted memory in South Africa deals with the born-free generation's interpretation of apartheid and the democratic transition. Moreover, she led a project on Vienna's Central Cemetery as a semiotic landscape.

Marlene Schwarz is a secondary school teacher for English as a foreign language, a researcher in applied linguistics and language learning, and an external lecturer in teacher training at the English department of the University of Vienna, where she also obtained her PhD. Her main interests lie in the areas of informal second language learning and vocabulary acquisition, in which she tries to bring together her research and teaching experience.